WITHDRAWN

The Dominican People, 1850–1900

JOHNS HOPKINS STUDIES IN ATLANTIC HISTORY AND CULTURE
RICHARD PRICE AND FRANKLIN W. KNIGHT, GENERAL EDITORS

The Dominican People 1850–1900

Notes for a Historical Sociology

H. Hoetink

Translated by
Stephen K. Ault

THE JOHNS HOPKINS UNIVERSITY PRESS
BALTIMORE AND LONDON

This book has been brought to publication with the generous assistance of the Andrew W. Mellon Foundation.

Originally published as *El pueblo dominicano: 1850-1900, Apuntes para su sociología histórica*, second edition, by H. Hoetink, translated from the Dutch by Ligia Espinal de Hoetink and published by La Universidad Católica Madre y Maestra, in collaboration with El Instituto de Estudios del Caribe de la Universidad de Puerto Rico. Copyright © 1972 by H. Hoetink

English language translation copyright © 1982 by The Johns Hopkins University Press

Printed in the United States of America

The Johns Hopkins University Press, Baltimore, Maryland 21218

The Johns Hopkins Press Ltd., London

Library of Congress Cataloging in Publication Data

Hoetink, H.
    The Dominican people, 1850-1900.
    (Johns Hopkins studies in Atlantic history and culture)
    Translation of: El pueblo dominicano, 1850-1900.
    Bibliography: pp. 239-43
    Includes index.
    1. Dominican Republic—Social conditions.
2. Dominican Republic—Economic conditions.
I. Title.   II. Series.
HN217.H6413   972.93   81-47610
ISBN 0-8018-2223-8   AACR2

To the Dominicans in our family

Ya ves, Compadre Mon, esta es la tierra
que despertaste. Todavía pierdo
más lo que vivo que lo que recuerdo.
   (Manuel del Cabral, *Compadre Mon*)

CONTENTS

In 1963, when I began the research that led to the present work, UNESCO published a study on the social aspects of economic development in Latin America. In this study was a list, prepared by experts, of urgently needed research; in this listing, priority was given to "historical studies at a national level of the political, social, and economic development of the Latin American countries, which might be used for comparison and synthesis."[1]

I started my research with the intention of describing only the period of Ulises Heureaux's *criollo* dictatorship in its sociological aspects. But I soon modified this plan: the first sixty years in the history of the Dominican Republic reveal so many interesting changes in all the social sectors that I decided to try to point out the relationship among these multiple changes by means of an integral description of the social reality. Beginning with an exposition of the changes in the agrarian and demographic structures, I compiled sufficient material through examination of the country's economic, political, and educational organization to be able to make a provisional analysis of social stratification, concluding the study with a description of the cultural "superstructure" and of family life. The only thing missing is a formal analysis of the country's foreign policy, although various facets of it are mentioned in other contexts.

The rise of the modern sugar plantation that occurs in this period, and the changes that it helped to bring about—such as the shift of the country's economic center of gravity to the South in the internal sphere, and the shift from economic dependence on Europe to dependence upon the United States in the external sphere—inevitably appear as a *leitmotiv* in all the chapters.

My first intention was to accompany the description of the social changes with a theoretical analysis in which I would study in detail the relations between the economic and sociocultural changes noted above. In an analysis of this type, attention could also be given to comparing Dominican evolution with that in other Latin American countries. In the period under consideration, the Dominican Republic and Haiti were the only sovereign states in the Caribbean archipelago, so that a study of their problems—especially the military, political, and economic ones—would have to involve comparisons with the independent countries on the South American continent, rather than with Cuba or Puerto Rico. Doubtless, such a comparison applied, for example, to the area of government loans (with the interests of local creditors opposed to those of foreign financiers), or to monetary complications, or to military and political organization, could. result in numerous illustrative parallels. Such a comparison could also show that certain aspects of technological as well as cultural and ideological development appeared earlier in the Dominican Republic than in some less readily accessible continental societies. It could perhaps be said that the very advantages of geographic position that determined the country's importance in the period of the conquest had not become disadvantages in more recent times. However, certain factors, such as the nation's agrarian structure or the problem of race relations in the period under investigation, lend themselves more to comparison with the Spanish-speaking countries of the Caribbean, although here too the difference in political systems continues to affect the clarity of the comparison.

Although I hope to publish a theoretical and comparative analysis like the one outlined above at some early opportunity, it seemed correct to me not to delay any longer in making the collected material available to those interested in the sociological aspects of the history of the Dominican Republic. I say "sociological aspects" because my choice of material to publish was motivated not by interest in the exceptional peculiarities of specific persons or situations, but by interest in precisely those aspects that permit understanding the cultural or social structures and processes. And although this work, as I explained earlier, certainly does not aim to be a theoretical analysis, I nevertheless believe that I have used a sufficient number of sociological concepts to make possible subsequent comparisons, generalizations, and abstractions.

Thanks to the assistance of Ligia Espinal de Hoetink, who also translated the Dutch manuscript to Spanish, this book has been provided with numerous notes and a bibliography. It seemed useful and proper to us to call the reader's attention in this way to the sources and books that, thanks to the efforts of their trustees or authors, have contributed to the completion of this study. From among the first group, I would like to mention here Lic. Vetilio Alfau Durán, and Dr. J. J. Julia of the Archivo General de la Nación, who gave me obliging and capable help with my archival work. From among the authors, I would like to mention by name Lic. Emilio Rodríguez Demorizi, whose exceptional work in compiling information has made so much important historical material so readily accessible; moreover, he has always shown me the greatest courtesy. I am also very grateful for interest and encouragement on the part of young colleagues and friends like Mario Bonetti, Franklin J. Franco, and Frank Marino Hernández. Finally, it gives me great pleasure to express here my gratitude to the Institute of Caribbean Studies of the

University of Puerto Rico and to its then director Dr. Thomas G. Mathews, who made possible my archival research in 1963 and 1964; the first six chapters of this book appeared, moreover, in this institute's journal, *Caribbean Studies*, and I am grateful for permission to reproduce them here, with slight alterations.

I hope that this book will be useful in three ways: first, that it will serve as a basis and point of departure for sociological research that would be concerned with present-day reality—because it is not possible to do a responsible contemporary study without taking into account the social and cultural reality of the recent past. Secondly, I hope that it awakens interest in sociological history. Thirdly, I hope that this study serves as a counterbalance to some recent publications, foreign as well as Dominican, that give the impression that the history of the Dominican Republic might be "unworthy" or might compare unfavorably with the history of other Latin American countries, or even that the country has always suffered a singular cultural poverty. It seems to me, on the contrary, that the epoch studied here is characterized by a notable number of figures and accomplishments of a considerable political or cultural level, which are even more outstanding when one considers the sparse population and the often turbulent circumstances of the period.

It is to be hoped that the promising young generation of practitioners of the social and historical sciences will continue studying the fascinating present and past reality of their country with enthusiasm, without exaggerated patriotism, but, above all, without unjustified scorn. In this way their work will be useful in the development of sociological "models" for the future, which will necessarily have to take into consideration the cultural and structural patrimony of the Dominican people.

CHAPTER ONE

Changes in the Agrarian Structure

INTRODUCTION: THE AGRARIAN SITUATION UP TO 1875

In 1844, at the end of the Haitian occupation, land ownership in the Dominican Republic could be classified as follows:

(a) Lands that had belonged to the governments prior to the proclamation of independence; (b) the extensive areas on which *hatos* [livestock ranches] had been established; (c) lands on which sugar plantations and other larger holdings had developed or where smaller private farms were to be found. On the first of these, the colonial sugar crop was produced, and they represented one of the most important items in the Colony's economy. However, these lands must not have comprised large areas, so that if some of them were considered of some importance in terms of their production, even that must have been relatively limited; (d) lands under control of the religious communities or institutions that, as times changed and after the independence of the Republic was proclaimed, were considered under State domain.[1] However . . . the Catholic Church continued to control the administration of some of its properties, even when it lacked the legal title that was later granted to it; (e) those that formed *ejidos* [communal lands] and that were assigned by the colonial government to the municipal councils of some towns on the occasion of their founding and that, later, the *Ayuntamientos* [Municipal governments] continued to possess, considering them communal property; and (f) the ones assessed with titles, censuses, tributes, chaplaincies, entailments, and so on, a group ended by the law issued by the Chamber of the Tribunate of the Republic on 30 May 1845.[2]

During the colonial era as well as the subsequent decades, the most important among the lands that were private property were the livestock ranches. Once mining declined at the beginning of the colonial period, raising cattle became the most important means of earning a livelihood. In the course of the seventeenth century, the number of livestock breeders increased. This was due to the fact that the inhabitants of the northern ports of Puerto Plata, Monte Cristi, Bayajá, and La Yaguana, whose cities had been destroyed under the Royal Ordinance of 1607 because they engaged in illegal trade with foreigners, founded new settlements, including Monte Plata and Bayaguana in the grasslands of the eastern part of the island.

In the eighteenth century, livestock raising received a great boost when the French section of the island, then at the apogee of its economic development, awarded the role of meat supplier to its eastern neighbor. The coastal section of the South, especially the area around Azua, continued to be devoted to sugar production based on traditional methods, but the North, the East, and the valleys in the western part of the country were dedicated to livestock. This division continued *grosso modo* in the three decades following 1844.

The almost total absence of means of transportation and roads obliged the rural population to lead an almost autarchical existence, which left no room for production for a national market, let alone for an international one, unless the production area was quite close to the natural ports (as in the case of the Azua sugar)—or when a product lent itself to the irregular, crude transport by the rivers (as in the case of lumber from the Línea Noroeste, south of Monte Cristi, and around Barahona).[3] Finally, where the agricultural products were of sufficient value and suitable for light transport, like tobacco and cacao, the problems of transportation could be solved, although only primitively, with the use of pack animals. Livestock, however, transported itself.

Besides the advantages of transportation and sales that encouraged livestock raising, also important was the limiting factor of the extreme scarcity of population, which demanded agricultural activities compatible with a minimum of personnel.

Thus, even in the beginnings of the colonial period, the rancher became a key figure in agrarian society.

> On these vast segments of land with their corresponding natural boundaries, the ranch owner, prominent because of his economic position in the region, erected on what was called the seat his *fundo* or manor house and other buildings where he lodged his family and servants . . . corrals, presses for making sugars and molasses, as well as his *conucos* [small plots] of land for the cultivation of secondary crops, the ones necessary for the subsistence of his family and servants. On the ranch, the fundamental, necessary economic elements for the acquisition of domain over the occupied land were created. Those elements of cattle raising and agricultural crops created the material conditions on which the legal claim of a family's new patrimonial rights was based. . . .[4]

One must recall that in order to receive the *Amparo Real* of the Spanish crown, which recognized a person's rights to his land, it was necessary to fulfill the requirement of having buildings on the land or having the land cultivated or stocked with livestock. Without a doubt, stocking the land with cattle was the easiest way to obtain the rights of possession, which generally became rights of ownership in the course of a lengthy occupation.

The population scarcity and consequent low value of the land; the absence of employees qualified to survey the lands; and finally the difficulty of dividing up a ranch among the heirs in such a way that each would receive a share of the grasslands, forests, streams, palm groves, and small agricultural plots that, only when combined, made possible the exploitation of the ranch: all these factors are commonly mentioned to explain the institution of the *terrenos comuneros* (common lands) that already existed, according to Antonio del Monte y Tejada, in the seventeenth century.[5] Instead of going ahead with the division of the ranch, each heir received *valores* or coupons, called shares or *pesos* and also *acciones de pesos*, which established the corresponding portion of the inheritance without splitting it up and in which a monetary unit (the peso), instead of a surface measure, was used as a unit of value. This last circumstance leads me to suggest, with the greatest reservations, yet another explanation of the *terrenos comuneros*: inasmuch as primogeniture existed, the eldest heir received the ranch undivided. But since in the primitive, autarchical economy of the ranch pecuniary means were usually insufficient to pay the other heirs their legitimate share, these heirs received *valores* expressed in monetary units.

In any case, it is certain that in the course of the generations possession of these shares did not remain limited to the descendants of the original rancher. The shares were traded among outsiders so that the land of the original ranch could be considered the property of a cooperative association without either management or a known number of members. Cooperative, since it was considered that all the *comuneros* (or shareholders) were free to graze their cattle anywhere on the ranch and to work any uncultivated land within the ranch: the share or *peso* did not give rights to possession of any specific land.[6] By the middle of the eighteenth century, there were already more than fifty *hatos* in the East whose lands had become *comunero* ranches. In the South the ranches of Peñón, Hato Viejo (in the Barahona *común*), and Cristóbal (in what is today the Duverge *común*), to mention only a few, had become *comunero* ranches by 1756.[7]

In the fertile north-central Cibao area, the most populated and the most dedicated to farming, the partition of lands by surveying and division gradually became more common. In the vast eastern section of the country, on the other hand, the institution of the *terrenos comuneros* continued to cause serious problems and abuses up until the current century. The low value of the land and the *comuneros*' difficulty in presenting collective opposition made usurping uncultivated lands easier for third parties who did not own shares.

In the 1870s Hazard observed the "curious custom, converted into law," that denied the buyer of a share any rights over the mahogany that might have been on the land. In order to ensure title over the share that he had purchased, the buyer himself had to engage in farming at that time, for if he abandoned his house and land for a year or more, "any other person" had the right to occupy the land.[8]

The *ejidos*, or lands of an ayuntamiento, or town government, were considered de facto as the common property of the inhabitants, or were rented to them for a nominal sum. Often this rental passed inadvertently into ownership,[9] if the lands were not given out as "donations or gifts."[10] Thus, in 1871, with a single exception, "all the land that is within the limits of the community of Baní is the community's property, and its members cultivate it. It is rented for small sums (from five to ten dollars) to those who want to take possession of it for purposes of farming or building on it."[11] In San Cristóbal in that same year, "it is argued that the lands belong to the community and cannot be sold. The public administrator gives each resident the land that he wants to cultivate."[12]

In 1871 it was estimated that the total amount of *terrenos propiedad del Estado* (state-owned lands) represented between one-fourth and one-third of the national territory;[13] the vagueness of these figures is due to the fact that the public archives repeatedly disappeared because of the wars and revolutions. It is, however, certain that during the Haitian occupation (1822-44) state ownership increased considerably because of the confiscation of numerous private and church-owned properties.

An index of how church property had again grown to considerable proportions between 1845 and 1871 is that in the latter year the priest at La Vega estimates that his parish possesses $100,000 worth of land;[14] by way of comparison, it can be pointed out that a plantation in the Cibao with more than a thousand acres "of good land, suitable for cultivating cane, coffee, cacao, cotton, and fruits," and including the buildings, could be purchased for $5,000.[15]

Regarding the size of the private lands, the scanty data indicate that the largest landholders were found particularly in two areas, the eastern meadowlands and the area west of Azua. In 1871 Don Domingo de la Rocha was considered the major *latifundista* in the country. He resided in the capital, and it was believed that he owned a sixth of the extreme eastern section of the island in El Seybo province. Moreover, the family of the then president Báez was considered in that year as one of the richest property owners in the region around Azua. "Outside these two districts, there are very few large landholders. Some with a thousand acres, and even ten thousand in a few cases. The rest is divided among small property owners."[16]

It is, then, apparent that after the eastern ranches that demanded little labor, the largest lands were the traditional sugar plantations in the South. Around Baní, some 100 presses were counted; around Azua, the estimates varied between 100 and 200.[17] With these wooden presses, one could "grind the white cane, filter the *guarapo* or cane-juice well, cook it, and finish it in great cauldrons made of tinned-copper or iron, clarifying or decanting it with leaves from the guava tree or with egg whites in order to make syrups for sweets"; sugar and brown sugar for domestic consumption were also made this way.[18]

Near Azua, there were at least twenty sugar plantations, among them Marchena's, "with some 600 acres, almost totally planted in cane, and we came to the conclusion that we had never seen a hacienda or plantation anywhere in such admirable condition. There was no overgrowth near its fences, nor were there weeds in the open avenues between its fields."[19]

A well-cared-for plantation was, then, a great exception. This can be explained by the scarcity of workers and the political instability, as well as by the fact of the circumstance that the dominant agricultural technique meant that one rarely found an agricultural enterprise tied to the only one piece of land. Thus, even in the fertile Vega Real, the fact that nine-tenths of the region was uncultivated made a "shifting agriculture" possible: "Instead of taking the trouble to plow and fertilize the land . . . , the natives prefer to clear the land to make other, new plantations,"[20] where they raised their tobacco and cacao for sale and their sugar, rice, and bananas for their own consumption. To provide themselves with meat, they turned branded hogs loose on the uncultivated land.

In this period, the plow was virtually unknown in the entire country. In Santiago the first plow was imported in 1898 by Juan Antonio de Lora, a minister in the Ulises Heureaux government. The use of this implement had little and slow acceptance: Don Eliseo Espaillat offered plows on credit to Cibao farmers, "and since such apparatus, according to them, conspired against their routine system, at the last minute these farmers cast them aside, and as such an obligation was of no use to them for the purposes of the payment, they relegated it to oblivion."[21] One must observe that, naturally, the mountainous terrain is less appropriate for plowing; here, the adze and the machete continued to be the preferred tools.

Summarizing the panorama of agriculture in the seventh decade of the last century outlined to this point, we can say that in an underpopulated country—the 1871 population was estimated at between 150,000 and 207,000[22]— a superabundance of land for farming led to the continuation of chaotic conditions with regard to the ownership of land. The deficient infrastructure, political instability, and scarcity of workers led to the predominance of cattle enterprises, which required a minimum of personnel, in the East and the West, and a "shifting agriculture" in the Cibao, where, nevertheless, there was also production for export. The traditional cultivation of cane for purposes other than home consumption existed only in the coastal section of the South. The primitive exploitation of fine lumbers was important, particularly around Barahona and Monte Cristi; honey and wax were also produced in small quantities. Only properties with between 1,000 and 10,000 acres were considered true *latifundios*; the number of private *latifundistas* was considered small. They rented out their lands or practiced extensive agriculture. The principal landholders were the state and the church.

In comparison with the more flourishing colonial period, during which a stable pseudo-feudal structure was, if not attained, at least pursued with considerable success, there had been a regression to more diffuse, confused forms of land ownership; to relatively more primitive agrarian techniques; and, accordingly, to the diminished importance of land possession as a criterion for social stratification.[23]

This regression, which in its social aspects could be called "democratization" or "levelling," was caused by the economic and demographic decline that resulted from the numerous wars and internal disturbances. It is also appropriate to recall that the Haitian occupier had carried out an enormous confiscation of property, not only ecclesiastical but private as well, and that this increase in state ownership had not been reversed by the governments of an independent Santo Domingo.

THE CHANGES

In this context of legal chaos, which was only tolerated because of the virtual insignificance of land ownership, a change occurred at the end of the seventies in the last century when large-scale sugar production got underway:

> Since some time ago, especially after the Cuban war broke out, agriculture has begun to come to life, with the establishment of large-scale cane plantations, in which large amounts of foreign capital imported by the Cuban immigration and also some considerable domestic capital have been invested, that have changed the face of the country, in which all kinds of agricultural enterprises abound today, now that the exporting done through its ports, not only of raw, centrifuged sugar, but also of tobacco, coffee, cacao, and other produce is considerable.[24]

Between 1875 and 1882, thirty "cane haciendas" were established. Four of them were "*centrales*," which received cane exclusively from hired *colonos* (tenant farmers). These were San Luis in Pajarito, founded by the Cambiaso brothers in 1881, with 2,400 *tareas* in cultivated land and 4,600 *tareas* to be cultivated, divided among ten tenant farmers; the San Isidro *central* in Pajarito, property of Hatton and Hernández and also founded in 1881, with 4,290 *tareas* cultivated and with twelve *colonos*; the La Duquesa *central*, established in 1882, of A. Bass and F. von Krosigh in La Isabela (San Carlos *común*), with 6,000 *tareas* ("installed, its machinery will triple results, and a railroad, already begun, will bring the machinery and the *colonos*' products to the sugar-mill"); and the Ocoa *central* of I. Heredia and Co. in Palmar de Ocoa (Baní *común*), started in 1882, with 3,000 *tareas* and fifteen *colonos*. Three plantations were "mixed"; the Constancia plantation of Heredia with Ureña in Pajarito, founded in 1878, which functioned with four *colonos* and lands of its own, 2,200 *tareas* in all; then Santiago Mellor's Porvenir plantation in San Pedro de Macorís, founded in 1879, working with twenty-one *colonos* and 1,200 acres of its own land; and the La Fe plantation of J. E. Hatton and Co., in San Carlos, which operated with 2,750 *tareas* and seven *colonos*, who possessed 2,250 *tareas* as a group.

The Esperanza plantation of Joaquín Manuel Delgado, founded in San Carlos in 1875, was already very large: 5,000 *tareas* and equipped with a "horizontal machine 16 inches in diameter, 2 Jamaican trains, 6 Laffertey centrifuges."

Out of these thirty plantations, only three were to be found in the North: two in the district of Samaná and one in the district of Puerto Plata; these three were among the first to be established (in 1877 and 1878) and were small (1,200 and 600 *tareas*, respectively). All the other plantations were in the South, to the west of the capital (one in Azua, three in Baní, and two in San Cristóbal); around the capital (six in San Carlos, five in Pajarito, two in Sabana Grande de Santo Domingo); and the rest to the east of the capital, including two in San Pedro de Macorís.

The two smallest plantations occupied 250 *tareas* each, the two largest 6,000 *tareas* each; the average size was around 2,000 *tareas*. The average sugar production was between 10 and 12 *quintales* [each *quintal* equals 100 kgs.] per *tarea*, although on good land they sometimes obtained 20 *quintales*.[25]

Among the owners there were persons with surnames that were not of Spanish origin: Italian surnames like Vicini; names that were apparently German like Bass, von Krosigh, Smidt, and Hachtman; and Anglo-Saxon surnames like that of William Read,[26] Fowl, Carol or Carroll, Hatton, and Stokes. Among the Cuban pioneers, we note Salvador Ros(s), who received a gold medal for his many merits from the city of San Pedro de Macorís in June of 1893. On that occasion Ross said that in the Dominican Republic he had not only managed to recover his fortune, but that "I have considerably enlarged it."[27] Shortly before, he had demonstrated his wealth by paying, along with his compatriot Juan Amechazurra, $200 for a box in the municipal theatre.[28] On the occasion of his marriage to "the distinguished lady" Orfelina Bazán in 1896, Rafael R. Deligne composed a commemorative poem:

> ¡Oh! la azucena floreciente en mayo
> abrió su cáliz rico de hermosura
> del espléndido sol a el alma rayo
> del aura matinal a la dulzura.*[29]

By 1882 a certain concentration in the ownership of plantations can be observed: Hachtmann, Peralta, and Hatton each possessed (a part of) two plantations. Vicini, who was going to make a great fortune in the following years and whose financial interests were to be closely linked to the Ulises Heureaux regime, was mentioned in 1878 only as co-owner of one plantation, but in 1887 he obtained permission to import "pichpen" (pitchpine) duty

---

*Oh! The lily blossoming in May / Opened its chalice rich with beauty / From the splendid sun to the quickening ray / Of the morning breeze to the sweetness.

free for four new plantations,[30] while in 1893 he is also mentioned as owner of the Angelina plantation in San Pedro de Macorís.[31] In the following year he receives a concession to establish the Central Azuano plantation, a concession renewed in 1897, when he also receives permission to open artesian wells necessary to irrigate the cane fields in the Azua *común*.[32]

The establishment of new plantations continued, then, in the decades of 1880 and 1890, notably in the region around San Pedro de Macorís and further toward the east.

North Americans began to be interested in the La Romana region. In a letter of 23 February 1888 President Heureaux confirms to Joaquín M. Delgado in Santo Domingo "that you are empowered by Sr. H. Newcomb to manage the affair of the purchase of lands in La Romana and to solicit from the government the renewal of the concession that it conferred upon Sr. Newcomb and his partners that lapsed because of the concessionaires' failure to meet their obligations . . . that I am ready to sell Sr. H. Newcomb twenty-five *caballerías* of land in La Romana, which, in accord with the sales offer that I made him, were settled on at $10,000–in American gold."[33] But in 1897 this region was still used principally for raising bananas by the La Romana Fruit Company[34] and not, as it is today, for growing cane.

Of the three most important sugar plantations in San Pedro de Macorís in 1889–namely, El Porvenir, Cristóbal Colón, and Puerto Rico–the last two had been established since 1882. The Puerto Rico plantation belonged to the Puerto Rican J. Seralles and employed 600 workers in 1893; bordering his sugar plantation Seralles also had a coffee enterprise.[35] In 1893 the Santa Fe sugar plantation was using a train to take workers back and forth from the city, and Salvador Ross installed a telephone line between his plantation and his warehouse in the city; Ross also had a Pullman car.[36] W. L. Bass of the Consuelo plantation in San Pedro de Macorís was also thinking about installing a telephone line between the *central* and the houses of his *colonos*. Bass's progressive ideas also appeared in his policy of distribution of benefits; as the newspaper put it, he made *colonos* of his workers, giving them 75 pounds of sugar as a bonus for each 200 pounds that they produced.[37]

By 1897 the mechanization of sugar transport was already quite advanced. Six plantations in Santo Domingo province had 110 kilometers of railway lines that year (the Santa Fe plantation alone had 30 kilometers and four locomotives to transport its product directly to the Ozama pier); five plantations in the San Pedro de Macorís district had a total of 108 kilometers; and three in Azua province had a total of 72 kilometers. The Compañía Frutera de San Lorenzo (Samaná Bay Fruit Co.) and the Compañía Frutera de La Romana, which raised bananas, also had railroad lines in that year, or were building them.[38] Moreover, the modern processing of the by-products had received attention: in 1885 a patent was granted to Robert Graham for a "device through which the waste-pulp of the sugar cane is instantly made into fuel."[39]

In the last two decades of the nineteenth century there were production increases not only in sugar, but also in cacao and coffee: between 1888 and 1897 sugar production was doubled, but that of cacao and coffee quadrupled, although sugar maintained its dominant place in the export statistics.[40]

In that period, cacao and coffee were preferred to tobacco, the traditional item for export from the Cibao, trade for which was completely in the hands of Germans. The prices on the Hamburg market were subject to extreme fluctuations, and the Dominican tobaccos, not very carefully cultivated, proved inferior to the Brazilian ones. Although in 1879 Luperón attributed the enormous drop in production (from some 100,000 *quintales* to 35,000) principally to the heavy rains that year,[41] in 1882 Heureaux indicated other causes: "I will tell you that Dominican tobacco would have retained its fame and held down the Brazilian and Colombian if the growers in the Cibao would have been more anxious about their future. They do not have to take all the blame: they suffered directly from the consequences of the frequent wars, and they have been victims of discouragement."[42]

But spirits did not fail completely with respect to raising tobacco. Thus, the government agreed in 1889 to Baron von Farensbach's[43] plan, by which he committed himself to establishing "model *fincas* or farms" in four or more locations to experiment with new tobacco seeds and to give instruction about these experiments. Farensbach would receive 75 centavos for each *quintal* exported; when the price rose to 15 pesos per *quintal*, thanks to Farensbach's activities, the government would levy an additional duty that would be given over to Farensbach.

Among the considerations that led to the approval of the plan, two items attract attention: first, that the state considered that in fact it was the government itself that should execute this plan,[44] and that it only turned it over to Farensbach because of lack of money; second, that there were factors apart from purely economic ones that motivated support for raising tobacco, since it "creates true citizens, free because of their customs and education, because each harvester is an owner, and even his subordinate employees retain the essence of citizenship in the kind of employment that they have in the preparation of that crop."[45] This thought must surely have been inspired in part by the social consequences of the establishment of the modern sugar enterprises, which we will deal with subsequently.

These efforts do not seem to have had much success, and in 1893 the governor of Santo Domingo issues a call to his province to follow the example of the Cibao farmers, who, tired of the "ungratefulness and caprices of tobacco, treacherous crop," devoted themselves to raising cacao and coffee.[46]

In November of that year Vice-President Figuereo signs a decree according to which everyone who plants cacao or coffee for ten consecutive years will receive $50 for each 2,000 plants in production; those who already have 2,000 plants are declared "exempt from all ordinary military service."[47]

Moreover, at that time, news about coffee cultivation arrives from the extreme western section of the country, from Enriquillo: since 1889, when lumber prices dropped on the European market, the Sres. Mota, who had created a source of work in the Barahona region with their lumber business, had turned to raising coffee on nearby lands. The Motas already owned more than 150,000 plants, four other growers had more than 60,000 bushes each. Moreover, there were many small property owners.[48]

There was also interest from abroad in investing in other agricultural products besides sugar cane. In 1888 permission was granted to Sres. Montandon, Descombes, and Co., "founders of a colony of foreign immigrants . . . in Sabana de la Mar," to import duty-free construction materials and equipment "for a rural *finca* for cacao, coffee and other produce, to be called La Evolución."[49] Three years before, a contract had been signed in New York with A. Boytel and Co. "via deposit of $5,000 at the Dominican consulate" in that city, in which "exemptions and other advantages were offered for establishing plantations for fruits, such as bananas, coconuts, oranges, lemons, on their own or through contracts with tenant farmers to whom they will advance funds, seeds and agricultural tools." As sugar was being quoted at a very low price on the market that year, the cultivation of "fruits, with which such profitable trade with the United States is carried on today,"[50] was considered quite advantageous.

Finally, it can be observed that the politicians, too, knew how to take advantage of the flourishing of agriculture. Around 1880 "Luperón liquidated his commercial house and gave himself over completely to agriculture—he planted 3,000 *tareas* of sugar and started a hacienda with cacao, coffee, and secondary crops and livestock and poultry breeding"[51]—while in 1896 Ulises Heureaux had "small plots of coffee" in Las Yaguas and Baní, and in that year he "ceded" lands in Puerto Plata to the Compañía Agrícola de Puerto Plata, which was directed by his friends and moneylenders Batlle and Cocco, and which was devoted to growing bananas.[52]

THE EFFECTS

Now let us consider the effects on the agricultural structure prevailing in the country of the rise of modern plantations, especially those for sugar—that is, the introduction of capital-intensive enterprises, rationally organized, that periodically employed a large number of workers and were oriented toward trade on the foreign market.

The system of *terrenos comuneros* that, as we have seen, had been maintained especially in the eastern part of the republic could not be continued when the sugar boom caused a rapid increase in land value. The titles of these lands were faked on a grand scale: "The co-owners' indolence in the exercise of the rights of their forbears over the land . . . favored . . . the surprising and extensive occupations carried out by persons who had never figured as co-owners of those lands, protecting themselves with false titles, by means of which large areas of land that now comprise extensive pastures and sugar cane plantations in the eastern region of the country were usurped."[53] "The progression of false titles in the *comunero* sites functioned in a direct ratio with the greater importance that the application of capital to agricultural development gave them, most especially in the cultivation of sugar cane."[54]

In that period the public surveyors were key figures in the process of formal recognition of property rights, for they had the authority "to judge the validity and adequacy of the titles that were presented by their claimants," as the Surveyors' Law of 1882 put it, echoing the law of 1848. According to this 1882 law, "students of the Instituto Profesional who had passed the second-year mathematics examination" could be surveyors. Often the surveyors received good lands in payment for their work.

Although the metric system of surface measurements was introduced in 1882, the legal problem of the *terrenos comuneros* continued until 1911, when the partition of these lands became compulsory, but with so many possibilities for evasion that as late as 1947 new legislation became necessary.[55] It was also in 1912 that the registration of private property became obligatory. Even earlier—that is, in 1867, 1875, and 1882—the creation of a national office of property registration had been ordered, but only for state properties.[56]

Thus, in 1889 it could still be remarked that the peasant had two enemies: "the *terrenos comuneros* and the open livestock breeding in all the agricultural zones."[57] Where population growth within the municipal limits had been very rapid, as in San Pedro de Macorís, the *ejidos* that the inhabitants had earlier cultivated according to their needs were given out as private property; by 1893 they were all covered with buildings.[58]

The fact that the arbitrary awarding of lands, which was sometimes formalized in appearance by the falsification of land titles, benefitted the foreign entrepreneur in particular and the fact that, overall, the entire sugar industry was sustained principally by non-Dominican capital—all this soon caused a feeling of irritation. Already by 1884 Pedro F. Bonó said in a letter to Luperón:

> I have seen, with my own eyes, the wicked doctrines reigning over the Cibao, and the destruction of its property and its agriculture. I have seen the transformation of the East; the titles to its property transferred almost for free into the hands of new occupants wrapped in the disguise of progress. Progress it would be, if it were a matter of the progress of the Dominicans, if the old peasants of the Santo Domingo *común* . . . were in part the owners of the plantations and the refineries; if already famed and wealthy as landowners, in the company of those who have done us the inestimable favor of coming to us, bringing us their money, their knowledge, their persons, their labor, they were sending their products directly to New York. But in place of that,

although poor and coarse, at least they were property owners, and today, poorer and made more brutish, they have become proletarians. What Progress does that show?[59]

Also in that same year Eugenio María de Hostos analyzed the Dominican agrarian situation profoundly: "We are going, apparently, before the wind," he writes:

calculating the number of all the sugar plantations founded in the entire Republic at 35, the land dedicated to raising sugar cane and the location of factories and machinery at 175 *caballerías*; the number of domestic laborers at 5,500, of foreigners at 500, and of machinists, sugarmasters, and other technical assistants whom the large-scale manufacture of sugar has made indispensable at 200. Taking capital of 40,000 pesos as the average value of the machinery . . . in each plantation; considering further capital of 10,000 pesos invested in each of them in means of transportation and cartage; computing the daily wages of all the workers in their various categories at 5,500 pesos; calculating the annual rent for land for these centers of production at 25,000 pesos; the interest on the capital applied to the machinery at 30,000 pesos; the annual production of sugar at 2,400,000 pesos; the duties on export at 183,750 pesos, the Republic owed the following to the development of sugar plantations:

1. The increase of its nominal capital to 21,088,750 pesos;
2. The economic valuation of land that only had a natural value and the regulation of land ownership, which used to be completely undefined;
3. The direct improvement of the work environment and the accompanying betterment of the worker;
4. The acquisition of modern procedures of production;
5. The rapid change from small to large industry;
6. The ancillary change from an almost exclusively domestic trade to an almost exclusively international one.

As a necessary sequel to the rapid increase in production and consumption, export trade increased, and the business of speculation prospered artificially. The progressive increase of the State's income, which has almost tripled, has been a favorable result of the first; the unhealthy development of puerile and ostentatious luxury is an unfavorable symptom of the second.[60]

After thus observing the immediate effects of the boom in the sugar industry, Hostos directs his attention to what could be called the structural effects. He notes the decline of livestock raising in the East and of traditional sugar production in the South: "The ranches have almost been wiped out by excessively avaricious mass exports; the sugar presses that dotted the fields of the South like ants have continued to disappear rapidly, and the worker in all these regions had been abandoning his small-scale production in order to become an agent of large-scale production. That is a bad thing."

Previously:

> they lived poorly, but on their own resources: the country lived almost totally on what the country produced. A little work was enough for the cultivation of secondary crops and raising their cattle, and the domestic markets offered a plentiful source of provisions for the public demand. Content in its poverty, the country consumed what it produced and nothing more. But the plantations came, the supply of work and the demand for laborers came with them. The old cultivator from the small properties became a day-laborer, abandoned his little plot of land, neglected raising barnyard poultry, the small agricultural industries; the rural economy, which whether by tradition or instinct had served to meet the needs of general consumption, gave way so much to the eagerness to earn in a few days the salary that one used to earn only in weeks . . ., and even months of work, and paradoxical as it may seem, the country was poorer when the State became wealthier. We have all felt here the daily consequences of that anomaly: we have all been starving . . . for those spontaneous fruits of tropical lands, which have been becoming rarer at each step of the way, and at the same time more expensive, and for those articles of primary necessity that have been becoming less accessible even as acquiring cash seemed easier.

After noting that the crisis in the sugar industry in the year in which Hostos writes is attributable in part to "what . . . the French define as *saison morte*" aggravated by the landowners' dependence upon New York merchants and bankers both in regard to sales and to supply of capital, the Puerto Rican sociologist goes on to a frontal attack against the sugar industry. "That industry that, thus, from the historical point of view, is abominable, was founded upon slavery. Slave the worker—the African—slave the labor . . .; slave the property, too, that was to a vast extent accessible only to the privileged." The principal basis of production, the land, was also cheap. Given the inexpensiveness of the first two fundamental factors of the industry, the easy task of monopolizing the benefits fell to the third factor, capital. However, the abolition of slavery and the slave trade made it impossible to "continue monopolizing the distribution of the wealth that the manufacture of sugar produced," and thus arose "the poorly-named *Centrales*." There, at least in theory, the requirements for a division of labor were met and the right of capital (as a factor of production) to profits was limited in favor of the labor and land factors. Since the owners of the *centrales* had to concern themselves only with the *processing* of the cane, they had to be industrialists and no more; the cultivation of the cane had to be in other hands.

The origin of the structural crisis, says Hostos, is in the fact that the sugar industrialists continued, as in the era of slavery, to affirm the monopoly not only over capital, but also over land and labor. The margin of earnings that they received thanks to this monopoly was exorbitant: even with the low prices of the 1884 market, Hostos estimates this margin at 16 percent. The crisis originates, then, "in capital's asking for a greater interest than that to which it has a right, and in seeking, anti-economically, earnings higher than it is legitimate to expect." Subsequently he affirms again, "It means nothing to the country for capital to increase, because the well-being of everyone does not increase." Hostos sees as a remedy, on one hand, the establishment of an agricultural bank for sugar producers, and, on the other, the foundation of agricultural colonies that, preferably occupied by immigrants, would concern themselves with raising various products, among them, cane. The sugar producer would leave the cane grower the freedom to diversify his agriculture.

Hostos's opinion that the cultivation of cane is inferior to raising beets is interesting. The beet is produced in lands "with a machine power that is unknown in the Antilles." This fact again shows the need to diversify agriculture, if, at least, one does not want to watch resignedly the ruin of many plantations, as in Puerto Rico and Cuba. Hostos ends his philippic against monopoly and monoculture by saying: "As long as we do not find a way for large and small properties, large and small capital, large and small industries to coexist, we shall be in permanent crisis."

Hostos's wise admonitions did not have an effect. Thus, the complaints about the scarcity of secondary crops continued. After indicating in his annual review for 1898 the need for improving the quality of sugar, coffee, and cacao by means of establishing model farms or by a provincial agricultural inspection whose inspector would have to "advise, even by employing coercion, the improvements that science counsels," the governor of the Santo Domingo province notes that it is necessary to encourage the cultivation of "secondary crops and those for daily consumption, whose lack is sadly observed to be detrimental to all classes, by not permitting any farmer or grower of secondary crops and with a family to go to work outside without leaving his *conucos* in good condition and in proportion to the size of his family."[61]

In the same year the governor of Santiago advocated lowering the transportation charges for secondary crops, some of which were found in abundance in his province, while there was a shortage of them a short distance away. However, the production of certain items for local consumption, such as rice, potatoes, and onions, was inadequate in Santiago as well.[62]

The scarcity of laborers and, consequently, the relatively high daily wages that the large agricultural enterprises paid (during the sugar harvest of 1893, they were paying two or three pesos per *tarea* in San Pedro de Macorís) occasioned an internal migration, partly permanent and partly seasonal, that explains the scarcity of traditional produce. Some people abandoned their *conucos* for good, others earned enough during the sugar harvest that they did not have to work much on their own land afterwards.

This geographic mobility caused uneasiness. The governor of Samaná complained in 1898 that the police force of the "great banana plantation of the 'Samaná Bay Fruit Company,' in Sabana de la Mar," was inadequate "to contain the unpleasantnesses that daily occur there, where, under the pretext of seeking work, all the malefactors from all points of the Republic come to take refuge."[63]

But not everyone was convinced of the appeal of this company as a boss. On 11 June 1893, a man named Marius wrote a letter to the editor of the *Listín*, in which he said, "The peons, sons of the country, are treated like animals that are not respected at all. Instead of paying them weekly or fortnightly, the fruit of their labor is arbitrarily withheld from them for a month and more, and as these unfortunate weaklings necessarily need some advances in order to buy their food, the Company gives them on account a kind of paper money *that it does not guarantee* to the public, so that they find themselves obliged to buy in the store that the Company has established and where they are sacrificed in the most indescribable, cruelest fashion."

Mentioned here for the first time is the notorious system of *vales* (vouchers), which was also going to spread to the sugar-producing region and was to be described later, in all its negative aspects, in the novel *Over* by Ramón Marrero Aristy.[64]

In the last decade of the nineteenth century, increasingly forceful protests were heard against vagrancy and corruption. This was due to the previously mentioned increased participation of the rural population in the cash economy (in which sums of money, subjectively large ones, were periodically delivered to people who had previously been able to cover their range of needs almost entirely with the products of their own land), and also to the uprooting that resulted from the increase in geographic mobility. In 1893, while making a layover at San José de Ocoa, Vice-President Figuereo confessed being "an all-out and cordial enemy of vagrancy, source of so many evils," and he gave "orders . . . so that within six months everyone today found in the camps without known employment will have his farmland in a perfect state of cultivation."[65]

The greater circulation of money among the rural population caused an enormous increase in the number of merchants and shopkeepers in the countryside, and various authorities attributed the "vagrancy" and "corruption" directly to these small entrepreneurs. It is worth citing, in this regard, the following paragraphs from a petition from the ayuntamiento of Cotuy to the National Congress in 1897:

> The spirit of corruption that is invading these regions, principally in our rural areas; the tendency to vagrancy that is developing in such a lamentable way among the peasants, who, now given over to revels, now to gambling and alcoholic beverages, no longer live for work nor for anything edifying and useful, but for licentiousness, immersing themselves more and more in a state of atrophy and demoralization, whose terrible and fatal results will not delay in making themselves felt if a remedy is not arranged in time, have compelled this Ayuntamiento, inspired by its desire for the public good and public order,

to direct . . . to that Sovereign Body the present lines in order to request:

Given that we consider the evils . . . noted above, whose major cause rests in the business establishments in the countryside because that is where fathers and sons gather together to abandon themselves to the open satisfaction of vices, without the rural authorities' being able to prevent it, let a decree be issued to prohibit said establishments in the countryside, with the exception of the so-called *bodegas* on the estates and of the cantinas at the cockpits, providing that these latter only sell on the days and nights that they are licensed for their dances and cockfights. This Ayuntamiento believes that in this way a decisive step can be taken in favor of public moralization.[66]

Three days before, and perhaps by mutual agreement, the ayuntamiento of Salcedo had proposed to the Congress the prohibition of commercial establishment in the countryside, under penalty of a $25 fine.[67]

The admirable concern for the *campesino's* spiritual welfare that seems to manifest itself in these petitions should not be viewed without a little skepticism. The material interests of the urban merchants, who were well represented in the ayuntamientos, also came into play. Thus, the following occurred: before the arrival of the sugar industry, the extensive rural zones that surrounded a small urban center relied upon the merchants residing in the town for their supplies. Even though the inhabitants of the countryside did not buy their articles directly from these merchants, the few owners of the rural *bodegas* nevertheless bought their merchandise in the nearby village. Thus, the rise of the sugar industry's "*bodega central*" hurt the village merchant in two ways. On one hand, the day laborer was tied to the *bodega central* by the voucher system, and on the other, the *bodega* obtained as clients the travelling vendors and the rural shopkeepers, whose number was increasing rapidly. The village merchant, whose capital was often limited, could not compete either in prices or stock with the large *bodegas*, which imported their merchandise directly from abroad. As the *bodega central* extended its radius of commercial action to the surrounding region, selling both wholesale and retail, the village merchant and shopkeeper saw himself deprived of a potentially important share of the growing cash economy.[68]

Naturally, the merchants' response to this challenge should have been to compete directly by modernizing their business customs, reducing their margin of earnings, working together more closely, imitating (or trying to imitate) in part the activities of the travelling vendors and the small rural shopkeepers. But their dignity did not permit them to take that route: they only tried to destroy through legal measures competition that they considered unfair. They expected to be able to promote some legal action not only because the established merchants were generally known as supporters of the regime in power, but also, and above all, because the travelling vendors and entrepreneurs toward whom their anger was directed belonged, for the most part, to the most recent group of immigrants to the country: the Arabs.

In a petition to the National Congress, dated 9 June 1896, seventeen merchants from San Pedro de Macorís remain silent about the corruption of the people and set forth their true objections in a direct fashion:

Our countryside is full of commercial shops. . . . There is no farmer who is not a merchant too, all of which significantly damages us, and this injury is augmented in the highest degree with the invasion in village and countryside, from door to door, of Arabs, who, given their commercial operations, have monopolized all the business, and have swept us away to the point of turning our commerce into a desolate, sad cemetery. Their warehouses are more important now than our firms, and given their absolutely minimal expenditures—for their manner of living is quite well known—omitting all expenditure that is not strictly necessary to the filthy, miserable existence to which they subject themselves, it is impossible to fight them. The importance of our businesses requires expenses and attentions from which theirs are exempt, and if we tried to compete with their prices, our interests would suffer. The commercial future of Macorís is in the hands of the Arabs, and we believe that the Arabs have never made any country happy, nor have they been the ones who have contributed to the importance that Macorís has today. We also believe that a people neither can nor should found its hopes for development and importance on that class of merchants; and that our civilized, illustrious Government should not regard with indifference the damage that they are causing us . . . and that will completely thwart business in Macorís, with harm to the interests of the State; we believe that [this damage] has some cause that our illustrious Government can investigate and combat, thereby demonstrating its conscientious and sterling rule.

We implore you, Illustrious Congressmen, that the establishments in the rural areas and sugar plantations be granted the right to sell provisions for the sustenance of their workers, with the exception of the right to retail fabric sales; and regarding the Arabs or travelling merchants, that they be prevented from importing merchandise, or that a heavy tax to preclude the inexpensiveness of their goods be levied upon them.[69]

It is well-known that the Arabs did not lose the war of competition, and not a few of the established merchants guaranteed their commercial success, in a subsequent generation, by entrusting the happiness of a daughter to a monied member of that same group that had previously been considered incapable of bringing about "the happiness of any country."

Grouping together the changes in the agrarian structure of the Dominican Republic in the last three decades of the past century noted here, it can be asserted that:

1. A transition took place from an essentially autarchical agriculture and livestock raising (with the marked exceptions of tobacco cultivation in the Cibao and the export of lumber and cattle) to a sugar industry that, with intensive use of capital, produced for the world market. The ex-

port of cacao, coffee, and bananas, raised in part by modern, large agricultural enterprises, also increased considerably.

2. As a result of the increase in land value, a crisis developed in the system of *comunero* lands, which had been established by a regression from the traditional, pseudo-feudal pattern of land ownership and the consequent possibility of dealing in the *acciones*. Out of this crisis, a clearly defined pattern of private ownership emerged—but not before our century, and at the cost of falsification and fraud.

3. The traditional forms of sugar production disappeared totally, and the livestock enterprises that employed few people disappeared in part, while the cultivation of traditional fruits and vegetables decreased noticeably.

4. The new, large agricultural enterprises were founded initially by individuals, the majority of them foreigners (particularly Cubans), and in a later phase by U.S. companies as well.

5. Mobility increased among the rural population, which obtained a greater share in the cash economy. From this the already established urban merchants benefitted only in part, for the *bodega central*, which tied down the workers themselves through the system of *"vales"* (probably introduced by U.S. companies), also obtained the itinerant Arab merchants as customers. This resulted in a reduction of the radius of commercial activity of the urban centers.

Needless to say, the changes in the nature and intensity of agricultural production outlined here affected all sectors of social life. In the next chapter we shall turn our attention to population growth and composition and to urban development in this period.

CHAPTER TWO

Changes in Demographic Structure and Population Distribution

THE NATIONAL POPULATION

The scanty data on the number of inhabitants in the course of the nineteenth century must, of course, be used with the greatest caution. But, at least, the general tendencies that they reflect are probable. In 1789 Moreau de Saint-Mery estimated the population of the Spanish part of Hispaniola at 125,000.[1] According to an 1819 census, in that year there were only 63,000.[2] The Haitian rebellion and its consequences for Santo Domingo (among others, the occupation under L'Ouverture from the end of 1800 until 1802); perhaps the French occupation under Ferrand as well; and certainly the subsequent period of "*la España boba*" (Foolish Spain) (1808-21) are factors that together make probable a balance in favor of emigration for the period 1789-1819. The next census data that I know of date from 1863; in that year an "ecclesiastical tribunal" estimated the Catholic population at 207,700. This figure was rejected as too high by the U.S. Commission of Inquiry for convincing reasons; in 1871, the commission itself set the number of inhabitants at 150,000.[3] In 1887, a new census was carried out by the ecclesiastical tribunal. In the time elapsed, considerable growth was apparent: the population was then fixed at 382,312.

Abad estimated the population in 1888 at 415,000 to 416,000 inhabitants.[4] An estimate of 486,000 inhabitants in 1897 confirmed this growth;[5] in 1898, Meriño calculated the total population at 485,000.[6] The decided population increase during the last decades of the nineteenth century that becomes evident in these figures is corroborated by the data on the changes in the geographic distribution of the population, as we shall demonstrate further on.

Moreover, the changes in the agrarian structure that we noted in the previous chapter make likely a rapid increase beginning in the seventies. A part of the population increase must be attributed to immigration. Thus, we shall now move on to deal briefly and separately with some of the principal groups of immigrants of the past century. We shall not limit ourselves to considering statistical data but shall also present materials that can assist our subsequent analysis of the structural and cultural changes in the period that concerns us.

IMMIGRATION

Methodists from the United States. Two years after the beginning of the Haitian domination (1822-44), President Boyer systematically began to attract North American freedmen to the country; the agent Jonathan Granville was sent to New York for that purpose. He had authorization to offer anyone who wanted to emigrate to the island of Haiti free passage, maintenance for four months, and thirty-six acres of land for each twelve workers. The estimates of the number of people who accepted Granville's offers vary between 6,000 and 13,000; it is certain, though, that a significant number of them came from an urban environment—the city of Philadelphia in particular was one of the places of origin most numerously represented. It is also certain that some of them went back quickly, as much because of their urban origin as because of difficulties in adapting caused by the new country's climate and culture; another portion, estimated at one third of the original number, died within a short time. However, in 1870, small groups of these immigrants or their descendants could still be found in various places in the country. The most important were then found in the capital and in Santiago, Puerto Plata, and Samaná. In this last location, about 500 to 600, some of whom had progressed to the point of becoming relatively prosperous farmers, were living at that time. For their religious organization, they received aid from the Wesleyan Methodist church of England; they had organized their own English-speaking school system, which compared quite favorably with the national Dominican system. In sum, they had come to form a duly organized foreign population nucleus that, with the cohesion its religion and language gave it, considered itself superior to the Dominicans and tried to avoid assimilation.

In that same year, the Methodist colonies of Santo Domingo and Puerto Plata had to a great extent already been "Dominicanized" with respect to language and selection of spouses, although they still had their own Methodist churches[7] and mutual aid associations, and in Puerto Plata their own school. For the immigrants residing in Samaná, this process of assimilation only came to be felt clearly in the last years of the century: President Heureaux's appointment of a son of colonists, General Anderson, as governor of Samaná province symbolized the recognition of the immigrant group within the national entity. Heureaux, who had been born in Puerto Plata and who thus knew the U.S. Methodists well,[8] always felt a sympathy for them that was perhaps also based on racial considerations. One of his daughters worked for a lengthy period as a teacher in Samaná.

Despite increasing assimilation, knowledge of the English language is quite widespread in Samaná even today. The Samaná origins of many members of the Dominican naval forces may bear some relation with this fact. We have no data available on the occupational composition of this group of U.S. immigrants; it is known, however, that President Boyer wanted to attract principally skilled craftsmen and farmers. It is also apparent that the educational level of this group must have been relatively high, and that in those places where there were enough of them to found their own schools, they knew how to maintain this level. This educational factor, as well as the group's Protestant work ethic (which was kept alive by means of religion) and the sober lifestyle that religion also imposed upon them—dancing, drinking, and smoking were forbidden—would all have favored their chances for social ascent and for occupying those positions open in the developing socioeconomic structure that required such culturally determined norms of conduct. But these possibilities were obstructed by geographic and social isolation (particularly true for the colony in Samaná). Then too, as the nongovernmental sector of the economic structure was crystallizing and being stabilized to a certain extent at the end of the century, upward mobility was blocked more than before if one had features that were too noticeably Negroid.[9]

Certainly one of the Methodist immigrants who had exceptional successes was Elijah R. Gross, who, having served under Boyer as colonel and later as director of the mails, was named a judge by President Santana, an office he still held in 1871.[10] We have already mentioned the political career of General Anderson.

In professions related to education and health care, the large number of descendants of Protestant immigrants was surprising. The first professional nurse was Mrs. Margaret Mearse of Puerto Plata, wife of a Protestant minister at the end of the century. In the eighties, few women from the capital were encountered among nurses. But more women from Puerto Plata and Samaná, as well as immigrants from Curaçao, St. Thomas, and the Turks Islands[11] were in this profession, which, it should be said in passing, did not enjoy great social prestige in the Dominican cultural environment.

The Sephardic Jews from Curaçao. Only after the move of the Real Audiencia to Cuba in 1799 as a result of the Treaty of Basel (1795) did Santo Domingo become a more attractive place for the establishment of Jewish immigrants than it had been under Spanish domination. It is not surprising, then, that in the first quarter of the nineteenth century some Jews had set themselves up in the eastern part of Hispaniola. The tombstone considered the oldest in what was the Jewish section of the Avenida de la Independencia cemetery in the capital says: *"Jacob Pardo, natif de Amsterdam, Age 46 ans, Décédé 6 Dec. 1826. Avec regret de sa famille et amis."*[12] Around 1830—that is, also in the period of the Haitian domination—the Rothschild commercial house of St. Thomas established a branch in Santo Domingo under the business name Rothschild and Cohen. But it is principally in the forties, and especially after independence in 1844, that the presence of Sephardic Jews coming, almost without exception, from Curaçao, becomes clearly notable. Surnames like

Pardo, Maduro, Naar, Crasto, Senior, Namías, de Marchena, de León, Curiel, and [Cohen] Henríquez all belong to families that, having fled the Inquisition in Spain and Portugal, arrived in Holland by way of other countries—France, Turkey—and from there set out for Dutch possessions in the Western Hemisphere—Pernambuco, New Amsterdam, Surinam, Curaçao. From these places, especially Curaçao, emigration to non-Spanish colonies of the Caribbean, such as Jamaica and St. Thomas, soon followed.

The first Curaçao Sephardim who left for Santo Domingo did not all remain there. They generally established their commercial houses as representatives of important Curaçao firms, but they themselves often left after a few years. This occurred with the Curaçaoan López Penha, who remained in the country for only a few years around 1845; some of his sons were the ones who established themselves there for good. According to Ucko, it was, on one hand, the political instability, and on the other, the inadequate religious organization that caused many of the older immigrants to return to Curaçao. From the authorities, they had enjoyed every protection, even in the first years. Interesting in that regard for a number of reasons is an official letter from President Santana dated 16 September 1846 and prompted by a complaint against some Jewish merchants in La Vega, from which we cite the following:

> The Council of Ministers of State meeting under the Presidency of the President of the Republic took note of a petition directed to the President by the District Prefect of La Vega, whose purpose is to demand that the Government take measures against some Jews who do business in that village; as a result, after a careful examination it was decided to direct the following response to the petitioners, by way of the District Prefect: Sr. District Prefect: I have at hand a petition, dated the ninth of the current month, that has been sent to me by you and some other officials and inhabitants of that Province, whose content has done nothing less than surprise me and places the Government in the position of having to use language that it would always hope to shun but cannot avoid after having calculated all the evils that might ensue if the causes that produce them are not cut off at the root in time. In the first place, as the foremost authority of that Province, you ought to abstain from signing petitions of any kind. The same principle ought to apply even more to the military chiefs. It would be well-deserved if they were subjected to a court martial in order to learn not to involve themselves in intrigues whose object they do not understand, but which is quite familiar to the Government, as I am going to demonstrate to you. It is stated in the petition that four or five Jews are doing considerable harm to the people because they purchase ounces of gold and the produce of the country at exorbitant prices, and so on. These words alone indicate clearly that it is not the people who complain, for there is no farmer to whom it would occur to complain because a Jew gives him a hundred pesos for a *quintal* of tobacco that a Dominican would

only pay him fifty for, in such a way that, far from redounding to the people's harm, it is a manifest benefit that will continue to increase to the extent that the number of buyers grows and they deprive the three or four well-known monopolists of the unhappy privilege of enriching themselves at the cost of the unhappy peasants whom they sacrifice. Those monopolists are authors on behalf of many others whose signatures appear in the petition because they are unaware of the hidden hand that guides them, but whenever they reflect upon their true interests, they will be convinced that they have been deceived in order to serve as the tool of passions as wretched as they are unseemly . . . : when some active, hardworking foreigner comes to our soil and does in a day what the natives do not do in a month because they do not stir themselves, far from persecuting him as the hidden authors of the petition would want, the Government, and all Dominicans interested in the good of the country, ought to protect and encourage him to the end that our [own people] might take his example and learn that wealth is the daughter of work and frugality . . . ; to desire in the nineteenth century, and in the middle of a free Republic, to persecute a peaceful individual and to prevent him from buying tobacco on the pretext of his religion is a scandalous abuse of the doctrine of Jesus Christ. . . . The conduct of those Dominicans would have had to be of another sort if, instead of listening to the cry of the passions, they heard the voice of justice and gratitude. Those four Jews whom they persecute there, and others who reside here, have been the first to hand over their funds without delay to defray the expenses of the war, at the very moments in which some Dominicans were not only doing nothing, not even making loans, but through their bad example discouraging the good patriots who showed themselves determined to defend the freedom of the Republic. . . . In this capital . . . there are more Jews than in any other spot on the island, and far from having experienced the least difficulty up to now, they go to the Church, attend all our ceremonies, and even contribute to the support of the faith with their alms . . . and the Church, loyal repository of the Christian faith, consecrates the fifteenth prayer of Good Friday to asking God for the conversion of the Jews, a conversion that cannot be attained with persecutions nor arbitrarinesses, but by means of kindliness and persuasion . . . [which] document will be printed and circulated by efforts of the Secretary of State in the Dispatches of the Interior and Police in order to prevent the evils consequent upon that kind of affair and so that the people shall know just what the conduct of the Government is in carrying out its sacred obligations. Given at the National Palace of Santo Domingo, Capital of the Republic, on the sixteenth day of the month of September of eighteen forty-six, third year of the Fatherland.[13]

As we shall later see in greater detail, the official attitude set in this early document in relation to immigration in general was always confirmed by subsequent governments. Concerning the Sephardic immigration in particular, this document touches upon two noteworthy points. There is, first, the financial support that the Jews gave to "the war" (against Haiti), support that must have been appreciated, of course, by the patriots. Moreover, in the following decades the Jewish merchants, established principally in Curaçao but also at St. Thomas, participated in financing politico-military enterprises, including internal revolutionary movements in particular. This happened, doubtlessly, upon the advice and intermediation of their representatives in Santo Domingo. Thus, in 1857, the Curaçao firm J. A. Jesurún and Son loaned $100,000 to the government of that time, also renting it the schooner *Amelia* for some 10,000 pesos.[14]

In 1866 President Cabral authorized Jacobo Pereyra to negotiate a European loan for a sum up to 400,000 pounds sterling, the loan contract that he signed in 1867 with the Paris bankers Em. Erlanger, however, was not approved by the National Congress. Simultaneously, Sigmund Rothschild had a power of attorney from the Dominican government. In 1868 Báez accepted the presidential duties again; his revolution had triumphed, in part thanks to the economic aid of J. A. Jesurún of Curaçao, whose bill for $37,145.80 was recognized as a national debt on 30 April of that year. The head of that firm, Abraham Jesurún, was the republic's consul in Curaçao during various periods, and he was named a general in reward for his accomplishments. In 1868 Báez entrusted Jesurún, along with the chargé d'affaires in France, Col. Adolphe Mendes, with negotiating a loan in Europe after the failure of the negotiations for that purpose that Jesurún had undertaken in the United States. The result of the contacts that they made in Europe was the unhappily renowned Hartmont loan (despite the fact that Mendes had offered warnings against the Englishman Hartmont). The agreement was signed in 1869, with the republic represented by the minister of the treasury, Ricardo Curiel, also the bearer of a Curaçao-Sephardic surname.

Without going deeply into the country's onerous financial history, we will limit ourselves to noting that in the eighties it was again a Sephardic immigrant, Eugenio Generoso de Marchena, who acted as the government's principal financial expert. It was he, undoubtedly supported by his Curaçao and Dutch connections, who signed in Amsterdam in 1888 the first agreement with the Dutch bankers Westendorp and Co., which regulated the debts to the holders of Hartmont bonds. At the same time, the agreement created, starting from 1 November of that year, the Caja General de Recaudación de Aduanas or General Office for Customs Collections (*La Régie*), which, staffed by Westendorp agents, would control the income from import and export duties during the thirty years that were to be the term of the 770,000-pounds sterling loan signed with Westendorp.[15]

Although it is not our intention to ascribe to the Sephardic immigrants and their relations residing overseas a monopolistic position with respect to the financial policy of the republic during the period that concerns us, we can, nevertheless, assume with considerable certainty that at least in certain periods they held the key positions.[16]

Let us return to the Santana document. A second point that attracts our attention is the fact that the Sephardim were, apparently, regular visitors to the Catholic church. Concerning this, it is appropriate to note that in a surprisingly short time—that is, two or three generations—the Curaçao Jews were assimilated into Dominican society. Since there is not known to have been any coercion to that effect, it is necessary to seek another explanation for that phenomenon, which was surprising for that group and that era. Ucko indicates that the group was too small or too dispersed to be able to maintain an organized religious life, including education; although the traditional religious holidays were celebrated, "the religious life was weak and not very enduring." He also mentions the rise of liberal Jewish thought (which caused a schism in Curaçao[17]) as one of the factors that encouraged religious indifference, while, on the other hand, their spiritual needs were satisfied to an increasing extent by Masonry, which was widespread in Santo Domingo: "They found Messianism again, as well as the Cabbala, with its mysterious speculations, in the pan-human ideal and the mysticism of Masonry." It is interesting to mention here that in the same year in which President Santana signed the document mentioned above for the protection of, among others, the Sephardic Jew Naar, a resident of La Vega, both their names appeared on the roster of a Masonic lodge.[18]

A third factor that, at least according to Ucko, explains the rapid assimilation of the Jews is the need that many of them felt to introduce "new blood" into their group, the endogamy of which was hampered by its small numbers. This feeling would have been influenced by "the appealing beauty of the Creole race." Certainly there were protests on the part of the Jewish older generation against these mixed marriages, which thus were sometimes performed with Jewish as well as Catholic rites. But with the passing of time, the Catholic part of the family generally proved dominant. However, in the families to which we refer, there was never any tendency to keep their partially Jewish ancestry secret. On one hand, their economic position already gave them social stability, and on the other—and this is probably the more important—the "Hebrew ancestry clearly verified its white origin, and the Dominican *criollo* attributed great importance to the white component of his lineage." One descendant of the Sephardic immigrants after another brought the theme of assimilation to Dominican literature. We should mention the verse drama *La hija del Hebreo* (1883) of Federico Henríquez y Carvajal, which describes the marriage of a Jewish man and a Christian woman, and chapter 12, entitled *"Los paisanos de Jesús"* ("The Countrymen of Jesus"), in the novel *La senda de la revelación* (1936), by Haim H. López-Penha (who, like many of his group—including the Sephardim of Curaçao—had received his education principally in Germany). In the latter work, the author presents a dialogue between a German peasant woman and a Protestant girl, granddaughter of a Jewish grandmother, developed in the tradition of Lessing.

The increasing assimilation of the Sephardim was accompanied by a reduction in their business activities, and it is tempting to see a causal connection in this. In the first decades of their stay, "the Hebrews began to prosper rapidly, and they occupied, more or less, the same place that the Spanish firms that were established in the Dominican Republic years ago retain today [1944]—that is, they were the owners of the large wholesale and retail business concerns. . . . However, their commercial prosperity continued to decline from the beginning of the twentieth century," says Ucko. As the Jews were being absorbed into the highest social stratum of the era, they were losing their economic ethos, adopting the latter's economic mentality, preferring to invest their wealth in houses and lands, and choosing traditional academic training as a doctor or lawyer for the male children in preference to a business career. To the extent that more important government positions were filled by them, their private commercial interest was being relegated to a secondary level.[19] However, it is necessary to point out here that some Jewish immigrants abandoned the country in the last years of the past century because of the then-current economic crisis, apparently preferring an opportunity for lucrative activities elsewhere to the economic instability of their status as members of a creole bourgeoisie.[20] Although the Sephardic immigration has not been very important in a quantitative sense—Ucko estimates that the number of Jewish families, at least in the forties, did not exceed twenty—we hope that the preceding paragraphs have convinced the reader of the importance that can be attributed to it in an economic, political, and social sense.

The Canary Islanders or isleños. Immigration from the Canary Islands took place, of course, as early as the colonial period. At the end of the seventeenth century, San Carlos was founded by *isleños* (Islanders). Quite soon this village situated west of the capital fell into decline, but in the mid-eighteenth century it was again infused with life by "hardworking, honorable" Canarian immigrants. By the end of the nineteenth century, San Carlos had come to form part of the Santo Domingo urban complex, even though it had conserved its own identity—geographically, by remaining outside the city walls; legally, by having its own communal police headquarters, town council, mayoralty, and registry; and socially, by having available its own schools and its own church "of solid masonry." In 1898, 10,000 persons lived there.[21] Almost all the inhabitants lived in *bohíos* (huts); there were only two stone houses.

San Carlos was also called the Mamey *barrio*: its local festival was that of the Virgin of La Candelaria, in February, when the *barrio* was decorated with mamey branches and the girls dressed in orange. Even at the end of the past century only one black family named the Caravallos lived in San Carlos: "They called them the 'dark-complexioned Islanders' because they were honorable, hardworking, and decent."[22] This last remark indicates that the population at that time was still distinguished by being predominantly of Canarian descent.[23] However, it does not seem likely that one can speak of endogamy within the group in that period: not a few of the distinguished families of the era were descended in part from *isleños*, although they had abandoned San Carlos as their place of residence. Accordingly, the image that dominates is one of a *barrio*, surprisingly homogeneous in an ethnic and cultural sense, where those *isleños* who had not managed to improve their economic position over the course of several generations remained together. Despite the favorable opinions generally expressed about the inhabitants of San Carlos with respect to their diligence and honesty, the majority of its inhabitants up to the present continue to form part of the category of clerk or shopkeeper, artisan, or small businessman. A detailed study could indicate whether, in effect, upward mobility led to abandoning the *barrio*.

At that same period, other colonizing was done by Canarian groups. The city of Samaná, which had been abandoned, was repopulated with Canary Islanders in 1756 by the Spanish authorities, who feared French expansion. In that same year, Sabana de la Mar, located on the southern coast of Samaná Bay, was established by *isleños*, to whom "plantations and cattle were given in order to establish a colony. Efforts to that end were so feeble that the village remained dormant, until during the Haitian Revolution a number of French refugees, seeking their own safety, established themselves there, creating several sugar cane haciendas."[24] In this same period of progressive Spanish policy, actively carried out in Santo Domingo by Gov. Rubio y Peñaranda, Monte Cristi and Puerto Plata were also repopulated with Canarian families. Furthermore, Baní, in the southern part of the country, founded in 1764 "by Spaniards, by Canary Islanders, and Dominican ranchers from the region," had such a predominance of *isleños* that it could be called "the Dominican Canaria, maintaining the purest Spanish lineage to the point that until only a few years ago there were scarcely any colored people there"—or, in Hostos's words, "a veritable ethnological parenthesis." Even today, people from Baní have the reputation of being able businessmen; moreover, the city has produced a significant number of intellectuals and politicians.[25]

In the 1880s and at the initiative of the Dominican government, a new immigration of Canary Island groups took place:

> The sixth of October [1884] this office [Section for Development] with the participation of the Ministry of the Treasury signed a contract with Sr. Andrés Sosvilla i Gonzáles to bring from the Canary Islands in the upcoming month of March, the greatest possible number of families or individuals intended for agricultural labor, for the sum of twenty pesos cash for each person from ten full years of age to sixty, and ten pesos from one to ten, under a contract whose terms were stipulated

under separate, sealed cover that contained the advantages promised by the Government and by the planters. . . . Charged to extraordinary expenses, the payment of 1500 pesos marked for the advance for each immigrant was made by the Public Treasury, according to the terms of the third clause of the terms agreed upon.

The government would take care of obtaining provisional lodging for the immigrants.[26] In March 1885, Hostos published an article where he reported: "It has just been ascertained that the first contingent for immigration has already left the Canary Islands for the Republic," expressing then his concern with the way in which the government was planning to receive them, and advocating, among other things, the creation of an Office of Immigration that would make possible more adequate planning of immigration ("a truly national plan"); he points out again the importance of agricultural colonies and makes references to the favorable experiences of Argentina and Chile.[27]

Finally, we find a reference to the immigration of this Canarian group from President Billini, in his message to the National Congress on stepping down from office that same year, reporting that the arrival had gone well, that thus had begun "a current of industrious immigration into the country," and that land had been given to the immigrants, who had already begun to cultivate it.[28] These were probably lands bordering on the sugar plantations, or if not, the immigrants were hired as *colonos* by some *central*.

From the Spanish Peninsula. It is not possible to treat cases of individual immigration here; to my knowledge, the choice of the republic as a place of residence by *peninsulares* (people from the Iberian peninsula) occurred on a large scale especially in the final phase of the War of Restoration (1865). Thus, many Spanish soldiers remained in the country at that time, while many of the civilian immigrants who had arrived in the country in the annexation period remained there after the reestablishment of independence. At the beginning these people suffered from persecution—in Santiago and La Vega, for example—and they had even been expelled from the latter city, a fate that had befallen certain Dominicans accused of collaborating with the enemy (*españolismo*) as well. In 1865 when Gregorio Luperón was governor of Santiago province and government representative for the Cibao, he permitted these Dominicans, "Spaniards, and Catalans" to return to Santiago. Although the Dominican masses did not want to accept the Spanish-sympathizing Dominicans, Luperón arranged for the *peninsulares* not to have to fear aggression any longer. That liberal attitude on the part of Luperón came to be profitable for the Cibao, for he saw that the merchants among them "brought money and credit, and could give action, progress, and life to the province."[29]

In the following years a number of Spanish immigrants accumulated great wealth. As early as 1871, it was noted that "some of the most prosperous merchants of Santiago belong to a country that caused the destruction of that city only six years ago."[30] About this growing economic and political importance, Luperón writes: "Step by step, the Catalans and Spaniards were taking over business and political influence in the Cibao, which caused most important consequences for many of them, who were ruined, mixed up in politics that could not give them any favorable result, because the circumstances that came to pass warned them to use the greatest moderation and prudence."[31]

In the sugar-producing city of San Pedro de Macorís, which was in the midst of all-out growth, there was also an important Spanish commercial colony in the nineties. Among the Catalan immigrants who came to enjoy considerable attention, we mention here Cosme Batlle of Puerto Plata, who came to be one of President Heureaux's most important moneylenders. He shared that position, as we shall later analyze more extensively, with several others, among whom we shall mention here the Italian immigrant Vicini and the Cuban immigrant José A. Puente from Sánchez.

Cubans and Puerto Ricans. The Puerto Rican Hostos, whose long stay in the Dominican Republic was going to be of such exceptional importance for intellectual life and particularly for education, arrived in the country 30 May 1875 through the northern port city of Puerto Plata. There was a *barrio* there inhabited almost exclusively by Cubans that was called "Free Cuba."[32] Numerous Puerto Ricans also lived in the city. The two groups of immigrants, "united with Dominicans who loved liberty, worked determinedly in favor of the independence of Cuba, then in armed rebellion, and the planned uprising of Puerto Rico."[33] Thus, Hostos found there his compatriot, "the noble, first citizen of Puerto Rico . . . the ever-exiled Doctor [Ramón E.] Betances," whom he points to as the teacher, guide, and friend of Luperón,[34] and who was to offer various services to subsequent Dominican governments from his residence in Paris.

At the beginning of 1874, the Cuban club *La Juvenil*, dedicated to "all who sympathized with the cause of Cuba," was founded in Puerto Plata, along with the *La Antillana* society.[35] Moreover, the *Delegación Revolucionaria Cubana* (Cuban Revolutionary Delegation) was also based in the city. "Thousands of Cubans devoted themselves to work, in the city or in the neighboring rural areas, at the same time that they were conspiring against Spain." Various members of the most important families of exiles—like Silva, Agramonte, Arredondo, García, Benítez, Fernández, Céspedes—established family ties with Dominicans. The political activities of these immigrants, stimulated even more by the leadership of Hostos (who also founded several magazines, *Las dos Antillas, Las tres Antillas,* and *Los Antillanos,* where he proclaimed his ideas on Antillian independence and confederation), led to pressures from Spanish authorities upon the president, Gen. Ignacio María González. The latter, obliged in part by a treaty of friendship with Spain that had just been signed in 1874, forbade the appearance of some of these magazines and ordered the Cubans to leave Puerto Plata. The opinion of the capital city newspaper *La Idea* that "the Cuban and Puerto Rican immigration [is] much more advantageous than the exchange of a treaty between Spain and Santo Domingo" could not be shared by the threatened president. This hastened his fall: Hostos, along with other immigrants, supported the patriotic society *Liga de la Paz*, which, under the leadership of Luperón, opposed González, and he wrote several documents that appeared with Luperón's signature. Hostos was even accused by the *Gaceta Oficial* of "taking up arms" along with the Cuban Pedro Recio and "of heading as chieftains the armed bands of Cubans that have recently been established in Puerto Plata without legal authorization." The rebellion against González—so clearly provoked and supported by the immigrants—succeeded in 1876, received the name of "Evolución," and brought relief to those foreigners who had remained in Puerto Plata. Many of them do not seem to have awaited the denouement. According to Luperón, the majority had left for Venezuela, Haiti, and Jamaica.[36]

Hostos too speaks of a "dispersion" of immigrants. But very soon a second wave came: "an immigration of capital that, fleeing the ruin that threatened it momentarily in Cuba and Puerto Rico, came to take up the advantage offered it by the free concession of land and the excellence of that land."[37] In the preceding chapter I have already noted the importance of this immigration, especially for the establishment of the modern sugar enterprises. In the discussions that originated around this spectacular agricultural transformation, not only the advantages and disadvantages of the rise of the modern plantations were debated but also whether this was due principally to a historical coincidence—that is, the sudden, "obligatory" Cuban immigration—or to the very liberal policy of concessions and tax exemptions. Pedro F. Bonó, the interesting amateur sociologist from San Francisco de Macorís,—supported the first opinion. He spoke of "privilegiomania":

> That foreign capitalists come and establish four or six sugar cane haciendas on fertile lands at prices that are almost a gift and on the shores of the ocean or of navigable rivers, bravo! That the masters find themselves surrounded by a population who were previously the owners of the land and who are now the laborers, that this very population, besides having become serfs, defend and guard these estates with Remingtons at their own expense, and that many do not care that the products taken out do not even pay for the Remington with which the peon defends the estate, and that here the bravos stop and pause for thought, bravo! . . . Meanwhile, the more I see the cane of Santo Domingo protected, the poorer I see the black man of Sabana Grande and Monte Adentro, and if it continues, the day is not far away in which all the small-property holders who up until today have been citizens will come to be peons or, more properly speaking, serfs, and Santo Domingo, a little Cuba or Puerto Rico or Louisiana.[38]

That sarcastic *ex-abrupto*, published in 1880 in *El Porvenir*, provoked considerable commentary and violent reactions, to which Bonó wrote in 1882:

> You see things coldly, and although it may shock and mortify our vanity and self-esteem, the original, unique cause of the recent development of the sugar industry in Santo Domingo is not due to the tax exemptions and monopolies that have been granted so liberally as well as onerously for years, to attract foreign capital to the country and even not to attract it; this development is due to the Cuban emigration, just as Cuba owed the establishment of its agricultural business to the French emigration from the western part of our island at the end of the past century . . . ; it is enough to note that without that first cause, despite the franchises from Carlos III and ourselves, neither the one island nor the other would have had the indispensable factor for any beginning of serious industry, that is: scientific, practical, wealthy, connected personnel, working in a known, virgin, docile, and appropriate environment.[39]

To this, *El Eco de la Opinión* answered, not without presenting facts:

> If it is true that a Cuban was the one who developed the first cane plantation in Santo Domingo, it is no less so that others of different nationality, and among them many Dominicans, like Abréu, Saviñón, Heredia, Sánchez, and Bona, followed in the same line, with American, German, and French capitalists, like Mellor, Hatton, Bass and Krosigh, Stokes, Contreras, Hartman, and so forth, coming later. It cannot be said that these last have come for the same causes as the first immigrants, because of the Cuban war, but that they have been coaxed by the exemptions conceded to the agricultural industry, exemptions that do not exist either in Cuba nor in the rest of the countries that they left in order to employ their capital here.[40]

In later years as well, Cuban immigrants continued to arrive in the country; it was not always a question of capitalists.[41] Thus, on 27 March 1896 a group of 295 Cubans arrived at Santo Domingo; of them 107 were heads of families. They represented the following occupations: agriculture, about 40; tailors, 5; businessmen, 6; landowners, 1; musicians, 1; beltmakers, 1; tinsmiths, 2; carpenters, 11; journalists, 1; barbers, 2; mechanical engineers, 2; sailors, 1; potters, 1; smiths, 1; bakers, 3.[42] In Puerto Plata in 1897 there was again a Cuban colony of considerable size.[43] It almost goes without saying that inasmuch as the immigration of Puerto Ricans and Cubans acquired a permanent character, their assimilation into the Dominican environment occurred in a very short time.

The Haitians. There is no doubt that in this period of superiority (or at least equality) of Haitian strength in the political and economic sphere, of long years of internal strife in Santo Domingo, and of scant vigilance along the border, uncontrolled immigration from Haiti took place. But I have not been able to find much data concerning it. Mentioned in 1871 only as one of the proofs of the "pacific character" of the Dominican people is the fact that "despite the national aversion that is felt for Haiti, there are at this moment many hundreds of Haitians who live peacefully and devote themselves to their activities on Dominican territory."[44] And in 1884, Bonó described the border region of the South as "exposed to a perennial, further progressive invasion of a foreign population (Haitian) that every day weakens further the Dominican element, which, defenseless and exhausted, will disappear completely from the region."[45] The rise of the sugar industry undoubtedly intensified the immigration of Haitian workers.

This provoked a reaction from the important spiritual and educational leader Francisco X. Billini, head of the Colegio San Luis Gonzaga, who directed a strong editorial in his newspaper La Crónica on 18 April 1885 against the arrival of even more Haitians. In this editorial he wondered whether the immigration could not be prohibited by using as a basis the same grounds with which Asiatic immigration was prohibited in the United States.[46]

Immigrants from the British, Dutch, and Danish Islands of the Caribbean. Besides the Haitians, workers for the sugar industry also arrived from the British islands of the Caribbean. Their number seems to have been sufficiently large to give rise to a criollo term as a designation for their group: cocolos.[47] Again, there are discussions in the press, as to whether their presence was desirable, that call our attention to them at the end of the century. Thus, an emotional article appeared in the newspaper El Distrito on 26 December 1898, advocating the prohibition of the immigration of cocolos–a suggestion that was indignantly rejected by a newspaper of much greater influence, Listín Diario.[48]

Several of these immigrants from British islands seem to have undertaken work as bill collectors, probably among the lowest social groups. The word inglés (Englishman) has retained the connotation of bill collector and appears as such in various expressions even today. We mentioned earlier the presence of immigrants from the Turks Islands among the nurses of Dominican hospitals. These little islands maintained frequent contact with Puerto Plata in particular; they were, along with St. Thomas, Curaçao, and Haiti, also important as a port of refuge for Dominican exiles. From the Dutch Antilles, there occurred not only the Sephardic emigration that we have already treated separately, but also an emigration of artisans, the majority of whom were people of color.

Thus, at the end of the last century, there was in the capital city the "second-class" barrio, La Estancia, located between Emiliano Tejera Street and Santa Barbara, and inhabited principally by Curaçaoans: "upright laborers, carpenters, woodworkers (both cabinetmakers and shipwrights), innkeepers, dealers in trinkets received via sailing-ships that arrived two or three times each month from neighboring Curaçao."[49]

Some of the Curaçao immigrants undoubtedly arrived in their new homeland by means of their relations with the Sephardim: thus, the Aruban Saludiano Fanduiz, who worked in the Marchena commercial house, which he left to go to the United States with the money he had saved in order to study medicine.[50] Members of important white Protestant families also emigrated from Curaçao to Santo Domingo at the end of the last century: surnames like Boom, Joubert, Schotborgh, and Evertsz are an indication of them. Curaçao marriages contracted by Dominican young women from good families occurred regularly; this was related to the international role played by Welgelegen, the Catholic boarding school for young women in Curaçao (in Habaai), during the second half of the last century. Finally, immigration took place from St. Thomas, especially to Puerto Plata; according to Martínez, surnames like Ashton, Mathieu, Palin, and Barbel would indicate Virgin Islands origin.[51]

The "Arabs". In the preceding chapter, we have already paused amply to study the importance of the group of Arab immigrants in commercial life, in terms of its development as a consequence of the agrarian transformation. We gave attention to the protests that the Arabs' itinerant business provoked on the part of the already-established urban merchants, who saw their sphere of commercial action reduced as much by the *bodegas* of the large agricultural industries as by the Arab travelling salesmen (who often bought their merchandise in the *bodegas*).

These protests did not lead to the government measures desired; on the contrary, these immigrants could also rely on official protection, at least at the highest level. That fear of international repercussions also played a part in the government's attitude becomes obvious in a letter President Heureaux sent in 1899 to the prosecuting attorney of the sugar center of San Pedro de Macorís—from which we cite the following passages: "The sentence that that Tribunal has handed down against the Arabs Señores J. Abraham and son is manifestly unjust, because these gentlemen have not harmed anyone or been the cause of damages. . . . If there had to be a sentence, it should have been decreed against the Minister of War, who was the one who pursued and had the cartdrivers seized. Let him strive by all the means that are within reach for us not to have international complaints because of matters of personal interest."[52] Complaints about the unfavorable business situation moved a writer in the eastern city of El Seibo to vent his feelings in the *Listín Diario* with the following verses:

> Solo nos queda una vía
> Para podernos salvar
> y es a menudo comprar

Billetes de lotería.
Lo demás es tontería
Pues aquí el bello tocón
No se consigue jamás
y el Seybo para atrás
Marcha como el camarón.*

The editorial staff of the paper noted that it was not only high prices, but particularly the "new store" (*bodega*) and the group of "travelling peddlers" that were paralyzing local business.[53] But the Arabs were not always involved in honest trade; thus, the *Listín* of 9 March of that same year observes that "a woman, Turk or Arab (it does not matter which), who was going around changing an ounce of false gold and taking advantage of the persons to whom she proposed the exchange for silver, has just been confined to prison." Some Arab immigrants sought and obtained Dominican nationality: "Joseph George, Nejib Joseph, Fehd, Trad, Abib, subjects of the Turkish Empire, are Dominican citizens from the 17th on," the newspaper announced in November 1893.

Nevertheless, six years later, there were still those who considered their stay in the country temporary. In an announcement in the newspaper, the Arab Miguel Pérez of San Pedro de Macorís bids farewell to Jorge Domingo, who "is leaving for our beloved Syria . . . and when happily treading upon the land of our forefathers, do not forget those of us who are waiting here, hoping to return to it."[54] According to Bueno, the first Arabs arrived at Santiago in 1897: Abraham Sahdalá and his nephew Avelino, decked out in Turkish garments; after them, members of the following families very soon arrived: Haché, Helú, Nazar, Tallaj, Jorge, Haddad, Sued, Khoury, Sahad, Ohai, Fadul, Bojos, Jacobo, Ramia, Zouain, Gobaira, Lama, Ega, Dumit, Tomás, Abinader, Elías, Girala, Diepp, Yunén, Apud, Sen, Sartú, Budajir, Abisadá, Feris, and Hagdala. "All these gentlemen, smiths by trade, united together, began to establish themselves on a small scale. . . . The greater part of them, with hardware in the Market (plaza), but on the basis of thrift and time, they began to set themselves up on a large scale."[55]

Selling on credit (with payments on Saturdays), even to clients of modest economic means, seems to have been one of the reasons for the Arabs' success. Once prosperity had been attained, "the Arab colony, quite unlike the Chinese, contributed greatly to the embellishment of the city of Santiago": the electric lighting for the Cathedral, the chapel of the municipal cemetery were Arab gifts. The Arab group has maintained its double loyalty even today; emotional ties with the country of origin are strong, a fact to which the subsequent immigration of relatives has contributed. But despite that, the

---

*Only one way is left for us/To be able to save ourselves/And it is to buy often/Tickets for the lottery./Everything else is foolishness,/For here a pretty penny/One never ever gets,/And El Seibo goes backward/Like the shrimp.

second and third generations of immigrants have not escaped a strong tendency to assimilation, and a visit to the unfamiliar country of origin often produces a certain disillusionment. Although even today many marriages occur between members of the group itself, one can definitely no longer speak about endogamy. The younger generation of the most prosperous immigrant families has lost the economic ethos of their parents (which is indeed still to be found on the capital's Avenida Mella) and has sought a career in the intellectual and semi-intellectual professions, which have brought some of them to important government positions during the last thirty years. What Bueno observes in Santiago holds equally true for the capital: among the descendants of the Arab peddlers, there are "lawyers, engineers, doctors, dentists, pharmacists, accountants, journalists," who, having grown up in an almost seignorial environment, feel irritation when they visit Beirut because of the obvious pecuniary interest and ability of their erstwhile compatriots.

The Italians. In 1875, Hostos observes that "the not-too-distant immigration of some hundreds of Italian families is an imminent fact."[56] I lack further data regarding the immigration of this group. But on this point, we can cite Bueno, who without difficulty mentions some thirty families that would have been established in Santiago before 1875. He remarks on how rapidly that group has been assimilated; how "almost all have married ladies of Santiago"; how through their business, agricultural, industrial, educational, and journalistic activity, this group has contributed to the cultural and economic growth of the city; and how this rapid absorption into the *criollo* environment explains the absence in the city of their own "*club de recreo*" (recreation center).[57]

The Chinese. According to Bueno, in 1898, there were only two Chinese in Santiago; the great increase in their number seems to have taken place later. At first, they were involved in operating laundries, then in the restaurant business, in which they occupy a principal place in the republic today. Bueno describes the group as extraordinarily cohesive and then argues: "The Chinese is extremely hard-working, respectable, cautious, intelligent, and prudent. In food, there is no limit to what he can do; however, he does not contribute anything to the adornment of the city where he lives; he is not festive; he does not go to the theatres, the cockpits, or the churches, parks, concerts, dances, racetracks, ball games, political meetings, lectures, funerals or processions; he does not celebrate marriages or baptisms, and everything that expands the spirit is for them a dead letter."[58]

Others. In the preceding discussion, I have limited myself to dealing with immigration that had a collective nature. Individual immigration did take place from various other countries. Thus, the tobacco business and sea trade with Germany attracted a number of Germans to the country; the sugar industry also attracted German entrepreneurs,[59] as well as some North Americans. Concessions for the installation of, among other things, the tele-graph led to the establishment of several Frenchmen. Also, at the end of the century Belgian (Bogaert) and Scots (Reid) technicians established them-selves in the country, sent there by companies involved in constructing rail-roads. Individual immigration also occurred from South American countries. Although not very important in a quantitative sense, the immigration of these educated and often well-to-do individuals had an influence that can still be observed in certain regions or economic sectors.

Attitudes Toward Immigration and the Plan for Immigration of Russian Jews. We have seen how at first steadfast objections were expressed in letters of protest or letters to the editor against Sephardic Jews, Arabs, Haitians, and *cocolos*; the arguments had economic and racial connotations, respec-tively. At times, the immigrants themselves also provoked antagonistic re-actions, such as when Enrique Vélez, a Spaniard naturalized as a Dominican, proclaimed publicly that without foreigners the republic would be a primitive country. This statement produced a heated discussion in the *Listín* in the summer of 1896. The flow of foreigners also caused vague feelings of malaise that were related to fear over the disappearance of a familiar and reliable environment. Thus, a Santiago newspaper wrote in 1888: "We find ourselves invaded by a multitude of individuals whose origins and conduct no one knows, and nevertheless, our city has placed in them its trust and the right to invite the principal families of this city from house to house."[60]

From both the protection that the government gave to the immigrant groups criticized and the initiatives taken by the government to encourage immigration, one can deduce the ideology that motivated the official atti-tude: the economic development and progress of the country are stimulated by attracting immigrants with education, preferably well-off, preferably from Europe. Even in 1875 Luperón was saying that he was of the opinion that the republic needed, above all, immigrants, who ought to be attracted by con-cessions, by the greatest possible number of rights, freedoms, and privileges.[61]

Once in the government (1879/80), Luperón appointed ambassadors in Washington, France, Germany, Holland, and Belgium, charging them with, among other things, encouraging immigration.[62] Moreover, he gave political privileges to the foreigners. Thus, Heureaux indicated in a letter to Hostos that the Constitution "considers the Antillians sons of the Republic, so long as they show that they want to make use of that right";[63] in 1892 it was decided that *all* foreigners would be eligible for municipal council seats.[64]

Indeed, Heureaux completely shared Luperón's opinions on the usefulness of immigration. In a letter to the latter, who was on a trip to Europe at that time (1882), he writes enthusiastically: "And so as you yourself are proving with the deeds of your mission, Europe already judges us favorably, industrial thought places us among the number of the countries that can be exploited by development firms, and in the country's interior, these are growing in an admirably rapid fashion, and capital and entrepreneurs are coming our way spontaneously." In this same letter, he recognizes the need to name consuls in Europe.[65] That very day Heureaux wrote to a friend in Puerto Plata about a plan for attracting Puerto Rican immigrants: "The entry of laborers from the neighbor island is certainly useful for Santo Domingo because they are skilled in the cultivation of cane and in other crops of this zone." Nevertheless, he advised urging the *Junta de Agricultura* (Agriculture Committee) to finance this plan with private means; the government did not have money. In other countries, "the Government promotes and pays for immigration, first because it has the wherewithal and then because it is reimbursed with large tax income, but here even a stamp tax, a customary matter even in barbaric lands, produced a terrible fuss."[66]

At the end of that month, the president writes again, pleased that "consumption increases daily, owing to the fact that immigration flows toward this capital city from all over."[67] In August of that same year, he reiterates to Luperón that "the spontaneous immigration that arrives on every steamer is doing a great deal of good, because the greatest part is made up of capitalists and hard-working men."[68] Six years later, he congratulates the consul in New York for the effort that the latter "is making, because capitalists from there come to help us raise up the country by developing the public wealth."[69] He subsequently thanks the first (European) subdirector of the Caja General de Recaudación for "your letter in which you set forth your ideas regarding the advantageousness of making European immigration flow toward these shores."[70] Eleven year later, the president is still actively concerning himself with immigration. In a letter to Abraham C. León, Dominican consul in Hamburg, he refers to a plan of the German minister Michaelis [?] for immigration of Germans, "towards which I showed myself favorable by indicating to him the Las Calderas harbor, where a city could be developed and German agricultural immigration brought, but he has not spoken to me about that again."[71]

The authorities' great interest in immigration does not mean, however, that they actively concerned themselves with the distribution and establishment of the recent arrivals. For example, the day laborers for the *centrales* who came from the rest of the Caribbean area were received by private *Juntas Directivas de Inmigración* (Managing Committees for Immigration), comprising the principal land owners or owners of *centrales* from a certain region. The agricultural colonies that Hostos had advocated and that were to be founded and encouraged by the government never went beyond being an idealistic dream, just as the author himself foresaw: "The country is still more for the exploitations that, cash in hand, are imposed with all the weight of silver and of gold."[72]

Within the dominant "ideology of development," the immigration factor played an important part; from the words of Heureaux that we have cited, one might retain the erroneous impression that the factors of capital and labor as such were exclusively the ones that were most appreciated in this context. There was, however, a third factor that comes to light pronouncedly in the writings of that era—namely, that of the good example that the immigrants were to give to the rest of the population, especially in regard to their work ethos. Just this was one of the arguments in favor of Hostos's agrarian colonies: they were to serve "as an economic, domestic, and civic example for the surrounding population."[73] Luperón also wanted "those [criollo] men" to learn from the immigrants. "Let them occupy themselves," he wrote in 1882, "with calling on all the immigrants ceaselessly and with trying to give them the biggest welcome possible . . . ; with teaching work to those unfortunate, ignorant men, disposed toward all the disturbances, who live attached to the State and are its parasites, for work is the only thing that makes one rich, and wealth is what gives independence."[74]

A fourth argument in favor of immigration was presented by Bonó. He was of the opinion that for construction of great projects, like the railroad in the Cibao, it would have been appropriate to attract foreign workers (who then would have been able to remain in the country), in order not to bring about disorganization in the Dominican population. The internal migration caused by these projects had only destructive results: the Dominicans abandoned their agriculture, gambled away their salaries, and returned "naked and sick" to their wives and children.[75] As we have seen, both Hostos and Bonó had grave objections to the capitalist operation of the sugar industry to the detriment of the population itself: "What Progress does that show?" Hostos added to this a sociopsychological objection that is, in fact, indispensable for understanding the social attitudes of the immigrant entrepreneurs: their double loyalty. "The owners of the soil have no other link with Dominican society except the soil. They are foreign capitalists, who at most take an interest in those agents of progress that are related to material interests, but who have none of the social incentives that demand a reconstruction in all the groups of society."[76] This point could be applied as much to immigrant merchants as to the plantation owners.

Nevertheless, the advantages of immigration were considered greater than its disadvantages. In this context, I would like to call attention to an interesting plan, which was never carried out, for immigration of Russian Jews in 1882.[77] At the beginning of that year Luperón, who had been informed during his European diplomatic mission about the pogroms in Russia and the conditions of the Russian refugees, sent a letter to the central committee of the *Alliance Israélite Universelle* in Paris, in which he recommended his country as a site for immigration. That letter was reproduced in various Jewish newspapers, including the Petersburg Jewish weekly, *Voshkod*. Arrangements were made to finance the passage; the barons Edmond and Gustave Rothschild took an interest in the project.

The Puerto Rican Betances, then secretary of the Dominican legation in Paris, prepared a significant list of Jewish personalities who could inform the alliance about the country: Baron E. de Almeida, Dominican ambassador to Paris; A. Pay, ambassador in the Low Countries; Léonce Bloch, consul general in France; Jacobo Pereyra, merchant and consul general in St. Thomas; Charles Coén, consul in Haiti; Charles and E. Pereira, merchants in Paris; Jacobo de Lemos, merchant in Santo Domingo; the brothers Maduro and M. Sibaver, merchants in Puerto Plata. Two hundred families in Europe appeared ready to undertake the voyage; a group of sixty persons recently arrived in New York from Russia requested and received from Luperón the information that three ways to obtain land existed: (1) cultivation of State land would *ipso facto* guarantee title to the land; (2) they could lease *terrenos comuneros* for an unlimited time; (3) they could buy land from private parties. In this letter, Luperón underlined again the guarantee of freedom of religion. Plans for receiving and helping the Jewish immigrants continued to be completed; a committee of Dominican planters made a study of the project. It seems that it was the death of Charles Netter, one of the directors of the alliance, on 2 October 1882 in Jaffa that prevented the realization of the plan. The change in the presidency in Santo Domingo (Father Meriño was succeeded by Heureaux in 1882) had not diminished enthusiasm on the part of Dominican authorities.

The Immigrants' Incidental Cultural Contributions. In our discussion of the various groups of immigrants, we have already indicated in part which places they occupied in the socioeconomic structure and in which direction their cultural influence was made felt. I will be able to devote greater attention to this in the chapters that will treat changes in the economic structure and the social stratification of the society in its totality. Similarly, immigrant figures like Hostos can only be placed in relief in an analysis of the changes in spiritual life and in the educational system. I will limit myself here to giving some curious examples in which the influences of immigrants on specific, limited realms becomes apparent.

Hostos asserts that the Cubans in Puerto Plata introduced the custom of promenading in public, which was previously unknown in the country, perhaps for "fear of small-town criticism."[78] Bueno is of the opinion that the accordion, which has become such an indispensable element in Dominican popular music, was imported in 1881 by the Italian Vitorio Steffani: "By around the year 1890, one began to feel the first sparks flying from the typical *merengue*."[79] The composer and folklore expert Julio Alberto Hernández believes, however, that the instrument was already known before then and that it had been introduced by German tobacco buyers.[80] Finally, the *kipper* (an Arab meatball) had been integrated, name and all, into Dominican cuisine.[81]

OTHER QUANTITATIVE DEMOGRAPHIC DATA

In 1888 Abad estimated the number of foreigners at 25,000. This was 6 percent of the population of 416,000.[82] In 1906 the number of deaths in the first semester was 2,852, of which 138 were foreigners, that is, something less than 5 percent.[83] This last figure corroborates Abad's earlier estimate inasmuch as a surplus of emigration was probable in the first years after the fall of Heureaux's regime. Information about the departure of many Cubans and some Curaçao Jews and Arabs was already being mentioned during the months before his death (1899), when a serious economic crisis prevailed in the country.[84] The political chaos of the subsequent years could have intensified this tendency. Deschamps gives data on Santiago 1906[85] (see table 2.1). For the male population, this represents a percentage of foreigners of more than 7 percent; for the total population, almost 4.5 percent.

Abad establishes natality at 30 per 100 and mortality at 13.8 per 1,000, from which results a natural growth rate of 16.2 per 1,000. Naturally, more males were born than females (in the first semester of 1906 in a ratio of 107.5:100); nevertheless, the female surplus that was noted in the country in the second half of the nineteenth century was considerable. In the Baní común, where 5,000 people lived in 1871, there were three times more women than men in that year.[86] The same proportion was pointed out in San Cristóbal común.[87] In 1888 Abad notes with emphasis the national disproportion between the sexes (which surely must have had some relation with the almost-permanent warlike state) and in addition mentions as demographic characteristics: "the increased number of single people, particularly among the inhabitants of the countryside, (although a great number of these lack only the civil and religious ceremony to complete marriage)"; the "considerable number of widowers and widows and the well-known excess of the latter over the former"; an "adequate longevity, with a noteworthy proportion of individuals of both sexes who reach and exceed one hundred years of age."[88] Some of these characteristics are shown clearly in the census data for Santiago in 1899[89] (see table 2.2).

Concerning the unconsecrated marriages in the Cibao, the U.S. Comission wrote in 1871 that "the marriage rite is generally quite respected, save, perhaps, among the lower classes, which declare that they cannot pay what the priest asks to celebrate the marriage properly, a sum that, according to what they say, varies between eight and sixteen dollars."[90] In Azua, 118 marriages were performed in the period from 1862-71, while no

TABLE 2.1. POPULATION IN SANTIAGO, BY NATIONAL ORIGIN, 1906

	Dominican	Spanish	Italian	Arab	Chinese	U.S.A.	Cuban	Haitian
Males	4,775	60	33	113	2	64	23	31
Females	5,624	31	–	80	–	28	13	20

TABLE 2.2. CENSUS DATA FOR SANTIAGO, 1899

Males	4,298	Single	6,358
Females	5,100	Married	1,065
		Widow/ers	248
		Divorced	7
		Children	1,720
Total	9,398		9,398

fewer than 2,580 children were baptized.[91] In the first six months of 1906, the ratio of illegitimate births in Santiago province compared favorably with that of the province of Santo Domingo and that of the country[92] (see table 2.3). From these figures, it appears that in this period the percentage of illegitimate births out of the total was the same for Santo Domingo and the country, that is, 58.6 percent, while for Santiago it was 48.1 percent.

It goes without saying that the data mentioned can serve only as an indication because of their scarcity and their possible margin of error.

TABLE 2.3. A COMPARISON OF LEGITIMACY RATES,
JANUARY-JUNE 1906

	Santo Domingo	Santiago	Nationwide
Legitimate births	864	787	3,952
Illegitimate births	1,226	730	5,615
Total	2,090	1,517	9,567

GEOGRAPHIC DISTRIBUTION OF THE POPULATION

In General. Of the more than sixty *comunes* that Meriño mentions in the country in 1898, thirteen had been founded in the period of the conquest. In the seventeenth and eighteenth centuries, a total of another dozen settlements were added. All the others were founded in the nineteenth century.

Of the settlements from the fifteenth and sixteenth century—Santo Domingo, Azua, San Juan de la Maguana, Bánica, Boyá, Seybo, Hato Mayor, La Vega, Cotuy, Bonao, Santiago, Puerto Plata, Monte Cristi[93]—the last two were evacuated in 1606 by order of the colonial authorities and were rebuilt in the 1750s. The inhabitants evacuated in 1606 from the northern coastal zone shortly afterward founded Monte Plata on the Congo River and Bayaguana, both in the province of Santo Domingo. Other cities established in that early period changed location in the course of their existence or after serious catastrophes (Santo Domingo, La Vega).

At the beginning of the seventeenth century, the Neiva *común* in the Barahona district was also founded. From the end of that century dates San Carlos, which soon fell into decay, only to be repopulated by *isleños* at the middle of the eighteenth century, just like Samaná and Sabana de la Mar. San Lorenzo de los Minas, founded five kilometers from the capital on the east bank of the Ozama by Haitian refugees, sprang up in 1719; the name evokes reminiscences of the West African fortress city of (San Jorge del) Mina and is also used to refer to certain Caribbean slave groups and their descendants who were shipped from that port. Also arising in the eighteenth century were Baní (1764); San Francisco de Macorís (1774), which grew up around a "hermitage devoted to Our Lady Saint Ann"; las Matas de Farfán (1780), which was begun as "an oratory or chapel on the east bank of the Macasía River"; San José de los Llanos; and Dajabón. The founding or reconstruction of a dozen settlements in the second half of the eighteenth century clearly illustrates the revival of the colony during the so-called restoration of colonial government.

Moving now to the nineteenth century, we see that it is during the Haitian domination (1822-44) that two new settlements arose: Altamira, in the Puerto Plata district, which was declared *puerto cantonal* in 1843 (it was not until 1889 that it was elevated to *común*); earlier, in the twenties, San Cristóbal had already come to be a town of some size. This was the consequence, above all, of the abolition of slavery in 1822, when the plantations of Nigua were abandoned and a part of the freed population established itself around the hermitage of the old San Cristóbal plantation. In the period 1844-61, three settlements appeared: Yamasá, Jarabacoa, and San José de Ocoa; this last was founded in 1844 and populated by refugees from the region of the Haitian border. Efforts in this period to make La Romana flourish failed twice "because of the lack of mercantile movement." During the Spanish period (1861-64) only the founding of La Victoria del Ozama is mentioned; in the turbulent following decade, only Blanco village is elevated to *puerto cantonal*, after having functioned in the War of Restoration as a "focus for the contraband trade that was carried on with the Turks Islands," and Guayabín in the Monte Cristi district is elevated to *común*.

Between 1875 and 1880, two towns arise in the Cibao (Tamboril and Esperanza) and one (Duvergé) in the Southwest. In the eighties and nineties, the rate of founding towns accelerates spectacularly: out of the total of thirty-eight towns founded or elevated to *puerto cantonal* or *común* in the nineteenth century, twenty-five are in the last two decades. For a dozen of these towns, it is possible to point out clearly the factors that encouraged their growth: the cultivation of sugar (San Pedro de Macorís, Montegrande, Mendoza, La Isabela, Haina, Sabana Grande, Villa Duarte); banana production, (La Romana); railway construction (Bajabónico, Villa Rivas, and Sánchez). Ten of the twenty-five new towns were located in the southern region of modern plantations; six in the Cibao; three in the center of the northern coast; two on the Línea Noroeste; two in the eastern El Seibo province; one was a railroad terminal and port in the Samaná Bay; and one was in the Southwest.

We can draw two conclusions from this data: (1) the large number of new towns in the last quarter of the century corroborates our data on population growth in this period; (2) the appearance and growth of new towns was, if not in an absolute sense at least in a relative sense, much more impressive in the South than in the Cibao. The supremacy of the Cibao is contested by the South in this period; the struggle between "tobacco" and "sugar" erupts—here, we are interested only in the demographic front. Let us look at the population development of the capitals of the two regions: Santiago and Santo Domingo.

Santiago and Santo Domingo. In 1871 Santiago had some 8,000 inhabitants. Its straight streets "generally formed right angles"; the houses in the central area were stone and in the suburbs wood, often roofed with palm. Located in the center of the tobacco-producing region, it functioned as a warehouse site for this product, which was transported from there to Puerto Plata with mules or horses. Many of its merchants were agents of commercial firms, predominantly German, established in Puerto Plata.[94]

According to a census, the city had 5,669 inhabitants in 1889. It then had 32 streets and 1,130 houses.[95] In 1890, however, the number of inhabitants was again estimated at 8,000.[96]

In 1899, the number of inhabitants had increased, according to a census, to 9,398.[97] Finally, in 1906, there were 10,897 *santiagueros.* The city then had "2 public libraries, 3 printers, 8 newspapers, 2 photographers, 15 tailors, 16 dressmakers and stylists, 7 lawyers, 1 engineer, 7 doctors, 3 notaries public, 3 dentists, 3 pharmacists, 5 music teachers, 42 musicians, 4 heads of machine shops, 2 teachers [of mechanics], 215 cigarmakers, 608 ironers, 389 laundresses, 230 cooks, 233 maids, 68 manservants, 704 seamstresses, 13 insane people, 2 blindmen, 15 beggars, 1 library, 8 pharmacies, 2 hotels, 61 varied retail stores, 87 groceries or retail food stores, 247 merchants, 108 business employees."[98]

The population of Santo Domingo in 1871 was estimated at 6,000.[99] Hazard, who visited the city in that year, called it "an old and strange place" where "no hand of progress" was visible; the plan of the city was, overall, still the same as in the days of the conquest, with many of the old monuments still existing within the city's walls—which had a circumference of some 4,500 yards. In the center there were many solid houses of masonry, low but wide, with large double doors for access, while in the poorer suburbs the houses were of wood or clay, and roofed with straw or palm. In the city, business activity seemed to be diminished; the exporting of some mahogany, dyes, fine woods, and some leathers from the East did not manage to make harbor movement lively. There was only one well-supplied store. "In reality, it is doubtful whether the city of Santo Domingo, under any circumstance, will ever become a great commercial center. . . . Even its position as capital will be contested, I believe, by the inland city, Santiago, which, located in the center of the island, in the midst of an agricultural region of the highest quality, with connections by waterway to all areas, will, aided by the railroad, have the decisive power on the island, becoming a second Chicago."[100]

By 1893, the population had increased to 14,072. The city then had

> streets, from north to south: 15; from east to west: 19; municipal districts: 6; Catholic churches: 14; Protestant churches: 1; public buildings: 33; houses of more than one story: 293; one-story houses: 2,354; institutions for public education: 20; for private: 17; public libraries: 4; bookstores: 4; national newspapers: 12; painting, photography, sculpture, foundry, smith, and machine shops: 6; lawyers: 20; notaries public: 5; engineers, surveyors, and construction supervisors: 12; doctors: 18; apothecary shops: 10; dentists: 4; charity homes: 3; insane asylum: 1; literary societies: 3; philanthropic societies: 10; recreation clubs: 6; philharmonic society: 1; religious societies: 6; coaches for hire: 23; private: 24; carts: 135; wagons: 11; commercial factories: 20; parks: 3; plazas and squares: 8; cemeteries: 2; public lighting (street lamps): 356; hotels, cafes, and restaurants: 11; clubs: 2.[101]

In 1898 Meriño set the population at 20,000.[102] For the year 1906, I have no population data available; we do indeed know that certain professions were better represented then than in 1893: now there were forty-seven lawyers, twenty doctors, five notaries, six dentists, eight engineers, four bookstores, two hotels, and four photographers.[103] However, one should not imagine the city in this period as very modern: anyone could raise pigs and goats in his house. There was only one municipal cart for collecting garbage; some individuals employed themselves picking up garbage for pay. The poor left their rubbish in the patios. Around the city there were large trash dumps with names like *Galindo* and *Mis Amores* that in times of drought produced dusty clouds that covered the city, so that some individuals sold water to keep the city dampened down. But when there were strong downpours, the irregular paving and the poor drainage sometimes caused serious floods—thus it happened that a child drowned in 19th of March Street during the May floods.[104]

From these data we can deduce that during a great part of the seventies and eighties, Santiago and Santo Domingo were, with respect to number of inhabitants, of almost equal importance, with numerical superiority probably going to the first city, which also had a more pronounced role as a commercial center. At the end of the eighties, however, the capital's growth was much more spectacular than that of Santiago, which resulted in a population two times larger at the end of the nineties. If we also remember that in the same period the *común* of San Pedro de Macorís grew, thanks to sugar, from a little village to a city of some 8,000 inhabitants, the demographic urban explosion of the South in comparison with the Cibao stands clearly illustrated.

The City That Stayed Behind. It is noteworthy that, excepting the three cities we just mentioned, the population increase manifested itself more in the foundation of new towns than in the growth of already existing urban centers. The cause of this must be sought in the fact that the new population concentrations, by being economically oriented toward the recently established large agricultural enterprises or the communications routes that connected with them, were subject to the determining factor of geographic position; in this sense, the older cities were in a marginal position or even completely inadequate.[105] Moreover, we ought to recall that the economic and agrarian boom was limited to certain regions.

A typical example of stagnation of a city in this period is represented by the very old town of La Vega, despite its location in the fertile Cibao. In 1871 with its (overly) large cathedral, its access avenues planted with grass, its streets that intersected at right angles, it made a true "urban" impression upon Hazard.[106] Its population was then 3,000.[107] Almost thirty years later, when it counted "21 parallel streets" and "73 city blocks," it still had no more than 3,406 inhabitants.[108] There were those who attributed this stagnation to a "punishment" by the Heureaux government for the part the town played in the 1886 revolution under the leadership of a member of the distinguished Moya family.[109] But against this idea of the "conquered city" can be adduced the fact that under the Heureaux regime La Vega was chosen as point of departure for the railroad to Sánchez.

More probable as an explanation of the stagnation of La Vega is the fact that the functioning of Santiago as a regional center did not need to be duplicated in the Cibao, while in the region surrounding La Vega the part of small-scale regional center belonged instead to Moca, which, situated between La Vega and Santiago, could be supplied more easily from the latter. Thus, "the hand of Progress" autonomously distributed its gifts in a capricious way. But "the higher government" also could—by the equally capricious route of political relations and friendships and with increasing financial means—help some poor town to get a zinc roof for the church, uniforms for the band, or a better fence for the cemetery.

The Village. Finally, in order to evoke the image of the typical "hamlet, the little Quisqueyan* village" of this period, we can direct ourselves with Hostos to the western border of the Cibao, where Jarabacoa is located:

> It is not a village like the rural, pastoral home of European villagers, nor the little township of the Yankee farmer, nor the half-rural, half-urban borough that gave rise to the municipalities, nor the nasty, backward country town that disturbs the sight and the heart on the highways of some regions of France, Spain, and England. Nor is it one in the sense that that has in the old nations, but the "*lugarejo*" [little village] in a special sense, like a pleasant diminution of "*lugar*" [village]. On the hills is the communal land; the little village itself, "one plaza is all of it. In a corner of the plaza, there is . . . a church of little

---

*Quisqueya was the Indian name for Hispaniola.

merit." . . . The rest of the plaza, a meadow; closed in on each of its four sides by a row of houses. Something like four streets, not completely closed in by dwellings, indicated instead by a few houses in the same row, continue—and not for a very long stretch—and extend the streets that begin in the plaza. The priest's house on the corner opposite the church; the sacristan's on the corner opposite the priest's; one store for everything, dry-goods and food, liquors and hardware, on the strategic corner where the line from the valley road comes together with the line from the series of houses that clusters in the direction of the confluence of two rivers; the troop headquarters, which is a simple hut in comparison with the store building, which is the best in the little village and is, in fact, a good wooden structure; another two or three houses a little less unpleasant-looking than the poor huts in the vicinity—that is the entire little village. Population, perhaps not even six hundred souls; the settlement, perhaps not a total of a hundred houses, slant-roofed and gabled huts . . . ; civilization, as it spread from the civilized countries to the uncivilized and from the cities to the little villages, was there, like anywhere, solidly represented by half a dozen egoists who prospered at the expense of half a thousand villagers and at the expense of the small farmers or rustics of the vicinity.

And through this last observation by Hostos, the Jarabacoa of the nineties takes on a certain symbolic value for the country in general, which, with its "boulevards such as neither New York nor Paris has, water such as neither the Altai, nor the Himalayas, nor the Andes has; a sky, like that of 'Turei,'" found itself subjected to such strong influence from the "civilized countries."[110]

CHAPTER THREE

Changes in the Communications Structure

THE "OLD" MEANS OF COMMUNICATION

"Our roads, by a proper definition, are not roads: those in the neighborhoods are paths; those in the savannas are cattle-trails; those denominated royal are nameless passages where absolutely no one has ever lifted a finger," exclaimed Pedro F. Bonó in 1881, and his complaint would continue to be justified for many years more. "Every old Dominican who finds himself obligated to make a journey," he continued, "spends the evening before as agitated as if it were the one preceding a battle. From the moment he sets out, he begins to ask everyone he meets: 'Can one cross the Yuna? How are the Corozal, the Piñal, the Egido, the Luisa? Is there a canoe on the Ozama? A boat on the Isabela?' If they answer him, 'Everything is dry, the rivers are low,' he breathes a sigh and hastens off, lest a storm upset everything if he delays."[1]

Attempts to improve the roads were left in the hands of private initiative; these efforts were numerous and generally unproductive. By 1846 a development corporation tried to improve and shorten the important link between Santiago and Puerto Plata, and during several succeeding decades, various projects with this aim followed upon one another. In 1879 Luperón gave a franchise to W. Lithgow and Co. for the construction of a road between those cities that had at least some success: thus, eight years later, Heureaux writes to Gen. Federico Lithgow: "The happy occasion of Wash[ington Lithgow's] bringing a loaded wagon to Santiago from Puerto Plata has been celebrated a great deal in Santiago and here [the capital], too—we shall see what comes of that experiment."[2] In other parts of the country as well (La Vega, Monte Cristi, Samaná), there were enterprising persons (Presbyter de Moya, Alfredo Deetjen, José Manuel Glas) who tried to improve the condition of the roads; their success, however, was temporary at best. In our period, only Gregorio Riva managed to give products from the Cibao a new exit to Samaná Bay by means of road construction and by navigation of the Yuna. Almacén village, which had been founded by him, was later called Villa Riva.[3] But generally it can be shown that during the second half of the nineteenth century, the road network was subject to few improvements or expansions. Even in 1887 the governor of Espaillat Province, located in the heart of the important Cibao region, observes that the communication routes "leave much to be desired in this province, just as it happens in all the rest of the Republic."[4]

By exaggerating a little, it can be said that the very same roads that the colonizers utilized were being used. Crossing the rivers could involve mortal danger; not infrequently, wills were drawn up before the beginning of some journey. To travel from the capital to the Cibao or to Higuey took three or four days.[5] It is not surprising that personal contacts even among the important leading figures were scarce: sometimes four years passed in which Luperón and Meriño did not see one another.[6] Land transport was carried out on horseback or by mule in this country that, though small, was passable only with difficulty. In the War of Restoration, for example, all the supplying of the army in all the cantons was carried out from Santiago by mule and horseback.[7] The *recueros* (or muleteers) who employed themselves in this type of transport formed a separate professional group, with special abilities and group ethics that enjoyed considerable fame: "They are a rough group in their behavior, and it is said of many of them that they are very coarse; but all leading a frugal, harsh life, and without exception, honorable and trustworthy. Merchants in Puerto Plata told me that is is normal to call out to any of these men passing through the street, giving him a packet of money, telling him, 'Give this to So-and-so in Santiago.' 'Write down the address for me,' he usually answers, and all the money would be delivered without fault to the addressee."[8] The "folklore" regarding the muleteer found expression in prose and verses, and in sayings with the flavor of the Cibao:

No impoita que faite aigo
pa yegai a tu detino;
la recua sale, y la caiga
se arreglan en ei camino.*

The German grand piano that Don Guillermo Knipping had taken from Puerto Plata to Santiago at the end of the century was transported in that way, but in this case, "it was necessary to carry it on [their] shoulders."[9] In fact, *within* the cities as well, moving [goods] was done largely by burro, even in the seventies: "There is nothing but some cart or other, drawn by mules, perhaps for private use, and with two wheels," writes Gómez Alfau about the capital.[10] Along with the *recueros*, or *arrieros*, there also existed the group of *prácticos*, who acted as guides for travelers.

An enterprising journalist counted the number of people and beasts of burden that entered Santiago on 6 September 1890 from 5 a.m. to 10 a.m. These data illustrate picturesquely this city's regional function:

from the direction of La Vega: 1,000 people with 896 animals

*It doesn't matter that something's amiss/For reaching your destination;/The mule team leaves and the cargo/Is arranged on the way.

from the direction of Puerto Plata: 417 people with 422 animals
from the direction of Gurabo: 750 people with 700 animals
from the direction of Otra Banda,
    Borbones, Rincón, Largo, etc.:   839 people with 238 animals

The animals carried "articles for everyday consumption, and tobacco, palm bark, pine and palm boards, cordage," and so forth.[11]

In the capital, a good part of local supplying was done by waterway: one of the largest markets was "the one on the shore of the Ozama, supplied by the peasants who lived on the banks of the Ozama and Isabela rivers and used native canoes for transport. Purchased there were charcoal, cowpeas, star apples, cashew fruits, guavas, tamarind, cassava, yams, caimoní, calabash cups, jinas, eggplants, sapodilla plums, mameyes, palm boards, and so forth."[12]

The good care of mounts and pack animals was important. When President Heureaux, making preparations for a trip, writes to the communal prefect of Guayabín, "Along with my General Staff, I am sending there Colonel José Eugenio Núñez with my horse and saddle mule. I ask you to make sure that the animals will not lack for fodder in whatever yard you might put them for me," he sends the same instructions to two other people in the same place just to be safe.[13] A good horse was, naturally, a favorite gift. Thus in 1888 Heureaux sent a horse to Tiresias Simón Sam, minister of war and the navy in Port-au-Prince,[14] and some months before his death, he writes to Tancrède Auguste, Haitian minister of the interior and police: "Seeking a memento to offer you on the occasion of the New Year, I have preferred to send you the only one of my battle horses that is left. It is an animal with good Andalusian blood, on which I have attained some victories. He still has spirit left for others, and I hope that if, unfortunately, there should be an occasion, it might be you who would obtain them."[15]

The transport of persons, internally as well as outside the country, also suffered from obstacles of an administrative nature: each traveler had to provide himself with a passport that was checked along the road. The governor of Azua province, for example, reported that in 1895 his province had issued the following numbers of passports:

in Azua	892
San Juan	1,272
Las Matas	1,173
San José de Ocoa	689
Cercado	344
Bánica	152
Total	4,522 passports.[16]

Among the "old" means of transportation also belongs, naturally, the sailing ship, used for commercial as well as military transport and for domestic as well as international contacts. With the commercial centers of St. Thomas and Curaçao, which were so important in the first half century of the existence of the independent republic, contact was maintained by schooners, sailing ships of small tonnage, which were also employed in transporting the numerous political exiles.

REGIONALISM

As long as the old means of communication that we have described were dominant, it was to be expected that the sociogeographic regions into which, for natural reasons, the country could be divided would be characterized by a large measure of de facto freedom with respect to the central government; this held true in the economic, cultural, and political realms. Each one of these regions, such as the Cibao, the South, the Línea Noroeste, or the East, could also be divided into subregions for which, *mutatis mutandi*, the same was true. When loyalty to the home region clashed with that to the nation, it was not uncommon for the first to come out triumphant. The formation of collective images and the creation of stereotypes about the inhabitants of one's own region and about those of the others were the ingenious psychological accompaniment of this regionalism: the *banilejos* (or people from Baní) were able businessmen, the Azuans had pretty handwriting, and so forth.

When Hostos wrote a laudatory article in the *Revista Científica* of 5 July 1884 on "The Province of Santiago de los Caballeros as an Example of Adhesion," it was inevitable that violent reactions would result. In the article, Hostos enumerated the heroic military and political deeds of that region: "In the civil struggles, the province that has most strenuously fought tyranny, the one that has most often battled against despotism, always the first to rise up in the name of principles has been Santiago de los Caballeros." In the following issue of the magazine appeared harsh criticism from an author behind whose pseudonym Jesús del Christo may have been hiding Father Meriño. His article was titled "The South as an Example of Love of Independence," and it not only underlined the virtues and military deeds of the South ("each span of land is a Thermopylae, and each man has the spirit of a Spartan"), but also mentions some characteristic, often-heard reproaches to the region praised by Hostos, observing that in the South "the revolutionary banner has not often been hoisted by ambition. The South does not have the reputation of being turbulent. Nor has the spirit of regional egosim darkened the light of reason there to the point of sacrificing everything for hatred of the men and preeminence of other provinces."[17]

In these reproaches is reflected the political reality of a *hierarchy of regions*, in which the Cibao had always been dominant, although without protests, resentments, and temporary replacement by other regions. We have seen how the Cibao's dominance with respect to the South began to lose its indisputable character in the last decades of the nineteenth century for economic and demographic reasons. Thus, the date of the argument between

Hostos and del Christo is quite interesting; moreover, Hostos's arguments advocating a patriotism as *inclusivism* and not as exclusivism in a subsequent part of this debate run parallel to, although they precede, a growing notion of national unity that had been made possible by improvements in the system of communications. Nor would it be coincidental that the national hymn of Prud'homme and Reyes received general acceptance precisely during these years.

For the moment, however, the Cibao actually was the region where the majority of the revolutions were begun and where governments were made and broken. *Puertoplateños* like Luperón and Heureaux both demonstrated, although in different ways, their preference for the northern part of the country. During the former's provisional government, Puerto Plata was declared interim capital and seat of government until a permanent government could be elected,[18] and during his government, on presenting a plan to dredge the South Ozama River, on whose bank the capital happened to be, he declared, almost apologetically, that the government's interest "in progress and material advancement is not limited to the local improvements of this province of the Cibao."[19] Heureaux, manipulating an utterly different structure of political and economic power eighteen years later, could hardly permit himself such public utterances and actions; his personal sentiments, however, were no less strong: "You know that I am from Puerto Plata, which is the only little corner where I want to have the right to be something personally," he writes to a minister.[20]

The unfavorable consequences of the poor communications, in both the political and the judicial realms, were clearly indicated by Bonó in 1881. All the barriers that exist in communications, especially between "the two strongest groups of the Republic," Santiago and Santo Domingo, he writes, "are the reason for which respect and consideration for the Government is rather nominal or sentimental. . . . Each one of these segments works limitlessly for its own interests," and thus there is always the threat of "violent perturbations that are settled only on the surface, for they presuppose the alternative dominance of the Cibao or the Ozama. These truces, for no other name can be given to them, morally and materially keep up a latent discontent on the other side, which is the first element that the ambitious and the troublemakers find at their service." And regarding justice: "The Court of Justice, highest tribunal of appeal and repeal, surely does not record in its thirty-six year annals even eight cases from the Cibao for crimes against persons; because . . . it has not been able with all its might to require from a witness from Guayabín or Sabaneta the superhuman effort of going a hundred-odd leagues at his own expense by the ill-starred trail, to declare in full session what he knows about such and such a robbery or murder." The Government, "sometimes parodying the Romans with their proconsuls in the remote conquered provinces or the kings of Orient with their pashas, when . . . Executive Delegations were created," has not been able to cure the illness with these momentary remedies; on the contrary, these "put the capital further from its provinces, leave it more isolated, weaker, and even impotent to exercise its mandate."[21]

NEW MEANS OF INTERNAL COMMUNICATION

For a strong, prolonged dictatorship like that of Heureaux, it was possible to keep the "violent perturbations" in the political and military realm under the surface for some time, but anyone who thought that the destructive forces of regionalism had been conquered for good was excessively optimistic—as was the author of a letter to the editor in the *Listín* of 6 January 1893, who was of the opinion that the situation in which "each city, each village and *común* was a little republic" and "everything was confusion and unrest" had been relegated to the definite past. In subsequent periods these forces would appear anew with unheard-of violence. This was not surprising, not only because the local loyalties were not to be eradicated so easily, but also because the communications innovations we are now going to describe—despite their importance and consequences for certain groups and sectors of social life—managed to reduce the isolation of the regions but did not eliminate it. For a large part of the population, the old means of communication continued to be the principal, if not the only ones. The new came to stay alongside, or put another way, was superimposed on the old: two "worlds" began to coexist, and the technical innovations of the "modern world" could as readily be put at the service of a greater central control and a more rapid mobilization of national resources and feelings as at the service of particularist loyalties, which the "old world" surrounded with so many lasting passions.

Railroads. Plans and concessions for the construction of railroads existed from early on, but the quite fragmentary realization of these projects had to wait until the eighties (see table 3.1).

Of the twelve projects grouped in the list, only two (both in the North) led to certain results in the nineteenth century itself.[22] European firms were involved in both. The first, the Sánchez-La Vega railroad with its branches (some 130 kilometers) was developed by private "Compañía Escocesa." The second, from Puerto Plata to Santiago (68 kilometers), was in the hands of the state company Ferrocarril Central Dominicano (Dominican Central Railroad); its construction was financed by transactions with the Dutch banking house Westendorp, which in 1892 turned over its interests and those of its representative Cornelius Jan den Tex Bondt to the San Domingo Improvement Co. of New York. An affiliate company of the latter, the San Domingo Railway Co., was involved in 1897 in the financing of the Santiago-Moca stretch, which was finished in 1909, and which, like the Moca-Salcedo line completed in 1918, was developed by the state company. Thus the history of railroad construction reflects the extremely important transition from European supremacy in commercial and financial interests to U.S. predominance; this transition began to take place precisely during the nineties, and we shall treat it in detail in the next chapter.

Bonó observed the railroads and the foreign investments they brought with them with his usual skepticism. In 1881 he wrote:

> Not having the capital, it must come from abroad, and being foreign, it can only be attracted to come by a good, sure premium, which the country will actually pay through well-organized arbitrage of principal bankers, outwardly velveted over so that its specific gravity will be less noticeable in customs. The rest, needing real securities for capital and interest, simple and compound, given the important factor of our discords, will not be able to apply on the basis of our autonomous fund alone, the only pledge of sufficient value that would be able to reduce the increases of said factor.[23]

In 1895 Bonó showed how the railroad had caused damages to "the *criollo* transport industries."[24]

Hostos, who as guest of the Scots engineer MacGregor made the trip from Sánchez to La Vega in 1887 even before the official inauguration of this line, expressed himself in more poetic terms: "And what a strange, what an exciting, what a moving apparition, that of the dragon of progress through the midst of the wild jungle that whole centuries have not been able to bring forth from its inertia." But, naturally, he had his objections: "The freight trains . . . take on passengers; and the passenger trains . . . have as their principal object freight."[25] He felt great admiration for the accomplishments of engineering; it had been an effort of great proportions: in 1885, the Public Works Section reported that 900 "men from the country itself" had worked on it.[26] Hostos had less admiration, and with reason, for the choice of Las Cañitas, whose name had been changed to Sánchez, as the railroad's point of departure. This place, located on the southwest shore of Samaná Bay, was, by virtue of being on swampy ground and because of the danger of cave-ins, much less appropriate than Santa Capuza, property of the great mover of the project, Gregorio Riva. A whim of the general director of the company, a Scot, determined the future of Sánchez. This muddy village was divided into a section surrounded with the company houses, and the rest, where already by 1887 some two thousand pioneers were trying their luck. A quarter of these were Dominicans, another quarter Europeans, and a half immigrants from the Virgin Islands, Turks Islands, and Curaçao.[27]

The Santiago-Puerto Plata stretch, although shorter, was even more difficult to build because of the mountainous character of the terrain. In 1896, the workers went on strike when they were obliged to work an extra hour for the same salary.[28] The inauguration of the railroad was celebrated in 1897 in Santiago with big festivals; on that occasion, President Heureaux observed that two events coincided there: "the rapprochement of two sister pro-

TABLE 3.1. PLANS AND CONCESSIONS FOR RAILROADS

Year of plan or start of construction	Route	Initiative of:	Nationality of interested entrepreneur of financier	Plan for financing or or exploitation	Year of partial or total inauguration
1866[a]	Neyba-Barahona	Davis Hatch	U.S.	To exploit Neyba rock salt mines	—
1867[a]	San Cristóbal-Ozama River	Félix Montecatini	?	?	—
1869[a]	Monte Cristi-Santiago	E. H. Hartmont	United Kingdom	Exploitation of neighboring land	—
1869[a]	Santiago-Yuna River-Samaná Peninsula	Fred. H. Fischer	U.S.	Exploitation of neighboring land	—
1870[a]	San Cristóbal-Ozama River	Shumacher and Angenard	U.S.	?	—
1870[a]	Ozama River-Azua-Las Caobas	Julian Grangerard	Dom. Republic	?	—
1879/80[b]	Neyba-Barahona	Luperón Provisional Government		?	—

1879/80[b]	Santiago-Samaná	Luperón Provisional Government	United Kingdom	Exploitation by Compañía Escocesa (A. A. Baird, Glasgow)	Sánchez-La Vega, 1887; La Jina-San Francisco de Macorís, 1895; Las Cobuyas Branch-Salcedo, 1909
1882-84[c]	"Barahona Railway"	W.A. Read	Immigrant from U.S.	?	—
1890[d]	Puerto Plata-Santiago	C. J. den Tex Bondt and Heureaux Government	Netherlands	Westendorp and Co., Amsterdam, loan for £900,000	1897 (Central Dominican Railroad)
1894[e]	Santiago-Moca	Heureaux Government and San Domingo Railway Co.	U.S.	1897 bond issue for £500,000	1909 (Central Dominican Railroad)
1896[f]	Moca-La Vega	Heureaux Government and A. A. Baird, Glasgow	United Kingdom	Baird loan for £80,000	—

[a] Academia Dominicana de la Historia, vol. 9, *Informe de la Comisión de Investigación de los E.U.A. en Santo Domingo en 1871*, preface and notes of Emilio Rodríguez Demorizi (Ciudad Trujillo: Editora Montalvo, 1960), pp. 100-101. This is a translation of the *Report of the Commission of Inquiry to Santo Domingo etc.* (Washington, D.C.: U.S. Government Printing Office, 1871) and will hereafter be referred to as *Informe*.

[b] Luperón, vol. 3, pp. 70ff. (see n. 1 of this chapter for full cite); also *Informe*, p. 269.

[c] *Actas del Congreso Nacional*, Sección de Fomento, 20 February 1885, Archivo General de la Nación (AGN).

[d] César A. Herrera, *De Hartmont a Trujillo* (Ciudad Trujillo: Impresora Dominicana, 1953), pp. 13-57.

[e] Ibid., p. 78.

[f] Ibid., pp. 79-80.

vinces, and the opening of a new breakthrough in the horizon for the Republic." In his memorandum of January 1898, the governor of Santiago was already asserting that, thanks to the railroad, "many individuals residing in the city are acquiring land in the countryside in order to devote themselves to cultivation of some produce or other." Once one could travel to Puerto Plata in four or five hours the value of the land had increased considerably.[29]

Telegraph. During the so-called "six-years" of President Báez (1868-74), the government was prodigal in granting concessions, as the plans for railroads have already shown. In that period of the adventurer-concessionary, one Levi Guilamo was granted—in 1870—the right "to build the telegraph lines necessary in the Republic."[30] Nothing resulted from this. In 1884, the National Congress approved a similar concession to Count Tadeo de Okza, who transferred it to the French company Société des Télégraphes Sous-marins. In the same year the work was begun, and in Santiago there was already an office of the "Cable francés" under the management of a Frenchman.[31] By the following year, schools of "practical telegraphy" were operating in Puerto Plata and Santo Domingo.[32] But the system's expansion was delayed: Monte Cristi was to be incorporated in 1890—thanks only to the $500 annual supplement from the important local business firm J. I. Jiménez—and San Pedro de Macorís in 1895. Azua came later,[33] and Samaná was liberated from isolation in 1898 by the connection with Sánchez, for which the people "spontaneously" helped out and put up the posts.[34]

When the minister of mails and telegraphs wrote on 12 May 1893 to Isidro Mendel, financial agent for the republic in Paris, requesting that he deal with some complaints with the principal company in France, the objections of a material nature—the slow expansion of the networks, the excessively high charges (20 centavos per word) that ought to have been reduced by half—were not the most important ones, although later he himself wrote to the Société that the government's greatest desire "is to see the entire Republic crossed by the telegraph network, symbol of progress and motor of wealth." His most serious complaints were due to the French company's political intervention:

> The violation of the secrecy of official correspondence, perpetrated by various employees of the Telegraph, particularly by Sr. León Escudier [the director], during the recent internal and international events, even while, on the other hand, he has been offering concessions or services to individuals who are enemies of the current situation. On the very same days, against the prescriptions of its Regulations and in violation of those established by the Law, the Company has thrown the originals of official and private telegrams into the streets, from which they have been gathered up by police agents and turned over to this Ministry, accompanied by the official police report, a copy of which I enclose.[35]

At the same time, the *Listín* found itself involved in a conflict with the telegraph company, for Escudier refused the telegrams that Arturo J. Pellerano Alfau, editor of the *Listín*, was sending in his capacity as "telegraph correspondent" for the Santiago newspaper *La Prensa*.[36] These telegrams dealt with a conflict between President Heureaux and the National Bank of Santo Domingo, an institution affiliated with Crédit Mobilier of Paris. This conflict was one of the "internal and international events" to which the minister alluded in his letter of complaint to Paris; we shall treat them more extensively later.

Here it is interesting to point out that the intervention of the telegraph firm manager would not have been based only upon feelings of solidarity with an equally French bank: there were also personal ties between the two institutions. Count de Okza, who has already been mentioned as involved in the French telegraph concession, was quite a good friend of Eugenio Generoso de Marchena, whose mediator he had been in 1888 in the transactions that led to the signing of the Westendorp loan. Marchena, in turn, used his efforts for the concession, arranged by the National Congress in 1889, for the foundation of a national bank by Crédit Mobilier. Later he was named inspector general of that bank in Santo Domingo. So then, when in 1893 Marchena, partly for political motives, ordered Heureaux's private account attached—the matter that was the direct motive, although not the fundamental cause of the conflict--the taking of sides by the "Cable francés" could be foreseen, although it was not any less illegal because of that fact.

Perhaps this conflict contributed in part to the decision to establish an independent "national telegraphic station" with its own training program. The fact that its apprentices in Baní and Azua would refuse to distribute telegrams in 1897 ought to be explained by the prestige that the new technicians ascribed to themselves. M. de J. Troncoso, member of a family on the rise, was chief of the Santo Domingo telegraph station in that same year.[37]

On the other hand, the importance of the telegraph connections was quite well understood by the internal enemies of the Heureaux regime: in 1899, several cases of "intentional damage" were noted, in which "groups of armed men had threatened them[the technicians] with death if they persisted in wanting to put the line in good repair."[38] The usefulness of the telegraph in political intrigue cannot be better illustrated than by referring to the "Código telegráfico" ("telegraph code") that Heureaux composed—according to what is said, in collaboration with a Puerto Rican journalist.[39] In successive sections on policy; war, mails, and telegraphs; orders on freedom and confinement; administration; embarcations and disembarcations, and coastal vigilance, customs, and ports; appointments, dismissals, resignations, licenses, elections; arrivals and departures, escapes, judicial matters; illness, death and reestablishment, fires, baggage, scandals, disturbances; the president on a journey to the vice-president, and so forth, all the important points of government were defined in questions and answers and then were indicated with ingenious code words. Also indicated in the same fashion were the names of important political figures and localities. As a political and military dictionary, this code is of great interest; we shall deal with it again later. It is sufficient to mention here, by way of illustration, some code words that underscore the political importance of the telegraph:

> *Hadena*—Without violence prevent the use of the telegraph by individuals, not allowing it except for trustworthy persons.
> *Hado*—Watch over the telegraph and look to see who sends telegraphs to . . .
> *Hager*—Is the wire cut between . . . and . . . ?
> *Hojalon*—If the wire is cut between . . . and . . . , send the correspondence by trustworthy express messenger. Let the messenger take care to try to avoid the places where they could surprise him.
> *Halis*—Make sure that the telegraph is watched over so that they do not cut the line on us. We need this means of communication at any cost.

Telephone. By 1886 a telephone conversation had taken place in the capital: on 7 January "at 5 p.m. the Rector of the Colegio San Luis Gonzaga greeted Sr. Nasson, administrator of the Electric Company, from his school by means of the telephone. Hurray for Progress!"[40] In 1888 Abad was already speaking of a "telephone network" in the capital. In San Cristóbal, "the pharmacist Luis Ruveno sought authorization from the government on 4 July 1891 for installation of a telephone from his home to the residence of Dr. F. Gonzáles on Republican Street."[41] We have already seen that in 1893 private lines were installed on the sugar plantations of San Pedro de Macorís. However, there was not rapid progress: even in 1898, one spoke of "a few telephone lines in the Capital and other spots."[42] In Santiago, the government installed the first line between the San Luis Fortress and the provincial governor's palace; it was in 1910 when an urban telephone system began to function as a private enterprise.[43]

Mails. With the exception of the new railroad routes, the distribution of letters and packages remained in the hands of muleteers or *dragones*, who, sometimes walking barefoot, at others mounted, followed their fixed routes. For a moderate salary (in 1895 the *dragón* who carried mail once a week from Cotuy to San Francisco de Macorís received 3.20 Mexican pesos per month), they ran great professional risks. Repeatedly, attempts were made on their lives. A correspondent from the *Listín* described in 1893 how a young mailman was lost: "A group shouted out at him: 'Who goes there?' and the youth answered serenely, 'A man.' The four replied to him: 'But not a man like us.' 'As much a man as those who are coming.' 'Well, we'll see about that.'" The *dragón* was killed, the mail remained intact.[44] It is not surprising, then, that the town governments often requested "some Remingtons" for the protection of the mail carriers.[45]

A great deal of correspondence continued to be distributed by trusted friends or by private messengers. Nevertheless, in the last decades of the century, the central government seems to have paid greater attention to postal organization: in 1889, the position of administrator of mails existed; in 1893, that of minister of mails and telegraphs; in 1899, that of manager of transport of correspondence. It is difficult to verify up to what point practical improvements were carried out; I have available only the information that in 1898 the transport of mail between Monte Cristi and Dajabón was carried out by coach,[46] but Hostos assures us that in the nineties the minister J. M. (Paino) Pichardo gave "the Administration of Mails not only a greater regularity of operations, but also [a] character . . . of tranquil austerity."[47]

Bridges, Harbors, and Plans for Dredging. In Santiago, bridges were built in 1882 and 1887 over the Nibajes and Gurabito arroyos, respectively, both with domestic capital. In the capital the Heureaux Bridge over the Ozama was built by a North American; in 1898 the government took charge of this bridge, and the financing of that transaction caused Heureaux concern: "Almost in the form of an ultimatum, the American government demanded from me by way of its Minister in Port-au-Prince the immediate payment of a sum on the Ozama Bridge, which was the property of an American citizen, that we had agreed by arbitration verdict would be paid in installments . . . ; there is no choice left for me but to choose between brutal coercion of the country or the immediate payment demanded."[48] The important Haina River, close to the capital, had to go without a bridge until 1912; the boat that was used to cross it was the joint property of San Carlos and San Cristóbal from 1892 on. For these *comunes,* the income from the toll was sufficiently important that they argued over exclusive ownership for many years.[49]

The Ozama port was also the object of speculative plans for improvement in those years. In 1885 an Englishman, Greenbank, received a concession for that purpose; because of a cholera epidemic in France, where the dredging equipment had been ordered, the projects advanced so slowly that an inspection commission was appointed.[50] In 1893 the port's development was in the hands of a private company, Muelles y Enramada del Ozama, S.A.; its president was J. B. Vicini and that year it paid a net dividend of 45 percent over the net balance earned in 1892.[51] In 1897 the concession for the wharf appears in the hands of Juan Antonio Read.

In 1885 mention is made of a contract between the government and the J. I. Jiménez concern of Monte Cristi, in which that firm commits itself to dredging the Yaque for a distance of three miles in order to improve the export (of lumber) from that region. By way of payment, the government transferred to Jiménez 10 percent of the customs duties during ten years.[52] Jiménez also promised to improve the harbor. In 1899, after a failed invasion, Jiménez, then the government's enemy, took refuge in Paris, and it turned out, at least in the government's opinion, that the concessions had not had any result: "Far from developing the District's elements of wealth with the abundant earnings that they have produced for him, he moved to Europe, squandered them, and now comes, as he did in Haiti, to seek out of disorder and public discontent the riches he did not know how to keep," wrote the *Listín* on 10 May 1899. (In November of that year, Jiménez was sworn in as president.)

Innovations in Urban Transportation; Electricity; Aqueduct. While in the seventies carts could scarcely be found in the capital, we have already seen that by 1893 there were 23 carriages for hire, 24 private carriages, and 135 carts available in Santo Domingo.[53] In Santiago "the first vehicle" was imported in 1879; the first carts appeared in 1881, the first carriage in 1890; the first gig was built for the doctor Don Eusebio Pons in 1894.[54] In 1897 the capital had an animal-drawn trolley, with a three-kilometer route, "half in the city-streets and the rest in the outskirts"; Monte Cristi also had one that went from the pier to the city.[55] In Santiago and the capital the first bicycles made their appearance in 1896; in the capital, there were complaints that year about the noise of the "*fotusos*" (*fotutos*?) [horns]; nevertheless, the first bicycle race was organized in November.[56]

Urban traffic was also encouraged by the installation of electric lighting in the nineties: in 1893, the capital's ayuntamiento requested permission from Congress to issue bonds for that purpose.[57] On 1 September 1896 the Ministry of the Treasury and Commerce decided to turn over to the government of the province of Santo Domingo "the sum of 221 Mexican pesos monthly at the rate of seven pesos 36 2/3 per day in order to attend to the expense of electric light for the citadel, military hospital, province government palace, police barracks, and so forth."[58] The Club Unión, recently founded at that time, received an exemption to import "four lamps for electric light" in the following year.[59] Materials for construction of an aqueduct for San Carlos and the capital that would contribute to making the streets more passable arrived in the country in 1893; in 1898, however, the work had still not been finished.

Dominican steamships. In addition to the sailing ships, steamships began to be introduced. In 1882 the merchant Vicini already had his own steamer.[60] At that time, the steamship *Presidente* already existed—the precursor of the steam gunboat of the same name that was purchased in 1889 and, along with the *Independencia* and the *Restauración*, built in England at government expense. These steamships also served for transporting public officials or persons related to the government. In 1893 the National Congress approved the construction for the Navy—for the sum of 45,000 pounds sterling—of another steamer that would be called the *16 de agosto*.[61] In 1899 there was another "national steamer" called the *Altagracia*. In that year, mention is also made of a meteorological office in Santo Domingo, managed by the United States.[62]

THE EXPANSION OF EXTERNAL COMMUNICATION

The Dominican Republic's contacts with the outside world were intensified and institutionalized in various ways during the last two decades of the nineteenth century. In 1880 the country joined the Postal Union.[63] Earlier we saw how during Luperón's provisional government (1879/80) ambassadors were named in Washington, Paris, the Hague, and Berlin. Moreover, diplomatic contacts were established with the rest of Latin America in 1880: "Is it not to be regretted that until now, already reckoning thirty-six years of independent life, we have not sought to sign treaties of friendship, commerce, and alliance with the sister republics of our own race? . . . With such an objective, Señor Santiago Ponce de León received instructions . . . to (prepare) a treaty of alliance with the noble Venezuelan people; and Dr. Aristides Rojas has been appointed Consul General of the Republic in Caracas."[64] The subsequent governments considerably increased the number of diplomatic and consular representatives. The majority of the ambassadors in Europe were not Dominicans, but members of European financial circles (frequently from the nobility) who had connections with the country because of a stay there or through business interests: Baron Emanuel de Almeida in Paris,[65] José de Escorisza in Madrid, John W. Reich in Hamburg, Baron von Farensbach at the Vatican—all belonged to that group. President Heureaux also kept up an extensive correspondence with people in those circles, like the "Baronesa de Wilson" in New York, who did *not* perform any official duty for the republic, and who probably belonged to the network of foreign informants that he had organized and that operated with considerable efficiency.

Also important for the country's reputation were the relations that the president maintained with certain organs of the foreign press, in the United States as well as in France. To the editor of *Le Nouveau Monde* in Paris, he wrote on 13 December 1892, "Considering what the efforts of your pen are worth in that Center, you can rely on the fact that in me you will always have a determined defender of your newspaper."[66] Contact with this growing network of diplomats, agents, and press relations could be effected more rapidly after the installation of the undersea telegraph cables that linked the country with the rest of the world via Haiti and Cuba and Curaçao-Venezuela and that had been installed by the Société des Télégraphes Sous-marins. Hostos mentions this in 1888.[67]

Regarding contact abroad by maritime routes, at first navigation with sailing ships to nearby commercial centers like Curaçao and St. Thomas predominated; then steamships began to establish direct contact with more distant ports. The "German steamship" from Hamburg occupied a significant place, given that city's importance for the Dominican tobacco trade. During the Baéz government, a valuable franchise was granted on 7 October 1868 to R. M. Funkhouser of New York to establish service between that city, New Orleans, and the republic and according to which 5 percent of the import and export duties on commodities transported by that route would go to the concessionaire.[68] Shortly afterward, this concession came into the hands of the New York firm of Spofford, Tileston, and Co.,[69] whose ship, "an old wooden steamer called *Tybee* [made] the round trip every 30 days, at a pace of 6 to 7 marine miles per hour";[70] the Clyde line was probably the successor of that *Tybee*. The favorable conditions of the franchise made competition practically impossible; in March 1893 the *Listín* showed that the New York connection was monopolized by that line, and it also took over a great deal of internal maritime transport.

In 1897 the overeseas connections by steamship were listed as follows:

> Ger. W. Clyde Steamship Co. (U.S.): departs from New York; calls at Turks Islands and Cap Haitien; stops at M. Cristi, P. Plata, Samaná, Sánchez, San Pedro de Macorís, Santo Domingo, and Azua. They make one voyage every 20 days; Herrera Sobrinos (Spain): from Havana to P. Rico and St. Thomas, calling at Puerto Plata on the 17 and 27 of each month; French General Transatlantic Co.: Puerto Plata and Santo Domingo twice a month, San Pedro de Macorís once a month; German steamship company of Hamburg: Santo Domingo, Puerto Plata, Monte Cristi, Samaná, Sánchez; La Veloce of Genoa (Italy): Santo Domingo once a month.[71]

The rise of the steamship represented a great reverse for the functioning of St. Thomas and Curaçao as regional supply centers for the Dominican market and as purchasing centers for Dominican products; the republic's commercial routes, instead of ending at the regional connection center, changed and became longer, ending in Europe itself and in North America.[72] Attempts like that of the Curaçao businessman León to keep up steamer contact between his island and Santo Domingo[73] indicated little understanding of what was occurring in the pattern of communications.

The fact that these steamers called at so many small Dominican ports had to do, presumably,with the tonnage, still limited, of these new means of transport. The transition from sailing ships to steamers as such still did not, in the last century, involve the decline of certain ports; that phenomenon occurred in a subsequent period, when foreign trade was concentrated in only certain harbors.

We see that *technological* changes (steamers, telegraph) reduced the country's dependence on the commercial centers of the Caribbean, but it was politico-economic causes that in the nineties made communication with the United States predominate over the link with Europe. In the next chapter I will attempt to analyze changes in the structure of economic power relations.

Here, I will conclude by establishing that, apart from the economic, financial, and political implications, which were not always perceived or understood, the almost general attitude toward technical innovations as such was optimistic admiration. The *Eco del Pueblo* of 1 March 1888 reproduced approvingly a remark from Gerardo: "The steamer, the telegraph, the phonograph, and the electric light, . . . I have here the sublime creations that have come to immortalize the great nineteenth century, the century of marvelous advances in all spheres of human knowledge."

CHAPTER FOUR

Changes in the Economic Power Structure

THE RISE OF NEW PRODUCTS

The greatest part of the state's income always consisted of import and export duties. With the caution that the limited credibility of the figures obliges, one can deduce from table 4.1 at least a doubling of that income in the last three decades of the century. This table also makes it evident that in 1884 sugar, as a new export product, produced for the state more than two and a half times more earnings than all export products combined had done in 1870.

The rise of the sugar industry is reflected in the increasing activity of the southern ports, as illustrated in table 4.2.

As one can see, Puerto Plata's income decreases even in an absolute sense, a fact that can be explained by the competition from the new Cibao port of Sánchez; in the South, however, the port of Santo Domingo appears unharmed by the new port of San Pedro de Macorís. The tendency is obvious: in 1896 the combined income of the two largest southern ports, Santo Domingo and San Pedro de Macorís, compares to those of the two northern ports, Sánchez and Puerto Plata, at a ratio of 7:6, while in 1869, the harbor income of Santo Domingo was less than half that of Puerto Plata.

TABLE 4.1. CUSTOMS DUTIES AND TOTAL STATE INCOME ($ GOLD)

Year	Import duties	Export duties	Total income
1861	355,044.40	56,503.89	478,768.43
1869	507,138.59	77,708.46	700,028.27
1870	601,393.64	71,419.20	728,605.59
1884[a]		183,750.00	
1888	1,195,531.11	280,645.93	
1895			1,382,703.00
1896	1,210,456.00	287,608.00	1,551,155.00

Source: 1861-70: *Informe*, pp. 359 ff. (see chap. 1 notes for full cite).
1884: Emilio Rodríguez Demorizi, *Hostos en Santo Domingo*, vol. 1, p. 160 (see chap. 1 notes for full cite).
1888: *Mensajero*, p. 149 (see chap. 2 notes for full cite).
1895/96: *Exposición*, pp. 179 ff. (see chap. 1 notes for full cite).
[a]Sugar only

TABLE 4.2. CUSTOMS DUTIES BY PORT ($ GOLD)

Year	Santo Domingo	Puerto Plata	Sánchez	San Pedro de Macorís	Monte Cristi	Azua	Samaná	Barahona
1869	179,363	396,865	—	—	?	?	?	?
1895	415,996	290,322	210,982	252,203	105,896	32,482	20,185	1,552
1896	505,048	368,687	244,684	221,298	99,182	28,560	28,695	1,908

Source: 1869: *Informe*, pp. 359 ff.
1895/96: *Exposición*, pp. 179 ff.

TABLE 4.3. EXPORTED PRODUCTS (IN *QUINTALES*)

Year	Sugar	Leaf tobacco	Cacao	Coffee
1888	406,147	175,636	9,730	2,552
1897	800,000	?	36,000	9,000

Source: 1888: *Mensajero*, p. 149.
　　　 1897: *Exposición*, pp. 179 ff.

Moreover, the fact that not only the export of sugar but also that of coffee and cacao increased considerably is apparent in the figures of table 4.3.

Finally, table 4.4 gives a sense of the distribution of export products among the various ports in the year 1891.

We will next attempt to analyze more systematically how some of the changes indicated by the preceding figures affected economic relations.

TOBACCO COMPARED WITH CACAO, COFFEE, AND SUGAR

The Influence of the New Products on the Merchant-Producer Relation. Long before the Cuban sociologist Fernando Ortiz wrote his famous *Contrapunteo cubano del tabaco y el azúcar*,[1] Pedro F. Bonó, retired in his little Dominican provincial town, was already reflecting upon the sociological and economic implications of the two products, tobacco and cacao, that were fighting for supremacy in the Cibao. Bonó went so far as to state, in a remarkably Ortizian way, that "cacao is oligarchic and tobacco is democratic." Tobacco is democratic, for without other capital than a piece of land, without machines, without personnel, any poor farmer can maintain his family by raising tobacco, for which he can easily obtain credit, since the crop only needs six months to be harvested. During the rest of the year, the family is sustained with the production of secondary crops "and who that plants cacao or coffee sees the beans in six months, and who that is naked will be able to wait years?" How easily credit is obtained: "Once an advance is obtained in St. Thomas, England, Germany, or somewhere else, each retail merchant, in person or through brokers and branches, establishes himself near the growers . . . He gives money, drygoods, hardware, and other assets to the farmer, by means of an indulgent usury . . . It is difficult to enumerate the advantages of these advances, the independence that they afford to work of all kinds and the comfort in which they maintain the population in general." And without formalities: "There are no mortgages or chirographic titles, everything is reduced to current accounts in the open, very badly kept by the merchant, who does not even give the farmer a duplicate or a copy." This has its disadvantages, especially for the producer: "Generally it makes interest on the assets advanced quite high, it makes the farmer imprudent and

TABLE 4.4. RANKING OF PORTS BY EXPORT DUTIES PER PRODUCT, 1891

Port	Total	Sugar	Tobacco	Cacao	Coffee	Abey	Lignum vitae	Dried coconut	Molasses	Logwood
Santo Domingo	1	2							1	
S. Pedro de M.		1								
Puerto Plata		3	1	2	1					
Sánchez				1						
Barahona						1				
Azua							1			
Samaná								1		
Monte Cristi										1

Source: Based on *El Eco del Pueblo*, 4 June 1891

inclines him toward crazy expenditures that in the end are his ruin and that of the small business. The military dictatorships that with rare intermissions have been the owners of the country have introduced a remedy worthy of their system, and it is this: that upon the simple say-so of the merchant, the farmer is recognized as debtor for any sum, and if he does not pay it, he goes to jail without any other verification."[2]

Despite these objections, which could be resolved with a notary law and a loan bank, Bonó sees tobacco as "the true Father of the Country. . . . It is the basis of our infant democracy because of the balance in which it maintains the fortunes of individuals, and from that it becomes the most serious obstacle for possible oligarchies; it was and is the firmest support of our autonomy, and it is ultimately what maintains in great part the Republic's internal trade because of the changes it produces in the industries that it promotes and needs,"[3] like the manufacture of palm-leaf fabrics, the textile, bale-tobacco, and transportation industries.

Compare to this such products as coffee and cacao, for which a great deal of capital is necessary, which need several years of cultivation, and which offer work to few sectors of the population: "The cultivation, harvest, and sales of cacao is exclusive. Our rancher and three or four laborers more employed in gathering, shelling, fermenting, and drying are enough for cacao, while in tobacco, they are all workers in action, all earning, all producing and consuming domestic products, and thus enlivening the society."[4]

Had the word been in fashion in his era, Bonó would not have hesitated to call sugar "imperialist"—this "colossal agriculture" that has seized "without any other preparation except the express monopoly of money capital" the *terrenos comuneros* of the provinces of the East, "with the destruction of an environment where a population of nomadic, itinerant customs, children of the pastoral profession and of the secular labor of mahogany cutting, could roam. This population that is the fief, or rather, the Nation itself . . . finds itself . . . pushed toward barbarism, and in such a way rendered unfit to help advantageously the capital that exploits it, that finally it will not be able to perform its duties of citizenship, nor to meet those as the head of family, and falling into pauperism, will require impossible services from the rest of the Nation or protection and shelter from abroad." So Bonó wrote in 1883. The total proletarization of the sugar workers could be stopped only by "making them if not partners, at least participants to a certain extent in the revenues they obtain," but Bonó did not consider such a solution probable, for "it asks for a self-denial that this capital does not have."[5]

Sugar's journey to the market was much shorter than that of tobacco; in the republic, the sugar producer was himself the exporter and often even the vendor of the product in the New York market. Meanwhile, tobacco went "from the grower to the broker, from the broker to the small merchant, from him to the exporter, from him to the commission-agent, who sells it to the manufacturer." For Bonó, the advantages that sugar brought with it in this sense were also obvious: the producer knew his market better, and he had a personal interest in the good quality of his product; the roundabout route tobacco had to take offered opportunity for fraud and speculation.[6]

The solution proposed by Bonó—the appointment of government inspectors—would not have managed to eliminate the speculating middlemen: the "democratic" character of tobacco production, praised so much by Bonó, harbored dangers that "imperialistic" sugar could evade. In the last instance, the internal market structure of each product was determined by its specific requirements of capital and labor. The "cheap" tobacco made possible a network of small- and medium-scale local intermediaries (as well as permitting the small producers' apparent independence); cacao and coffee already demanded larger assets, and they offered opportunities to exporters, fewer in number, but more capitalistic. Lastly, sugar required such sums for its processing that only the foreign market could provide the necessary credit. Thus, although it is certain that on the scale tobacco-cacao-coffee-sugar, the first product was in fact surrounded by a larger network of relations in the internal market than the last, we should not forget that in all four cases one is dealing with export products, whose value and credit were ultimately determined abroad. In that sense, too, the small tobacco grower in the Cibao was the subject and at times the victim of "imperialist" commerce, but it is also certain that, with his own land and without a "dead season," he was not a prisoner of the proletarization that threatened the sugar worker in the South.

Changes in the Economic Relation between the Entrepreneurs and Government. The internal structure of the tobacco trade was described briefly and clearly in 1871: "After Puerto Plata, Santiago de los Caballeros is the most important city of Santo Domingo. It is a city of merchants who govern the lesser merchants of the interior and who, in their turn, are governed by the foreign merchants of Puerto Plata and St. Thomas."[7] The merchant contributed to the financing of government in two ways: indirectly, inasmuch as the customs duties for import and export formed the most important source of state income; and directly, because many merchants acted as moneylenders for the government, in return for which they were often granted exemptions from the import or export duties. Not infrequently it was also stipulated through a contract that a fixed part of the customs duties of a certain port would serve as amortization.

Although the individual moneylenders always continued to offer their services, at the same time a collective institution of lenders, the so-called *juntas* or *Compañías de Crédito* (Credit Associations or Companies), organized in each port by local merchants, found acceptance. Not infrequently these *juntas* took charge of payment of the state's fixed expenditures in their territory in exchange for (a part of) the customs duties. In the capital the first *Junta de Crédito* was formed in President Báez's term by the latter himself; by 1879 the government's debt to this *junta* already totaled a "half million," according to Luperón. Luperón's own government also stimulated the creation of these *juntas*. About the one in Puerto Plata (a lucrative institution in which he also participated actively), he wrote: "As it was not possible to cover a budget of expenditures without having a solid, constant base of revenues, the Government had to promote the establishment of the *Compañía de Crédito*, which would furnish resources to attend punctually to the ordinary and extraordinary expenditures of each province. Indeed, on 1 February [1880] the Minister of the Treasury signed a contract with several individuals of this city [Puerto Plata], by virtue of which they were pledged to form a *Compañía de Crédito* that would supply the sum of $16,000 monthly at a rate of $4,000 each week, charging a premium of 10 percent on amounts advanced and receiving the proceeds from all the revenues of this Customshouse." The investment of these $16,000 was carried out in the following order:

Budget for ordinary expenses of Santiago province	$3,469.70
Budget for ordinary expenses of La Vega province	$2,667.80
Budget for ordinary expenses of Puerto Plata province	$7,643.25
For extraordinary expenses	$2,219.25
Total	$16,000.00[8]

If we consider that in those years the harbor income of Puerto Plata still reached probably around $300,000, the appeal of such a contract for the merchants becomes self-evident. In 1880 it was decided that the *Compañía* in Santo Domingo would cover government expenses in Santo Domingo, Azua, and El Seibo provinces. Moreover, in Samaná, and Luperón government made a contract with a *Compañía de Crédito* that had to pay $60 a day.[9] In 1887 Heureaux founded a new company in that same city, this time consisting of "various merchants from Puerto Plata, represented by Mr. Cosme Batlle," who, in addition to a loan of $170,000, would also pay $174.60 daily "to meet the expenses of Samaná and Sánchez."[10]

In that same year, the principal (lumber) merchant of Monte Cristi set himself up as a *Compañía de Crédito* "to approve the contract dated 1 April last signed between the citizen Admor. of Monte Cristi representing the government and J. I. Jiménez and Co., constituted as a *Junta de Préstamos* in order for the latter to supply the Government the sum of seven thousand pesos in one payment and that of seven thousand three hundred twenty-nine pesos, ninety-three centavos, over four months beginning from the date of the contract. Said company will also provide the sum of one hundred pesos monthly for the office expenses of the *Junta* itself." The interest was 3 percent a month.[11]

It was to be expected that as long as it was so lucrative for the merchants to make loans to the government, they would be opposed to efforts to seek sources of credit elsewhere, unless they could profit in some way from these international manipulations or keep their interests safe in a satisfactory way.

In 1883 Luperón, in the name of the government, had agreed on a loan of 12 million francs, as well as the establishment of a national bank, with Eugenio Pereira, president of the Compagnie Transatlantique. But "after this contract was approved and sanctioned, it was postponed indefinitely, given the distorted versions of those who formed the capital's *Compañía de Crédito*, who were opposing any institution for credit to the State, since it would not be theirs."[12] Already on 5 May 1882, Heureaux had placed emphasis on the necessity of such a bank: "I can assure you that if the Bank is not established, I do not dare take over the Presidency: we are extremely short of resources, this *Compañía* [*de Crédito* of the Capital] is extremely hard up; it will be owed $100,000 at the conclusion of the presidential term and in Puerto Plata at least $50,000 will be owed, a total of $150,000. If the Bank is set up, our path remains open, and it is to encumber to the Bank 70 percent of our customs receipts as guarantee on the amounts that it advances and to rescind the contracts with the *Compañías*, leaving them 30 percent in order to amortize the outstanding debt."[13]

In the following years Heureaux also continues to be, sincerely or not, of the opinion that straightening out finances would be possible only by liquidating the internal debt to the *Juntas de Crédito*, and this by means of a foreign loan. Luperón, however, had abandoned this point of view in 1887, five years after his diligent activities in Paris: the loan that was then going to be signed, without his cooperation (with Westendorp, Amsterdam), seemed less attractive to him, notwithstanding the arguments Heureaux adduced for him: "I want to clarify our financial situation, to alleviate the country's internal credit, and to assure credit; the country owes 700,000 internally and pays 443,000 in interest: do me the favor of telling me whether the country can continue to pay that interest without risks of ruining its creditors. It is necessary, then, to look for a loan that would permit the Government to liquidate its internal debt and to free the capital committed and the public Treasury from the enormous interest that it pays."[14]

The Westendorp loan as it was finally signed in 1888 had many characteristics in common with the transactions that the governments had always arranged with local merchants. Customs control that would be exercised by a "General Office for Customs Collection" (*La Régie*), managed by representatives from the bankers, was to assure that the annuities of 55,654 pounds sterling were produced for thirty years. At the moment when the contract was signed, this annuity represented less than 24 percent of the customs duties. The interest on the loan of 770,000 pounds sterling was 6 percent annually and could thus be considered—even with a bond issue at 75 percent—as quite low in comparison with the usurious interest of the local *Compañías de Crédito* and individual financiers. The fact that the Netherlands government was appointed arbiter in case of conflict and that foreigners would then be the ones who had control of customs doubtless wounded the sincere nationalist feelings of some people. But it is difficult to escape the impression that among the many who protested—including several immigrant-merchants whose nationalist sentiments were, to say the least, poorly developed— there were also those who had the powerful motive of fear because of damage to their own lucrative position as creditors. Moreover, subsequent Dominican historians, often linked to this group of merchants, barely noted the hypocrisy of the protests, since they also knew the later evolution of the *Régie*, which led to the Americans' taking it over.

For the commentators of 1888 that development was, naturally, hidden; the obstinacy with which someone like Federico Henríquez y Carvajal, tied closely to the Sephardic merchants in the capital, argued in favor of internal debts and against foreign debts,[15] as well as his declaration in favor of the abolition of duties on sugar export,[16] seem explainable only in part by his patriotic sentiments. Fear for the interests of the *Compañías de Crédito*,[17] whose credits were paid partly in cash, partly in Westendorp bonds, and partly in bonds from a new "Consolidated Debt without interest," played an important part, just as it must also have determined Luperón's opinion.[18]

Thus Heureaux managed to break the power of the *Compañías de Crédito* in exchange for foreign obligations. This absolutely does not mean that the system of contracting debts to *individual* merchants had been eliminated. On the contrary, in the eighties and nineties a number of private lenders who managed to place themselves in the forefront are increasingly evident. Perhaps Heureaux thought that by pitting the individual financiers against one another he would find himself less exposed to pressure than in the case of the companies. Facing them, he had available only one means of pressure, which was the argument of the companies' own interests: "If [the *Compañía de Préstamos* of Puerto Plata] refuses to make the necessary advances to us, it will not be possible for us to guarantee the capital that it has in the Government's hands; for this we rely on peace, this is maintained with money; if they cannot supply us with that powerful agent, everything is at stake: peace, Government, and Capital." He also argued that "it is necessary to stamp out the rumors of conspiracy . . . so that those who lend their money to the Government retain confidence, and thus resources are obtained to attend to those same people."[19]

Thus as president-debtor Heureaux had stood up to these powerful collectivities, a fact that did not prevent the president as a private individual from sharing—as did Luperón—in some of the profits of the *Compañías*, as was the case in his native city of Puerto Plata. For Heureaux complained in 1887 to the great merchant Cosme Batlle: "As I ought to have a share in the quotas, something of the 6 percent [interest on a loan of $310,000] ought to fall to me, but Don José [Ginebra] has only agreed and arranged (as a courtesy) that I collect the share that properly belongs to me from the 40 percent of the Export duties from 1 November '86 to 30 September of the current year."[20]

The earnings obtained from these and similar transactions, as well as the liquidation of the moneylenders' collective associations in the nineties, put Heureaux in the situation of acting himself as a lender to the state in cooperation with other individual financiers. Thus in 1896 a loan contract was approved "with the Gen. U. Heureaux and Sres. Santiago Michelena and the Successors of C. Batlle for one hundred thousand Mexican pesos, which sum will be deposited in the Central Office in order to cover the January deficit and expenditures of the current month of February."[21] And in the following month Heureaux and Santiago Michelena again loaned 140,000 Mexican pesos to the state, immediately receiving for themselves 16,000 "by way of discount and commission on the above-mentioned sum."[22]

If we observe in greater detail the origin and economic activities of the state's principal local financiers in the last two and a half decades of the past century, it is not surprising to find them at the beginning in the traditional tobacco region, above all and especially in the port city Puerto Plata. Names like Cosme Batlle, Tomás Cocco, and Ginebra appear in the forefront. The firm of the first of these, a Catalan immigrant, continued in its function as creditor during the entire duration of the Heureaux regime. Batlle was active in the functioning of a *Compañía de Crédito* in Samaná,[23] as we have seen before, and he had already established himself in 1888—like Cocco—in the new port of Sánchez in such a way that we can assume he benefitted from the rise of cacao and coffee as export products. Heureaux's relation with the Batlle firm was such that the president believed he could freely avail himself—although not without protests—of the firm's bank account: "I am very sorry that these little drafts for a small amount that I have drawn on you have placed you in such great financial embarrassments in order to pay them, but I believe that neither those nor this last one for $600 to Bilín Martínes will bankrupt you. This is the last, last, and last, and it comes because I could not avoid it, I was pledged to it beforehand because they don't want drafts except on Cosme: what to do?" he wrote in October 1887.[24] Many months later he continued, "Regarding the repeated orders that you give me prohibiting me from drawing on your account, I will tell you . . . I will not draw more, I repeat it to you again. But Raffin has put the knife to my throat and it is from this position that I have resorted to my angel of salvation, which is you."[25]

By 1888 a part of the Batlle earnings belonged to Heureaux: "I hope . . . that the 8,437.50 balance in my favor will be sent to me according to contract via the Clyde steamer."[26] In 1891 Cosme Batlle had almost completely taken over the role that the *Compañía de Préstamo* had played in the Cibao: "to supply monthly, on the Government's account, to the Treasury Administrators of Puerto Plata, Santiago, Monte Cristi, La Vega, Espaillat, and Samaná the amount of the budgets of said provinces and districts, starting with the current month of January, the Government promising to turn over to Sr. Batlle all the promissory notes and liquidations that under the heading of the 65 percent of the duties on import and export, etc., have been generated from the first of the current month and that are generated in the following one."[27]

Heureaux also had monetary dealings with the Monte Cristi lumber firm J. I. Jiménez, already long established, before their relations were chilled by disagreements. The president admitted the evasion of customs duties: "I have arranged with Don Juan Isidro Jiménez the way in which he ought to effect the introduction of the commodities of which he spoke to me."[28] But along with these "traditional" merchants, various new merchant-immigrants, also in the Cibao, began to emerge as lenders, such as the Cuban José A. Puente, who had established himself in Sánchez and was surely involved in the cacao and coffee trade. In 1899 he was still making deals with the president, who in that year gave instructions to the customs inspector at Sánchez to make a reduction of 25 percent on "everything that Sres. José A. Puente and Co. and García, Sánchez import."[29]

However, and completely in accord with the economic changes that took place in the country, we see slowly appearing as new, important lenders individuals connected with sugar production in the South. This change, which appears clearly in the nineties in particular, not only represented a move of the economic focus from the Cibao toward the South, but also meant that the *producers* instead of the *merchants* began to act as creditors and that the *immigrant* character of the group of financiers became even more apparent than before.

One of the most important representatives of that group was undoubtedly the Italian J. B. Vicini. Although he was making important transactions in the country by the beginning of the eighties—at that time he had at least one ship of his own and in 1882 he had an office in New York[30]—his rise as a major sugar producer and financier coincides with the regime of Heureaux, to whom in 1882 he had already loaned significant sums of money.[31] In 1893 relations between them were so intimate that Vicini was acting as Heureaux's representative:

> By reason of your having signed in my name the contract that I copy in its entirety: Between the signatories Sr. Charles W. Wells, in the name of and in representation of the Santo Domingo Improvement Company of New York of which he is Vice-President, and Sr. J. B. Vicini as proxy of General Ulises Heureaux, owner of the credit that will be mentioned further on, the following has been agreed upon: First. The company commits itself to paying Sr. J. B. Vicini the sum of one hundred fifty thousand pesos in current silver in the following manner: from the month of May next the sum of two thousand ($2,000) monthly through the *Caja de Recaudación* at each month's end for two consecutive years, and at the end of the two years, the Company will pay the outstanding balance of the $150,000 in cash in current silver in a single payment. . . . I take pleasure in giving you the most affectionate thanks

for having represented me on that occasion, requesting that you continue to represent me in order to collect the sums to which the contract involved refers."[32]

In the same year Vicini paid more than half the "war expenditures" that the president had had to make, a sum of almost $38,000 in gold. The rest was paid by the Santo Domingo Improvement Co.[33] In the subsequent years Vicini continued to lend large sums to the state, generally with a 5 percent commission and with 2 percent monthly interest. In February 1897 the amount the government owed him was $394,872.53.[34] In 1898 Heureaux shared in a loan to the government, participation that "is represented in the name of Don Juan B. Vicini." At the time of Heureaux's assassination, Vicini, with $400,000, was by far the president's biggest *criollo* creditor.[35]

In that same year, 1899, the export duties on almost the entire sugar harvest were turned over to Vicini: "The Government has concluded an agreement with Señor J. B. Vicini to the effect that the yield of the export duties of all the sugars that are shipped through the port of Macorís or through any other under jurisdiction of that District will be turned over to the aforesaid Sr. Vicini or his agents, with exception of the yield of the duties on sugars that are shipped from Santiago W. Mellor's Porvenir Plantation, up to the sum of $40,000 in gold, and the yield from the duties on sugars that the Señores W. Biedermann ship, up to the amount of $29,000 in gold."[36]

Vicini was also concerned with monetary affairs: in 1892 he presented a bill "for the minting of the currency,"[37] and in 1897 he was also involved with the minting of silver coinage. After the dictator's death, he believed he had to excuse his actions by depicting his relationship with the president as not very friendly; he had, he wrote on 28 November 1899 in the *Listín*, often warned Heureaux against his monetary policy and perhaps for that reason the president hated him so much, "having received more than evidence of the hostility with which as Chief of State he acted against my interests." Of such "evidence," however, there is no proof in the archives.

In addition to Vicini, certain sugar producers such as Thormann, Biedermann and Co., Ellers Friedheim and Co., and Santiago W. Mellor, all of San Pedro de Macorís, acted as moneylenders for the president.[38] Mellor's death in 1898 was quite inopportune for Heureaux, as he wrote in a letter to Isidore Mendel, minister plenipotentiary and financial agent in Paris: "I had counted on Don Santiago Mellor, planter from Macorís, for the advance of a considerable sum on the duties on his harvest for this year, a sum that I intended to send to you. But it was unfortunate that on the eighth of this month Don Santiago died suddenly, without leaving a power of attorney."[39]

In the last years of Heureaux's government, Bartolo Bancalari, an Italian merchant established first in Samaná with his partner Gisbert, and whose interests also grew in other parts of the country, also became an important lender. In order to liquidate what he owed, the president sometimes had to contract other debts with a competitor of the person he was paying off:

"I am requesting that you be so kind as to deliver to Don Bartolo Bancalari twelve thousand pesos (national currency) charged to my account."[40] Or, to slight the interests of old creditors: "as soon as you finish paying off the Griessen matter, set aside a monthly portion of $2,500 in cash on importation and $2,500 in gold on exportation, sums that you will deliver by means of receipt to Señores Gisbert and Bancalari of Samaná. All this must be in confidence and with the necessary precaution so that Puente and Batlle do not stir up difficulties nor believe they have grounds for complaints,"[41] Heureaux wrote to the customs administrator at Sánchez.

Among the *criollo* creditors with whom Heureaux had, at the time of his death, debts of more than $100,000 were numbered, along with Vicini, Bancalari, and Cosme Batlle, Perrelló and Petit in Monte Cristi, and Pou, Rodríguez, and Co. in the capital. Among the creditors for smaller amounts we find names such as Eug. Abreu, J. A. Lluberes, J. de Lemos, T. Pastoriza, E. Mayer, A. T. Ricart, and Manuel A. Rodríguez.[42]

In the last two decades of the century, some industries in which the president also had financial interests had emerged. Thus in 1885 franchises were granted to M. E. Grullón and R. R. Boscowits for the "large-scale" production of vermicelli and pastas.[43] In 1898, a "petroleum refinery" existed in La Romana, for which one Enrique Dumois had obtained the concession and for protection of which all importing of "gas" or refined petroleum "that did not have a strength of 150 degrees and up" had been prohibited.[44] In 1899 this refinery appears in the hands of the capital city merchant Lluberes. The Dutch financier den Tex Bondt received permission in 1898 to set up an ice factory.[45] The Scot A. D. Baird, who arrived in the country for the construction of a railroad, appears in 1898 as manager of the Samaná Bay Fruit Co. (and the following year is unmasked, in that capacity, as a smuggler).[46]

In 1899 General Heureaux had interests in the following industries and firms:

1. one-third part of Empresa Muelle y Enramada, Santo Domingo, of which Bancalari was the administrator and Vicini one of the major stockholders;
2. one-third part in the vermicelli factory of Pou, Rodríguez and Co.;
3. one-third part in the Dutch schooner *Leonor* of J. M. Leyba (a Curaçao Sephardic Jew and Dutch consul) and J. Willems;
4. 133 shares in the National Bank of Santo Domingo, in the name and in the hands of C. W. Wells, New York, for $66,666.66 in the New Jersey San Domingo Brewery Co.;
5. the German Hamburg Mercantile Society (Viñamata and Huttlinger, directors);
6. the Puerto Plata pier and the soap factory of Puerto Plata;
7. the "Yaque" firm (J. I. Jiménez) in Monte Cristi;
8. 62½ shares in the Samaná Bay Fruit Co. (the shares were "in the hands of E. Demorizi");

9. the firm García, Sánchez and Co. in Sánchez;
10. the Azua Pier (John Hardy, U.S.A., manager);
11. the "West Indian Public Works" of the Italian L. Cambiaso;
12. the San Francisco de Macorís Railroad.

Moreover, the general received a bonus of five cents in American gold on each *quintal* of sugar exported by the Central Azuano of J. B. Vicini and an equal amount per *quintal* from the Central Quisqueya of Juan F. de Castro in San Pedro de Macorís. From W. P. Clyde in New York, manager of the important shipping line, he received a sum of $5,000 American gold annually. P. A. Lluberes denied the fact that Heureaux owned a third of the shares in the banana plantations and in the petroleum refinery in La Romana, and Salvador Ross denied the president's participation in the San Pedro de Macorís pier.[47]

From all these data can be deduced the extent to which the president was personally involved in the entrepreneurs' activities; it is also evident that there was no clear division between the groups of sugar producers and coffee, cacao, and tobacco merchants on one hand and the other merchants, the financiers and builders of small industries and harbor projects, on the other. The money earned with the cultivation and trading of export products was willingly invested in part in the manufacture of consumer products and in the private financing of infrastructure projects, since both investments promised and yielded large profits in periods of political stability. Meanwhile, on the other hand, the sums earned with financial speculation, with construction and commercial transactions were readily invested in the purchase of agricultural enterprises and real estate, as was also the case with Heureaux.

Thus there arose in those years a wealthy, united group of merchants, producers, and financiers that, if surnames are taken as a guide, consisted in part of "old" Dominican families (Abreu, Ricart, Rodríguez, Grullón, and so forth), who, moreover, had only attained prosperity in these years, but that for the most part was composed of immigrants of Cuban, Curaçaoan, and European origins. With this group, a Dominican bourgeoisie, in the sociological sense, was begun, as I hope to show in greater detail in a subsequent chapter.

Notwithstanding the aforesaid, the ambiguity of the relationship between Heureaux and "the merchants" should not be underestimated. The president, always armed with the "suspiciousness" indispensable for political dealings, recognized his "friends for money" as such at every moment; indeed, the relationship was one based on a system of exchange with implicit sanctions: the government needed the merchants as moneylenders; for the latter, political stability was important. The president could use his apparatus for sanctions arbitrarily in order to create difficulties for the stubborn; business could, by means of economic pressure, cause the president financial embarrassment. It was, in a few words, an unstable alliance that was only maintained while the mutual advantages were considered greater than the mutual distrust. A little note hurriedly written in pencil by a Sra. Dubocq to Canon Nouel reveals the fear that could seize the well-to-do classes: "Don Carlos, for God's sake, please take care of this matter. On leaving Mass, Salvador told me that Lilís [Heureaux] wants a sum of money but that he gives no guarantee—tell me if that is true. Gregorio Billini told him. It is tomorrow that I must take that money from the Pou firm, and I have it on my mind; I ought to leave on the twenty-seventh, and what shall I do? You are the only person in whom I trust and with whom I am candid: tell me what to do. Reply or come here if it is possible."[48]

But there were also many tributes to the president on the part of the moneylenders. In 1893 in the Le Figaro exhibition hall in Paris the armchair that Cosme Batlle had ordered as a gift for Heureaux could be admired.[49] In 1896 Tiffany's in New York made him a sword of honor that was going to be offered to him by the National Congress,[50] and even in 1899 "Sr. José A. Puente [a Cuban] in his own name and in that of General Heureaux, gave the outgoing Ayuntamiento of Sánchez the sum of 2,671.50 odd pesos of gold that the Council owed to the commercial house José A. Puente and Co. of that City, so that the incoming one would not find any obligation."[51] But in that same year of economic crisis, according to Rufino Martínez, "two of his capitalist good friends, one from the capital and the other from Puerto Plata, upon seeing that the Government's insolvency was an incurable ill, suspended credit and began to demand the payment of accumulated interest."[52]

Heureaux, for his own part, dreamed in 1899, the last year of his life, of a complicated intrigue with which he would bring to justice all those who had enriched themselves so much under his regime and who were beginning to threaten it; in a subtle way, perhaps he allowed this dream to exercise its influence when he wrote the Italians Bernardini and Marietti in Puerto Plata: "For my part, I wish you luck, health, and prosperity, so that the country too may collect part of the benefits created and enjoyed by you."[53] His assassination in July of that year put an abrupt end to that dream; when Vice-President Figuereo found himself compelled to resign by August, he also blamed the moneylenders: "A government exhausted of money [was] surrounded by creditors who suddenly assumed an intransigent attitude towards the unfortunate country that they had, in their majority, contributed to burdening with debts in the face of a people almost starving."[54]

The Merchant and the Community. At the level of the lesser organs of the government—provincial governorship, town council—economic relations with the merchants were, on a smaller scale, a reflection of the central government's. The prosperous municipalities could permit themselves to make contracts on bases equal to those of the president. Thus Isaac D. de Marchena committed himself to San Pedro de Macorís in 1885 to build a Catholic church, receiving in exchange, among other things, five centavos for each *quintal* of sugar exported by the *común*.[55] Moreover, the largest cities bene-fitted from the merchants' gifts and initiatives destined to beautify or im-prove their *"patria chica"* (or native region). The creation of parks, the building of fences for cemeteries, the construction of churches, the creation of a corps of volunteer firemen were often the results of such activities. The constantly repeated pattern of setting aside specific future income for fi-nancing certain projects we also find here; sometimes the yield of certain agricultural enterprises was bequeathed for a charitable purpose. Thus, the Hospital San Rafael in Santiago also owed its existence to the well-known merchant José Manuel Glas "because the latter had ceded to it the usufruct of the two ships that belonged to him."[56] If during festivals of the Virgin of La Candelaria in San Carlos, "the arrogant *barrio* of Pendón defeated the legendary *barrio* of Mamey, this latter received money from E. Hatton, administrator of the neighboring La Fe plantation. The inhabitants of the first *barrio* then sang:

> El mendigo mameyero
> alegrar sus fiestas quiso
> y a *mister* Hatton, sumiso,
> le fue a pedir su dinero, etc.[57]*

The smaller, poorer *comunes* depended, naturally, on the generosity of the central government.

Compared with this occasional philanthropy of the merchants was their eagerness for profit, which few sentiments mitigated: a small drop in the value of the Mexican peso, which was in common use, was the motive for the merchants in Azua to increase their prices immediately by 50 percent, and a salary increase of 50 percent for some groups of employees in 1899 led to a rise in prices of 200 percent in the capital.[58] Nevertheless, this eager-ness for profit was not accompanied by rigorous bookkeeping, by efficient billing techniques, that is, by economic accuracy and punctuality. The code dictated by the culture in commercial traffic scarcely permitted such things; the risks that this represented, along with the dangers of political instability and the scant loyalty of the immigrants toward the country and the people, go far, perhaps, to explain the large margins of profit that they appropriated. In any case, it continued to be common to dun a respectable customer for a bill of a few pesos in the following way:

> It is not this exigency that prompts it, but rather the lack of pecuni-ary resources; thus, then, I hope Your Honor will pardon me once con-vinced that it is not any other motive that has compelled me to call your attention to such a small sum, which ought to have been awaited until Your Honor had paid in full whenever circumstances permitted or

*The beggar from Mamey/Wanted to cheer up his fiestas/And, meek, to *Mister* Hatton,/he went to beg for his money, etc.

at your pleasure. Because I have determined that this step will not alter the friendly feeling that we profess for one another, I beg that Your Honor continue as up until now to grant your favors to your most affectionate friend and servant . . . .

After a long wait, this could be written with less circumlocution: "I believe that you have already investigated the way in which to pay me, as you had me told the last time, because it is now a year that you have owed me on that account, and you should consider that I cannot grant credit for such a long time."[59] Moreover, the buyers readily spent any small sum that remained after the purchase (*el pico*): "If what was purchased cost them 97 centavos: And in what shall I give you *el pico*? Give me whatever you like." In the countryside, a whisker from a mustache sometimes served as a pledge for loans, without anything more being set down in writing.[60]

It was a Sephardic immigrant who dared to confront these customs: on 15 July 1893, Eugenio de Marchena placed the following "important notice" in the *Listín*: "As disavowing any debt that is not backed up by a document seems to be becoming a custom, and since another baneful custom is that anyone who takes credit in the commercial houses never signs I.O.U.'s, I am notifying my numerous customers that starting on the first of September all those who owe me debts must either pay me or they will have to sign an I.O.U., whatever the sum, for I do not wish to leave my own family in poverty by not taking this necessary precaution." It was also an immigrant who introduced more aggressive methods of advertising: Ostertag, who sold cream of malt, decorated a wagon with boxes of that product, something that was commented upon favorably in the newspaper. And finally in 1893, the delivery of a sum of 10,000 Mexican pesos for a life insurance policy with "El Sol de Canada"–Canada Sun–was a novelty acclaimed by the *Listín*.[61] But it does not seem that at the time these innovations were considered as anything other than curiosities.

The Government's Economic and Administrative System. Let us now turn to the Government's economic activities and operations. As has already become evident from many of the items mentioned previously, the separation between the president's private means and state finances was vague, fluid, and often nonexistent. In a letter to his then moneylender and agent in St. Thomas, Jacobo Pereyra, Heureaux jumps easily from the plural (government) to the singular (private): "We are, that is, I am a little hard up for money, and a great deal is being spent in these days of elections . . . could I obtain a private loan . . . for $10,000, payable in six months and under my responsibility?"[62] But that possibility was also used in the opposite way: in 1887 he notifies another foreign financier, John Wanamaker of Philadelphia, that a personal debt "has been incorporated into the Government's account."[63] A loan made by the same Wanamaker later in that year, to be amortized by the export duties from San Pedro de Macorís and Azua, was considered, nevertheless, "a deal of friend to friend rather than of Government."[64]

Also in that same year Heureaux declared himself personal guarantor for the debts that Dominican merchants had contracted with the Brondsted house in St. Thomas.[65] However, when he began in the mid-nineties to act as a creditor of the state, a division between the public person and the private was indeed created in the contracts. Nonetheless, even in those years the vague separation of those spheres continued to exist, although in another sense. This cannot be better illustrated than with an annotation from 12 November 1896 in the *Libreta de Hacienda y Comercio* (Treasury and Commerce Account Book), according to which Heureaux had borrowed a sum of 307,271.87 pesos from Successors of Cosme Batlle during his journey through the Cibao "in order to meet Public Service expenditures and other personal expenses." The commission charged with preparing the description of the inventory after Heureaux's death spoke of: "the natural predisposition in many persons to consider that whatever General Heureaux possessed must have belonged to the Nation, by mistakenly supposing that a perfect separation did not exist between the two patrimonies, because of the apparent confusion of the two conditions, public and private, that coincided in the deceased.[66]

But the commission was mistaken in the implicit idea that such an "apparent confusion" could only be found in the "deceased" and that a "perfect separation" had really existed and was the rule. This was not true: the identification of the president with the state and the country, not only in an economic but also in a political sense, had already existed before—and would continue to exist after—Heureaux's regime. It was a consequence of what Max Weber calls a "structure of patrimonial authority," which we shall analyze in due course. It is interesting to note here how Heureaux, perhaps unconsciously seeking a counterpoint against that identification, liked to make comments that carried the separation between the person and the office to the point of the ridiculous; many anecdotes testify to this. He was already practicing this in 1882, a little before his first presidency: in a letter to President Meriño he wrote of himself: "Situation of Lilís, this unfortunate finds himself entirely ruined, obliged to pretend to be what he really is not, he owes at least $2,500 . . . , for in order to help us, this poor friend has had to make great sacrifices, in the Government as well as in the Loan Companies."[67]

Meanwhile, the fact remains that from 1897 on Heureaux personally financed the budgets of various *comunes* such as El Seibo, Azua, and Barahona. It is unnecessary to say that in 1899, when the country was plagued by serious droughts and an economic crisis and when the existence of the regime was rightfully feared for, the lack of separation between the economic spheres, private and public, became a vital necessity for political functionaries. Heureaux distributed $6,000 in gold to some merchants to buy articles of primary necessity in the U.S. in order to sell them with a 10 percent maximum profit. He put a thousand yearling cattle up for sale to stabilize the price of meat; he even gave rice to the merchants so that they could sell it at fifteen centavos. Moreover, the governor of Santo Domingo, Pichardo, slaughtered cattle from his own ranch to combat the shortage, just as, here and there, a merchant friend (Manuel Cocco in Puerto Plata) decided to establish a "store for the common people."[68] But here one is clearly dealing with desperate measures, which illustrate, moreover, the extent to which the leading figures of such a political system fear its collapse and how they are prepared to avoid it by risking their private capital. Since their own lives could be at stake, it was not possible to think of a division between the private and official spheres.

That a mixture of private and public funds often occurred at lower levels as well fits in with the patrimonial system. The president expected that, if it were necessary, the employee responsible would pay for public expenditures from his own funds; the promise of a reimbursement at an opportune moment was to be considered a sufficient guarantee. "I have taken note," writes Heureaux to the treasury administrator in Azua, "regarding what you tell me about the $1,950 that the Cashier's office sent you, and it surprises me that you would only destine that sum to the extraordinary expenditures of the Province, when you could have met those already made with your personal credit, confident that, as I have done other times, I would attend preferentially to covering your liabilities."[69]

The fact that certain government posts produced bonuses in favor of the private resources of the employees also formed part of the "economic code" of the patrimonial structure. In the rare case in which the employee sacrificed this right, that appeared in the newspaper: "The Municipal Treasurer of Santiago had generously waived on behalf of the *común* the 4 percent of the last municipal loan that he is entitled to. Which amounts to $600 Mexican pesos."[70]

The concept of corruption, the definition of which is usually based on the separation between public and private means, is scarcely useful in such a structure. Even when that separation was the ideal norm that the individual had, there was always insecurity about the duration of his employment to encourage him to take advantage of his post. When the hero of one of the stories of José Ramón López—written in the period we are considering—is appointed customs inspector, he says: "My mother, my blessed mother, so honorable her whole life, also found out about my appointment and came to congratulate me. 'Take advantage of it, son,' she exclaimed with a voice veiled by weeping. 'Take advantage of it. God offers very few opportunities in a lifetime.' 'Mama, don't worry. The salary . . .' 'What salary, boy! The salary is nothing in comparison. . . .' 'Ah, no. Not a centavo more, not a centavo less.' 'Son,' replied my mother with painful distress, 'son, you're going to go back to the days without bread and the nights without light. Think of the future, think of your children. . . .'"[71]

Finally, it is difficult to use the "normal" definition of corruption because for a long time it had been traditional for the government to make gifts in money or in goods, whether periodic or not, to individuals without the latter having to make any material return. At times, in order to justify these gifts, services offered to the state in the past were pointed out, but at least just as often it was a matter of individuals who had to be persuaded by means of gifts to desist from taking sides against the government. In a country where the number of governmental functions was very limited, the government—or the president—thus acted as an organization of calculated philanthropy, which was naturally always mixed with political aims. As can be seen in a letter from Heureaux to Luperón, the latter had tried, after a fashion, to formalize the system of gifts, calling them "*asignaciones*" (or subsidies):

> I do not venture to reply to your ideas regarding the system of Government that you say I have introduced; I believed that you knew that before my coming to public affairs, the country was dominated by corruption, and if I am not mistaken, it was the virus that infected the masses to overthrow the Government of Don Ulises [Espaillat]; and as the country has continued under the sway of those same customs, in the Provisional Government you had to invent the expedient of *asignaciones* to divide the sums that are distributed in gifts and valuables more equitably. By continuing that order of affairs, it has become corrupt to the point that everyone wants to live off the State, and you, when you have been in power, have distributed considerable sums for the same purpose, but since you have not had the necessity of materially assuming the responsibility for these acts that you condemn, you blame me and accuse me without reflecting for a moment that the Republic has been turned topsy-turvy by others and that I have come to govern, finding it in Chaos.[72]

Furthermore, sometimes these gifts were not enough to keep someone calm: "My friend Manuel María Almonte, who due to a matter of $500 with Geneva has let himself feel inclined toward the ranks of those discontented because of money; this is not strange: here, there, and everywhere is felt the malaise produced in the souls of our friends by the fact that the Government or I cannot satisfy their aspirations for money despite the salary or *asignación* that they enjoy. . . ."[73]

The custom of paying government salaries regularly in cash did not exist in the last century. In its place, *hojas de sueldo* (salary sheets) were often signed and used as means of payment with a variable rate of exchange. It must have also been the insecurity of the financial situation that made the higher employees and the members of the parliament frequently demand *daily* payment.[74] In 1893 the cabinet daily received payments that varied from $17.06 2/3 for the vice-president of the republic and his secretary to $10.33 1/3 for the minister of foreign relations.[75]

For the year 1889 we have budget figures available. The total expenditures of $1,408,543 were divided among the departments in the following way: Treasury and Commerce: 39 percent; War and Navy: 31 percent; Interior and Police: 14 percent; Justice: 6.5 percent; Public Works: 5.5 percent; Public Instruction: 3 percent; Foreign Relations: 0.5 percent.[76] But public administration continued to be extremely defective and erratic. It was only in 1896 that it was decided to record the most essential information in an organized way:

> Inasmuch as the formation of a statistical table regarding the customs flow of the Republic is notoriously necessary for the purpose of thus preparing and giving a basis to the reform of the tariff laws and other projects of general interest and singular importance that the Executive Authority has in mind, it is resolved: to entrust to Señores Hipólito Billini and Federico Henríquez y Carvajal the collection of all the statistical data on customs operations in general with respect to the years 1895 and 1896; to remunerate the gentlemen cited with a monthly sum of $200 national currency each until the termination of said project.[77]

The installation of scales in the principal trade centers was also called for. Moreover, in 1896 a new treasury law was approved with the aim of "introducing a system of internal order regarding accounting." As "first fruit" it was mentioned proudly that "all the fiscal accounts of the Republic that the Ministry of the Treasury has been able to present to the National Congress have been submitted already examined and approved by the Honorable Tribunal on Accounts."[78]

The Monetary System. In his *Reseña general geográfico-estadística*, José Ramón Abad stated in 1888 that "calculation and speculation had brought to the markets of the Republic a mass of coinage inferior to the one that existed before" and noted that Santo Domingo had become "the receptacle for all the mintings of trash."[79] Federico Henríquez y Carvajal wrote in 1886 in his *Mensajero* that the "monetary question" was causing the country difficulties from 1883 on; in apparent response to allusions already published, he continued: "It is not only the Hebrew merchants who have speculated with the introduction of the [Peruvian] *sol* and 80 centavo fractions of South and Central American pesos," to which he immediately added that the introduction of these currencies was perfectly legal, given that money is only a commodity. Moreover, he was of the opinion that the conversion of all foreign money into "national currency," which would involve a loss of 15 to 20 percent, would put the sugar exporters in great difficulties.

The change carried out in earlier years from U.S. currency to the peso, especially the Mexican one, had harmed principally the workers: "Eduardo has been earning $50 a year since 1873, in which U.S. silver functioned as the norm, but since 1879 he has received it in Mexican silver. He has continued to lose, then, the difference produced by the agiotage."[80] Heureaux thought in 1887 that "the introduction of foreign coins that occurs is not to be feared because of the shiny ones or ones full of holes, which can be said to have disappeared from the neighboring Antilles and which cannot by their nature be the object of great speculation; what ought to be feared is the import of Grenadine, Prussian, and Chilean *pesetas*; for that already lends itself to strong speculations. The introduction is prohibited and punished, and on this coast it is difficult for it to occur, but it is necessary to pay considerable attention to the steamers that come from Colón, for there is a plethora of that coinage there."[81]

In that same year, from Paris, the Puerto Rican Ramón E. Betances presented Heureaux a plan "that has as a goal the introduction of a national currency in this Republic," to which the president responded courteously but cautiously: "Offhand, only one observation occurs to me," he wrote, "and it is that before signing a contract for the minting of currency, the law should be issued to establish types, values, and so forth, calculating it on those of France, Belgium, and Italy, and even Venezuela, in order to keep entry into the Latin [Monetary] Union open."[82] But already in 1888 a law on minting Dominican currency was issued, in which the National Bank, recently created by the Crédit Mobilier, was singled out as the bank of issuance for the "*dominicanos*," which would be worth 25 percent less than their prototype, the franc, which "produced relative alarm in certain guilds and some uneasiness in the majority of the production centers of the country."[83] In November of that same year the National Congress decreed that each 100 units that were owed to the public treasury were to be paid in the following manner: "80 in Mexican pesos at the rate of 100 centavos each or in Chilean and Peruvian pesos at the rate of 90 centavos each, or in 'National Bank of Santo Domingo' bills at par, of those that are circulating by virtue of the Resolution by Executive Decree of 21 December 1881; 10 in silver coinage, 10 in national currency of nickel."[84]

In 1892 and 1897 new emissions of silver coinage took place, in which, as we have already seen, J. B. Vicini was involved. It was to the 1892 issue that Luperón's criticism would have referred when he spoke of "coins of debased silver and nickel, which are not quoted in any way on the foreign markets, minted in Brussels without any official contract."[85] In the nineties there were also new emissions of paper money involving the Santo Domingo Improvement Co.

The growing crisis in the Dominican monetary situation can be reduced, to my way of thinking, to the following causes: first, Abad's correct observation that because of the introduction of foreign "bad money"—and in perfect agreement with Gresham's Law—"good money" had gone out of circulation; second, and closely linked to the preceding, the eagerness of some merchants for monetary speculation; third, the increasing international devaluation of silver during those years; fourth, inadequate government policy, which encouraged inflation with new emissions and loans and which more and more emphatically undermined confidence in the currency.

In 1893, the year of the great North American crisis, a decree was promulgated according to which a tax of 20 centavos had to be paid on each foreign silver peso imported, import of a peso in fractions was assessed with 30 centavos. In the preamble to the decree, it was noted "that the depreciation of foreign silver money produces conspicuous damages to the interests of the Nation and to those of individuals," and that the government should do everything "to shelter the public interests from ruinous speculations." However, the decree would not take effect until ten days after its promulgation, and, furthermore, resolutions exempting various merchants from the measures were immediately passed.[86] In 1896 the free importing of Mexican pesos was permitted again because of the great shortage of them.[87] In the law of 17 March 1897 it was established anew which coins were considered "common currency": nickel coinage; the republic's franc-type coins; its bronze coinage; minted coins (issued) and National Bank bills, guaranteed by the government, in which the common currency-American gold relation was set at 2:1, and the common currency-Mexican silver relation for "obligations between private parties" at 1:1,[88] but by then this type of resolution could no longer provide any effect. Already by the following year, it was necessary to resort to an emergency measure: "Starting 1 December 1898, export duties will be collected in U.S. minted gold, and, lacking this, in drafts drawn by the exporters on foreign markets. . . . Of each hundred units of export duties, 20 percent will be collected to be turned over to the National Bank of Santo Domingo or to its agents for the amortization of the bills issued by the Bank itself,"[89] but the catastrophe could no longer be avoided.

At the beginning of 1899 Heureaux traveled to the principal cities to come to an agreement with the merchants on new types of exchange rates: the common currency-American gold relation was now fixed at 3:1. In his message for that year, the president announced the importing of gold coins and the cancellation of national paper currency (called "*papeletas de Lilís*" or "Lilís's pawn tickets" by the people).[90] He also pointed out some of the causes of the crisis:

> There was not, then, any reason for the renascent panic since the last emission of bills by the Bank, and one must attribute it to the inadequacy of the economic notions of the majority of the country, which sees dangers in an emission limited to a figure lower than the daily needs of the population [The emission was $1.6 million.] This disregard of good economic principles places the public fortune at the mercy of the first moneychanger who aspires to raise the rate of exchange. By making an offer higher than the quotation of the day, he establishes a new rate, spreads the alarm, and from one moment to the next all the merchants are getting ready . . . setting higher prices for their articles. And while that occurs the rate for day-wages . . . remains

almost unalterable, making the situation of the worker and the artisan one full of anguish.

The June 1898 invasion attempt by J. I. Jiménez, which was not in itself important, continued the president, had had repercussions abroad, which scared away the capital necessary for new financial operations. "These difficulties in the foreign market, worsened by the economic and financial consequences of the war waged by the U.S. and Spain, principally in waters and territories that neighbor our own, were reflected in a dangerous rise in the internal market, and taking the occasion of the new monetary system being introduced into the country, and even more so the recent emission of bills from the National Bank, they caused a groundless panic among the public and in every way worsened the economic situation."[91]

In April, a national commission that would be in charge of the exchange and burning of the devalued bills from the National Bank was appointed. This operation was to be possible because of a loan from the Englishman F. H. Morris.[92] During his journey in the Cibao, the president promised that same month that in July the bills would be exchanged for gold at a rate of four to one, which could be considered attractive for the merchants who had been availing themselves of rates of eleven to one and more. Meanwhile, there was a shortage of small change—*las motas* (or little specks); in the capital as well as in Puerto Plata, bills were issued for small change. Prices reached absurd heights: in Azua, a pair of shoes cost $22, a pound of rice 50 centavos. A serious drought struck various parts of the country simultaneously, increasing the scarcity and high prices of articles of primary necessity. In July, Heureaux left for the Cibao, where thousands of bills were burned, which caused a drop in the price of gold and a rise in the value of the *"papeletas de Lilís."* In Moca a hundred thousand bills had to be changed for (vouchers for) gold. On 26 July Heureaux was assassinated in that city.[93] By 1 August an anonymous group of merchants proposed setting the exchange rate at 3 to 1, which Federico Henríquez y Carvajal, president of the capital's ayuntamiento at the time of Heureaux's death, rightly protested because of the high profits they would make.[94] During the provisional government of Horacio Vázquez, installed on 4 September 1899, the *"papeletas de Lilís"* were taken out out of circulation by means of monthly sales with an exchange rate of 5 to 1.[95]

Changes in Economic Relations with the Outside World. In accord with the pattern of communications as described in the preceding chapter, the foreign financial centers during the first four decades of the republic's existence were found within the Caribbean area, that is, in Curaçao and St. Thomas; on both islands, it was principally Sephardic bankers, like J. A. Jesurún and Son and Jacobo Pereyra, respectively, who supplied the loans. Of the two large loans that the republic arranged outside the Caribbean area before 1890, the Hartmont loan of 1869 was the result of contacts that Jesurún, in cooperation with the French financier Adolphe Mendes, had made in Europe, while the Westendorp loan of 1888 was prepared by the Curaçao-Sephardic immigrant Eugenio G. de Marchena. From Heureaux's papers, it can be seen how even well into the eighties he kept up his contacts with the Pereyra firm as private creditor and agent. In addition, Wanamaker and Brown of Philadelphia and Federico Hohlt in Hanover later began to act as his principal private lenders abroad; the latter had commercial interests in the republic. However, it can be said in general terms that European financial influence in the country, which continued until the nineties, was based on a network of relations that the Sephardim from the Caribbean maintained in Europe. It is not, therefore, surprising that this group, since it was oriented toward Europe, would resist increasing North American penetration, which finally cost Marchena his life.

The rise of North American financial predominance, although perhaps inevitable in light of the new sugar industry, with its New York orientation, was accelerated by the debacle of the Westendorp banking firm of Amsterdam. After the loan of 770,000 pounds sterling in 1888, this firm had loaned another 900,000 pounds sterling in 1890 for the construction of the Puerto Plata-Santiago railroad line. "The moral climate in which its dealings with the Dominican government evolved would be the principal cause for the employees of *La Régie*, under whose protection they were enriching themselves, wallowing in the mire, of managing so many fraudulent operations, to neglect intentionally their duties regarding sending money to the Amsterdam firm, it being impossible for Westendorp to know the correct liquidations on the services of the loans."[96]

Both Heureaux and Marchena had appropriated considerable sums from the loans for themselves. On 31 July 1889 the former wrote the latter: "But despite whatever may be said regarding the distribution of the yield from the loan, the only part that has fallen to me from it are those 5,000 pounds sterling that you designated for me; I already have a love for them such as you cannot imagine. . . . I have nothing to do with anyone but you, and you are the one who answers to me for these little pounds. Moreover, I warn you that I do not want you to send them to me on accounts of the government or of Westendorp or of anybody, but in cash addressed to my personal attention." In that month the same Marchena requested for the second time within a short period a sum of 1,000 pounds sterling, which caused the indignation of the minister Gautier. Nevertheless, Heureaux wrote: "As for me, you know that I have never bargained over the stipend necessary for the services that my friends do for me, but it is strange that a man as rigorous as you in questions of numbers and accounting [would complain] just because a matter for which those unfamiliar with it required explanations is not cleared up immediately, especially when the verifying documents that were missing in the account that you sent to Don Manuel [Gautier] had not been delivered. . . ."[97]

We saw before how by giving exemptions from customs duties Heureaux hindered, to say the least, the administration of the *Caja de Recaudación*. The director of *La Régie*, a member of a distinguished Amsterdam family, C. J. den Tex Bondt, was without a doubt one of the principal culprits in the bankruptcy of the company that he represented. Although at the beginning he had some disagreements with the president, later he became his accomplice in numerous financial arrangements, to the point that in 1891 an agreement was signed between den Tex and the government according to which 35 percent of the customs duties went to Westendorp and the rest to the government. Although it had indeed been remarked in the 1888 contract that the annuity to be paid would equal no more than 30 percent of the nation's customs duties, the fraudulent administration of customs had meant that the percentage had to be increased considerably in the meantime. When Westendorp in Amsterdam denied den Tex's legal authority to sign such an agreement, the firm then no longer had any alternative but to notify the holders of its bonds that fraud had been committed, which led to the collapse of the Westendorp house.

The Amsterdam firm then transferred its contracts to a U.S. consortium led by Smith W. Weed, the San Domingo Improvement Company, which also took over the contract signed between den Tex and the government for the construction of the Puerto Plata-Santiago railroad.[98] By a decision of 31 August 1892 the Dominican government determined not to recognize this transfer, which was to have taken effect on 1 September and of which the government had been ignorant.[99] "The 35 percent of the customs receipts . . . will be turned over to the Consul or Consuls of H. M. the King of Holland or to the persons whom they designate, who will guard said deposit until another arrangement to the contrary is determined."[100]

However, on 12 January 1893 Pedro J. Garrido, Genaro Pérez, Augusto Franco Bidó, and Manuel de J. Galván were invited by the president as "a most select representation from among the jurists of the Country" to give their opinion on the transfer, since within a short time a commission delegated by the American consortium was to arrive in the capital. The jurists made favorable and speedy recommendations; by 24 January they received some words of gratitude from Heureaux, as well as the four thousand pesos that their recommendation had cost.[101] New contracts signed with the Improvement Co. served to calm *criollo* creditors like Vicini, Batlle, Lemos, Abreu, and Lluberes. With its affiliated companies, the San Domingo Railway Co. and the San Domingo Finance Co., the U.S.-based Improvement Co. dominated the greater part of Dominican financial life after 1893.[102] It should be noted that a large number of Europeans in Belgium, France, Great Britain, and Holland continued as holders of bonds of the consolidated Dominican foreign debt.

One important financial institution in the country continued, for the moment, to be European: the "National Bank," which, as we saw earlier, operated with French capital and of which Marchena had been named inspector general. Rather than entrust the creation of this bank to Crédit Mobilier, Heureaux would have given preference to Westendorp,[103] but he had finally accommodated Marchena, who had already made the preparations for the bank's establishment. The opposition of Marchena and his European connections to the usurpation of financial power by the Improvement Co. culminated in 1892 with the presidential candidacy of Marchena, who simultaneously made known a plan in which he had obtained European interest and that would prevent American penetration: a consortium of Englishmen, Frenchmen, Germans, Dutchmen, Belgians, and Spaniards would liquidate the republic's debts (undoubtedly by means of control of customs); a reserve of 5 million pesos would be kept in the National Bank of France; the monetary system would be incorporated into the gold standard; Samaná Bay (used as a lure by many presidents, Heureaux among them, in their political and credit dealings with foreigners) would be rented to the consortium.[104] But Heureaux did not allow Marchena to win the elections. The latter responded by making the National Bank suspend credit to Heureaux and his government, blocking, moreover, Heureaux's accounts. The latter then transferred his funds to his creditor Lemos and won a suit that the bank had begun against him.

The bank's refusal to allow Heureaux access to his funds led to the famous scene in which the authorities forced their way into the bank, an affair that in turn produced a visit from the French Navy; this was repeated in 1895, that time based additionally on the illegal imprisonment and murder, respectively, of two French citizens. This last appearance of the French fleet was observed by three U.S. warships by way of defense of the Dominican government and of the Monroe Doctrine, so that the conflict ended with a financial indemnification by the Improvement Co. In this same year the concession for the National Bank was transferred to the Improvement Co. Already in 1893, Marchena had been captured during an escape attempt; in December of that year, he was shot. Heureaux wrote in December 1893 in a report to Isidore Mendel, financial representative in Paris:

> Don Generoso: This friend disembarked in this port on 27 October, right afterwards he gave himself over to his efforts at electoral candidacy, by striving to have elected—throughout the whole country and in the space of three days before the meeting of the primary Assemblies—the electors who were to elect him President of the Republic. He lost the primary election. [This] nullified the pretensions of Marchena, who in believing the opposition very strong and the connections that he brought from Europe very influential tossed aside all foresight and prudence and proclaimed himself owner of the country, to such a point that the newspapers of Europe called him the savior of educated Dominicans.

Writing of the conflict with the National Bank, Heureaux concluded: "We shall see how we come out of this affair, of which the sole cause is Don

Generoso Marchena by being a *know-it-all.*"[105] Luperón also expressed an unfavorable opinion regarding Marchena: "There exists in the Dominican Republic the mistake of believing that any man who knows something about numbers is an economist; thus, the governments almost always appoint, by what misfortune we do not know, as Minister of the Treasury somone who has done poorly in his own affairs, who then, naturally, manages those of the State even worse. Heureaux eagerly took it upon himself to give Marchena a fine reputation for honesty and ability, but the results proved the opposite."[106] It is difficult to prove that Marchena was more inept or less honest than other ministers.

Irony demanded that in the last year of his life and of his government Heureaux did everything possible to free himself from the power of the Improvement Co. and tried to arrange a contract with a European consortium like the one that Marchena had sought in 1892. Through his financial agent in Paris, Isidore Mendel (former president of the Chamber of Commerce and president of the Banco Comercial in Santo Domingo, with whom Heureaux had already arranged loans as early as 1887),[107] he had been put in contact with the financier Gerónimo Becker in Brussels.[108]

When repeated financial transactions with the Improvement Co.'s exorbitant interest rates only seemed to worsen the economic and financial crisis—the company did not comply at all with the exchange rates required by the Monetary Conversion Law of 1897—an interview finally came about between Heureaux and the company's vice-president, Charles W. Wells, in Nassau. On 14 January 1899 Heureaux wrote to Mendel about this meeting: "I went principally to obtain the assurance that since the Improvement Company does not meet all its obligations either within or outside the Republic, it would be prepared to withdraw whenever I found someone who would help me to regularize the economic situation, by liquidating the Improvement Company's rights. He had to agree to it, and thus I have been able to confirm to Sr. Becker the authorization to begin negotiating."[109]

To his minister Teófilo Cordero y Bidó, Heureaux wrote three days later:

> The negotiations that the Government undertook for developing its economic plan are already quite advanced, and are only awaiting the Government's ratification. . . . For more extensive information I am transcribing for you a copy of the translation of a letter dated 18 December last that I received from Sr. Gerónimo Becker: "that through my efforts a group of financiers has been formed that . . . has accepted your [Plan's] principle completely although amending it with the following reservations: 1st, Complete liquidation of the Dominican financial situation; 2nd, Complete leasing of customs, that is, redeeming the above-mentioned customs from the 'New York Improvement Co. of New York' and from any party that might at present have a right to them for any purpose; 3rd, Concession of the National Bank on conditions that will be examined subsequently by mutual agreement. Upon the bases mentioned above, the group that I have managed to form is

disposed to supply the *amounts necessary* for the good functioning of your operations. I send you these lines after having seen Mr. Mendel in Paris. I introduced him to Sr. Lagge, who has made a special effort in the formation of the Financial Syndicate. . . . Mr. Mendel has received us very well, and . . . has promised us his most active support." . . . I received from Sr. Wells the following telegram referring not only to the positive outcome of the negotiations entrusted to Sr. Becker, but also to those that he is pursuing personally, for economic ventures of great usefulness to the Republic, with the Halifax Bank, one of the richest in London: "I am referring to your arrangement or contract with Becker: everything has been agreed on and signed *ad referendum*, pending approval from you. The first installment will be made in July, against delivery by the National Bank." The arrangement with the Halifax Bank is still pending. All the probabilities are, then, not only that by the middle of the year we shall collect all the bills, with minted gold entering into circulation in place of them, but also that all our foreign debt will undergo a favorable modification, which would enable us to attend comfortably to public service. I forward this news, that the incertitude regarding the economic course that we shall follow might cease completely.[110]

A vain hope, this last one, as we know. The assassination of Heureaux made impossible a return to European financial dominance, supposing that this would have been feasible. The convenience of an influence less close by and less monolithic than that of the United States must also have been understood by Heureaux in the last months of his life.

At the time of his death, Heureaux's most important foreign private creditors were J. Sola and Co. of New York, Fed. Hohlt of Hanover, and I. Mendel of Paris. It was rumored of this last that he had bonds worth $500,000 in safekeeping for Heureaux and that, therefore, he owed that sum to the heirs. Something similar was said of Wells, "and there is sufficient knowledge to be able to affirm that the Central Railroad Enterprise, the National Bank of Santo Domingo, the *Caja General de Recaudación*, and the San Domingo Finance Co. of New York owe the Heureaux Estate an account of securities and stocks," but the local offices refused to give information. It could be said with good reason that "the tendency to hide and to retain goods from the Heureaux Estate is being demonstrated everywhere and in various ways." (Even the attorneys of the Heureaux Estate Inventory Commission, Enrique Henríquez and Casimiro N. de Moya, had withdrawn more than $10,000 in gold "for a transaction agreed upon with the State . . . of which transaction said attorneys have still not given an account.")[111]

Agreements were finally reached with the Heureaux government's *criollo* and foreign creditors. In 1904, German, French, Italian, and Dutch warships arrived at the Dominican coasts to emphasize their citizens' claims. At the urging of Secretary Hay of the United States, the Dominican government then asked the American government to take charge of the task of collecting

TABLE 4.5. VALUE OF IMPORTS BY COUNTRY (IN %)

U.S.	Danish Antilles	Gr. Britain & colonies	Germany	France & colonies	Belgium	Dutch Antilles	Italy & others
45	12	11	7	7	5	3	2

Source: *Exposición*, p. 184.

customs income, in order thus to arrive at a satisfactory agreement with the various creditors. Thus, U.S. politico-financial domination became a definitive fact for the next forty years. Irony would have it that Santiago Michelena (a merchant born in Puerto Rico and considered a U.S. citizen), who had made a great part of his fortune during Heureaux's regime, was the agent for the collection of customs revenues.[112]

In the nineties began a period not only of U.S. financial influence, but also of growing American commercial influence. In 1891 a trade agreement with the U.S. was signed according to which Dominican products like sugar, coffee, and hides could be imported into the United States duty-free, in exchange for the free importing of, among other items, meats, flour, and machines. Protests from European trading partners, especially from Germany, did not have the desired effect. In 1899 the *Listín* complained because of the quality of the numerous articles imported; it spoke of a "miserable nutrition for this people. The Yankee provisions are leading to a tomb for each consumer. The butter, the lard, the cod, the cheese, the ham, everything that is imported from the U.S. is a threat to the health."[113]

In 1897 the value of imports was divided among the trading partners (see table 4.5).

What Heureaux wrote in 1893 to his friend Mendel, that "the theatre of financial relations is going to be the United States of America rather than Europe,"[114] could be extended to the theatre of trade relations. Only the export of products like tobacco, cacao, and lumbers remained oriented principally toward Europe in this period.

It is thus not surprising that when, after Heureaux's death, the republic received considerable attention in the U.S. press, the *Daily Inter Ocean* headlined an article, "Santo Domingo Governed by American Citizens," while the *New York Herald* was counted among the papers that advocated military intervention in the country.[115]

CHAPTER FIVE

Changes in the
Apparatus of Sanction

THE ARMY

When in 1844 the Dominican Republic declared itself independent from Haiti, the latter country attempted for a number of years to affirm the "indivisibility" of the island by means of arms. This permanent threat from a superior—certainly in a numerical sense—enemy obliged the president-*caudillo* Pedro Santana to create a rigorous military organization. In November 1844 he decreed that every Dominican had to perform military service, with the reservation that the following "are exempt from forming part of the frontline troops: 1st. Married men with children, as long as they have not abandoned their families. 2nd. Only sons of poor widows and elderly parents, as long as they are supporting them. 3rd. Those less than fifteen years old and older than forty. 4th. Merchants."[1] Some months later, a "superior police force" was organized, along with the military judicial courts—both supposed to guard against, among other things, espionage and betrayal to the enemy, "any scandal against public morality," any disturbance of religious ceremonies, and "any injurious attack by word or in writing against the acts of the Government or public employees in the performance of their duties."[2]

In July 1845 compulsory military service was extended even further: "From the age of fifteen years up to forty-five, all Dominicans are called, while the current war lasts, to do their part in the frontline corps without appeal: the Government will know how to give distinction to those who appear voluntarily. . . . Only public employees, invalids, and those older than sixty years are excepted." These last only had to perform guard service in cases of emergency.

Men between forty-six and sixty years, as well as foreigners who had resided in the country for more than three months were supposed to serve in the civic guards created at the same time. The colonels and lieutenant colonels of the guard were appointed by the government, following the suggestions of the district prefects of each *común*; the officers of the guard would wear the same uniform as those of the permanent national army.[3] By 1846 it was obvious that the permanent mobilization of the guards would lead to the dismemberment of economic life, and again more attention was paid to the formation of a permanent, professional army.[4] Besides, the rigor of military service must have brought about the fact that large numbers tried to evade it, as is readily deduced from the rewards promised to those who appeared voluntarily: Santana promised to include their names in a register that would be called the "Summary of the Most Distinguished Patriots."[5]

The extent to which all these directives were carried out is difficult to verify. The complaints about the lack of sufficient regulation also continue in the following years. But it is certain that in that period of regular battles with the Haitian army, in which sometimes hundreds and not infrequently thousands of men fought on both sides, the Dominican army attained a reasonable degree of efficiency. The regular army consisted of eight to ten thousand men; of these, two regiments were found in the capital, each with some one thousand men, plus a brigade of artillery with five hundred men, three hundred "artillery workers," and two hundred cavalrymen. "In a moment of unexpected invasion, the Government . . . could immediately send one or two regiments to reinforce the borders of the South without leaving the capital unarmed"; it was never necessary to send auxiliary troops to the Cibao, which was more populated.[6]

When the country was annexed to Spain in 1861, the army was reorganized, as is natural, according to the Spanish model. Thus the "War of Restoration," which started two years later to finish in 1865 with reestablishment of independence, could not (at least at the beginning) be a conventional war, but a *guerrilla* (or guerrilla warfare) of small bands against the Spanish colonial army, into which the old regular army of the republic had been incorporated. "With enormous efforts, and until the big war could be begun, Luperón wanted to undertake [the guerrilla warfare] that so confounds governments. This consisted of bands of patriots dispersed among the forests and difficult passes to harass the enemy from advantageous spots without ever letting themselves be caught. In this way, the peasants became soldiers, making use of their special tactic, which tends to cause so many annoyances to the enemy." Their armaments were poor: "some with lances, others with old rifles; several with blunderbusses from every era, others with pistols of every kind, the rest with their machetes, and not a few with clubs."[7]

The departure of the Spaniards meant the sudden absence of an organized army, as well as the loss of almost all war materiel.[8] The lack of political stability and continuity in the following fifteen years resulted in the fact that many well-intentioned efforts at military reorganization were limited to paper. Around 1870 there were only some five more or less regular battalions with a total of fewer than 2,000 men.[9] Luperón proudly mentions that as minister of war in the Espaillat Government he concerned himself in 1877 with the organization of regular battalions and of the civil guard, which had fallen into decline, to the point of succeeding in having the active force number 1,200 men.[10]

In 1880, during his own provisional government, Luperón introduced certain measures anew. Thus, a military service of three years for men eighteen years of age was created, and the establishment of permanent schools and academies in the garrisons was decreed.[11] All this did not mean that in the period 1865-80 military activity occupied a subordinate role in social life: to the contrary. Still, in the period 1844-61, when the country was threatened and attacked by an external enemy, the military apparatus under the direction of the president-*caudillo* Santana had the characteristics of a national *organization*—with a hierarchy dominated from above—that succeeded in subordinating to the central authority and to the national ideal the loyalties of small groups that surely appeared. What occurred in the period after 1865 (and even during part of the Heureaux regime) was a passive restructuring, which gave the military structure the characteristics of a *marketplace*, in the sociological sense. The army broke up into small groups that, competing, offered their services in the political marketplace. The curious phenomenon of the *criollo* "general" then stood out more than ever.

Earlier in the struggle against the Haitians and the Spaniards, high ranks had been lavished on those who distinguished themselves militarily, but in the next fifteen to twenty years an enormous inflation took place in the "officer" corps. As Gautier coolly observed in 1870: "The continuous state of war that has afflicted this country for many years has caused the creation of an excessive number of officers who do not belong to any specific corps, but who offer their services at the head of our militia in extraordinary cases. Since the Republic is unable to give them any other reward, it has granted them their grades or ranks."[12]

The "market" character of the military organization was observed clearly by the U.S. Commission of Inquiry that same year: "[The men ambitious to attain supremacy in the Republic] have received military titles granted by the chiefs of various governments or revolutions, the rank of each one depending principally on the number of partisans that he could bring to the leader whose cause he had embraced. In the anarchy produced in this way each vicinity has shown a tendency to group itself around its boldest or ablest men. The union that thus began in war continues in peacetime, and as the political institutions are weak, that union often becomes stronger than the law or political customs. From this arises an [unemployed and restless] class whose importance depends upon commotion, ready to augment whatever disorders that might appear." Furthermore, because of this, it was possible for "certain capitalists [from neighboring islands] to make investments in prominent revolutionaries as if . . . dealing with a business matter . . . with the certainty of running great risks, but with the possibility of obtaining great profits."[13]

If by 1865 it was normal for a carpenter and a bricklayer who worked for Luperón both to have the rank of colonel,[14] and if in that same year there were already forty-five generals registered in the Ministry of War, by the end of the seventies there were, according to Luperón, more than a thousand dispatches of appointment as general, issued principally by Presidents González and Cesareo, "who, with cowardly proclivity, wanted to win over partisans for themselves." Some did not have military experience; the majority lacked the "spirit of order, and without any discipline, were living and wanted to continue living without working, at the expense of the Public Treasury."[15] The number of generals mentioned by Luperón does not seem incredible if it is recalled that in 1881 there were in San Cristóbal alone twenty-three generals who signed a political document.[16] Much less acceptable is Luperón's accusation that President Heureaux was the first—in 1887—to bribe enemy generals;[17] such an occurrence was inherent in the "marketplace" character and could scarcely be called corruption. Even in 1882 Heureaux was complaining that the generals were causing him considerable expenses: "regarding my financial embarrassments, imagine how I will be, all the generals, chieftains, & c. appear, supposedly to come to agreement on the elections, and to get rid of them one has to give them handouts."[18]

In the 1892 elections Heureaux's control over the country was already so strong that he dared to write to the governor of Barahona: "You announced to me that Gen. Alejo Ruiz was thinking of coming over to this Capital; I will appreciate it if you advise this friend as well as others who want to come here to postpone their trips to another occasion, for at present, given my shortage of resources, I will not be able to take care of them in anything that they request of me, nor even to furnish them something for travel expenses." This did not mean that he did not, in general, cultivate his relations with those friends. Invalid military men sometimes received provisional payments (officers 30 centavos a day, soldiers 20). Heureaux paid for coffins, gave out Panama hats, money, "finished lumber from two thousand pines," cloves, champagne and liquor, and exemption from import duties to friendly generals, all this on the accounts, in most instances, of his merchant friends,[19] not to mention here other types of favors in real estate transactions, legal matters, and jobs for these individuals. Also numerous were the generals who received a pension (around 30 pesos a month), an indemnity, a "*pago de haberes*" (or credit) or an *asignación*.

For his part the president relied on their support in case of crisis: his personal correspondence with them, carried on independent of the official authorities, was intended to increase their loyalty. In 1887 he wrote to four generals in Moca: "Since in this life everything is accidental, it is my duty to prevent the accidents that might come to favor the hidden plans that friends and opponents might have set in motion . . . and I am prepared for it, and I advise you to prepare yourselves with considerable prudence and secrecy so that these preparations do not give away their executors as indiscreet and alter the normal political state of Moca . . . hold steady, and oil the carbines gently." Some years later, he wrote to a general friend in Puerto Plata: "I recommend that you keep alert, sleep little, and sharpen your sense of smell."[20]

The image of these generals, as the literature that dates from this period or deals with it describes them, is one of aggressive, poorly educated *campesinos* who were recognized or feared as natural leaders in their rural environment, but who, even when political fortune placed them in high and influential positions, did not easily attain in the urban environment the social acceptance of the merchants and of the intellectual group related to them. (Note, however, that among the generals there were also more educated landholders.)

José Martí, who visited the country in 1895, gives us a nice description of a general, with "a wide Panama hat, cotton drill outfit, parasol with an iron handle, and quite swarthy, with rustic mustache and sideburns," who acknowledged that "About this politics, I don't know much, but here in my heart I seem to know that politics is like a duty of honor. . . . Because for me, either everything or nothing."[21] According to Vigil Díaz there were "two warlike archetypes: the gunfire general who sacrificed himself for his political cause, and the hustler general, cautious, roguish, braggart, turncoat, without personal or collective courage but richly equipped for betrayal and utilitarianism, with a perfect instinct for self-preservation since he is never seen fighting in the vanguard."[22]

"The *criollo* general," writes R. Emilio Jiménez in his excellent *Al amor del bohío*, "was always a fellow much taken with his reputation, and commonly crafty, obstinate, ignorant, arbitrary, and given to lovemaking besides. They gave him credit everywhere even though he did not pay, out of admiration or fear . . . one had to keep him happy in hopes of earning his favors . . . The general's wife was quite respected, and his mistresses, too—as a measure of prudence for some and camaraderie for others. His weakness was the golden buttons on the Sunday jacket of elegant blue wool. Generally he was a cock-fight fan, a smoker of good creole tobacco ordered especially for him, a coffee-lover, a womanizer, and fond of drink. . . . When in opposition to his orders, they argued with him in legal terms, he ordinarily answered: 'I command it,' and gravely twisted his mustache, seat of his manly self-respect."[23] The superstition so widespread among the population also extended to the generals. Thus, it is said that Gen. Pablo Mamá could not be hit by any bullet, that he was "bewitched." Heureaux himself, who according to popular belief could only be wounded by silver bullets, always sent the superstitious Gen. Eulalio Malojo "special" ammunition. If the generals were like this, what were the soldiers like?

The peasants, who had to supply the greatest part of the soldiery and who often refrained from cultivating more land than was absolutely necessary out of fear of the army or the "revolutionary bands," had had since the creation of the republic a terror of the "recruiting" that carried off boys of fifteen years and more from their homes. In fact, the system of recruitment consisted "of detailing groups of soldiers with orders to seize any youth they found in passing and to conduct him to the Fortress." Married men were exempt, a fact that sometimes increased the number of marriage contracts; a *compadrazgo* with the local military prefect could at times bring relief, but for the majority of the peasants, recruitment was a "contribution of blood, which was collected by blows from rifle butts in manhunts through the forests." According to Hostos, this was the reason that the good arable lands near the villages were unoccupied and that the inhabitants built their *bohíos* scattered throughout impenetrable regions.[24]

The privileged youths from the villages had more opportunity to escape service: they could obtain a letter of exemption from the governor or join the firemen's corps, but the peasant sometimes reached the point, in exchange for such an exceptional favor, of yielding "the hand of a pretty girl to a coarse rural official." Such arbitrary acts were common, and recalled in the collective memory is the general who after a victory did not want jobs or sinecures, "contenting himself with asking only that they have 'considerations' for him"—that is, freedom to carry off women for himself, to put people in jail, and to kill other people's animals that he found on his property.[25] It is not surprising that Luperón described "the meager battalions" of the seventies as "composed in the majority of criminals . . . , enemies of society, of property, of laws; they stole the rifles and the ammunition to sell them at any price, just as they sold their shoes and clothes to meet the exigencies of their vices. Lacking their salaries, without discipline, and without military honor, they were incorrigible,"[26] and they continued to be so for a considerable time.

Still very far off was Luperón's ideal: a small army with special training that would give the soldiers "grave bearing, with that certain elevated character and pride of great men and celebrated captains," so that they would retain for the rest of their lives "the habits of order, of valor, and of self-denial, temperance in weaknesses, the habit of moderation, reason, and firmness in all the serious matters."[27]

One can imagine what the entry of the victorious revolutionary bands into a village must have meant: "thousands of dirty, barefoot, ragged, evil-smelling peasants, weapons shouldered, shouting raucous *vivas* and *mueras*, . . . the ruinous vengeances and repressions" and, naturally, "the harvesting of the merchants who sent out orders on the Chief's account . . . the appointment of the Ministers and the typical job-hunting tactics of the provincial politicasters, who had helped—with money, service, or weapons—and who now overflowed the city."[28]

Only the word "thousands" seems exaggerated in this citation: the "glorious battles" were, for the most part, affairs of no more than four to five hundred men in each band, and not infrequently only a few dozen,[29] but naturally these battles were extolled in the political bodies. For example, the "grand army" of General Guillermo in 1865 consisted of 400 men; the capital surrendered to Guillermo and, as he was an illiterate, a French immigrant wrote the declaration of the city's surrender for him. During the important Moya revolution of 1886 in which parts of the Cibao opposed Heureaux's election, the number of dead and wounded reached at most 600.[30] In that civil war, "the most complete morality" reigned; the two groups bought cattle and ammunition instead of seizing them, as was the custom, and "the combatants killed each other in the battles, and left each other alone outside the struggle." This code of conduct and this courtesy were not uncommon: when during the War of Restoration, the hated Spanish brigadier Buceta took shelter in the house of Don Juan Chávez, "out of respect and consideration for this honorable farmer and his estimable family, [the patriots] ceased fire."[31]

But even while the ideal of courtesy and gentlemanliness was pursued in situations of psychological and social control, there were also fixed in the culture characteristics of cruelty that appeared on other occasions. Thus there was, according to the indignant "Popular Declaration" of 4 August 1865, General Pimentel, "forgetting that he lives in the midst of a Christian society, with sun and good day, . . . putting the head of General Polanco on parade like the town crier through the streets of Santiago. This is the greatest of the insults that can be offered to a people in the midst of the nineteenth century."* Thus, too, Luperón in a gesture of cruelty inspired perhaps by his reading of the classics, had executed an official messenger as a "corrupter" because the latter had brought him the dishonorable proposal of entering Spanish service.[32]

A pattern of such cruelty in persons of high and low rank, within and outside the military apparatus, continued to be characteristic of the society in the later years as well.

> El soldado que no bebe
> o no sabe enamorar,
> qué se puede esperar del él
> si lo mandan avanzar,†

the people used to sing, but "the blind war ardor" also manifested itself in cruel, aggressive conduct, "in fiestas ending up in shooting, started up on purpose to acquire renown among the skirts, or in the gambling houses after a provocative *'coca'* [blow to the head], or an insolent crude remark."[33] In the popular imagination arose subsequently what anthropologists call a

---

*In 1931, in Mao, the head of Gen. Desiderio Arias was offered to Trujillo, who showed himself displeased and ordered it joined to the body again. See R. D. Crasweller, *Trujillo* (New York: Macmillan, 1966), p. 94.

†The soldier who doesn't drink/Or know how to conquer women,/What can be expected of him/If they order him to advance?

"figure of concentration," named "Concho Primo," in whom all the virtues and vices of the part-time soldier of the second half of nineteenth century— "of the time," then, "of Concho Primo"—began to converge. The contemporary poet Manuel del Cabral was inspired in this popular tradition with his "Compadre Mon."*

It was precisely the inadequacy of the army in those years as a national separate organization, united in the multiplicity of war actions, that caused the fact that the *entire* society was, to a certain point, "militarized"; thus, just as it was difficult to draw a boundary between army and citizenry *as institutions*, so it was difficult to do so between the military man and the citizen *as persons*. The citizen had military equipment and pretensions; the military man had the behavior of citizen-merchant when putting his abilities up for sale. Elements of military "culture" became widespread throughout the entire society; even today the military greeting between citizens, which was probably more common earlier, has not disappeared: "¡Hola, jefe!" "¡Adiós, general!" "¡Qué tal, teniente!"[34]

We saw that in the last two decades of the century there were still numerous "generals" with whom Heureaux kept up frequent contacts. But it was to be expected that Heureaux—although himself in many ways in terms of descent, experience, and behavior the prototype of the *criollo* general—would try during his long regime to strip the military apparatus of its "marketplace" characteristics, to encourage its professionalization, and to guarantee the loyalty of the military men to the state—and thus to himself—in an organizational sense as well. Certainly at the beginning of his regime he could count on that loyalty only in part, when the soldiers came from his own region: "If you can bring me 30 or 40 military men on the steamship," he wrote in 1882 to the governor of Puerto Plata, "bring them to me; here I have only 22 soldiers and 4 officers left—everyone deserted when the last garrison from Santiago was sent out. You will understand that I always need to have our own people, for we should not trust the ones from here."[35]

The irregularities in the distribution of the daily rations to the soldiers caused him many difficulties; in 1887 these amounted to $1 for generals, 80 centavos for captains, 70 for lieutenants, 60 for soldiers.[36] In 1889 Heureaux wrote to the treasury administrator of Monte Cristi: "With the aim of avoiding the abuse of the buying and selling of rations that brings with it disorganization of the military service, you will arrange that each soldier will have his salary delivered to him personally or that in your presence each battalion chief will do so for his respective subordinates."[37]

A General Yimi (Jimmy?) Clark had been attracted the preceding year to organize the "military branch" in expert fashion: "I have recommended to him completely eradicating the sale of rations and the fatal system of some subaltern officers of making soldiers desert so that they have occasion

---

*(Buenos Aires; Losada, 4th edition, 1957).

to collect the ration for their own benefit; I have also charged him with maintaining the officers and soldiers of the regular budgeted corps in the best state of decency and discipline."[38] And although the president of the National Congress told the president in his *Message* in 1889: "Regarding the organization of the Army you have said: 'Everything is there to be done!' and 'The law of conscription approved in this legislature can be a powerful aid for undertaking that organization, if other current circumstances . . . do not prevent embarking upon that arduous enterprise immediately,'"[39] in the following years there was surely some organizational improvement.

In this, Heureaux concerned himself with the most minimal detail: he oversaw the purchase of armaments and personally wrote a letter of complaint to the supplier of this same equipment in Liege; he even gave orders for taking the measurements of a second lieutenant for his uniform. Before undertaking a trip to a remote region of the country, he maintained correspondence about the equipment of the soldiers who were to accompany him, requesting that they let him know by telegraph if there were not enough shoes. In short, he was vigilant, and he gave practical advice: "Take special care for me with the troops from Samaná," he wrote on 27 January 1899 to the commandant of arms of Puerto Plata, "teaching them to keep their clothes clean and to use and shine shoes. It is also necessary to drill them in military exercises with all the firmness necessary, since the discipline that there used to be in Samaná has been relaxed. . . . There are no drums, but you can get them by fixing drumheads of untanned goat leather to the old pots that you must have."[40]

The nature of the internal conflicts implied that the most common military operations retained their *guerrilla* character. The orders in the key to the *Código telegráfico* refer principally to "small, fleeting guerrilla attacks," "skillfully planned ambushes," and so forth. Attached to these orders was tactical advice not to make complicated plans of attack, for "with troops that are not perfectly organized, complicated plans never give results," and psychological counsel such as: "Don't use the . . . force in any formal operations; as it was defeated recently, it must be demoralized—arrange an easy little victory for it." Attention was also given to theoretical training: in 1895 500 copies of a "Rules for the Tactical Instruction of Mountain Artillery" had been printed.[41]

In that same year José Martí observed one of the best-known battalions organized under Heureaux in Santiago: "The soldiers, resplendent in blue drill and kepis, pass on the way to Mass in the new church, with the silk banner of the Battalion of the Yaque. The soldiers are black, and the officers: mestizos or blacks."[42] This battalion, formed in 1887 after the Moya revolution, consisted of some 800 men, whom the people called "bull-dogs." "General Lilís [Heureaux], when he had the chance to visit that Corps, said to them in greeting, 'How are my sons?' To which, very happy, they replied with the greatest affection 'Very well, dear papa.'" General Lilís did not fail to put a one *"clavao"* coin into the hands of each of them. Many soldiers were known in the region by their nicknames: Francisco the Rabbit, Pedro the She-Cat, Colá the One-Eyed, and the commander Victoriano the Stingy.[43] In 1896 a military hospital existed in the capital.[44]

In comparison with the preceding decades it was certainly correct to say of the army in 1899 that, thanks to greater resources, it was well organized, trained, armed and supplied, and adequately paid.[45] It seemed that in the nineties "the revolutionary attempts died in their cradles, and the ever-so-many generals were going out of style,"[46] and that the honorific title "Pacifier of the Fatherland" (with all its connotations, including the negative ones) had been bestowed on Heureaux justly. It is necessary to recall, however, that the military organization created by Heureaux attained only an inadequate degree of professionalization and that, with regard to loyalty, it was too attached to his person to be able to survive the fall of his unipersonal regime. His death meant the resurgence of the "marketplace" character of military affairs.

THE NAVY

The processes of organization, disorganization, and reorganization of the navy were, as can be expected, parallel to those of the army. Under Santana the creation of what was proudly called the Dominican fleet was arduously encouraged. In 1847 this consisted of one frigate with twenty cannons, two brigantines with five cannons each, and seven schooners, of which three had been seized by the government from individuals.[47] The Genoan J. B. Cambiaso is mentioned as "founder of the National Navy" and its commandant in those years. Of the nearly eighty "heroes of the Dominican Navy" that Rodríguez Demorizi mentions, there were in fact several leading persons (Barbaro, Corso, Demorizi, Maggiolo) of Italian descent, just as there was also a major Curaçao influence (Evertz, Glas, Jansen, Naar, Van Rheen).[48]

In 1852 instruction in sailing was begun in the Colegios Nacionales. Of the Navy that had proved its importance for the transport of munitions, supplies and troops for the army as well, nothing remained after the War of Restoration: "Our ships were disarmed and sold."[49] In 1877 "although no warship existed," Luperón "ordered . . . the recruitment of navy brigades with their training school."[50]

After other efforts that had little success, a Nautical Academy that started with twenty students was founded in 1894 under the direction of the Spanish officer Luis Martínez Viñalet.* Among the later directors was, in the nineties, the Curaçaoan Gerardo Jansen, who was also professor of mathematics

*An exception must be made with regard to the Academia de Náutica, founded in 1875, which did successful work for some time under the direction of Román Baldorioty de Castro. See C. N. Penson, *Reseña histórico-crítica de la poesía en Santo Domingo* (Santo Domingo: n.p., 1892), p. 25.

in the Instituto Profesional and held other important posts in the field of education.[51]

In 1893, a special subministry was created for war and the navy.[52]

In 1899 the first large naval vessel, the *Presidente*, had already been purchased; in 1894, the cruiser *Independencia*, built in Glasgow and outfitted with electric lighting, arrived, 176 feet long, "in the style of a yacht." Lastly, the war steamship *Restauración* reached the capital in 1896, also coming from England; "it displaced one thousand tons and had three cannons per side, one in the bow, and two machine guns in the stern."[53]

Thus, during the Heureaux regime, the navy was better constituted with regard to material and discipline than previously. Here, too, the president nevertheless kept a watchful eye on each detail. In 1893 he noted to the commander of a maritime operation that he should always have alongside the *Presidente*'s port and starboard pieces and machine guns "the number of shells necessary for an emergency situation. All in their corresponding boxes, taking care that the rain does not deteriorate said ammunition."[54] The pride of the new navy, the *Restauración*, was lost in 1899, shortly after Heureaux's death, when a pilot in connivance with revolutionaries let it sink near San Pedro de Macorís. Just as the army had been "dismembered" after the dictator's death, the same fate befell the navy, whose other ships were lost through poor maintenance and whose organization fell into decline.[55]

PUBLIC ORDER

The one who is leading the revolutionary movement from abroad is _____ . See what kind of behavior his family, friends, and partisans are following: and thus we can know what his plans are. Put a skillful person in charge of it, one of those who do not get themselves mixed up in politics and who are politicians from head to toe, so that he gets close to one of the suspects and skillfully finds out what there is to know.

It is now necessary to develop a policy of attraction and benevolence. Circumstances are eminently delicate, and any forceful measure may produce a most serious disturbance of order. Strive, then, to attract and to calm the dissidents for the moment, flattering them and appeasing them in such a way as to gain time at any cost, but this is to warn you that you should not maneuver so that our opponents come to believe that you fear them and that thus we accelerate what we are trying to avoid.

Through confidential reports, I have learned that _____ is displeased. It is best that you see him and that you attempt to content him. He is a friend whom we should not lose.

The seriousness of the circumstances obliges me to tell you that now is the time to have done with the policy of attraction and leniencies. Shoot anyone who tries to disturb the order or to induce anyone else to disturb it; and finally, anyone who loans resources of any kind to our opponents in order to disturb the peace. It is necessary for you to capture_____. It is preferable to take him dead because this individual is a constant threat for society.[56]

These orders from the government's *Código telegráfico* reveal with what psychological depth and also with what toughness the Heureaux regime sought to maintain public order—with all that this implied in terms of spying, betrayal, treason, punishment, and reward. As in so many other sectors of public life, Heureaux was not a *deus ex machina* here either: all these activities had been carried out from the beginning of the republic, sometimes with passion yet at the same time out of necessity, by all the subsequent governments. It is only thus that Heureaux succeeded in perfecting the security system, and at least in part in codifying and institutionalizing it. The long duration of his regime is partly due to this, even as this lengthy duration encouraged the codification and institutionalization.

But all the threads of the organization always converge in Heureaux; he was the only one who could supervise the totality of the activities and concern himself with everything. He instructed Governor F. Lithgow of Puerto Plata on how to interrogate a conspirator: "If he says that he has not been in contact with anyone, he is an accomplice." He scolds the authorities in Moca because they did not immediately execute an "enemy of the situation": "such useless people, those Mocans . . . , a better opportunity will never offer itself." He intimidates a general friend: "I have learned that you are living the life of concubinage, that you keep as a mistresss a little girl 15 years old. What an atrocity, a man so old and burdened with responsibility . . . Father Pichardo has told me this. . . ." He calmed down his agent Pereyra in St. Thomas about exile activities in Curaçao: "For I have an agent among the enemies themselves, of the best quality, and this is not an easy thing to discover." He gives "advice" to his ministers: "Make an effort not to arrest politically insignificant people because few advantages result from it, and the care that must be displayed in curbing and watching over them is increased. . . . Make an effort at attempting to obtain the capture of fugitives, employing in all of it more cunning, craftiness and activity than force itself. The big roundups get underway only laboriously and very noisily, and almost never attain their ends. Ambushes and small detachments give more results. In politics and when order is disturbed, it is almost always necessary to cauterize and afterwards to spread salve on the sore, that is, to render the guiltiest ones impotent and to try to regenerate the rest."[57]

Heureaux incited intrigues among the governors and the commandants of arms and surrounded both with loyal informants; according to what is said, he was accustomed to going on trips disguised as a soldier to see whether his orders were conscientiously obeyed.[58] Although we cannot believe everything that the biassed Sumner Welles says about Heureaux—and although we ought to look at his account that "in each village he kept a mistress in whose house he was put up" and from whom he received local intelligence as poetic hyperbole instead—his information on the extensive internal and external network of agents that comprised the principal islands of the Caribbean and reached New York, London, Berlin, and Paris does not seem disputable to us.[59]

One could not, however, speak of a perfect organization, not even in the last years of the regime, given the many objective obstacles, in either what concerns the formal services for public order or in espionage.

We read of the province of Santo Domingo in 1898: "The Government Police of this capital (Public Order and Nightwatchmen) fulfill their duty entirely, although the lack of Organic Regulations and of services that lay foundations for and facilitate their important action by assigning duties and responsibilities makes itself felt. The Municipal Police . . . is helped to advantage by its headquarters chiefs and twenty-five guards. The lack of police that is felt in many of the *comunes* is to be regretted. There are some in which there are none, and other important ones in which there is only a single guard." There was also in the province a rural police, with its inspectors-general, inspectors, petty and auxiliary justices of the peace, of whom there were, respectively, 9, 74, 233, and 96. Lastly, there was a National Militia and a Firemen's Corps, these last also lacking the necessary regulations.[60]

This is the place to note how much value was attributed to the external appearance of the bearers of authority and to their services, clearly as a means of encouraging distance, admiration, and respect. Thus, Luperón was proud of having ordered in 1880 "musical instruments from the Lefebre house of Paris" for the bands of the principal *comunes*, as well as "European-style uniforms for all the Military Corps."[61] In the subsequent years, too, emphasis continued to be placed on music and color. Each self-respecting *común* placed in a prominent position in its list of petitions to the Superior Government a musical band in order thus to brighten up the popular concerts in the plaza or the park. The battalions and corps of firefighters (Santiago's consisted of 180 volunteers in 1898) had their own bands, sometimes with directors brought from abroad. With respect to uniforms, Heureaux took the prize with his French marshal's gear, his many decorations, and his Sword of Honor. But his ministers' dress uniforms, made by a Madrid tailor, with their shell batons and their buttons ordered in France, also helped to underscore visually the importance of authority.

JUSTICE

The formal organization of justice was already well regulated quite early on. A Supreme Court in the capital with a president, four judges, and a solicitor general named for five years by the Senate from a trio of candidates submitted by the electoral college; in the province or district, a tribunal of first resort with a judge and a district attorney designated by the executive power; finally in each *común*, a mayor designated by executive authority who performed the functions of justice of the peace: here in broad strokes is the scheme in effect during the period that we are studying.[62] However, the quality of justice was always threatened by two factors. On one hand was the inadequate legal education that existed in the country for a long period. Until chairs in various branches of the law, which were occupied by figures like Hostos and Nouel, were created in 1880 in the recently founded Instituto Profesional, the training of jurists had been a matter of private classes followed by an examination before the Supreme Court. Carlos Nouel in particular had distinguished himself over many years as a private teacher,[63] but, needless to say, in this way only a few had been able to receive adequate training, and only in the eighties was it possible to improve the quality and quantity of Dominican jurists, trained in the French law that had continued to exist in the country since the period of French domination.

The other danger for "independent" justice, the intervention of third parties, which had been observable since the creation of the republic, certainly did not decrease in those same eighties—that is, during Heureaux's regime—although there was generally an attempt at maintaining propriety. As a politician without direct reponsibility, Luperón, first Heureaux's protector and then his enemy, never had difficulty in confronting the president with the ideals of the modern state.

In the first years of his regime Heureaux still bothered with answering him, although not without complaining: "You will have the kindness to excuse me for the fact that I am not using the normal form of responding to your letter point by point, neither to your advice, which I esteem so much, nor to your enlightened reflections, which I respect, nor to your requests, to which I shall give my attention," he was still writing to Luperón in 1888. "It is not my intention to argue, since I would have the worst of it because there are thoughts that like yours relative to justice make their own way alone in the realm of theory, but when it comes to practice, one must at every moment run up against the drawbacks that are so prolific in this unfortunate country . . .; justice in our land, notwithstanding the effort that men of good will make so that it will be a reality, is nothing but a myth." Heureaux noted in this regard the work that it had cost for "the Tribunal of Santiago to try the case of the Espaillats," members of an important family from that city who were suspected in 1887 of committing an attack on Gov. Miguel A. Pichardo.[64]

In fact, the Espaillat trial had been a delicate matter for Heureaux; he had asked the governor himself to abandon the city temporarily and then had written to Juan Tomás Mejía, minister of justice:

> Do me the favor of convincing the Honorable Judges of Santiago that the peace of the locality . . . depends on how they conduct themselves in this matter, for if they do not condemn the Espaillats in order to have a legal reason for taking them out of that city, war will be inevitable. . . . I have already penetrated the Supreme Court and as they are

conservatives, they have promised me to confirm the verdict of the Tribunal of Santiago out of political convenience; I had them at my house yesterday, Don Pedro Garrido behaved well. I hope that both Father Meriño and friend Glas will be useful to you there, without forgetting that although both of them are interested in peace, the responsibility for maintaining it does not weigh upon either of them, and perhaps they think more with the heart than with the head.

For additional security, Heureaux addressed himself to the merchant Glas in a separate letter: "May God will that the Justices be inspired with what is convenient! They more or less must know that for the convenience of the peace of that province, it is convenient to apply that part of the Scripture: 'If thy right arm offend thee, cut it off and cast it away from thee.' "[65]

Three times in this short letter we find a form of a key word in politics and society: "convenience"–the penetration of which into justice was inevitable. The prudence with which the president behaved before the highest bodies of justice is clearly explained by the fact that Luperón still believed in the nineties that "there is no justice outside the Supreme Court (and some local trial courts)."[66]

But in the lower-level judicial bodies Heureaux often intervened (usually via the governor) in favor of the brother of a general friend, of a trial judge friend guilty of abuse, and so forth. Sometimes through his intervention a prisoner was set free, and a job was given to him right away. He also intervened when a punishment or a "patent"* for a poor friend seemed excessive: "Leandro Espino, a friend of mine, who has a little shop on those fields, with a value of only $30–there they charge him $100–as patent–how is this? for I would like to assist this friend, and I will have to help him pay." And "Señor Rafael Martí has revealed to me that he has been imprisoned on account of five cows that recently gave birth that he was supposed to turn over to Sr. Saldaña. If that is the only reason that you had, I will appreciate it if you return his freedom to Sr. Martí, for that is not an adequate reason for imposing such a penalty on him."[67] As can be seen in the "Judicial Matters" section of the *Código telegráfico*, all these interventions had to be carried out with considerable tact "in such a way that neither is your intervention noted nor do the judges feel offended," and the possibility of negative results from an intervention was taken into account.

Nor was the influence of the exective authority limitless in the designation of judges. To his loyal collaborator Gen. Pedro Pepín, governor of Santiago (described, not without prejudices, by Sumner Welles as "an illiterate Negro, fierce and cruel in all his undertakings"[68]), Heureaux wrote on 6 February 1893: "You have a great deal of the blame for the appointment of Polanco. The Electoral College sent its *ternas* [slates of three], and you should have been well represented there so that someone who in your judgment must not

---

*Under an 1889 law, "patents" were required to be able to practice a profession.

be suitable did not figure in them. . . . Against my wishes Luis Pichardo was appointed President of the Tribunal of Moca; against my wishes the personnel of the [Tribunal] of Azua—composed in its entirety by enemies of mine—was appointed."

Sometimes, curious "autonomous" tribunals arose: "At the foot of the Santo Cerro, in the Province of La Vega, there exists a blood Tribunal in the house of the Mayor José Taveras, where he has stocks and jails for imprisoning men and women. It is said that the presumed criminals are brought to that newly-minted Inquisition and before the aforementioned official and a secretary who assists him, tortures and other numerous torments are performed on the victims, until they confess what the tribunal of blood wants—a tribunal that other friends of the aforesaid Mayor form."[69]

But the official judicial bodies also knew bursts of cruelty: in 1893 in a San Pedro de Macorís in full-blown sugar activity and with many immigrant-adventurers, the number of murders had increased considerably. "Neither do the Petty Justices dare to send [for] the witnesses of the crime, . . . nor do the latter dare to testify out of fear that the guilty party will be free again and sate his desire for vengeance on them, as has happened several times." For that reason and because of the imminent "great sugar harvest," the judicial and governmental authorities met and decided to execute suspects without further ado. The Supreme Court, however, disapproved of this proposal "with the aim of erasing the stigma . . . that makes the Republic lose its civilized status, placing it among the number of those unfortunate peoples who vegetate in barbarism and are ruled by force." In the following years, the criminality in that region continued on the increase: in 1899 the National Congress forbade the importing of revolvers into that district and a tax of $300 was required from liquor dealers.[70]

Earlier I mentioned the intervention of third parties in the activities of the judicial branch. Yet, it would be incorrect to focus exclusively on the influence on the part of the executive branch. Indeed, the "patronal" structure of the society implied the fact that other persons and groups were also constantly active in intervening on behalf of their protegés; as far as "apolitical" groups are concerned, we ought to think principally of the church and Masonry. Regarding the latter, Deschamps observes that it often succeeded in "returning the prisoner home" or obtaining "pardon for the condemned man."[71]

In 1897 the judicial authorities of Santiago province tried eighteen civil cases, two commercial cases, eleven criminal cases, and fifty-eight delinquency cases.[72] As is to be expected, only a small portion of all crimes were brought to justice; police organization was far from being adequate to investigate all the crimes committed in the countryside; moreover, the peasants did not want to cooperate: "as witnesses . . . they talk too much, but they deny having seen what they saw and having heard what they heard. . . . They saw the victim on the ground, but did not see him fall . . . ; he who dwells in the countryside has to get along well with everyone. Hence they are so caring."[73] *

There were many robberies: "Just as almost all go into the government to steal, so almost all the inhabitants of the countryside and the suburbs go to someone else's plot of land or the neighboring patio to steal. Hence neither petty theft nor cattle-theft seem to be crimes . . . ," wrote Hostos, observing that in these economic crimes, armed aggression was rarely resorted to. However, weapons, in the hands of so many people, were often used in anything that seemed to be an attack on personal dignity: "a word, a gesture, a look . . . a boast of bravery, a long-brewing envy . . . ," in such a way that one had to be very careful about "armed ignorance" in social relations."[74] Federico García Godoy, governor of La Vega province in 1890, was not principally looking for the explanation of this aggressiveness in ignorance; he spoke of "the sad tendency (particularly in those peoples of Iberian origin) to resolve by means of weapons questions that can and should only be elucidated in the peaceful, serene setting of the law."[75] His emphasis on cultural inheritance stands out when we look at how much aggression, even among the members of the urban elite, had death as a consequence. Thus acquiring almost a symbolic value is the item in the newspaper that in the club La Esperanza de la Patria (The Hope of the Fatherland) the youths Soriano and Deetjen, "on account of a disagreement" had turned to arms, resulting in the death of the first, as well as the fact that the second was absolved.[76]

Let us attempt to recapitulate some conclusions about changes observed in the apparatus of sanction. Regarding the army, the navy, and the police, the fluctuation in the degree of their organization is noteworthy. What Santana created in the period from 1844-60 was lost during the War of Restoration and remained missing during the following twenty years, and only Heureaux in the period 1880-1900 was able to reorganize it with greater resources and thus in a more impressive way, although he was unable to avoid its subsequent decline. That the long regimes of strong *caudillos* generally meant an effective military organization is a well-known fact. But it is useful to observe that this military apparatus is as much the "result" as the "cause" of their long regimes.

As for the military and police apparatus, and for justice as well, it can be said that in the last decades of the nineteenth century, their professionalization and the consolidation of their structures was increasing and that the "marketplace" qualities stood out less. As loyalty before the "state" was identical in the patrimonial structure with loyalty before the *caudillo*, the fact that the disappearance of the latter would lead to great damage to the

---

*In civil disputes the *campesinos* often sought justice before the "rural council," a "moral authority" recognized by themselves in their region, to whom they presented their inheritance matters, and so forth. See. R. Emilio Jiménez, *Al amor del bohío*, 2 vols. (Santo Domingo: Editora Montalvo, 1927), vol. 1, pp. 277 ff.

organization built up causes no surprise. This is especially valid for the military sector, which was so intimately linked to the political sector of the society that the resurgence of active political groups had to cause immediate dismembering of the armed sector according to the new political divisions, resulting in a rebirth of the "market" character. For justice the fall of the *caudillo* was less fatal because its symbols of loyalty were instead united to a formal set of sacrosanct legal rules that the jurists themselves could adapt little by little to the changing situation. Although the professionalization of jurists was not really complete, the formal separation between judicial and executive power, as well as the respect for "lofty," complex judicial activity, in comparison with the armed activity in which almost everyone was involved, made the judicial organization more stable than the military (Moreover, in any regime the possibility of revolt of the judicial branch is reduced, so that flexibility here is a matter of convenience.)

This also held true *during* the Heureaux regime. But it was only a difference of degree: the typical structural and cultural characteristics of the society as a whole—patronage, personalism—continued to corrode the sought-after ideals of "objectivity" and efficiency in military, police, and legal activities. It is fitting to ask whether in comparison with the North American and European societies of that time this corrosion was *extraordinarily* noteworthy.

CHAPTER SIX

Changes in Political Ideas and Structures

"There are peoples of our origin [Latin American] who have made costly, gloomy, and retrograde revolutions, with the exclusive aim of setting themselves up as equal to the hybrid government of England and as a copy of the parliamentary Republic of the French," wrote Hostos in 1900—when, after Heureaux's death, one of the numerous plans for a constitution was being debated. Hostos's positive suggestions (a presidential council, communal and provincial autonomy) perhaps speak against his not very practical mentality, but his rejection of "the constitutional traditions of European origins that have ended up drying out our societies" was founded on a lucid analysis of reality. And two things—his suggestion of new political experiments and his rejection of imported, admired models—were implicitly based on the idea that a society's own culture and structure demanded political institutions of their own.[1]

Hostos was sufficiently idealistic to think that these institutions could be created by an autochthonous scientific elite; after their rise, these people would maintain human and political freedoms so that they would not be less but merely different from what was the case in Western Europe.

Bonó, the *criollo* sociologist, was less cosmopolitan than Hostos but perhaps for that reason had a more realistic notion of the feasible. He abandoned all idealism and believed in a social-historical determinism: the colonial period had been "positively despotic"; the Haitian domination had been so, too, in the modern form of military dictatorship; the first Republic (1844-60) could only fight Haiti "by consolidating that very dictatorship," while the Restoration "undermined all the traditional hierarchies, the intermediate ones, and made new elements that have stirred up anarchy in the upper stratum of society join in leading the country." Thus, says Bonó, Dominican society was organized for despotism; subsequent events have resulted in the polishing up of that form, and "we shall have, whether we like it or not, rebellions and more rebellions; dictatorships and more dictatorships; because, besides being the universal remedy to which peoples and Governments have appealed in the supreme hours of their existences, ours do not lend themselves to any other." What is needed is "unity, homogeneity in the social impulse." The only thing that can prevent "the dictatorships from stifling the dictators, and anarchy from destroying the Republic" is "transaction" between peoples and governments, between classes and parties.[2]

More than the two preceding men, Luperón was a man of political action, but at the same time one who did not want to exchange his protected position in Puerto Plata for the risks of a presidency in the capital, and who as director of a political movement preferred to choose the token figures who had to govern the country in his name. He demonstrated in his writings and speeches a predictable ambiguity. On one hand, he liked to pose as an altruist and idealist who, already covered with glory as a hero of the Restoration, wanted to push his country rapidly toward the political level of Western Europe.* On the other hand, he shows himself a man who knew the limitations of his own environment completely. On rejecting the candidacy for the presidency in 1876, he wrote: "And as it would be necessary either to use the machete or to manage the intrigue, and from whichever of these methods, I would cease to be worthy of the presidency; before attaining it without honor, I will remain content with my honor at home." And when Espaillat, the Europe-oriented Santiago pharmacist who was elected president that year, had been deposed after a short time, Luperón skeptically observed: "Espaillat was not a good President because he was loyal, honorable, and moral, and he was not a squanderer or traitor. This is a harsh, severe reality, but it is true." At the same time, however, he was blaming President González for the fact that, according to the latter, "our constitution encloses two Constitutions in one: the one . . . with freedom written down, and the other with unpublished tyranny."[3] Almost twenty years later, when he had already lost all his influence over his original protegé Heureaux and was living in exile in St. Thomas, naturally, little of his idealism remained. Latin America consisted, according to Luperón, of "republics without republicans, worse governed than in the times of the viceroyalties, without being determined on the progressive action of modern democractic principles."[4]

Thus political ideas wavered between realism and idealism, between what seems possible here and what was admired elsewhere. The use, at times simultaneous, of two frames of reference, the *criollo* and the foreign-modern one, led even the most liberal among the politicians to a kind of political schizophrenia. The right of revolution at any moment was recognized, even when one was dealing with elected governments. The "liberal" politican Deschamps was expressing the general opinion when he wrote (without referring to any current episode): "Revolution is a right. . . . Congresses and governments are nothing, then, but emanations of the people, and from such a point of view, when the congresses and governments are not attentive to the inspiration of the totality of the citizens," the latter have the right of revolution.[5]

This idea of total popular sovereignty, which could naturally make governments fall via leading spokesmen, we find clearly in the proclamations reject-

*"In favor of democracy, as in the U.S.A., Switzerland, Denmark, Holland, and Belgium" (See Luperón, vol. 2, pp. 11-15. For complete cite, see chap. 1 end notes.)

ing presidents (often call *Popular Declarations*). In the 4 August 1865 statement against Pimentel, it was declared: "From this moment on, we disavow the authority of General Pedro Antonio Pimentel as harmful to the interests of the nation, and *in the exercise of our sovereignty* we invest with full powers the worthy General José María Cabral so that he might immediately take supreme authority as 'Protector of the Republic.' "[6] In a similar fashion, "various citizens" regularly requested one countryman or another to take over the presidency. Sometimes it was even asked of them to become *dictator* (for life)—as in the case of Luperón in 1866 and 1879—a term that obviously lacked negative connotations, in contrast with the term *tyranny*, although generally the objective difference between the two forms of government was not made very clear. "The necessities of the war [of Restoration] and its dangers had imposed the dictatorship of the governments that followed one another during its course," wrote Luperón, "but never tyranny, which cannot be justified under any circumstance."[7]

THE POLITICAL PARTIES

In the decades following the second independence from Spain (1865), there is constant evidence of the existence of two large "parties," called the *azules* and the *rojos* (or the "blues" and the "reds"), the first of which was also known as the National or Liberal party. These parties were originally based, to a certain extent, on the two great *caudillos* of the first Republic, Santana and Báez. The *rojos* were Baecistas who after 1865 also acted—and sometimes successfully—in favor of Buenaventura Báez's return to power. The *azules* were the old followers of Santana (who had died in the meanwhile), augmented with a group of politico-military leaders from the Cibao who arose during the War of Restoration—like Luperón, as well as, at least at the beginning, followers of the southern general José María Cabral.

From quite early on, Gregorio Luperón declared himself leader of the blue group. In 1868 he was proclaimed the party's chief,[8] and his authority remained intact until the eighties, although there were attempts to smash his influence. When in 1873, at the end of Báez's "six years," a certain discontent arose within the *rojo* ranks, the latter obtained support from prominent members of the *azul* party, who showed themselves disposed to break their ties with Luperón. This group of unhappy "reds" and "blues" supported the (successful) revolution of the governor of Puerto Plata, González, and in popular parlance was called the *verde* (or green) party. Very soon, however, opposition to González's presidency lead again to a recognition of Luperón's leadership, and in 1876, upon González's fall, the majority of the green party again divided itself between the reds and blues.

After the short-lived Espaillat government, the presidency briefly fell back into the hands of González, who found himself obliged to turn it over to Báez, the leader of the reds, that same year. In 1878, the latter had to escape to

Puerto Rico because of a revolution; the southern leader of this revolution, General Guillermo, proclaimed himself chief of a provisional government in the capital. Simultaneously, González, who had ingratiated himself with Luperón, headed a provisional government in Santiago. With Luperón's help, González won the elections, but his refusal to name Ulises Heureaux, Luperón's henchman, as governor of Puerto Plata led to a revolution, directed again by Luperón, that resulted in 1878 in a provisional government in Puerto Plata. In this government Luperón's protegés–Heureaux, Fed. Lithgow, Alfr. Deetjen–held important positions. However, General Guillermo, a native of the country's eastern section, had also taken up arms against González, seizing possession of Santo Domingo; in 1879 after elections he was proclaimed constitutional president.

Like his father, Guillermo had been one of Báez's loyal generals and could be considered a *rojo*. He was from an utterly humble social background and must have felt threatened by Gen. Manuel Cáceres, a more educated Cibao native, who in his own region was considered Báez's successor. Cáceres was assassinated during Guillermo's government; this was only one of the atrocities of his regime.* Once again "the soldier of democracy," Luperón, proclaimed a revolution, which, with Heureaux's help, led to Guillermo's flight to Puerto Rico and to the establishment in 1879 of a provisional government under Luperón in Puerto Plata, with Heureaux its delegate in the capital. When Pedro F. Bonó rejected the candidacy for the presidency that Luperón had proposed to him, Luperón chose Fr. Fernando Arturo Meriño, a highly influential prelate and considered an *azul*, who governed from 1880-82 and was followed by Heureaux (1882-84), with Casimiro N. de Moya of La Vega as vice-president. This was the country's twenty-ninth government since 1844.

To this point, this dry enumeration has helped to establish that after 1874, the *rojo* party had no leaders of national importance available, although at the local level there continued to be important *rojos* like Manuel María Gautier in the capital or Generoso de Marchena in Azua; that Luperón seemed to have the decisive influence in the naming of *azul* presidential candidates– (Espaillat, Meriño, Heureaux) and could also determine the destiny of less loyal presidents (González, Guillermo); and that in these years Heureaux's importance–as minister, as the government's delegate–was increasing to the point of culminating in a presidency in 1882. But regional loyalties continued to be an important element in the presidential selection. Even in the sixties the Cibao's political supremacy had created fears in the South that the capital would be moved to Santiago;[9] in 1882 Luperón was warned by Bonó that "it is four years now that Cibao has been dominating completely, and Santo Domingo is not so accustomed to such a clear domination that it will

---

*Some see Heureaux's hand in that assassination; Heureaux was assassinated in 1899 by Ramón Cáceres, Manuel's son. See P. Troncoso Sánchez, *Ramón Cáceres* (Santo Domingo: Edit. Stella, 1964). He considers this supposition unwarranted.

endure it peacefully much longer," adding then the interesting idea that it was precisely the new sugar plantations that had sprung up that were making it more difficult than before for the South to rise in armed rebellion.[10] But this increasing economic importance of the South made "compromising" with it more necessary for the Cibaeños than before; in this connection, Bonó also spoke of the need for compromises with the *verdes* and *rojos*, a fact that seems to argue for the thesis that geographic divisions had a certain importance in the party system, at least in the sense that although the two large parties—the *rojos* and *azules*—had followers in all parts of the country, the *azul* leaders came mainly from the Cibao and were directed, in the person of Luperón, from Puerto Plata.

The need for "compromises" emphasized by Bonó was also seen clearly by Puerto Plata's Heureaux. To the degree that he was obtaining a certain independence of movement as a strong man, he increased his tendency to choose collaborators of various political tendencies and geographic origins, and vice-versa, a fact that led at the end of the eighties, as we shall see, to a break with Luperón. Thus it is tempting to see Luperón's loss of political power in those years and the rise and long duration of the Heureaux regime, which found its financial bases more and more apparent in the South, not as an accident of history, or only as a proof of disloyalty, or as a personality clash, but in relation to the economic changes that took place in that period of the republic.

To the extent that it is possible to analyze them, the political parties did not acknowledge any formal organization, governing boards, lists of members, formal meetings, or statutes. Decisions were made by the party's *caudillo*, generally after consulting with regional "big-shots," among them merchants, generals, and intellectuals. By way of illustration let us look briefly at the decision-making process when Pedro F. Bonó was asked again, this time in 1884, to offer himself as a candidate for the presidential elections (an invitation that, moreover, was rejected by him anew). With a single exception, a letter from the intellectual M. A. Cestero from the capital, all the correspondence Bonó received in relation to this matter came from the northern part of the country. In October 1883 the French-speaking priest J. F. Cristinacce wrote him from Puerto Plata: "I am authorized on behalf of General Luperón, your friend and mine, to tell you that in the upcoming elections you are his candidate and the candidate of all his friends. . . ." In November Luperón insisted that Bonó make a decision; "From all the villages of the Republic, the most important citizens ask me to indicate the Candidate who ought to be president." Later that month Luperón wrote him again, pointing out the "bastard ambitions" and "dangerous pretensions" of others and urging Bonó to become active. "Go to Santiago, publicize your program," he urged, asking Bonó, however, to leave the vice-presidency untouched in his "governmental system . . . for we need this post to place one of the most serious candidates after you."

Right after another letter from Father Cristinacce, in January 1884, Bonó received a very confidential letter from a member of his family, the important merchant J. M. Glas of Santiago. Glas informed Bonó that Luperón had argued for Bonó's candidacy in a meeting of twenty-five individuals. In this meeting General Heureaux had indicated that the *caudillo* of the Línea Noroeste, Gen. Benito Monción, had declared that "Luperón's will had already been done several times, that now it was his turn and that he wanted [General] Segundo Imbert [of Puerto Plata] named at any cost." Glas himself had proposed in that meeting that all the *azul* party candidates ought to meet in Santo Domingo along with the "most sensible and famous thinkers from there," and, to avoid conflicts, they could single out a compromise figure whose nomination could be presented "to the most illustrious thinkers of the Republic" before being publicized.

President Heureaux had said in private "that he was not for any of the aspirants nor for entirely civilian candidates." This preference of Heureaux's for a military candidate undoubtedly strengthened Bonó's decision to reject the candidacy. The following month Luperón wrote again that "your candidacy has been welcomed by the men of some importance in all the towns of the Republic to whom I have written proposing it and completely accepted by public opinion almost universally. The next day Luperón wrote, "You do not know the maneuvers of the ambitious, which are always pernicious. You are not inured to their struggles; leave them to me, and I will answer for the triumph." The following day Father Cristinacce tried to clear up Bonó's apparent fear about Heureaux's opposition: "Lilís's little entourage has little weight in the decision." On 17 February Bonó received a letter from J. M. Glas in which the latter informed him that he was going to withdraw from the scene now that there was no certainty about Bonó's candidacy. On the eighteenth Bonó received a letter from W. Quesada, a Luperón opponent in Puerto Plata, who noted that the latter himself had always had the prudence to reject the presidency.

After a late, encouraging letter from Dr. Tió y Betances of Samaná, in April Father Cristinacce briefly described the situation that had arisen after Bonó's refusal. Luperón then seemed to support the candidacy of Imbert from Puerto Plata against that of Moya (from La Vega) and Billini (from the capital).[11] It is clear that decision making was reserved for a few people; a candidate like Bonó was willingly entrusted with the development of a program, but the *caudillo* watched over the occupancy of certain key posts that, in fact, were always held by the same small group of leaders. Moreover, it was in this year of 1884 that the *azul* party was for the first time presented with more than one candidacy, a fact that already points to the weakening of Luperón's power. The conflict within the party between the traditionally powerful North and the up-and-coming southern and eastern areas was marked even more clearly when Imbert and Moya combined their candidacies, opposing Billini, who was seconded by Woss y Gil, a native of the

East; this latter combination came into power.

Various historians, among them Sumner Welles,[12] see in this disintegration of the *azul* party only and exclusively the hand of Heureaux, who would have brought it about by means of skillful manipulations. This seems to me too great an honor for the astute general, although it is certain that he opted in favor of Billini-Woss y Gil after having seen that Luperón supported the opposite set of candidates. Nevertheless, on making this decision, Heureaux found himself in the excellent company of the influential Father Meriño, himself from the South, and it is not surprising that Luperón would see Meriño as a greater culprit than Heureaux: "The Party that struggled against Spain in defense of the independence of the Fatherland, called the National Liberal Party, acknowledged only Luperón as chief, from 1863 until the Billini elections in 1884, in which the honorable Doctor Meriño, going outside the discipline of the group that had brought him to supreme power in the Republic and later to the Archbishopric, presented Billini as a candidate, and along with Heureaux, made him triumph, completely disregarding any agreement with the chief of the party."[13]

Again, in 1886 two lists of *azul* candidates were presented: Heureaux-Imbert and Moya-Billini. This time Luperón realized that he had to support the candidates with greater possibilities. When, after Heureaux had come out the winner, Moya began armed rebellion, the former knew that he had to crush Moya's group of followers, thus formally beginning his dictatorship, which he had earlier exercised behind the scenes. The presidential term was lengthened to four years in 1888, and the system of direct elections was replaced by one of electoral colleges, which were easier to manipulate.

The 1888 elections led to Luperón's presenting himself for the first time as a presidential candidate, in a desperate attempt to maintain his influence. Moreover, for the first time, the power struggle between Luperón and Heureaux was formalized when the latter also offered himself as a candidate and won. Shortly afterward, Luperón abandoned the country in order to fight the regime from St. Thomas as an Heureaux opponent. At the end of his life, in 1896, he was visisted by Heureaux, who made him return to Puerto Plata, where his funeral was organized by the dictator with great official splendor.

Although in the first Heureaux government (1882-84) some prominent *rojos* like Wenceslao Figuereo and Generoso Marchena had been included,[14] something that must have occurred with Luperón's approval, the latter saw particularly in the composition of the Billini cabinet the signs of an increasing penetration by "reputed *rojos*": "While they told the *azules* that they were *azules*, they sought to place all the *rojos* well and to make many true *azules* lose their standing and to persecute them. Thus Señor Gautier, leader of a *rojo* group, found himself instructing Marchena to work on dividing Heureaux and Luperón." For that reason, Luperón spoke bitterly of "an unknown plan . . . to benefit a deadly oligarchy."[15] Thus Heureaux's collaboration with prominent *rojos*—whose leader Báez had died at the beginning of the eight-ies—and with the remainder of the *verde* party, among them ex-President González himself, formed a counterbalance against the traditional power structure of the *azul* party. In fact, important former Luperón collaborators in Puerto Plata and Santiago also saw—especially after the failure in 1887 of the Moya revolution, one of the few failed Cibao revolutions—that their political future was with Heureaux: "the greater part of the leading men who directed the [Moya] revolution in the province of Santiago . . . , when they met in the home of Don José Manuel Glas at a banquet that this gentleman gave for General Heureaux, lavished praise upon him, declaring that, given his popularity, he should not keep on depending upon Luperón's counsel and opinions, advising him to work for himself and offering him their sup-port, Señor Glas in the lead." To which Luperón added: "But there is no reason to be surprised at this event; Dominican history is plagued by similar inconsistencies."[16]

It is difficult to answer the question of whether at some time there were clear differences between the *rojos* and *azules* in programs and ideologies. That only the *rojos* were "annexationists," as has sometimes been asserted, is difficult to prove. That the *azules* represented more liberal spirits is plausi-ble up to a certain point, for the Cibao, where, as we have seen, this party was strongly represented, counted among its political elite a number of men who by their education were strongly oriented toward Europe. The influence of the cosmopolitan Hostos and of Betances on this group, Luperón included, should also be pointed out. In political practice, however, these lofty ideas had scant opportunity to be realized; the rapid fall of the progressive Espaillat was symptomatic of the situation and made it so that for a considerable period various intellectuals with similar ideas—among them Bonó—refused to engage in the political struggles. The "doctors" depended upon the "gen-erals," and the Europe-oriented intellectual had to consider the available human material and the structure and culture peculiar to his country. "If I had been elected president," sighed Bonó, "which ones would have been my ministers of State, my communal chiefs, my governors, and my Con-gress? The very same ones of last year and today. And when I had been able to repair this rusty, out-of-order machine, would I have been able to make the people who consider themselves wise and who lead this society under-stand that they are nothing but ignorant and corrupt? . . . [The Dominican Republic] does not have the conditions necessary for being autonomous under the pure democratic banner."[17]

It was Luperón who brought home from one of his European journeys the term "socialism." In his autobiography he uses it once in a positive sense to indicate that the republic "as its founders made it, is despotic and oppressive; the nation, as Providence has made it, is socialist, to such an extreme that fifty years of torments have not been enough to destroy social equality."[18] But he uses the term in a negative sense in referring to a group from Puerto Plata, led by his old friend Juan V. Flores, that was criticizing the *Compañías de Crédito* (in which Luperón had interests), calling them "communists, socialists, and anarchists."[19] In an equally negative way, Luperón wrote in 1885 to his friend Valverde: "Today the socialists and visionaries swarm throughout the Republic, preaching in their leaflets demoralizing doctrines and social war." The "liberal" journalist E. Deschamps considered this expression sufficiently curious to publish it in his newspaper *La República*; he confessed that at first he had had to look up the word *socialismo* in a dictionary, but, of course, Luperón had just returned from Europe. . . . In Santo Domingo these new terms made no sense, wrote Deschamps, for here there are only two parties: the tyrants and the democrats.[20] Indeed, the parties in this period were nothing but diffuse conglomerates, communities of interests, generally with a single leader at the head, and under him a barely-crystallized hierarchy of leaders—groupings in which mainly regional interests were united. Elections were only held after successful revolutions in order to give a certain legality to the new status quo so as to resolve internal competition within the "party" in an "honest" way.

The other party did not participate in the elections and was never represented in parliament. The political group to which one belonged was "democratic," the other "tyrannical." It is not surprising, then, that one could change parties continually: "Any *azul* today from whom they take away job or pension . . . will be *rojo* tomorrow."[21] A family belonging to one party liked to have *por cálculo* (for prudence's sake) a relative in the other who could serve as "guarantor": "Don't worry, gentlemen, for I am your guarantor."[22] Bonó was of the opinion that the variableness of political sympathies was influenced by the city-country antagonism: the inhabitant of the countryside would "almost always" prefer a party different from the one the city people supported, as a consequence of the exploitation to which the country was subjected by the city.[23] But his thesis is difficult to prove. In general "the masses" followed (as J. M. Glas explained to Bonó) the political directions that their local leaders, their "trustworthy men," gave them.[24]

The governors also openly influenced public opinion. On 15 June 1892 there appeared in *El Eco del Pueblo* an advertisement addressed "to the People" by the northern governors, in which they announced that they would meet together with "many enlightened and important men" in order to come to agreement on a presidential candidate: "until . . . that moment, keep your opinions secret and hold back your efforts."

On political issues, however, the mass of people was not apathetic and always had an interest in politico-military events. They received information on these events by means of popular singers and poets like Juan Antonio Alix, who commented on current affairs in their *décimas* (stanzas of ten octosyllabic lines).[25] The *campesinos* were cautious in their opinions: "In politics they talk a lot, but they say everything in a roundabout way, experts on the fact that an imprudent opinion can bring about unpleasantnesses for them," says Jiménez.[26] It seems to me that this caution was not limited to the peasants; it was part of a complex of attitudes that embraced the whole people with respect to politics and originated in the internal instability. I will return to this theme further on.

The politics that influenced social life so profoundly precisely because of variableness could hardly be kept out of the activities of the numerous associations, particularly because party organization was so extremely diffuse. An association could, as did the Liga de la Paz, evolve from a cultural club into a political pressure group (Espaillat's presidency was fostered by this group); it could also, as did the Sociedad Republicana, lose its principal political function and attempt to limit itself to cultural activities. The continually changing political constellation made these changes in function common, without avoiding, however, the result that the existence of these associations was ephemeral.

The financing of political affairs, like their organization, was not tied to definitive rules. The *criollo* or foreign capitalists, persons or governments expected to take advantage of a political movement, were all potential financiers. If it was a "European combination" that made possible the country's independence in 1844,[27] little doubt should exist about the importance that the German tobacco merchants and their Dominican representatives attributed to the success of the War of Restoration and to the failure of Báez's plans for annexation to the United States.[28] Thus in 1870 a group of foreign merchants in Puerto Plata helped generals Luperón and Cabral with $8,000 in their struggle against Báez;[29] in St. Thomas a Revolutionary Committee was founded for the same purpose with money from merchants from the island. In Curaçao, the financier Luis Oduber offered money to Luperón "under the guarantee of [Venezuelan] President Guzmán Blanco"; President Nissage of Haiti also feared the American annexation and facilitated services for which, after the successful outcome, he was paid the sum of $290,000.[30]

An invasion by General Guillermo from Puerto Rico in 1881 was financed by the Casa Gallart of Ponce and encouraged by the Spanish authorities, who considered the presence of the Cuban general Antonio Maceo in the country undesirable.[31] For his electoral campaign Heureaux appealed to the Haitian president Salomon: "I deplore it that circumstances oblige the Government to trouble both Your Excellency and his Government with such frequency, but the notion consoles that perhaps not very far in the future the next government may be in a position of reciprocating to Your Excellency if Your Excellency finds himself in the situation of using the services of the Dominican government, for the establishment of a National Bank in this capital that will permit us to regularize our financial system is almost certain."[32] To what point the "government" and "party" were one can be deduced from the letter that Heureaux wrote a month later to Luperón in which he exhorted the latter, who was at that moment in Paris, to do everything possible to carry out the establishment of a National Bank: "The

Party will collapse if it does not obtain a solid base that will enable it to regularize its financial system."[33]

In a previous chapter I pointed out the "marketplace" character of the military organization, and the *criollo* and foreign financial interests that supported certain generals in their attempts at revolution, even putting them up to it. A similar thing can be said of the party system and its functioning, since in reality it was impossible to draw the boundaries between internal military and political conflicts. Given that the political triumph generally was preceded by a successful revolution, military bands formed part of the political factions. The marketplace character of the military structure was the reflection of a similar political constellation, and just as during a strong, prolonged regime like Heureaux's, great efforts were taken to make the military a true "organization" of the state, the elevation of the "official party" to a government organ and the elimination or absorption of opposition factions could also be considered as part of an effort to take their mercantile character away from political activities.

The difference between the *azules* and *rojos* lost political importance by the last decades of the past century; instead, one was a Lilisista (a supporter of Heureaux) or opposed to him. When after Heureaux's death new *caudillos*–Jiménez, Vázquez–who led their own political factions arose, the continuity with the party system of the nineteenth century seemed completely broken. *Personalismo* always creates, according to this reasoning, new groupings. What else could be expected of *caudillos* who had both arisen from the political struggle against Heureaux and whose parties showed no clear ideological differences, other than the intention of settling up accounts, of breaking with the recent political past? Nevertheless, the reality was more complicated: since anti-Lilisismo had centered principally around the person of J. I. Jiménez–his initial wealth, his business and political contacts in Europe, his attempt at invasion in 1898 enhanced his reputation– it was predictable that the remaining number of Lilisistas would feel more attracted to Horacio Vázquez, especially after the failure of a 1903 attempt by Alejandro Woss y Gil to reestablish a true "Lilisista" government.[34]

It is tempting but dangerous to postulate a historical connection between Lilisismo and Trujillismo. In fact, it was Ulises Heureaux, Jr. who in 1933 published the first great panegyric to Rafael Trujillo, in which he pointed out the similarities between the latter and his father:

> Each of them was born in a modest family . . . , both embraced a military career with robust faith and active will, men made by their own efforts, their own character, and their own constancy. . . . "Trujillo President! It cannot be!" cried some. However, it had to be! "That black President again! Impossible!" wrote the friends of Heureaux. And that black man, whose talent was superior to that of many whites who taunted him, returned to Power. In both cases triumphed talent activated by the sword and the sword upheld by talent. Among those

peoples . . . , as Bolívar said, "servile in chains and haughty in tumults" and that it is necessary to govern with a strong, stern hand in order to deal with the intransigents . . . men of that makeup are needed. . . . Trujillo put Heureaux's method into practice: go yourself, don't send somebody else. We can say that Rafael Leonidas Trujillo Molina is justly entitled to be the brave, gallant continuer of the policy that, for the welfare of the people and the enhancement of the Republic, Ulises Heureaux began in 1882. . . ."[35]

Thus quite early in the Trujillo regime Puerto Plata had offered him the Sword of Honor that the "Pacifier of the Fatherland" had received earlier, and also quite soon the popular imagination created stories that had as a subject a meeting between the legendary Heureaux and the boy Trujillo.

POLITICAL *CAUDILLISMO*

Caudillismo or personalism is a phenomenon produced by the overall culture and structure of a social conglomerate and that consequently is manifest in all the social sectors and institutions. I hope to be able to analyze it as such in its general characteristics later. Here I only want to give attention to its most familiar facet, that is, the political, and to emphasize some traits of a cultural and psychological nature. The *caudillo* is always a hero, and one could speak of an *ideology of heroism* upon which *caudillismo* as a social phenomenon bases itself. "God," writes Luperón, "in his infinite wisdom has made heroes so that the memory of them might serve the oppressed as a lesson of triumph against their oppressors."[36] The hero sought his inspiration in classical antiquity. Luperón was one of the many who—in the home of his guardian—came to know the works of Plutarch, "which purified his sensibilities, and engendered in him the love of truth, liberty, justice, and national glory."[37] In fact, he liked to compare the country's recent history with that of ancient Greece and Rome: "The cowardice and baseness of a decadent Rome are often reproduced in the Dominican Republic." As is natural, classical history was interpreted in terms of heroism; the individual was more powerful than any socioeconomic determinant. "The same qualities that determine the character of the governors also determine the character of nations. Regarding the institutions, no matter how good they may be themselves, they are not sufficient . . . to maintain the national character at a lofty level. The citizens, taken individually, and the spirit by which they are dominated are what determine the moral situation and the stability of nations."[38]

Luperón attributed to himself the ideal qualities of the hero: "Never has any man had more control over himself, more constancy in his will, or more determination in his purposes." Of the *caudillo* Santana he wrote admiringly that "he was austere, upright, sincere, and impassioned about order to the point of being inexorable."[39] These ideals of firmness of character and self-discipline could only be attained in part through education; to make them a reality, *suffering* was also necessary. Thus, Luperón's accomplishments were seen as the result "of the efforts, the labors, and the sufferings of this man," and Espaillat's traits were attributed in part to "banishment, persecutions, prison, philosophy, and study."[40]

These heroic qualities of order and discipline that could lead to glorious deeds in politico-military life were in sharp contrast to the characteristics of the popular masses, devoid of "spirit of order or of thrift."[41] The *distance* between the hero and this mass, the *vulgo* (or common people), had, of course, to be great; although the hero not infrequently originated from among the common people themselves, he necessarily had to keep himself above them.

> Often, they [the heroes of the Restoration] are called popular. Unfortunate he whom the *vulgo* loves and whom the common people exalt, because the love of the *vulgo* is the path to the scaffold. We deceive ourselves a great deal when we speak of popular love, for the *vulgo* does not love. One without constancy cannot love; and where there is no conscience, there is no love! . . . The heroes' most imminent risks are their victories. The more they distinguish and elevate themselves, the more difficult they find their movement among the *vulgo*, because their herosim makes them supreme, gives them another form with which they no longer fit among the people, and admiration and envy bring about their misfortune! As they no longer fit into the group, destiny, with signs of evil antipathies, prepares them a disastrous end in the shadows![42]

Since in this conception the leaders—no matter how heterogeneous their social origin—knew themselves to be so clearly distinct from the people, the idea that that "people" should not have access to any real influence in political affairs is not surprising. Referring to the delicate relations with Haiti, Heureaux formulated this idea very clearly in a letter to the Santiago merchant Glas: "The political thoughts that the Government has for maintaining international harmony or for saving the rights of the Nation in any hour of conflict cannot be abandoned to the common people who do not know how to measure the distances that exist between throwing words to the wind, whether well or poorly strung together, in the cafes, the literary gatherings, or the public plaza, and working and solving problems with the responsibilities of duty and conscience as a respectful Government."[43]

For the hero, in his role as political leader as well, the greatest ambition was to cover himself with *glory*: "The presidency, my dear general, does not gratify me," wrote Heureaux to Luperón in 1882, "for it cannot give me more than a title, while I am eager for something more: I need fame and glory, and my aspirations are constantly in pursuit of them."[44]

As the definition of heroism was so subjective but at the same time so essential, the political necessity to distinguish clearly between the false heroes and the real ones required attention; not all those who acted to obtain "fame and glory" in the politico-military struggles could be considered the same. As Luperón wrote: "Unfortunately, the Dominicans are generally impassioned to the point of rashness, always struggling between the extremes of volubility and ambitions, which have improvised so many heroes in no other part of the world. There ambition obtains what, with effort, genius attains in other places. It is undoubtedly from this that the misfortune of the Dominicans is born. Without sense, or judgment, or prudence, or experience, the sons of the Dominican Republic hurl themselves like gusts of wind in pursuit of audacious adventures, which always cause their own ruin as if the future did not interest them at all."[45]

Moreover, the *caudillo* who had ascended to great heights continued to refer, with no small satisfaction, to his sufferings, and in a culture saturated with an Iberian Catholicism that did not fear intimacy with sanctity it is easy to reach the point of comparing oneself to, even identifying with, saints, apostles, or even Christ. Complaining about lack of money, Heureaux wrote Cosme Batlle in 1888: "There are days that I want to die, but God does not want to take charge of me; those who want to take over that prerogative don't suit me, and for that reason, I have to walk with the cross toward Calvary." The following year, asking a minister to reconsider his resignation, Heureaux wrote: "Nobody better than I can ask others for sacrifices, for I am the one most sacrificed of all. I would appreciate it if you returned to occupying your easy chair and helped us bear a little while longer the cross that who knows how much longer I will have as a burden." And in another place he wrote, "Here things are going well, and I continue playing the role of Christ."[46]

The narcissism that has equally deep roots in this culture we also find in an obvious form in the *caudillo*. At every moment one's own superior merits are boasted about without any modesty. We already saw which personal qualities Luperón found in himself without a moment's doubt. Heureaux, too, liked to mentioned his own generosity, magnanimity, and benevolence, as well as the "power of my foresight and calculation" and "my way of being"—this last was to serve as an inspiration to others.[47]

It is easy to trace the relationship between this narcissistic emphasis on one's own altruism and other excellent qualities and the dominant patron-client structure: the recruitment of clients by means of praising one's own good qualities was permitted to the (potential) patron in this culture. Also, those who still belonged to an enemy political camp had to be encouraged to switch political color through the understanding and magnanimity of the *caudillo*. "There are neither victors nor vanquished" is even today an obligatory expression for any political leader after a successful seizure of power.

Heureaux expressed the relationship between narcissism and patronage well when he wrote of himself as "always obeying an impulse of generous sympathy that makes me solicitous of men who have been singled out by error or by misfortune."[48]

Perhaps it is also possible to point out here a relationship between the narcissism and the legitimacy of the political *caudillo*. Certainly in the turbulent period that we are analyzing this legitimacy had very weak institutional roots. With insurrections, revolutions, elections, and installations disputed from the beginning, the ruling *caudillo* had only a weak formal sanction of his leadership. The rapid change of party and the generally brief duration of the presidential terms also eliminated the factor of permanency or tradition-in-a-strict-sense as legitimizing elements. Thus, there was a marked tendency to attribute the legitimacy of political authority to providence or—in reality, the same thing—to history, thereby giving it the role of selector, of autonomous instrument of choice. Moreover, the *caudillo* saw history as collective consciousness—in fact, as the opinion of posterity, which would bring him to account for his actions. Thus Luperón rejected a proposal of revolution against González "because I cannot justify myself before the country or before history."[49] The awareness of being the chosen one of history, of destiny, accentuated the leader's narcissism and also caused objective changes in his actions, since the national leader occupied the peak position in the society's patron-client structure. "I have always considered," wrote Heureaux in 1892, "that the particular mission that might be reserved for me by destiny should contrast with the impatient arrogance of my adversaries and it is in obeying that special consideration that I have been able to make myself superior to it, in the temperance of my character."[55]

Finally, the concern with the appearance of person and clothing that seems to be a readily observable expression of narcissism at all social levels also characterized the *caudillo* who, like Heureaux, had a haircut every three days and who placed "the greatest attention" on the care of his clothing.[51] The emphasis on the showy uniforms of the bearers of authority also had a social function, which was to increase distance from the people and therefore respect for the government.

"The government" was, in reality, only one man, who, naturally, called himself that ("As government, I want to retain my authority"[52]), and who was also considered just that by his ministers. Thus, these latter men accepted his decisions "by order of the Government" or by "prior consultation of the Government," indicating with this term the President.[53] This idea fit perfectly into the partrimonial structure of authority, in which official functionaries formed part of the team of the ruler's personal servants. Just as the division between private and government finances was vague or nonexistent, according to what we have seen elsewhere, so a division between the *caudillo*'s personal power and the power of the government was scarcely possible in such a structure: the *caudillo* was the State itself. As Francisco Sánchez already said of himself "aloud, though without boasting" in an 1861 proclamation against Santana: "I am the national flag."[54] At the same time, the national territory was the *caudillo*'s property: "Tomorrow," wrote Heureaux in 1893, "I will meet with President Hyppolite [of Haiti] in Manzanillo Bay in *my* waters."[55]

This identification, person-office-state, led in a man like Heureaux to semi-ironic, "counterpoint" remarks, long since incorporated into the folklore about Heureaux, in which he emphasized *ad absurdum* precisely the division between person and office in the political realm as well, distributing favors as "Heureaux" on the condition that "the president" not find out about it.[56] But these were nothing more than humorous attempts at "playing" a double role. Thus at the top of the political power structure, the strands of patrimonialism, patronage, and *caudillismo* converged, the first two forming the structural network, the last a complex of attitudes and values determined by the culture, while the three factors mutually upheld one another. In the *caudillos*' honorific titles—in themselves a form of flattery from the clients to the patron—were included the virtues attributed to them, which simultaneously represented their implicit obligations toward the country and the people, their clientele: Liberator of the Homeland (Santana), Great Citizen (Báez), Protector of the Republic (Cabral), Peacemaker of the Homeland (Heureaux), and, in our century, Father of the New Homeland and Benefactor of the Homeland (Trujillo).

The adulation of the already established *caudillo* fits within this system; it is necessary to flatter the protector to receive his favors. During Heureaux's regime, this adulation could be observed at all levels: on the part of the intellectuals who in their speeches, poems, and open letters praised the leader (even saying of Vice-President Figuereo, "It is said that the head of a great man is a kind of Olympus from whence grandiose ideas come forth . . . ; in Figuereo this appears confirmed"[57]); on the part of the merchants who made gifts to Heureaux or who placed his image on their products;[58] on the part of the people, who carried his portrait in the patron saints' festivals.[59] Laudatory books were written about Heureaux,[60] and streets, bridges, parks, and a district were named in his honor.

This does not mean that every viewpoint favorable to Heureaux was based exclusively on calculating adulation. There were important intellectuals, such as F. A. Delmonte, F. G. Billini, César N. Penson, and A. Pellerano Castro among others, who knew how to express their desires for a renewal of Heureaux's mandate in rational terms: "If we were to return again to setting out in electoral struggles that still, in our political school, do not represent anything but the prologue to civil wars, we would have undone . . . and without advancing a step in the democratic system that we pursue, all the good that the country has reaped in favor of national progress in these last years. Thus, the continuation of General Heureaux in the Presidency of the Republic is required, not by force, but by reason. . . ."[61] But flattery predominated, and it was exceptional for anyone to dare or consider it necessary to express his disapproval in writing, as in a poem in Deschamps's journal *La República*, in 1884, that began like this:[62]

A un Adulador
¡Alza gusano vil! ¡No desgradado
Te arrastres a los pies de ningún hombre
Por más que al orbe su grandeza asombre
Por más que sea temido y respetado!*
    etc.

On the other hand, *caudillismo* was so widespread as a cultural fact that those who were declared enemies of Heureaux and who said they abhorred all dictatorship expressed their admiration for *their caudillo* in the customary way. Thus José María Nouel, exiled in Curaçao, wrote his father with great admiration for his "intimate friend," the Colombian general Avelino Rosas, "every bit a man,"[63] and Luperón could keep writing respectfully about "the illustrious Venezuelan Guzmán Blanco."[64]

Heureaux's death thus could not mean the end of a political system in which patronage, *caudillismo*, and patrimonialism were fundamental. Only a few names changed, and the degree of political organization and stability temporarily decreased. Partly as a result of that, the margin of freedom of the press and assembly temporarily increased. Just they did sixty-five years later at Trujillo's death, after Heureaux's death mobs gathered, destroying his portraits and changing the names of streets named in his honor to "26 July," the date of his assassination. Also, individuals' homes were attacked (among others, that of the Fiallo family), provoking an open letter of protest from the poet Fabio Fiallo. Many attempted to deny that they had collaborated sincerely with the regime, but as Leopoldo Montolío noted, it was almost impossible to think of revenge "because all of us have contributed to the excesses that brought the Republic to the stage in which we see it now." He also opposed personalist flattery: "We do not want to go on hearing this 'Long Live So-and-so' . . . with respect to the nations, these men or those are not worth anything; everything depends on their principles."[65] But regarding this last point, Montolío was a voice crying in the wilderness: already by 15 September, J. I. Jiménez was being saluted thus: "Hail, Illustrious Regenerator of the fatherland!"[66]

Should the rapid transfer of loyalty from the dead *caudillo* to a new one, with all the hypocrisy that this implies, be censured as an immoral thing? It seems to me that the system offers few alternatives outside of "The king is dead; long live the king!" When the protector disappears, the clientele finds itself obliged to look for a new one who can offer "guarantees" and

---

*"To a Flatterer": Rise, vile worm! Do not, disgraced,/Creep to the feet of any man,/ However much his greatness may astonish the world,/However much he may be feared and respected!

"protection" in exchange for "loyalty" and "services" while he holds power. But the abrupt character of the transition and the affection, sometimes genuine, for the deceased create an initial ambiguity that was sketched clearly and courageously by Rafael J. Castillo in an "open letter":

> You know very well that I was nothing more than a loyal friend of that Government and that I served it faithfully, as I will do tomorrow for any other that gives me guarantees and grants me the protection that my well-known services to the country merit. . . . I continue to believe that in everything love of order and peace guided [Heureaux], and far from censuring him in death, as have done so many who admired and applauded him during his life, I defend him where I can do it without being heard by the liberators. If he raised his head and saw how so many of his friends deny him, what a barrage he would give them. A pity that he does not come back to life. More than a few would die of the fright.[67]

HEUREAUX'S "*CRIOLLO* DICTATORSHIP"

In the political thinking of Heureaux, as typical *criollo* dictator, ideological principles were scarcely possible. Even quite early in his political career he determined his political attitude toward the "liberals": "It is necessary to be liberal to deal with those who respect rights and freedom, and it is necessary to be strong to resist the force of the volcanoes that erupt from the hearts of those who are liberals for convenience's sake."[68] In that same year, 1882, he wrote about democracy with a similar sense of relativity, calling to memory the attitude "I respect but do not carry out" that typified the Spanish colonial authorities' view of orders from home: "I have paid my homage to the democratic republican principle; I respect it, although I do not use it in certain, selected cases."[69]

He explained his antipathy to political theories in a letter of 27 June 1882 to his friend and minister of war, Miguel A. Pichardo:

> All the theories sound good on hearing and when they are invoked to puff up principles, to proclaim liberty, to decree order, and, lastly, to assure national independence, they are always applauded, but on putting into practice the definition of any of these problems, inconveniences that the executive has not foreseen and that contradict his will and his desires almost always appear; however, there is no shortage of a few blessed poor in spirit who try to enjoy the kingdom of heaven. And I say this because Santo Domingo would be God's chosen land if at its age as a free and independent Nation, and short of time and men, so many rosy promises could have been fulfilled. For my part, I pledge that the day these miracles are realized I will confess before the altar of the Fatherland having been one of its worst sons, and at the same time I will bless for all the centuries the regenerator of a people whose aspirations are greater than its capacities.

This peroration against the theoretical, idealistic man was really directed against Luperón; earlier Heureaux had already reproached his lack of realism, which he attributed in part to the long journeys that Luperón made through Europe, that "civilized, powerful world that you travel. . . . If you were here in the saddle, you would see at each step the inertia, the obstinacy, the hostility, the resistance of friends and non-friends . . . , in sum, such a heap of obstacles that to remove them it would be necessary to dispense with all law and in its place establish an army and a guillotine. And even that way we would not obtain a complete result, because although we might wipe out the hostility, the inertia would remain, and in politics this last is more pernicious than the other."[70]

In 1888, when the break with Luperón was already almost total, Heureaux described to a friend a second motive for Luperón's idealism:

> The General [Luperón] does not want to understand that our situations are not identical, given that I assume the moral and material responsibilities of the Government, being the target of the shots from the intransigents from all the circles of my personal adversaries and from impertinent, ungrateful conspirators, while they only search out him who today finds himself more distant from public matters, when they want him to sponsor them and to guarantee them with the *arriére-pensée* of his falling out with me. . . . You know him and know that for him there is neither law nor procedure except what his heart dictates, and no, no, it cannot be that way, the scripture teaches us that Cain killed his brother Abel. Why? Out of envy! And Abel was esteemed for being good.[71]

Thus, then, neither ideology nor sentimentalism fit into Heureaux's politics: "With regard to politics, I have no loves. I follow a course to reach the attainment of my goal, counselled by my character and the dignity that should serve me in every case, even as the basis for that funeral oration that should be spoken over my body, if circumstances permit it. This is the guideline that I have drawn for myself; I do not make a policy of affections nor of parties. I will gather up men where I find them, I will appraise them, and I will treat them considerately in accord with the conduct that they follow with me."[72]

This line of conduct has two aspects in regard to the selection of collaborators; on one hand, it was completely opportunistic and "rational," judging everyone by his abilities and aptitudes; on the other, the private element, the loyalty to the *caudillo*, was, in the last instance, decisive. The two aspects were emphasized by Heureaux in his correspondence; he wanted the "unification of all . . . to guarantee the peace and to accommodate men rationally in positions that will be compatible with their aptitudes." He said repeatedly, "Well, before everything, I am an opportunist," and held that "political ability comprises many different things, but among them there are points that should not cease to be noticed, such as attraction, dissembling, prudence, persistence, without ceasing to be opportunistic under any circumstances . . . ; in the country in which we live, the day that they know how to find a man's turning point, they *straighten him up*, and then one comes to be a nullity like all those who have been put to the test." Other Heureaux sayings: "Do not forget the dissembling that is appropriate in dealing with our adversaries; it is necessary to have a smile on one's lips in order to push them to the kiss of Judas." And "In trust is the danger"; "The time of prosperity is the time to get ready to save." Political opportunism was also praised in public, as in an 1888 editorial: "The established politics of opportunism . . . have been fertile in results."[73]

It is not surprising that a man who spoke so pleasurably about his "cold, mature calculation" and who wanted his acts to be inspired "by loyalty and efficiency" would find Machiavelli favorite reading: "The desire to acquire instills in hearts the same passions as the desire to govern, these words spoken by Machiavelli," and "Wait for the future, this is uncertain, as Machiavelli says." Talleyrand's maxim that words were given to conceal thoughts was also frequently cited by Heureaux.[74] But, with his own *bons mots,* he had little reason to envy them in evocative power: "You know very well that I am like the crab: I scratch myself on the inside, but nobody knows when I do it," and "You know that I am like the monkey: when grabbing hold, I don't let go." His distrust of "these Dominicans" he expressed this way: "I am quite afraid that they'll squeeze the juice out of me and then throw me on the fire like bagasse."[75]

In his recommendations about the appointment of collaborators a part was played by his quite subtle psychological judgment, which seemed to give a curious dialectic to the rationale of his decisions: "Liriano suits us, because his very defects oblige him not only to be loyal, but to live constantly alert," he wrote of Gen. Francisco A. Rodríguez (alias Liriano) in Dajabón. A more general tendency to dialectical thought can be deduced from his observation in a letter to his trusted friend Pedro Pepín, governor of Santiago, that "in politics each thing engenders its opposite."[76] Luperón, too, during his provisional government had appointed people whose objective qualifications were as minimal as Liriano's (although it must be remembered that Luperón wrote the following judgments of Federico Lithgow many years after the latter's appointment and was embittered by what he considered his betrayal): "Lithgow, without discipline, insubordinate, unruly . . . , arbitrary and violent . . . , trampler of society . . . , tough and course; . . . there is no tyrant more cruel and calamitous than this adventurer. Luperón, who did not know where to employ him in order to avoid his doing damage to others, named him Minister of Foreign Relations."[77]

Heureaux saw political activity as artisanry, the political apparatus as a tool, the political structure as a delicate but static whole, as an altar that should not be shaken so that the saints would not topple, or as a "national

monument, poorly built, to be sure," or as a fabric in which it was necessary
to "straighten out . . . certain strands that disturb the organic harmony of
things," or even, in extraordinary cases, "to spin a bit fine."[78]

It is obvious that the need for "efficiency" inherent in this artisanal,
static conception of politics not infrequently clashed with the requirement
of "loyalty," since that could only be demanded if the dictator showed
himself "consistent with his friends." The *"amiguismo"* (or cronyism) was
irrevocably tied to "loyalty" and was often harmful to "cool, mature calculation": "Although I am a man who judges politics a matter of calculation,
it is not possible for me to cease having a heart to love those who support
me with their sword and help me to realize the good of the whole," he wrote
in 1888. He formulated the ambiguity between calculation and heart more
explicitly that same year in writing about solutions to problems "that will be
rational and advantageous to my friends and to the country."[79]

When Washington Lithgow of Puerto Plata was troubled, doubting whether
he would be able to obtain from the Congress the concession for building a
highway, Heureaux wrote him: "Don't alarm yourself—you know that I
am your friend and the Government is, too—so, then, trust in us just as we
trust in you, for we are called to help one another." To Federico Lithgow,
who out of political motives had said that he did not have the ability to hold
a ministerial position, he wrote: "You say that you are not suitable to assume
a Ministry. Do you think I have just come from France? We have all been
brought up together and in our country, in service we are all good for anything." In turn, Heureaux said that he was convinced that his "true friends"—
whom he distinguished quite clearly from his friends for money or for convenience—"did not compromise themselves, not even with Jesus Christ."[80]
Finally, it should be noted that in the past century, the preamble to an official appointment always began with the words, "Because of aptitude and
other circumstances. . . ."

Although Dominican thinkers of this period often spoke of Latin Americans as a cultural category, it was not common for politicians to refer specifically to other Ibero-American societies or situations. Only when Heureaux
argued in 1887 for the need to change the electoral system and the duration
of the presidential term did he come to write that "We feel the need for these
reforms here just as it has been felt in all those Republics of South America
that had the same term and the same system."[81] The exile Pepe Nouel in
Curaçao considered that regimes like Heureaux's were inspired by the Venezuelan dictator Guzmán Blanco: "It seems that this man's imitators abound
in the American republics," although "what has occurred . . . in Santo Domingo has not occurred in any other country. Not even in Honduras and
Coasta Rica, which find themselves in identical political conditions, in
terms of civil wars, murders, and robberies." Nouel also said that "In politics,
we are more backward than the Haitians; at the least, they have an excess of
what we lack: patriotism."[82] The slow and inadequate contacts with the
majority of the South American countries in this period allowed for little

concrete information. Here it is important to note that in the second half of the past century the status of republic was still considered sufficiently curious to give the countries of the Western Hemisphere a certain solidarity toward a predominantly monarchical Europe: in 1893 the *Listín* observed emphatically that "in the whole world there were twenty-seven republics and twenty-eight monarchies.[83]

The parliament's role in the *criollo* dictatorship was in accord with the nonideological, artisanal character of the political system; the delicately established power structure was not to be unsettled by violent opposition. In the words of the president of the National Congress on beginning a new parliamentary year: "[The National Congress] will maintain the harmonious equilibrium indispensable in the governmental mechanism, . . . in its heart, you will not find hostility, nor prejudices, nor systematic opposition, an evil that would please the instigators of bad faith and the unthinking instigators who, some by understanding it all too well and others by not understanding it, seek to undo the dignity of the mandate and to break the equilibrium and the harmony from which the greatest amount of the general good should result."[84] The freedom that the "loyal" members of parliament could permit themselves in their tidy criticism of specific government actions is, therefore, surprising. But the president also had an interest in a harmonious relation with these distinguished followers, often intellectuals. Complaints about pressure and election fraud perpetrated with the help of military men were brought to light with great emphasis by some deputies and were studied quite comprehensively according to the rules of the game, although, of course, the result could be predicted beforehand.[85] The president's attitude toward the parliament was comparable to his attitude toward judicial power; he was fully aware of his personal power, without making emphatic demonstrations of this power in public. Informal pressure was more effective and did not contradict appearances.

In matters regarding the civil government at lower levels, the smaller *comunes* (that is, the great majority) were an example of lack of power, particularly economic power, a fact that provoked many litanies from Hostos, with his great expectations of the autonomous municipality, although perhaps that very lack of power was the reason that "the Executive's interference in the municipal elections is much less coercive and effective than in the others."[86] In 1898 the governor of Santo Domingo wrote: "It is to be lamented that all the municipalities have not yet been penetrated by the duties that the position they play involves. Everyone awaits an impulse from above to move and for everything to be done for them, and this in matters that are of interest to their own *comunes*."[87] The year before the problem of central political power had been explained for a foreign public in elaborate language, which, nevertheless, seems modern to us.

> The Dominican Republic finds itself in the same situation as many other new countries, short of population and rich in territory, in which

it is necessary on many occasions for central power to replace local action, specifically for preparing the elements that, later, will have to constitute municipal life. The aim is for the public right to be in harmony with the democratic right, and without sacrificing the latter, as was done in ancient societies, to advance toward the moment in which the political autonomy of the State is fully established upon the solid, imperishable base of the economic and administrative autonomy of its municipalities.[88]

Thus, three quarters of a century ago, the status of young nation and underdevelopment were already being invoked in a not unconvincing way to justify the political structure.

I end these notes on Heureaux's regime as an example of a *criollo* dictatorship with some facts about his death—in part because they are little known, in part because they are not lacking in sociological relevance. Even quite early in his government he speaks of himself as "an armored man," who "at the height at which I find myself," could alone give himself "guarantees" regarding the safety of his own person; in fact, never "can we set aside suspicion in a land in which true loyalty is scarce in the majority of politicians."[89]

In the crisis year 1893, with Marchena's attempt to attain the presidency just cruelly frustrated, with the minister González exiled in Puerto Rico, with politicians like Luperón, Casimiro de Moya, and his young relative by marriage Horacio Vázquez in active exile, Heureaux's father became uneasy. The son responded: "My dear *papá*, don't worry about the behavior that many citizens continue to follow, for I don't sleep and I am prepared for any eventuality."[90] At the end of 1898, after the sensation of J. I. Jiménez's attempt at invasion and with the deteriorating economic and monetary situation already pointing toward a dramatic denouement, a rumor of Heureaux's death arises during his trip to Jacmel, Haiti. His friend Washington Lithgow urges him to take precautions, but he responds: "It would be too much work to be excessively cautious, and I would not have time for my affairs . . . Besides I have seen that being on the offensive gives the same or more results as being on the defensive, and thus I have preferred the first. God orders things, and when He passes sentence, Carnot, Canovas, the Empress of Austria, and so many other great people, painstakingly cared for and attended, fall. As long as He has need of a man's life, not even a downpour of dynamite could destroy him."

On the same day Heureaux reproached Don Jacobo de Lara, treasury administrator in Moca (and a relative of young Ramón de Lara, one of the conspirators in the Heureaux assassination), for paying out extraordinary rations; he was—"in order to maintain order"—to halt this practice immediately. Also on the same day he writes calming the Puerto Plata commandant of arms, who warned him against conspirators in Cap Haitien: "Strong governments like mine are not brought down with conspirators' threats."[91]

J. I. Jiménez's "subversive publications" in the foreign press did not worry Heureaux either, as he wrote to the German Federico Hohlt on 14 January 1899. The homogeneity and efficacy of his regime had never been greater. He asked his relative J. I. Marsán in Cap Haitien not to give any credit to rumors of his death. The fact that a (Haitian) friend would have been greatly saddened on hearing a notice of his death did not surprise him; this friend had had no motive for resentment and could not do anything "but mourn the disappearance of one who up to now has always proven that he is a good man."[92] But the man who had written eleven years before: "No matter who may be President, I shall rule,"[93] was assassinated on 26 July 1899.*

Three days afterward, in the great tradition of classical heroism, a cyclone lashed the capital, and on the thirty-first, the Venezuelan Guzmán Blanco died in Paris. Heureaux's body, brought from Moca by the governor of Santiago, Pepín, was interred in the cathedral of Santiago in a metal coffin that one Don Jacinto Ramírez had ordered made for himself. It had not been possible to embalm the body, wounded by six bullets, to take it to Puerto Plata. Along with the clergy the "Nuevo Mundo" Lodge also participated in the funeral procession. There were wreathes from, among others, the minister Teófilo Cordero y Bidó with the words, "Your grievous death eternizes the immense and tender feeling with which I love you," and from the ayuntamiento of Santiago "to its adopted son." There were telegrams to the vice-president from Porfirio Díaz, from William McKinley, and also from the San Domingo Improvement Company: "Deepest sympathy we are ready to help and support you and well-being country." At the moment of his death, wrote the newspaper, Heureaux had come out of Jacobo de Lara's house to give alms to a beggar. On 31 July appeared a judicious manifesto from Vice-President Figuereo:

> What there is in the country, more or less, is glorious edification of some days of truce, rescued from the vertigo of our fratricidal disputes. It was not, therefore, possible to bring to a conclusion these necessary and honorable improvisations of the national grandeur, of which various railway lines and many additional telegraph networks and the creation of a [naval] squadron and the organization, outfitting, and maintenance of armed forces on sea and land and the improvement, lastly, of all the public services are patent testimony; it was not possible, it could not have been. It was also necessary, and had to be indispensable, to consume in that extemporized grandeur for the Nation the State's credit, which in the end has been impoverished under the blows of accidents beyond all prediction, like everything that originates from fatality that, because it is an invisible force, no one can contain."[94]

---

*A curious item: Members of two families (de la Maza and Cáceres) were involved both in Heureaux's assassination and in Trujillo's.

The apocryphal stories related to Heureaux's death are numerous, set down perhaps most evocatively by Rufino Martínez. But real facts could also inspire the popular imagination: had Heureaux not signed a contract with the Barcelona sculptor Pedro Carbonell to make a tomb "with a larger than life-size equestrian statue of him," and was the sculptor not "directing the labors on the sepulchral project when the death of the one who ordered it took place"?[95]

THE POLITICAL VOCABULARY

The absence of clear ideological motivation as well as the rapid succession of the majority of the regimes in the nineteenth century created a general feeling of incertitude and instability reflected in the key words of the political vocabulary of that time. Here we have the word *situación* (or situation), which indicated the government as well as the period of government and which reflected the fluid character of alliances and formations. One was a friend or an enemy of the *situación*; a *situación* was developing; one spoke of the first days of a *situación*. The term *reaccionario* (or reactionary) had no ideological connotation. That anyone who acted against the reigning *situación*, the government, belonged to the forces of reaction fit into the neutral, mechanical interpretation of political activity.

We already saw that words like opportunism, convenience, suspicion, dissembling, and malice did not have a negative connotation; on the contrary, they were considered inevitable traits and attitudes and thus estimable in political behavior, which was also always characterized by calculation, coldness, prudence, efficiency, compromise, rationality, and "*mucho tino*" (or "a good feel for things"). In the word *político* (or politic) as an adjective, all these terms converged. "Un hombre muy *político*" indicates (even today) of someone that he knows how to move ably and successfully among many, sometimes antagonistic, groups. The fact that such a person does not necessarily have to be "a professional politician" reinforces the idea that what is being dealt with here are qualities that were considered necessary and desirable in the entire people. Each one had to keep himself afloat in the political turbulences, had to make friends with new *protectors*— no matter at what level—when the old ones had lost their power, and had to seek out new clients if the old ones had abandoned him. One always sought *garantes* (or guarantors) for himself and wanted to be one of the protector's *recomendados* (or favorites).

Under these circumstances, everyone was political; just as the people were militarized, so were they politicized, and the qualities mentioned here were part of the national psychology and still are. Thus it is incorrect to attribute political caution only to the *campesinos* and to believe that only they "say everything in a roundabout way"; this was valid for everyone to a greater or lesser extent, and the fact that these traits were also observed in the humble peasant proves to what point this group of the population was involved in the changing political events.

Needless to say, the terminology regarding revolutions was extensive. Like hurricanes, they frequently received names, and like these tropical storms, they had a clear, limited, but scarcely predictable route: the valiant partisan "*salió para la revolución*" (set out for the revolution), just as the conformists "*votaban por la plaza*" (voted for the town square—where the current authorities usually resided). It is not surprising that meteorology influenced the political vocabulary: in a threatening political *situación*, one spoke of "storm winds." Political imprisonments were called *cabalongas*, after the brand name of a contemporary dog poison.[96] Alarming reports about a revolution were called *bombas* (or bombs); those who launched them were *bomberos* (or bombers). In opposition to them and to calm spirits down, the government launched *bombas oficiales* (or official bombs).[97] Often, the *bombas* were invented by the exiles, who lived in hopes of better times; one such hope was formulated as follows: "Here I have my *political capital*, the *interest* on which I will some day collect for my own satisfaction and your honor"[98] — a remark that illustrates the interesting combination in political matters of, on one hand, the apparent "marketplace" characteristics and, on the other, emphasis on personal honor and dignity.

CHAPTER SEVEN

Changes in the Organs of Cultural Transmission

EDUCATION

With help from the material compiled to this point, we shall concern ourselves in the following chapter with social structure and mobility. But first it is necessary to establish an idea of the development of those institutions (with the exception of the family) that concern themselves with disseminating knowledge.

At the beginning of the seventies the republic's educational institutions could only be described as not very advanced. Even in the time of the first regime of Buenaventura Báez (1849-53), primary schools and two "*colegios centrales*" had been founded—one in Santiago, the other (called the Colegio de San Buenaventura) in Santo Domingo. And by 1848 a seminary that was to be maintained by the rent from some state-owned houses and profits from a plantation had already been established. But these institutions did not enjoy an uninterrupted life. The amounts, sometimes imposing, that the parliament voted for secondary and primary schools in various *comunes* were generally not paid out. In reality, the expenditures for public primary instruction had to be defrayed by the poor town governments themselves: in 1871 there were twenty-one such schools, which cost a total of $8,686, in the country. It is necessary to note that a rich *común* like Moca paid $600 for its school for males, while San Cristóbal could not pay more than $72.[1]

The fact that the government rarely paid its contributions to education notwithstanding, it is of interest to see how the state planned—even before 1861 and without changing its judgment over the course of the years—the distribution of these contributions: more than $13,000 for higher education, contrasting with around $4,000 for primary education, and more than $7,500 for the capital, in comparison with some $9,500 for the rest of the country. Pedro F. Bonó, who was minister of justice and of public instruction in 1867, thundered violently against such a biassed distribution of state monies, which only worsened "that leprosy of ignorance that is so terrible." But his exhortations on behalf of a more equitable subsidy policy had no results at the time. In that year he estimated the number of pupils in the public primary schools at 720 and that of the private schools at 600. "From those who know how to read and write," he wrote, "subtract: 1st. Men who by their age are presumed to have learned before independence; 2nd. foreigners; 3rd. sons of the city of Santo Domingo, residing in that *común*; 4th. youths who have learned in Europe or some other place abroad; 5th. sons of the natives of the City of Santo Domingo, or sons of foreigners, whom their parents . . . have taught themselves; and see what is left."[2] In 1867 Bonó also established chairs in law and medicine at the Seminario Conciliar, which was operating again at that time and which gave instruction for free. The latter chair was held by Dr. Betances, but political vicissitudes did not allow this initiative a long life either.

More successful and stable even in those years was the San Luis Gonzaga private school in the capital, directed by the presbyter F. X. Billini. In 1867 this *colegio* gave free instruction to two boys from each of the provinces, "with preference," according to the way the minister interpreted it, "to sons of simple soldiers killed in the war of independence."[3]

First we shall look at the quantitative changes in the system of instruction, analyzing the data from certain *comunes*. In San Cristóbal in 1871 there was one (private) school for males with twenty-nine pupils who paid one peso per month to the teacher; of the 15,000 inhabitants, some 400 knew how to read and write. In 1882 the same *común* had three private schools for males and two for girls, with a total of 224 students, as well as six public schools with a total of 286 students—a surprising number that the astonished Hostos attributed to the civic sense of a number of persons (Pina, Cordero, Reynoso, and Pérez).[4] In Baní in 1871 there were two (public) schools with 75 students. The percentage of illiterates in the *común* was estimated at 80 percent; in 1882 there was one more school.[5] In Azua in 1871 there was one private school and one public; in 1882, 296 pupils were attending school, which points to an approximate number of five schools. The percentage of illiterates in Azua was around 80 percent.[6] The impression of national progress is even clearer if we compare the maximum of 1,500 pupils in 1867 with the 6,535 (3,861 males and 2,674 females) who were receiving elementary first- and second-grade instruction in 1883 in a total of 101 schools for males and 74 for females. Between 1883 and 1897, an estimated 50 of these schools was added to the existing number.[7] Moreover, in 1898 Father Meriño wrote with satisfaction that "since a few years back . . . elementary schools for both sexes have spread throughout the whole country."[8]

But it is appropriate to ask whether the increase in institutions for primary instruction was also greater than the growth of the total population in those years. In 1867 there were 30 schoolchildren for each 3,000 inhabitants and in 1883 some 30 per 2,075 inhabitants; in 1897 the proportion remains the same.[9] If these estimates are correct, one must conclude that in the last three decades of the past century there was at first a considerable relative increase in the number of students, but that this rate of growth could not be maintained afterwards, owing in part to the notable population growth. It is also interesting to see whether the increase in the number of primary schools favored certain provinces or cities.

Santiago, which had three schools in 1867 and eight in 1871, had thirty-two in 1898. However, the number of this city's inhabitants, as we saw earlier, had not grown in those years at much more than 15 percent. With 1,410 students (782 males, 628 females) in a total population of some 9,400, that is, 30 per 210, the situation in this city was ten times more favorable than that of the country in general. The percentage of illiterates also compared favorably with that of the nation.[10]

In 1867 Santo Domingo had six primary schools, in 1871 eight, in 1893 thirty-seven "establishments for education"; the greatest number of them, naturally, were primary schools. In 1898 the city had 1,046 students, that is 30 per 600 inhabitants; although the proportion was not as favorable as that of Santiago—the growth of the capital had been much more spectacular—its situation was three times more favorable than that of the whole country.[11]

Not very far from the capital the situation was miserable. "The school statistics are truly disheartening," wrote the governor of Santo Domingo province in 1898. "There are *comunes* like Llamasa, Guerra, and Palenque in which there is not a single school because the town government does not have the income to take care of it."

Inevitably, the conclusion is that the larger *comunes* that had enjoyed the increase in prosperity were the ones that made disproportionate use of the total increase in the number of primary schools. With regard to accessibility of primary instruction, the contrast between the countryside and the city became more apparent in these years: as deduced from its policy of subsidies, the central government had always had the intention of favoring the cities, but it had not been able to realize these plans because of the lack of money in the first thirty-five years after 1844. However, as prosperity increased and as the cities were the ones principally benefitting from it, the government policy became in a sense almost automatic.

Of the little private schools, of which each *barrio* of the capital had one or more, with twenty-five or thirty students, some were limited to teaching reading, spelling, arithmetic; others also taught "arithmetic, geography, grammar, physiology, world and national history, and the good manners in the 'Manual de Urbanidad y Buenas Costumbres' by Carreño." Physical punishment reigned: "For the least fault of discipline or for not knowing the lesson by memory: the strap, the slap on the hand, standing long hours over the bench, palm-bark ties on exhibit during class and sometimes in the entryway to the school building. They tell how some cruel teachers customarily made the delinquent kneel down on a *guayo* (a grater)." The school hours were from 8 to 12 a.m. and 2 to 5 p.m;[12] but in 1898 several schools had a total of almost 180 days off.[13]

Over the course of the years protests were raised against the severe corporal punishment; in the General Law on Public Instruction of 1895 anyone who applied these punishments was threatened with immediate dismissal. In the same law, in addition to the usual subjects, general ideas of agriculture and of hygiene, Christian morality, refinement, and social duties were also made obligatory for "complete primary schools."[14] But in 1899 the governor of Santo Domingo had to recommend again that "classes in agriculture" be given in the schools; that same year (perhaps because corporal punishments had been formally eliminated) the schools published the names of students with good and bad conduct.[15]

The tendencies of the time to modernize education—which we shall look at later in more detail—were opposed not only to the traditional method of instruction (with its emphasis on collective memorization) but also to the traditional curriculum. The skeptical—and realistic—Bonó did not accept the educational modernism in its entirety, and today his criticism seems enlightened in certain aspects. After criticizing, in 1884, the province or district capitals that requested and demanded universities "before their children know the spelling-book and their adolescents Spanish grammar," and after pointing out that the farmers and cattlemen were the ones "who pay for the schools almost completely" while they themselves "generally lack free primary schools," he spoke of the understandable opposition that modern pedagogical ideas provoke—for which reason in fact an anarchical situation had arisen, "which ultimately neutralizes and negates the efforts of the old and of the new." Then he continues: "By its form and content, public instruction up until now has not produced true workers, but aspirants, more numerous each day, to public employment; youths without careers, without discipline for any long conscientious effort, imperfectly trained for scientific careers, and only good for joining an office to swell the budget or for putting themselves behind the counter of a dry goods store to sell merchandise, to the great desperation of the women whose work they take away." In fact, instruction of girls had not improved either, according to Bonó:

> In the lower grades the national traditions of plain sewing of shirts, of stockings, Christian catechism, and homemaking tasks have been abandoned completely, replaced in great part by laces, oratory, and tapestry. The Government should not protect nor public opinion encourage such ill-informed aspirations of poor parents, of all our proletariat . . . ; for the moment they are not going to send their daughters to the Legislative Chambers, nor as ladies of a gothic Court to those of Flanders, nor as experts to the Gobelin factory . . . will these poor lacemakers and tapestry-workers without dowry, without trousseau, be able to be the happy wives of the government clerks who await them, with infinitesimal, arbitrary, and fleeting salaries?[16]

One can see, then, that it was possible to express a just criticism of the "modernizing"—and sometimes poorly understood—tendencies because they alienated primary school pupils from their environment (the "ideas of agriculture" notwithstanding) and because they did not respond to their immediate and future needs. On the other hand, however, modernization as advocated and partially realized by Hostos produced important impulses in the spiritual life of the republic. In order to study them, we must now leave the subject of primary education.

When in 1879 during Luperón's provisional government the legislation that created the normal schools—drafted by Hostos in Puerto Plata—was passed, some private schools at the secondary and higher levels were already operating in the capital. There were the previously mentioned Colegio Seminario Conciliar Santo Tomás de Aquino directed by Father Meriño; the Colegio San Luis de Gonzaga (1866) of Francisco X. Billini; the Liceo del Ozama of the poet José J. Pérez; a school for girls, El Dominicano (1867) of Román Baldorioty de Castro. In Santiago, the Colegio de la Paz of Manuel de Jesús de Peña y Reynoso had already existed since 1872.

Hostos's prolonged stay in Santo Domingo had quantitative as well as qualitative repercussions in national education. Besides the capital's normal school, of which he himself was the director, similar institutes were established—although sometimes for a short period—in La Vega, Santiago, and Puerto Plata. In Azua and Santo Domingo, preparatory schools were founded; in 1881 the Instituto de Señoritas, involved with training teachers, was established by Salomé Ureña de Henríquez. A year before, and perhaps as a reaction to Hostos's activities, after a prolonged interruption university education was reestablished in the Instituto Profesional—from 1882 on—under Meriño's direction. Hostos collaborated in this institute as professor of public law and political economy. (In 1887 Hostos published his *Lecciones de derecho constitucional*, in 1888 his *Moral social*. His posthumous work *Tratado de sociología*, published in 1904, has had numerous editions, the last in 1941 in Buenos Aires.)

Hostos's qualitative influence in Dominican education was the emphasis on Comte's positivism as interpreted by the Spanish Krausistas, Hostos's teachers. Evolution opposed to the Creation, reason opposed to revelation, experiment opposed to dogma, rationalism opposed to traditional rhetoric: here are some of the topics that must inevitably have brought Hostos and his followers into conflict with the conservative circles among the intelligentsia of the era.*

In his newspaper *La Crónica* the director of the Colegio San Luis Gonzaga, Billini, first severely attacked "the science that moves away from God, proscribing God from the schools" and attributed to that the increase in criminality after 1881. He believed that the Hostosians "did not have the freedom to profess publicly either irreligion or atheism, because the perfect order of society, which is moral order, on which its nature is based, is injured." Billini's school had not produced large numbers of graduates between 1866

---

*And not only that of the era: in 1918 and again in 1954 the press took surveys on Hostosian influence in the country, and the reactions—favorable or unfavorable—not infrequently reveal emotional interest. See *La influencia de Hostos en la cultura dominicana. Respuestas a la encuesta de El Caribe* (Ciudad Trujillo: Editora del Caribe, 1956).

and 1884: "five priests, five teachers of primary and secondary education, with degrees, and other young men in the commercial course." In addition to Latin, Greek, Spanish, English, and French, his school taught world history, geography, cosmography, physics, chemistry, arithmetic, bookkeeping, geometry, music, and calligraphy. But the emphasis seemed to fall on subjects like "sacred history, philosophy-ethics ('Arguments against utilitarianism'), theology, and rhetorical ones: oratory, exordium, proposition, confirmation, arguments; oratory division: forensic oratory, judicial deliberative; political oratory, parliamentary, sacred."[17] The power of persuasion of Hostos and his arguments and Billini's flexibility are to be admired, since after some time (around 1885), the latter withdrew his charges of "school without God" from the normal school and, moreover, introduced a program with Hostosian points in his own institution.

The Hostosians found a more perservering, more powerful, and thus more dangerous opponent in Archbishop Meriño, who did not let an occasion pass in the eighties to fulminate against the "materialistic rationalism (that is positivism and liberalism)." In his attacks he linked together under the common denominator "liberals" the "freethinkers, anti-Catholics, renegades, indifferent, and atheists," equating materialism with sensualism and therefore with concupiscence.[18] It is noteworthy that Hostos himself recommended Meriño in 1882 for the rectorship of the Instituto Profesional, and that the latter supported the spread of the normal schools during his presidency (1880-82). Still, the good relations that this prelate maintained with Heureaux must surely have precipitated Hostos's departure in 1888. On 26 December 1888 Heureaux wrote his minister Gautier: "I celebrate as is proper the departure of Doctor Hostos from the country. From there some friends have telegraphed me, proposing Sr. Don Fed. Henríquez to me to replace him, they say, so that he will abandon journalism and with it the opposition he continues to offer us in his paper. God having helped us in getting rid of Hostos, I don't want Don Federico or anyone else who is not a good Christian coming in."

Hostos returned to the country in 1900, after Heureaux's death in 1899; he died there in 1903.* A harsh blow to his work came in 1895 when the General Law on Public Instruction stipulated that the divergence of methods between the normal school and the "Escuelas Superiores" had to disappear. The same law created in Santo Domingo and Santiago *colegios centrales* whose permanent personnel would consist of a director (100 pesos monthly), a secretary-professor ($37.50), and a janitor ($7.50), with a sum of $4.00 monthly for expenses for materials; the monthly stipend would be 10 gold pesos for each hour of class. The new normal schools that were to be estab-

---

*But in 1896, disgusted by clerical opposition in Chile, a country he called the "victim of the spirit of imitation," he was disposed to return to Santo Domingo, despite Heureaux's presence. See Emilio Rodríguez Demorizi, ed., *Hostos en Santo Domingo*, 2 vols. (Ciudad Trujillo: Imprenta J. R. vda. García Sucs., 1939), vol. 2, pp. 261 ff.

lished in each provincial capital would pay $50 to their directors, and to the assistants $15 each. Furthermore, Provincial Committees on Education were established.[19] This counterreform did not mean that the ideas Hostos defended so gallantly disappeared from the country with him, just as they had not entered the country exclusively via him either. Nineteenth-century positivism, as well as materialism and rationalism in their various forms, had already existed in the country since long before, and it is possible to point out at least one of their manifestations, skeptical anticlericalism. These ideas continued to exercise their influence by way of Masonry, to which Hostos also belonged; against this influence at times not even Meriño's opposition could have an effect, as is demonstrated in his vain opposition to the Divorce Law of 2 June 1897, promulgated by Heureaux with the help of the deputy Leonte Vásquez.[20]

If Hostos's scientific ideas had not created a certain elitism, something similar to that of the Mexican *científicos* in the period of Porfirio Díaz, the notion of being a disciple of the revered teacher and of being, along with him, the target of criticism would have sufficed to encourage a cohesion among the *"normalistas"* that practically gave them the characteristics of a sect. Thus there was the *tertulia* (or gathering) in the Parque Colón, "made up of elements chemically *normalistas*, enemies of Lilís."[21] John Pieters, a bricklayer from Curaçao and a popular singer, criticized the supposed snobbery of this group in the newspaper:

> Si porque eres normalista
> te firmas Bartolomé,
> yo manejando mi plana
> me firmo John Pietersmé.*[22]

But the clearest evidence of the characteristics of *normalismo* as a "social" movement is undoubtedly the personalism around Hostos, who rightly— although perhaps to his own regret—can be called the group's *caudillo*. A more interesting proof that *caudillismo* was not limited to the purely political sector can hardly be found in this period. "Many called him father; many he called sons." Especially in his last Dominican years and in conjunction with his plan for a general law on public education (1901), violent debates took place; outstanding among the opponents was the presbyter Rafael C. Castellanos, a student of Meriño, who was attacked in turn in *El Normalismo*, the press organ of the Hostosians. The quarrel was not limited to verbal encounters: in that period the "fervent *normalista* Pelegrín L. Castillo" was "assaulted by one of the obsessed sectarians of the opposition minority." Hostos's slogan "Civilization or Death" thus acquired a special significance, which he can scarcely have desired, but which was made inevitable by the "excesses of the defense" of his loyal friends who had elevated him to *cau-*

---

*If because you are a *normalista*/You sign yourself Bartolomé,/Wielding may trowel,/I sign myself John Pietersmé.

dillo in this "first great contest of thought." That the maestro's death coincided with an "atmospheric disturbance" fit into the heroic framework in which this *caudillo* of education had been placed.[23]

The growth and improvement of education in the country itself did not prevent education abroad from continuing to be considered desirable. For girls one immediately thought of nearby Curaçao, where since 1853 in Habaai the Franciscan sisters of Roosendaal ran the Welgelegen boarding school, which was attended by numerous young ladies of "good family" from the nearby republics. President Heureaux, who visited Curaçao several times (he owned some houses there), had given a lamp to the school, and in the nineties he maintained regular contact with the mother superior, Josefina Ricart, a Dominican. Not only did Heureaux's daughter Dilia study there, but he also wrote numerous recommendations for friends (Gen. Manuel Jiménez, Ernolio Mayer, Carlos Nouel) whose daughters were going to Curaçao and returning later to their country, sometimes with a husband.

For young men, Europe continued to be the preferred area for studies. In the previous generation there had been several young men, especially from the Cibao, who had enjoyed an education in some European country—Benigno F. de Rojas had studied in England, Pablo Pujols in Spain, to name only two—but starting in the eighties the number of students abroad, not infrequently making use of scholarships or other presidential favors, gradually grew. Thus in 1887 Francisco Henríquez y Carvajal had the opportunity to study in Paris at Dominican government expense, acting as mentor for sons of Heureaux and the minister Gautier.[24] Heureaux's other sons were sent to Germany and Spain for study—one in mechanical engineering, the other to enter the Escuela de Guardias Marinos; after being unable to find a good Spanish teacher in Hanover, the first youth was also moved to Spain. Heureaux lamented this change "because I prefer German education to any other."[25] This opinion was surely not exceptional if one considers the Germanophilia of Latin America at that time.

The number of sons of poor, unlettered families who by means of (presidential) scholarships managed to receive intermediate and academic education is difficult to determine but should not be underestimated. Several of the country's private schools were aided by the government with gifts or exemptions from customs duties, with the specific aim of offering in return education to children from families with limited economic resources.[26] Petitions like the one in which Brigade General Montero asks money for his son José Eulogio to enter the College of Engineers in Segovia so that later he will be able to make himself useful in the building of fortifications are constantly encountered in the *Actas del Congreso*. Another petition—exceptional in regard to the type of study—is that of Manuel María del Orbe, who wanted to send his nine-year-old son to a European conservatory.*

---

*The son, Gabriel, became an excellent violinist. The father had built his own piano in three years, "the Moca piano" that Hostos describes admiringly (Rodríguez Demorizi, ed., *Hostos en Santo Domingo*, p. 239).

Between 1888 and 1900 the Medical Jury that had been established to give certificates for the practice of medicine did so to fifty-two persons. Of them, twenty-nine had received their training abroad: six in Paris, seven in Madrid, six in Havana, two in Edinburgh, one in Dublin (the last three came to the country for the construction of the Samaná-Santiago railroad and remained there), and one each in Barcelona, Naples, Maracaibo, New York, Philadelphia, Connecticut, and Maine, respectively. The twenty-three doctors with local training had studied in part in the Instituto Profesional; others had prior, dubious instruction and diplomas like "Practical professor of the third class."

Let us look thoroughly at some cases of obvious mobility among the doctors of that period. There was J. F. Alfonseca, a native of San Cristóbal, who, living with an aunt in the capital and working as a shoemaker, obtained a scholarship from President González. He left for Paris but had to return after the fall of González; a new scholarship from Vicini gave him the opportunity to finish his studies. There was the case of Salustino Fanduiz, a poor Aruban immigrant, who by working in the Casa Marchena saved the money to pay for his studies in the United States. José F. García, a son of Gen. Hermógenes García (whose brother became wealthy as a merchant in Sánchez), received a scholarship from Heureaux. Finally Rufino Otilio Meléndez, illegitimate son of Francisca Urraca Vidal, who did laundry and kept a tavern, received economic aid from Heureaux's physician, Dr. Felipe Urraca, apparently a relative, three of whose sons were also graduated as doctors. The help of political or commercial protectors as well as that from well-to-do relatives was what permitted at least 10 percent of the graduates in the period with which we are dealing to complete their studies (to the extent their biographies are known).[27]

In an earlier chapter we already noted the improvements in the training of lawyers with the reopening of the Instituto Profesional; previously their education was carried out largely in private, and the Supreme Court gave them diplomas. Undoubtedly there must have been in this group a mobility similar to that of doctors.

As we saw, the improvement in the teaching of law did not result in a perfecting of justice throughout the country; thus, a positive effect on the public health situation as the number of doctors increased and their training improved was not to be expected either. The doctors continued to be concentrated in the growing cities, and both the rural and poor urban populations had to continue resorting to popular remedies, the numerous healers, and some practitioners. These last did not dare to demand a fee from public employees, since they were vulnerable for not possessing a certificate from the Medical Jury.[28] In the nineties Santiago had a hospital established by the merchant Glas; in 1898 Santo Domingo had a military hospital in addition to San Lázaro, a "hospital for elephantiasics," an insane asylum, and various charity homes and asylums, which, it can be supposed, concerned themselves in a primitive way with medical attention.

In that same year the Instituto Profesional comprised three faculties: law, medicine, and mathematics, and also offered classes in philosophy and pharmacy. What was missing here and in other parts of the country was interest in the technical and laboratory aspects of the training. Some curious examples can illustrate this failure, as well as the ignorance that was a consequence of it. The Instituto Profesional had "one microscope . . . but it was said that it was broken, and it was only used while a German professor, Weber by name, who taught how to operate it, was in this capital." The fact that an advanced student of medicine would seriously try to prove the theory of spontaneous generation by growing "tiny animals in a flask of more or less clean water, stopped with a cork" is not surprising either.[29] There was also the "invention" of a perpetual motion machine based on some little cans full of liquid that Don Juan B. Rodríguez of Jánico realized; between 1885 and 1888 this gentleman demanded and obtained the attention of high officials. "It is quite true," wrote Heureaux to the Santiago merchant Glas in 1888, "that Don Juan B. Rodríguez of Jánico wrote to me and that he sent me a species of Treatise on perpetual motion that I read with great interest and I even gave it to competent persons to read in order to devise criteria regarding his projects. It was well accepted, and friend Rodríguez was respected as quite competent in physics and mathematics." On 24 August of the same year Rodríguez again advertised his invention in *El Eco del Progreso*: "Exposition submitted to the consideration, justice, honor, and dignity of the High Authorities of the State and Corps of Representatives or Consuls of the other Nations." His device was authorized by the priest, the district prefect and other leaders of his village, Jánico.[30]

Better proofs of scientific modernism could be found in those years in the lengthy polemics that occupied the ordinary press over Darwin's theory of evolution, over the causes of tuberculosis, and especially over hygiene, a fashionable theme, on which long articles taken from the European press were published.

Returning for a moment to education we should note the institutions established especially for artisans, often at their own initiative. "La Alianza Cibaeña," an association founded in 1884 at the initiative of Eugenio Deschamps and others, had three schools four years later, when President Heureaux was named an honorary member of the association. Moreover, in the capital there were night classes for artisans that, like other educational institutions, received a subsidy from the government.[31] (One of them, the Escuela Nocturna para la Clase Obrera, was founded by Hostos in 1888.)

THE PRESS AND THE ASSOCIATIONS

It was an old custom for the organs of the press also to receive subsidies; this had been regulated by Luperón in a decree[32] that promised each newspaper the sum of forty pesos per month. In later years the amount varied, but the principle was maintained. Naturally, political prudence was recommendable to the editors of newspapers, but even under Heureaux's regime the editor of *El Teléfono* who had written about the "incompetence, malice, or private influencing of the Judges of Law" was declared innocent by a court.[33]

The press subsidy can scarely be considered as cause of the noteworthy number of newspapers that appeared in the principal cities.* The capital city paper *Listín Diario* had a circulation of a thousand copies in 1893; in that year a total of twelve periodicals came out in the capital. In Santiago, whose first daily, *El Día*, had appeared since 1891, between 1852 and 1900 sixteen periodicals were founded—twelve of them in the last quarter-century.[34] Despite the fact that they did not all enjoy a long life, their number is testimony of an irrepressible eagerness for communication. Generally it was a matter of the activity of a single person, and the journalist also worked in the educational or governmental apparatus. The name of the publication—*La Reforma, La voz del Cibao, El Dominicano, La Paz, El Derecho, La Redención*—often indicated a good part of its ideology or program. In this inventory we are not including the numerous little newspapers of sensationalism and scandal that with names like *Cójanlo* (*Grab it*) and *La Bomba* (*The Bomb*) disseminated local gossip and undertook violent personal attacks.

Equally noteworthy is the number of associations that characterized social and intellectual life. In 1893, the capital, with a total population of fourteen thousand, had three literary, ten philanthropical, six recreational, six religious, and one musical associations.[35] In Santiago, too, the number of associations with names like La Caridad (Charity), Amantes de la Luz (Lovers of Light), Amigos del Adelanto (Friends of Progress), and so forth was large. The exclusive social group Club Santiago was established at the beginning of 1895, a year after the capital's Club Unión, which had parallel aims. A village like San Cristóbal had in 1895 the societies La Aurora del Pueblo (The Dawn of the People), for "the development and enhancement of the *común*"; La Esperanza de la Juventud (The Hope of Youth), for "licit recreation and diversions"; Independencia, "to oversee the progress of public instruction"; and a company of theater amateurs, who organized performances after 1885.[36]

Hostos, whose many journeys enabled him to see the Dominican phenomenon in the Latin American context, was also surprised by the multitude of private associations: "How have these associations been able to be born, to grow, and to be maintained . . . in a social environment so weak and a political atmosphere so violent? . . . That poor country . . . has a spirit of association that has survived all the coercions." He praised especially the Amigos del

*However, Joubert confesses that a paper like *El Repúblico*, of which he was co-editor, could only exist thanks to government support. He praised the Heureaux regime, which never required a laudatory article about the government. See E. C. Joubert, *Cosas que fueron* (Ciudad Trujillo: Imprenta J. R. vda. García Sucs., 1939), p. 116.

País (Friends of the Country)—founded as a political instrument against the annexationist plans of President Báez, limiting itself to cultural goals—which "holds public meetings in which the members read or discourse before the gathering of persons of both sexes"; the Prensa Asociada (Associated Press) with readings and speeches and music; and La Sociedad Republicana, whose aims were at first political, but which later was the owner of the theatre in the capital.[37] The number of "ladies' clubs" was also noteworthy.

It must be observed that the "spirit of association" was not unfamiliar to Hostos himself: during his Dominican period he founded two associations and was made a member or honorary member of eleven more.

Along with these formally organized societies, there were the *tertulias*, conversation clubs that met informally but frequently in a fixed site to discuss current affairs. In the capital during the nineties there were the *tertulias* of the silversmith José Lamercí; of the barber Lechuga; of the central pharmacy of Don José Mieses, presided over by Doctor Alfonseca "of Paris"; of Papá Juan, where the Syrian colony met; of the Petit Riche, where the *horacistas* (political followers of Horacio Vázquez) later congregated; of the Malú, opposite the statue of Columbus, where "in familiar and tropical cordiality" gathered "aristocrats and democrats, ministers and governed to play checkers and drink coffee."[38] Many of the provincial associations were in reality *tertulias* that met once or several times a year and organized public events.

MASONRY

Masonry occupied a prominent place in social life. Introduced in Santo Domingo under the French general Ferrand in 1803 and active in the Spanish and Haitian periods, it managed in 1858 to found an independent lodge, the Gran Logia Simbólica of the Dominican Republic; the Supreme Council of the 33rd Degree, which took charge of the direction of the Dominican lodges in 1866, has recognized the autonomy of the Gran Logia Simbólica since 1890. Between 1858 and 1900 a score of lodges were founded throughout the country.[39] Of all the presidents of the republic in the nineteenth century it is known for sure only that Father Meriño was not a Mason; of some it is known by oral tradition that they were Masons. The great majority—among them Santana, Báez, González, Espaillat, Luperón, Billini, and Heureaux—were Masons; the first and the last two were Masons of high degree. The number of politicians, poets, educators (Hostos among them), journalists, and businessmen who were members of a lodge is so overwhelmingly large, their position in the social life of the period so prominent, that it can be said without exaggeration that Masonry brought together the leading circles of the republic in a highly effective network. This did not prevent antagonisms of a political or other nature among the Masons, but the call to a "brother" or *"frercito"*—as Heureaux preferred to call his fellow Masons—undoubtedly had an effect little less than that based on blood or ritual kinship.

Hostos emphasized that it was not only the "leading circles" that were found in the lodges: "that institution's members, rich and poor, perennially helpless or powerful for a day, high and low, young and old, . . . make the lodges a meeting center all the more frequently inasmuch as . . . many are teachers in the free, night schools that all the Masonic centers have, and almost everyone participates in administration, support, and overseeing of them."[40] In addition to this educational work, there was the charitable: in 1878 the Gran Oriente established two Aid Committees that covered between them the entire country and were supposed to offer help not only to "families of brothers disabled for work by reasons of age, illness, or accident," but also where the brothers "for causes contrary to their will find themselves abroad," a clear reference to the many political exiles.[41] The lodges also established or helped maintain hospitals, asylums, and cemeteries. It is not astonishing that the Masonic lodges would have received aid from the government, for example, with exemption from tariff duties.*[42]

The ideological world of Hostos and his colleagues, as we already indicated, was not very far removed from that of the Masonry of the period, and this is confirmed yet again by the fact that the German Karl Christian Friedrich Krause (1781-1832) is considered one of the principal philosophers of the Masonic movement.[43] This philosopher, by way of his Spanish followers, the Krausistas, was the major influence on Hostos's scientific education. Krause's ideas on Masonry's duty as caretaker of morality, alongside the state as keeper of order and the church as regulator of religion, we find reflected in Hostos's activities. It must be made clear that in public life he turned over the task that Krause awarded to Masonry to the elite that he wanted to create by means of his educational system. It also seems to be in agreement with the Krausistas' ideas that Hostos—although he did not hesitate to judge Protestantism as "more advanced in the religious evolution than Catholicism"[44]—would demonstrate tolerance for Catholicism and for religion in general in his opinions and public actions, desiring, however, that some day religion might come to be compatible with reason.[45]

That same type of tolerance, fortified perhaps by the small scale of the social environment and—during long periods—by the absence in the lower Dominican clergy of tendencies toward fanatical social isolation, may explain the fact that in the period that we are analyzing many personal and even organizational ties existed between the clergy and Masonry. Only during the Spanish Annexation (1861-65) had Masonry been proscribed by Monsignor Bienvenido Monsón: "from the pulpit, in pastoral writings, and at their

---

*Masonic contacts were not limited to national borders. In the last years of the century the Restauración Lodge No. 11 of Puerto Plata maintained correspondence with seventy-eight foreign lodges. (Enrique Deschamps, *La República Dominicana: directorio y guía general*, 2 vols. (Santiago: n.p. [1906?]), p. 195.

deathbeds, without heeding the circumstances of the country, where for more than half a century Masonry, like freedom of religion, reigned, they were pitilessly excommunicated, in the course of which considerable goodwill among the very ones who had brought about the annexation was estranged." Indeed, also during these years, the "Dominican clergy, influential in the villages and powerful in the countryside," had "to submit itself to new discipline that went against its habits and diminished its preponderance, soon becoming an enemy of the annexation and making the arbitrary oppressors unpopular."[46]

When after the Restoration both the clergy and Masonry recovered their old liberties, the tradition of cooperation was able to continue. In the capital it was customary for many years that only the Masons carried the image of Saint John the Evangelist in the Good Friday procession, and in Santiago until 1886—and the disappearance of this custom perhaps reflects the growing influence of Meriño, recently promoted to Archbishop—"the Masons attended the events of Holy Thursday and Good Friday in proper full dress to act as guardians for Jesus Transubstantiated. . . . The Masons of the first to third degree carried their patron Saint John the Evangelist, those of the fourth to the thirty-third [degree] accompanied the Holy Sepulcher, and bearing the ribbons that hung down from that was the privilege of the thirty-third degree." Under these circumstances there cannot have been generational conflict when in the twentieth century two Masons of high degree (Nouel and Beras) saw their sons become archbishops. In this century and the past one it happened that Catholic churches were built with help from Masonic gifts; it also happened that the building for the Respectable Lodge "Nuevo Mundo" No. 5 in Santiago could be completed thanks to a loan of five thousand pesos from the presbyter Manuel Zenón Rodríguez. In the nineteenth century there were at least a dozen friars, presbyters, and priests who were simultaneously Masons.[47]

RELIGIOUS ORGANIZATIONS

Contact of the clergy with the political authorities was also common and not infrequently symbiotic. Father Meriño, the highest-ranking prelate and one of the prominent figures of the *azul* party, was in close contact with the government as much before as after his presidency (1880-82). Especially in the eighties he worked in unison with Heureaux. In the unsettled year 1887 the president showed gratitude for his cooperation both in words and in cash: "Thanks for your very good reports, I [am sure] that you will do as much as is humanly possible to work in favor of peace and harmony among your political and spiritual sons. I know that you understand a great deal and are too sagacious to know how to fathom the abysses that the conspirators form . . . . Regarding the $200 that by virtue of the plan are indicated for the Archbishop, they have not been reduced . . . and I pray to God that we are always capable of fulfilling such a sacred obligation."[48] And on 15 September of that same year:

> I desire more than anyone else that your visit produce great benefits, as I expect it to, as much in the religious, as in the social, as in the political, and you can be certain that I and my government will not waste any opportunity to make available to you effective aid to keep safe the principles of the Dominican people. I trust in the goodness of God that will have permitted me to await your return in peace, for the celebration of the Holy Father's Priesthood Jubilee, and I do not doubt that you will always take something from the Government, for the Government, when you and the Church are involved, has the duty to be accommodating and meet its obligations.

In the same year Heureaux asked Meriño not to give up the rectorship of the Instituto Profesional, alluding obliquely to the Hostosianismo whose influence was on the increase: "The necessity for you as the premier Leader of the Church . . . to be at the head of the Republic's teaching institution, where the struggle becomes indispensable in order to avoid, with the light of truth in hand, the triumph of the errors that aspire to be truths, nothing less than permitting morality and conscience the irrational freedom of the beast that runs wild across the plains. No, Señor Rector, you cannot, you must not abandon the chair."[49]

The following year, the year of Hostos's departure, Heureaux published a "Message on Teaching of Christian Morality in Educational Establishments." Commenting on this document to a friend, Heureaux indicated clearly which functions he was awarding to religion: "I do not allow religion to fall back: it is in part the restraint on the passions."[50] For his part, Meriño was always convinced that "Order is the first element of society; it is its base and firm support. Without it, the union of the members is impossible, because it is the true support of the moral force of institutions and the regulator of social movement in the use or exercise of communal or individual right."[51]

Despite the fact that Meriño and Heureaux were basically in agreement over the aim and the task of the state and of the church, they had differences of opinion over certain matters that both generally considered as belonging to their respective jurisdictions. As early as 1888 Heureaux was complaining to Luperón that "about that very same Father, whom I respect and esteem, and whose elevation to the Mitre I took so to heart, I already have complaints that would have drained the heart of another who was not of my character."[52] And Meriño's tone was violent when in 1897 he severely—and vainly—attacked the law that made divorce possible; we have mentioned it previously. In his protests against this "sign of decay of wholesome customs," he even allowed a threat to be heard: "And in particular, We, who have always blessed God because during the exercise of Our episcopal ministry We have seen the most inalterable harmony reign between the ecclesiastical authority that We wield and the civil authority, anticipate the alteration of such smooth, pleasing, and beneficial relations with justifiable anxiety, obligated as We are to the fulfillment of very sacred, impretermitable duties, obeying God before men."[53] But Meriño had to continue his opposition to what he considered antireligious ideas even after Heureaux's death—and then with greater urgency—as in December 1899, when a law of separation of state and church was proposed. All this indicates the almost inevitable character of the secularizing tendencies of the period, which reflected events in Europe and especially in France. The rhetorical question that Meriño posed himself in his pastoral letter—"And, indeed, in a people Catholic by its origin, education, constant practice, and inalterable tradition, is it conceivable to separate the Christian from the citizen?"[54]—was answered in the name of the rural population, which was also conservative in these matters, by the popular singer Juan Antonio Alix:

> Que siga la religión
> Del que fué crucificado,
> Siendo siempre del Estado
> Y también de la Nación.
> La general opinión
> Del pueblo dominicano,
> Y de todo ciudadano
> De criterio y de valer
> Dice que así debe ser,
> Porque el pueblo es soberano.*[55]

At the provincial level one encountered the same cooperation between spiritual and secular leaders that was usual at the national level. Several priests, following Meriño's footsteps, served as informants for Heureaux (Fathers Luichín in Guayabín, Antonelli in Dajabón, and several more.)

About the visit of one of Heureaux's governors to Jánico, the village priest wrote the following report to the Vicar-General: "The [patron saint's] festivals are going as I and you wanted. General Pepín ate here today, I made the Ladies of the village make him a manifesto so that they could sign it, and a girl would bring the petition on a tray. Finally we obtained our goal, he has donated a Holy Christ. Now it is up to you to activate the matter. You will speak with him. I recommend that you do it as if it were a matter of your own." And, indeed, shortly afterward the vicar ordered from Larrier, in Alwy, France, a "Christ in clay, with all the accessories, inscriptions, nails, etc."[56]

The pastoral work in the countryside was carried out practically without control from above. Only occasionally did some high prelate like Meriño

*Let the religion/Of the One who was crucified/Always continue to be that of the State/And also of the Nation./The general opinion/Of the Dominican people/And of every citizen/Of discernment and of worth/Says that it should be so/Because the people is sovereign.

visit a remote region, and then he was kept busy with his multiple duties: "the confirmations abound, and with them, as is quite natural, the heat and the perspiration."[57] "If [the church in La Victoria] is an old ranch, this one [in Sabana Grande] is a deserted shanty. The people here think of re-building it, that is, building it again, but there is something like apathy or negligence. [Monsignor Meriño] has spoken some of marriage, of the good that it does for societies, of the morality and advantage of it. He spoke of cohabitation or concubinage, of the evil it occasions society, of its immorality and inconvenience. Some have already come to speak of getting married (notice, some cohabiters). Monsignor provides them dispensations from banns, kinship, and whatever may be necessary. Monsignor is seen and heeded. You know that his word magnetizes, you know it: it will also break this cursed chain of concubinage, so common in our villages, so harmful in our families, so dishonorable in our societies."[58]

The priests themselves sometimes could not resist the temptation of concubinage. Heureaux occasionally made use of the possibility for moral blackmail that this type of relation offered. Thus on 29 July 1882 he wrote the humble Reverend (and journalist) Don Gabriel Moreno del Christo in El Seibo: "I must also let you know that here in the Church circle some charges of lechery scarcely honorable to your personality are being made against you . . . that this has climbed the stairways of the Archepiscopal Palace . . .; here, the charges: 1st. That there is a man there who is a thief and of wicked conduct, and that you live constantly visiting that house because of being enamored of the daughter of that malefactor—named Nepomuceno Peralta. 2nd. That Sra. Catalina Zorrilla has found herself obliged to move her daughter to another house because of your tenacious pursuit. All these things, my dear friend, make me think a great deal about you, especially when I am so jealous of your good name and reputation, please keep quiet about this letter, be prudent and judicious, meanwhile write me and tell me what this is all about."[59]

Father Quezada in Jánico seems to have had similar difficulties. In the same letter in which he asks permission from the Canon (and Mason!) Nouel to perform marriages of cohabiters in his parish for free, he refers to "the matter of Juana Núñez, I swear on the ashes of my mother that it is untrue. Besides, send here to ask whether they know a certain Rosa Pelitón, and if they know that any woman is here on my account. Enlighten me about what I am going to ask you, in this matter I am an ignoramus. . . . Being twenty-three years old, what did that young woman want? Perhaps she is a minor?" Although he even had his horse ready to order to flee to Haiti, his case seems to have been settled with money. The priest continued lamenting afterwards: "Now, how did Santamaría remain in his post? And Moscoso, and Santeliseo? Believe me that I am the most unfortunate, for such things only happen to me."[60]

The absence of supervision and social interchange encouraged other weaknesses similarly. Thus in the San Pedro de Macorís of 1874, still a small village, the priest was accused of "using violent means like the whippings he administers or the fear that he instills in the sinners, whom he obliges to confess or get married without having prepared themselves as the Church orders."[61] And in 1896 Fr. Eliseo Bornia provoked a scandal in Baní: he had placed a little mirror in the altar to be able to spy on the parishioners. When one Alfredo Martínez did not kneel at the right moment, Bornia sent a cleric to compel him to go down on his knees. This dispute came to involve even the president, and it finally ended with a suit by the priest against the *Listín*, which accused him of immoral conduct. The newspaper won in the local court; later, the suit was settled out of court.[62]

We have available the accounting of a priest from the village of Mao, possibly referring to a month in the year 1893:

Baptisms 45	56.25
Marriages 2 (1 charity)	9.00
For an exemption from banns	5.00
First-class burial	16.00
Responsory for a body in the Church	2.00
Sent by Father Honorio	14.00
	102.25

Deductions	
To the bell-ringer as usual	10.00
To *idem* for the burial	1.00
To the sacristan for *id*.	1.00
To the lay brothers for *id*.	0.75
To the sacristan and to Lolo for the responsory	0.75
To *id*. for incense	1.00[63]

The economic situation of rural priests was not very favorable. It is true that they received some income for religious services, and thanks to old customs like that in the name of San Isidro, patron saint of agriculture, they received a part of the harvest, but they had to turn over a considerable portion to the higher clergy. This sometimes provoked reactions of bitterness, in which the priestly "career" was lamented:

> For around ten days or more an official letter from the Vicar General in which he tells me that I should go immediately to Santo Domingo to receive orders from the higher clergy has lain in my power, and for want of money with which to undertake the trip, for I do not earn a centavo, I have not been able to go to the call that is made to me. Therefore, I hope that you, indulgent as ever with one who will never be able to reward you for the many favors that you have known how to offer me so spontaneously, will see a way to send me some Masses with which I might be able to carry out my journey. Perhaps they will be the last Masses that I will offer, for I am disposed to resign from this

career, which has only offered dismal disenchantments, before putting up with the injustices from the despot [Vicar General Tejera] ... for I have always believed, as the Holy Book says, that man does not live by bread alone. If that fiendish man continues in the Vicarage, I do not doubt that there will be a schism in our Church very soon.[64]

Just as medicine involved unauthorized practitioners who must be distinguished from the primitive popular healers, so, too, the church had its unauthorized representatives, who, nevertheless, kept the official church as a model and who ought not to be confused with the witches and other practitioners of magic. Thus, in various places in the country sprang up hermitages that had no official authorization and to which the faithful brought money and where certain saints were worshipped.[65] Attending church and ritual devotion were predominantly a women's affair. In the old capital city church Regina Angelorum, 1,154 women and 16 men received Holy Communion during the month of June 1884.[66] But where religion and social life coincided outside the church, then the participation, including masculine, was practically general, and the close tie to government was reaffirmed at the same time. This was demonstrated especially in *Semana Santa* or *Semana Mayor* (Holy Week), which was usually paid for, according to tradition, by the government, which generally—and also according to tradition—borrowed the necessary amount from some important merchant. In the capital, to take it as an example, a procession was held daily: on Sunday, that of Jesus into Jerusalem, later that of Jesus in the Garden, on Holy Monday, religious services to Jesus on The Column, under the sponsorship of its brotherhood, led by the prestigious Guerrero family, owners of the image. "From Holy Wednesday at ten in the morning the church sounded the curfew until more or less the same time on Holy Saturday, a great retreat was observed in the city, nobody raised his voice, no one who dared to sing or to play any instrument was heard anywhere." The police busied themselves with maintaining the silence. No horse or vehicle was permitted entry into the city. The few animals that went through the streets had hoofs tied with rags. Public offices and cafes were closed. "The ritual tolling from the churches was done with the instrument called the *matraca* [a wooden rattle]. The military drums were out of tune. The flags, including those of the consulates, waved at half mast." The religious ceremonies in the cathedral finished, a company of soldiers went out to go through the streets, "playing happy marches and shooting, in passing, at the Judases hung from house to house."[67]

"Each parish had its societies or brotherhoods, presided over by a pious person whom they called The Commissioner and empowered to collect annually . . . the funds for the patron saint's festivals as well as to draw up the program for these festivals that was printed and circulated in advance, the nine days of Masses, *salves*, reveilles, sung hours, etc., being divided among the wealthiest worshippers. Printed *décimas* and *seguidillas* that . . .

were going to kindle popular enthusiasm were also circulating. In those days the festival church did not rest, for there were many Masses celebrated, *salves*, sung hours, distribution of alms, concessions of indulgence, confession and Communion, fulfillment of promises, vows, baptisms, marriages, sermons, etc. On the exterior, the church was adorned, as was the *barrio*, with flags, strands of cut paper in all the colors, simulating fringes and chains. Some houses displayed special decorations, made with *guáyiga* or with cocoanut palm. If the procession was overtaken by nightfall on account of the many motets, the neighbors brought their lights and glass-shaded candles to the doors and windows."

These festivals of the *barrios'* patron saints lasted nine days; eight of them were organized by the devout, and the ninth by the church. Each *barrio* tried to outdo the other in its festivities, and the entire city participated in each *barrio* festival: "These were days of total mirth and carousing, heavy eating and drinking days . . . After midnight, they often made the *sancochos* and *locrios* [or meat stews], made with the chicken or turkeys that good-humored youths stole from other *barrios*. . . ." There was a street band with guitar, *güiro*, and tambourine that played *danzas* and *carabinés* for dancing in the afternoon (after everyone had attended the High Mass in the morning). In the elegant houses there was a piano, violin, and sometimes a harp, and waltzes, *danzones*, and *danzas* like *"La tentación"* and *"Tus ojos"* were played.

Sometimes running bulls through the streets was organized, with a jury and patronesses; they sometimes tied fireworks on the animals' tails. Finally, there was also a small cannon that was taken from *barrio* to *barrio*, operated by some gunners "almost always captained by a little mulatto nicknamed *Chago*." It is not surprising that the seriously ill were taken to more tranquil places during the festival days. The *barrio* of San Carlos had the fiesta of La Candelaria (Candlemas) in February, San José had its in April, in July that of Nuestra Señora del Carmen in the *barrio* of that name; in October the *barrio* of San Miguel had its, in November that of Santa Barbara. In addition there were the fiestas of the New Year, the Three Kings, Our Lady of Bethlehem, and La Altagracia (patroness of the country) in January; Independence Day and Carnival in February; Holy Week in April; the "noisy cross festivals" of May, when the crosses that were permanently located in plazas, streets, and crossroads were decorated with flowers and garlands; Corpus Christi in June, when many rockets and firecrackers were tossed; in August the fiesta of the Restoration; in November San Andrés on the thirtieth. On that occasion the elegant ladies and gentlemen tossed eggshells filled with perfume; the common people filled them with *agua de tuna* or aniline. The fiesta was earlier called *carnavales de agua* (or water carnival) and ended—like the majority of the fiestas—in stone-throwing fights. In 1897 President Heureaux, accompanied by a minister, travelled along the Ozama in a little rowboat to reach some distinguished capital city residents (who had wanted to escape the fiesta in a boat) and to get the citizens wet and shine colored lights on them. In November there was also the Novena for the Dead, with a nocturnal "procession of the bones"; finally, in December there was Christmas Eve. And we have still not mentioned all the festivals: thus, in June there was the festival of San Juan and San Pedro with its bonfires and processions, on muleback, in which riders mounted on mules leaped over the bonfires.

The influence of so many fiestas on the economy, as well as on the economic mentality, was subjected to judicious criticism by Bonó: "The Dominicans set aside three quarters of the year, comprising: Sundays, days of both commandments, the commandments of vigil, those of general and particular patron saints, the three days of the four solemn festivals, those of the advocate saints of the societies of illnesses of the eyes, throat, and molars, births, earthquakes, lost objects, etc., imposing on their abstinence not the holy and pure religious idea of prayer, good works, or retreat, but attributing to the act of useful, honest labor imminent and fortuitous punishments for having done it on the day they believe in observing. In such a way that this belief takes away from work its holiness and imparts a sinful character to it, the opinion being current among the workers and laborers that whosoever works on one of those festival days incurs traumatic wounds or negative results in the work itself because of his idolatry."[68] In March 1899 Leonte Vásquez presented to the Congress a proposal for a law to reduce the number of holidays; it was he who had also sponsored the divorce law two years before. In defending his proposal he emphasized the fact that many workers were prepared to work on those days, but that they were not allowed to and consequently found themselves obliged to go without income.[69]

Thus, the political, social, and economic sectors of the society were subjected to the profound influence of the church as a social organization on one hand, and on the other, and undoubtedly equally important, to the totality of convictions and beliefs that were considered by the people or segments of it as commendable by being evidence of Catholic faith. The silence of the church in this regard was interpreted, it seems correctly, as approval.

Not much news reached the local press about the activities of the small group of Protestants, largely descendants of the North American Methodists who came to the country in the twenties. Their ranks had recently been reinforced by immigrants from the British Isles and the Virgin Islands who had established themselves on the sugar plantations. In the capital, they had abandoned the English language for Spanish. In June 1893 Josiah Robertson gave a lecture in the capital city's Protestant church: "Education Considered with Regard to the Development and Enhancement of Man"—a characteristic subject for this group that placed so much emphasis on study. In the same year we read about plans for new quarters in the capital. The surnames of the leaders—Hamilton, Phipp—indicate continuity beginning with their settling in the country seventy years before.[70] It was in the twenties and thirties of the twentieth century when the various Protestant communities were organized nationally, replacing their old ties to the British Methodists with cooperation with North American evangelical organizations—the same pattern of rising North American dominance and European decline that we found in the economic realm.[71]

THE ARTS

Literary life reached noteworthy pinnacles in the second half of the nineteenth century. The quantity of literary production had already been great during the whole century, although the emigration of an important part of the elite during the Haitian period resulted in a certain setback; in the biographies of Dominican literary figures—almost all participants in politics, like everyone else—exiles that underscore the notable intensity of intellectual contacts with Cuba, Puerto Rico, Venezuela, and the rest of Latin America appear in every case. But in a qualitative sense it is the second half of the century that can be called exceptional both for the quality of the works and for their chronological precocity within the respective genres. It was Pedro F. Bonó, so talented in many facets, who published his "novel of manners" *El Montero* in Paris in 1856, an early date for this "realist" work.[72] There is also *Enriquillo* (1879), a historical novel by Manuel de Jesús Galván that deals with the beginning of colonial society and the role of the Indian rebel leader Enriquillo. (Recently it was included by UNESCO in its series of representative works of world literature, and it has been translated into English by Robert Graves and into French by Marcelle Auclair.[73])

Finally there are José Joaquín Pérez and Salomé Ureña de Henríquez, the latter applauded by the Spaniard Menéndez y Pelayo as the country's first great woman poet. We are not writing a history of literature and thus we refrain from mentioning the names of the dozens of others who contributed in this period to the undoubted flourishing of Dominican letters. Regarding the social and political dimensions of their production, we would like to limit ourselves to pointing out four clear tendencies: interest in the Indian past; interest in the customs and language of the people themselves; emotional solidarity with neighboring peoples still under colonial rule in Cuba and Puerto Rico; and a faith, expressed poetically, in progress, in the possibility of improving the society of the future.

The literary search for the roots of a national identity found its parallel not only in the successful work of the painter and sculptor Abelardo Rodríguez Urdaneta, but also in the impressive work of the historians of that period. After Antonio del Monte y Tejada, in Cuban exile, wrote in 1853 his *Historia de Santo Domingo* (published in 1883 by the Amigos del País Society), a work that described only the colonial era, there came José Gabriel García, "the father of national history" with his *Historia* (1900), in which he described contemporary history up to 1876. This work, along with the one by Luperón, *Notas autobiográficas y apuntes históricos* (1896), has determined in great part the judgments and prejudices of the Dominican intelligentsia in relation to the historical process of national liberation and the phenomena that accompanied it, both regarding the actors who appear in it and the nature of the historical interpretation: the latter is—in accord with reigning social thought—of an "aristocratic," heroic character.

Returning for a moment to poetry, we ought to note how tenuous the demarcation between "elite" and "popular" poetry was in a country where everyone wrote verses from time to time. In Rodríguez Demorizi's work *Poesía popular dominicana*[74] appear the names of various "official" poets. Several of the verses of José Joaquín Pérez were put to music in his time and "were sung by the people."[75] A typical popular poet like Juan Antonio Alix (1883-1917) was later placed in the ranks of the great national poets. Alix, who commented on current political and social topics in his *décimas*, thus informing the lower social strata in a delightful way, "published his compositions on leaflets that circulated profusely throughout the whole Republic. These flyers, so much in demand, were the money that Alix brought to his village marketplace in search of daily food. Among the market-vendors and peasants of Santiago he was an idol. The *campesino* could bring no better gift on return to his *bohío* than a '*décima* by Juan Antonio,' and not a week passed without the celebrated poetry's becoming known and recited in the entire region."[76]

In their turn, the "elegant" poets often wrote occasional poems, as did Fabio Fiallo in praising the beauty of a singer from one of the Spanish zarzuela companies that in that period began to visit the country with some frequency, as did other foreign artists and even circuses.[77] In the nineties, numerous literary critiques, generally referring to French literature, appeared in the periodicals, and the death of Verlaine prompted someone in the little village of Sánchez to a lengthy statement against "*decadentismo*."[78] Even from quite early on Fiallo had contacts with Rubén Darío, but it was principally European literary figures who continued to attract the interest of the Dominicans. J. J. Pérez translated Thomas Moore, César Nicolás Penson translated from the Italian, and Manuel Rodríguez Objío, to mention only these three, translated works of Victor Hugo.

While in 1871 neither a bookstore nor a library existed in the Cibao,[79] in 1899 there were in Santiago alone two public libraries, three printers, and one bookstore, and in 1893 in the capital, four public libraries and four bookstores. There was an agent of the Curaçao book store and publisher Agustín Bethencourt and Sons, which published books and music for the entire surrounding Spanish-speaking area and also imported European works. Moreover, European books were imported from the United States, as can be seen in an order written in French from Bonó to the *Courrier des Etats Unis* in New York, in which he orders works by, among others, Molière, Rousseau, Diderot, Pascal, and La Fontaine, and French editions of Goethe, Shakespeare, and Swift.[80] Foreign literature could also be obtained in the country. In the *Listín* on 22 January 1893 the book and music store of Abraham Curiel and Pereira (two Sephardic Jews) advertised having in stock works by Balzac, Dumas *père*, Espronceda, Flammarion, Benjamin Franklin, Victor Hugo, Lamartine, Edgar Allan Poe, and Schiller.

President Heureaux always had two books on top of his desk: Machiavelli's *The Prince* and *Amalia*, a historical novel by Marmol, "in which the era of Rosas in Argentina is portrayed."[81] He also ordered other books and music from Curaçao, often for his relatives, and he supplied foreign libraries that requested books on the republic. Ulises Heureaux, Jr. (1876-1938), educated in Paris, wrote some novels of French orientation and some plays, which established his reputation as a literary man; he did not share his father's interest in war and politics. In this case, then, these two types of vocation were divided between the two generations, an exceptional instance, given that the common thing was for generals to be poets and vice-versa.

The predilection of the literati for the word rather than for the idea, for form rather than for content, for "saying well" rather than for "what to say," so apparent in the type of aristocratic culture that concerns us, was criticized with little restraint. A director of operettas who passed through the country spoke of "the colonial vices: trivial politics, bad verses, and worse speeches."[82] And again we cite Bonó, who devoted the following words to this topic: "In my country . . . the letter has been spread more widely than the spirit; form comprises everything, the ideal of saying well is pursued, style is corrected, extolled, given excessive veneration on its own terms, void of sense, in details of infantile trivialities and phantasmagorias. There are editorials in periodicals, there are speeches whose phrases and periods resemble Olympian Jupiter in the midst of lightning bolts and thunder, and that once wrung out do not let loose a drop of judgment." He found a functional explanation for the abundance of poets: "If public education . . . has produced nothing truly useful, individual initiative, . . . finding the routes of public usefulness totally obstructed, has slipped on to the only open path in which the inspired talent of a tropical people could be developed. Literature, especially poetry, is a favorite occupation (of our youth); but, oh! it should be the complement of our general culture. . . , while today it only appears in our situation like the failure of a languid plant that has not been able to grow, become strong, and ripen." But Bonó did not want to halt the avalanche of poems because one great poet would perhaps be enough "to present with decency and grandeur to future generations our unknown and until now unfortunate Nation."[83]

THE IMAGE OF EUROPE AND THE UNITED STATES
IN THE LEADING GROUPS

On 19 December 1896 the journalist Eulogio Horta published in the *Listín* a "mental photograph" of himself that seems to us illustrative of the preferences of his educated contemporaries:

Favorite object:	Woman
Favorite prose authors:	Voltaire, Renan, Gautier, Paul Bourget
Favorite poets:	Musset, Byron, Lamartine, Henri de Regnier, Julián del Casal
Favorite musicians:	Chopin, Schubert, Bellini
What books do you like to read from time to time?	The "Buddhist Catechism" of Sumangala
Favorite book (outside religion):	Dictionary
Aspiration:	The best culture
Favorite occupation:	Reading
Favorite historical character:	Bolívar
Favorite fictional character:	Hamlet
Where would you like to live?	Paris
In what period?	The present
What is the most admirable quality man has?	Valor
What is the most admirable quality woman has?	Beauty
What do you hate most in both?	Hypocrisy
Who would you like to be?	Marcus Aurelius
What is your nightmare (*bête noir*)?	Financial distress
Your distinguishing characteristic:	Impatience
Your favorite pleasure:	Conversing with an intelligent woman
Your motto:	*Nitus in adversum*: struggle against adversity

The temptation to take this self-portrait as the topic of a socio-psychological statement is great, but we limit ourselves here to pointing out to what extent the cultural predilection for Europe, especially for France, turned out to be impervious to the conflicts that in that period characterized the relations of France and its representatives with the republic, including with the newspaper on which the journalist was employed. Indeed, European economic dominance did not lead in the Latin America of the past century to an antipathy toward European culture, any more than the subsequent U.S. penetration resulted in a complete change of course in the Latin Americans' cultural preference.

The journey through Europe was then, as now, in what can be called the humanistic-aristocratic tradition, the crowning moment of education, and it could be used as an argument when explaining a political preference, as is seen in the manifesto from "several citizens" of Monte Cristi who supported Luperón's presidential candidacy in 1888: "Because General Luperón has visited the civilized regions of the Old World more than once, he has felt the astonishing progress that is occurring in every sense in those advanced regions; and it is quite natural to assume that anyone who loves his country, as the general loves his, will once in power attempt at least to copy in it something of what he has seen and felt in nations advanced in civilization, like France, England, Germany, and other states of civilized Europe."[84]

Nor did Luperón himself, who also knew the United States—the Irish riots coincided with his stay in New York—and whose brother had fought in the U.S. Civil War with the soldiers of the North, hide his admiration for Europe. He was of the opinion that Latin America and France formed a "true community of aspirations, similarity of races, in sameness of political sentiments." He respected the "orderliness and method of the European peoples" (although at the same time he observed in Aix-les-Bains that "princes and potentates of the world" came there "to spend so many thousands of pesos on some waters that are perhaps no better than those of Bánica"). To the extent that his political star was fading, and as Heureaux continued tightening his grip on power (a fact that Luperón attributed to the approval of the United States), his criticisms of that country became more bitter, and he mourned the decline of the importance of Europe in Latin American politics. As he wrote in 1893:

> Unfortunately, the situation of Europe with armed peace, always with the prospect of war, has forgotten the affairs of America, almost growing accustomed to letting the U.S. government create the entanglements that it wants against the other, Latin American republics, threatening to absorb some and to ruin others, which will occur if they do not agree expediently on a mutual security pact, in order to oppose the inclinations of the Republic of the stars and stripes formally, threatening it with withdrawing all the commercial dealings that they do with it, cutting off diplomatic relations. It is the one that with its freebooters, its money, and its intrigues maintains Heureaux's tyranny, just as it maintained that of Balmaceda in Chile. Spain, France, England, Holland, and Denmark, for the preservation and security of their American colonies, would be at the side of the Latin republics. Mexico would recover part of its territory, and Haiti, Colombia, Chile, and Venezuela would require the U.S. to return to them the sums that it has wrested from them with unlawful claims.[85]

The image of the vulgar speculating Yankee was not infrequently confirmed by reality. When in 1888 the consul Astwood dared to propose that the remains of Columbus be exhibited to the U.S. public for money, Manuel de Jesús Galván wrote a letter to Luperón expressing the fear that "the squared-off, triple-soled shoe of the Yankee speculator" would be in greater demand than "the elastic Greek cothurnus."[86] President Heureaux did not know either Europe or North America, and though he also shared the existing preferences ("I have always lived in distrust of the Yankees," he was already writing in 1882[87]), his characteristic irony and skepticism did not falter on this subject either: "I do not doubt that your short stay in Europe will permit you in the future to be an improved worker (in politics)," he wrote to a politician friend, who undoubtedly must have felt annoyed by the word "short."[88] Heureaux preferred the "tranquil" life of Santo Domingo rather than the European, which (also) had its political vicissitudes: "In this land of promise one lives more spontaneously than in the volcanic great world: there goes Gambetta and loses his good eye, von Moltke and is ruined, the first for being too excitable and the second for being so Saxon."[89] He preferred to compare his enemies to the bandits of Calabria rather than referring, as was commonplace, to situations in Africa or Turkey.

But the general rule was that admiration was felt for the Old World, almost as a cultural monolith, an admiration with which the feeling of respect for some individual U.S. statesmen and thinkers expressed almost out of obligation could not compare.

However, there were those who, like the poet José Joaquín Pérez, saw Europe as a setting sun and North America as the "new gladiator":

"Y Europa, la vetusta madre estéril,
que el vigor de otra savia necesita,
sin más fé en sus conquistas, caerá débil,
ante este nuevo gladiador vencida."*

But perhaps it was just this emerging feeling of decadence within Europe itself at the end of the century, which seemed, in contrast to its previously undisputed cultural and technological supremacy, like an enigmatic peculiarity, to which the romantic Dominican intelligentsia was sensitive and which only served to increase the complex power of attraction that the Old World exercised over it.

---

*And Europe, the ancient sterile mother,/Who needs the vigor of other vital fluid,/Without more faith in its conquests, will fall, faint,/Before this new gladiator, vanquished.

CHAPTER EIGHT

Changes in the Social Structure

SOCIAL AND ECONOMIC STRATIFICATION

The image a society holds of its own social stratification is determined in part by cultural factors. In a society where a great diversity of ideologies may exist, there will simultaneously be a great number of such images, whose influence will not necessarily be similar, given that their social importance depends upon the position occupied in the social stratification by those professing each image. In a society like the Dominican one of the nineteenth century, where political ideologies were professed, if at all, in a scarcely conscious way, the image of social stratification was rather homogeneous, influenced principally by—or forming part of—the Hispanic or Mediterranean cultural heritage, which could perhaps be summed up best—in its conception of society as well—with the term "aristocratic". We could call it that in order to distinguish it, in a schematic division into two sections, from the "democratic" image of society.[1]

Characteristic of the "aristocratic" social image is the emphasis on the social distance between groups, as well as on the rigidity of the boundaries between them, and on the immobility of the social whole, while in a "democratic" culture the fluidity of social stratification is proclaimed, the opportunities for social ascent are considered great, and the distances between classes reduced. Present in the "democratic" social concept is the tendency to underestimate the socioeconomic importance of the groups at the extremes of the social scale and to consider—in the familiar social division into three strata—the middle class the most important, the most numerous, even the purest in a moral sense. On the contrary, the "aristocratic" vision prefers to divide the society into two groups: above, the thinking class, *la gente bien* (or the people of good breeding), *la gente culta* (or civilized people); below, the *vulgo*, the lower class, the unfortunates. By observing the upper class carefully, it is sometimes possible to divide it in two as well—in Santo Domingo the familiar division between those of the first rank and those of the second—but always on the premise that the truly rigid dividing line is the one that sets apart the two preceding groups. The language underscores the division by creating pairs of synonyms in order to allude to the upper groups with one

165

and to the lower with the other: *niño-muchacho* (upper-class boy/poor boy), *angelito-muertico* (or dead little angel/little corpse), *bien nacido-mal nacido* (or wellborn/lowborn), *dar a luz-parir* (or to give birth/to bear).

This cultural predilection for the drastic elimination of intermediate categories, of intermediate routes, of compromises is also encountered outside the strictly social realm. It is worth noting the preference for *"dilemas"* (or choices between extremes) in the *criollo* use of language, which Ramón Emilio Jiménez illustrates with numerous examples.[2]

The language also reflects the emphasis on distance: measure the distance, keep one's distance, those above, those below, this order comes from above. The language itself shows a great distance between solemn or sacred language and the daily or profane. The first is not limited to religious or other social occasions of an "official" character; instead, it is also used on important occasions in the family circle. Nor are the *"cultos"* (or the civilized) the ones who master the ceremonial idiom, for "anyone (even the illiterates)" can *say a few words* in a similar extraordinary situation, using "words, expressions, and turns of phrase that no one would dare to employ in everyday speech." Such a repertory is called *un dominguero* (that is, for Sunday use) in some regions of Latin America.[3]

As we already noted in a previous chapter, the emphasis on distance, determined by the culture, is closely tied to formalistic and narcissistic tendencies, and in nineteenth-century society these three characteristics appear on all social levels. The social distance between spouses and between them and their children was—at least in name—quite great, and also (and specifically) the child from the poor rural regions of the country was supposed to kneel down on the road if he met his godfather and to ask his blessing, while the latter would never omit taking off his hat on meeting his *compadre* or *comadre*. The "singular peasant courtliness" that Jiménez describes was part of that aspect of Dominican popular culture that was formalistic, an emphasizer of distance, "aristocratic."

It is apparent that the "aristocratic" image of social stratification that we have described is founded as much on a totality of cultural ideas deeply rooted and resistent to change as on a social reality—or an abstraction of it— that ought perhaps to be located in the Spanish middle ages. What interests us here is how an image of such stratification could be maintained in a period like the second half of the nineteenth century, when one could speak in the Dominican Republic of notable social mobility and of a stratification that was being extended and complicated.

Regarding politico-military mobility, we already spoke of the heroic ideology, which also justified the status of hero—and especially so—for persons with origins among the common people. The qualities of military and political "opportunism" and of knowing how to take advantage of the opportunity to cover oneself with glory were the ones that, along with a personal history of suffering and the corresponding self-control, could place a person in a leading position. This bonus to whoever knew how to make use of "opportunity" implied a recognition of the vicissitude, of the lottery nature, of the caprice of destiny as a determinant in the individual's career. As the fortune of the sectors devoted to industry and commerce was linked in such a close way to the politico-military apparatus—recall the "marketplace" character of this last—it was not surprising that here, too, individual mobility would often be seen as the result of a personal relation with fortune, rather than as reward for a sense of thrift, industriousness, or other "puritan" virtues, whose secret the circles of recent immigrants seemed to guard up to that time. Thus—and not without reason—in this type of society it was a heroic ideology that emphasized destiny rather than a Calvinist-Darwinian type of ideology, more a faith in the variability of fortune than in the regularity of social reward, that legitimized mobility. And as what was legitimized in each case was an individual, and not a group of individuals in similar circumstances and with equal "opportunities" or even "rights" to compensation, the growing mobility could be reconciled with the rigid image of stratification that the "aristocratic" culture imposed.

It is necessary to add that, as Bonó says in another context, "Revelation is the only thing that should guide us, our analytic power has not yet reached an adequate level."[4] This observation fits in perfectly with what Karl Mannheim says in relation to the preference of aristocratic culture for morphological thought over the analytical, and the significance of revelation, rather than rational argument, as a source of truth. This model of thought operates—also as a consequence of real or imagined social distance—in terms of social complexes, without paying much attention to process or to analysis. It can be illustrated well with a passage, with the indispensable classical comparisons, from an 1888 manifesto in which "various citizens" of Monte Cristi, idealizing an earlier period in the republic's history, recall "when being the Chief of State was something like a semi-God, and the capital of the Republic with its chiming, its brilliant uniforms, and its lofty domes, was, especially for us, the poor *cibaeños*, a sort of Rome of Popes and Caesars"[5]. This is a fantasy on the ideal political hierarchization that finds its parallels in the fantasies on social stratification—classico-aristocratic images from which only a few thinkers of empirical, scientific orientation, like Bonó and Hostos, or political leaders of skeptical-political orientation, like Heureaux, escaped.

Undoubtedly, the political and social convulsions that began in 1790 in the French part of Hispaniola and that, with respect to Santo Domingo, reached their temporary climax with Toussaint L'Ouverture's invasion in 1800, had profound consequences for social stratification. A sizable emigration of members of the highest social strata, with their capital, began. Ferrand's active economic policy between 1804 and 1810 may have produced a momentary economic recovery, but the period of *"la España boba"* was once again one of economic depression, and it has been said that "the widespread poverty was such that distinct classes almost ceased to exist; the purchasing powers of the *hacendado* and the free mulatto were on a par."[6] It must be noted alongside this item that sometimes it is precisely economic levelling that makes social dividing lines more rigid.

Over the effects of the Haitian domination (1822-44) opinions are more divided. The classical opinion is that expressed in the 16 January 1844 manifesto by the Trinitarios (members of La Trinitaria, a pro-independence secret society organized in 1838). According to this manifesto, Boyer:

> obliged the principal and richest families to emigrate, and with them the talent, the wealth, the commerce, and the agriculture: he kept away from his counsel and from the principal positions the men who could have represented the rights of their fellow citizens; he reduced many families to indigence, seizing their properties in order to add them to the Republic's domains, and to give them to individuals from the western part, or to sell them to them at the very lowest prices. He burned the fields, destroyed agriculture and trade, despoiled the churches of their wealth, contemptuously trampled and humbled the ministers of religion, took away their incomes and rights. Later, he issued a law so that the goods of absent persons, whose brothers and relatives are still living submerged in misery, would go to the State . . . he prohibited the commonage of the *terrenos comuneros* . . . in order to make use of them in favor of his State, ending the breeding of animals and impoverishing a multitude of heads of families.[7]

Hostos's opinion, although also severe, attempts to see the favorable part as well:

> The African wave beneficently swept away slavery, the privileges of caste and those of origin, and kept in suspension the Caucasian elements that could resist it in such a way . . . that the Haitians' sway over the Dominicans during the twenty-two years could be better considered as a social fact than as a political event. That predominance did considerable damage to civil society because it was the predominance of the barbarians during which the constitution of the family and of property, the progress of ideas, and the course of civilization suffered a profound illness; but it did the political society the inestimable benefit of democratizing it and equalizing it to the point of erasing from mind and customs the notion of privileged authority and the caste difference. Thus, thanks to that, when the hour to expulse the Haitians struck, a Government of equals, for whites, blacks, and *mestizos*, could be formed, without the whites' arguing with the *mestizos* or the blacks over their political and social elevation, and without the *mestizos* and the blacks' being discontented about obeying white men as leaders.[8]

In our day Juan Bosch has defended an opinion that is completely opposed to Hostos's "democratizing" theory: since Boyer's regime was *latifundista*, "in the Dominican section, the old colonial group of the large landholders was reinforced." These last, supported by members of the Dominican clergy, were precisely the ones who desired the country's independence, after the overthrow of Boyer by his most liberal opponents in 1843.[9] The fact that under Boyer a rural code that actually reestablished a system of forced labor was introduced seems to support Bosch's theory. On the other hand, there can be no doubt that the departure of people and capital in this period must have caused sufficient damages to the economic structure for it to be unable to recover in the short term. Thus, Bosch's opinion that "during the Haitian government the country had recovered from its earlier misery" seems exaggerated.[10]

It also seems likely that the Haitian period would prompt important social changes, possibly similar to the ones that Hostos points out, but more research on this topic is necessary. After the social structure had attained the beginnings of stability in the First Republic (1844-61)—in a period of little less than economic stagnation, but in which the threat from Haiti led to a certain degree of solidarity—the annexation to Spain and the War of Restoration afterward (1863-65) caused new social disturbances that Hostos as well as Bonó considered grave. According to the former, the annexation came at a "social moment that . . . would have favored the formation of a modest, obscure, through strong and lively society," and it "interrupted normal development and with the war provoked the jumbling of the worst with the best social elements, bringing about the predominance of the worst."[11] Bonó pointed out that *caudillaje* (or bossism) had its first opportunities for proliferation with the Restoration, "when the intermediate classes . . . extant [during the First Republic], all their wealth lost with the fires and devastations of the war, and discredited by the Annexation to which they almost all contributed, in utter political defeat until today [1895] . . . have been unable to regain their old position as preponderant class, with respectable credentials for leading and restraining."[12] Although these observations seem to refer only to the political system, their possible validity would extend outside the limits of that system: as we saw earlier, political, military, and economic fortunes were closely linked, and a success in one of these sectors represented a victory for one's comrades in the other two and a defeat for one's competitors in the marketplace system that predominated in the three sectors. In these three social sectors the political and the military were linked in such a way that even for analytical purposes, it makes little sense to attempt to differentiate painstakingly between them.

The War of Restoration, carried out on the Dominican side without an organized army and presenting, instead, the character of a popular guerrilla war in fact gave a considerable number of persons from the lower social strata the opportunity to ascend the politico-military ladder rapidly; after the victory as heroes of the Restoration they—and sometimes the second generation as well—could demand some national distinction, with the corresponding rights to material reward. Figures like Heureaux, Luperón, and Guillermo (whose influence was short lived) came from marginal social groups, a fact that had not been the case (or at least not to such an extent) with the earlier *caudillos* Santana and Báez. The former, once their prestige had been won and their abilities as leaders demonstrated, managed to maintain their influence in the country in the following decades, manipulating, at least at first, the moral sway that their status as *Restauradores* gave them in the face of leaders from the highest social groups, who, according to Bonó's observation, were compromised as *españolizantes*.

In a social system like the Dominican one, the individual maintains many close ties with family, at least to the level of second cousins, then with ritual kin—co-parents and godchildren, whose number increases as the individual's social importance grows—as well as with neighbors and to a certain extent with those who belong to his *patria chica*, and finally sometimes also with his *"frercitos"* in Masonry. In such a social system the lives of many are influenced if one of them achieves the politico-military ascent that we are treating here. Occasional material favors to maintain or improve one's position are periodically given, almost as an obligation, by the one who has risen. This last person will fill the largest possible number of positions of trust with old friends and relatives whose personal loyalty to him—the primordial requirement in this system—is proven.

He will bind his old acquaintances to his person, granting them *asignaciones* and pensions from the public treasury, and giving their sons "recommendations" for business or scholarships in order to prepare for a profession. In turn, those whose situations have been improved by their protector's influence can favor numerous individuals within their extensive network of social relations—something that is expected of them. In this way "the cortege of men who have in the Dominican Republic come out of the poor, hardworking class and have distinguished themselves in various paths of life," a group described by Luperón and to which he considered himself to belong,[13] could, each of them, determine the social and economic position of a number of people.

The total number of those being favored this way was undoubtedly large enough to be considered a *social* phenomenon. However, this *politico-social mobility* had few long-term consequences as long as political and revolutionary regimes alternated rapidly, as was the case in the seventies. The ascents were rapid, but the period of favoritism was minimal, and in his fall the politico-social protector dragged down the majority of his clients. Hostos did not speak idly of the "sudden social and political ascents that the crises of revolution favor." It is interesting to point out that he considered this abrupt mobility one of the causes of what he called "a species of secret respect for oneself that dominates in all [the Dominicans] and that sometimes exacts consideration for everyone."[14] It was only in the eighties and specifically during Heureaux's regime that the system of favors began to operate for the permanent benefit of a larger number of political clients. The principal cause of this fact is the long duration of the regime. Those who during this period managed to keep themselves in a politically favorable position had the opportunity to consolidate the economic position improved thanks to political protection and to give their children an education or a career that, along with the economic means they would inherit, would make them acceptable as marriage partners within the strata they had earlier considered "higher." Other factors that made the social and economic advantages of the political favorites during Heureaux's regime more permanent were first, the growth and improved organization of the governmental apparatus, including the army, and second, the country's economic growth during the last two decades of the century, which created new positions in numerous sectors of the society, while at the same time the expansion and improvement of the educational system could provide a larger number of persons with the abilities required for the new positions.

But with this last factor we move away from the type of mobility inherent in this politico-social system and begin to discuss the type of mobility inherent in the economic changes of the period: *structural mobility*. The rise of the modern plantations; the increased, modernized production of coffee and cacao; the increase in the number of small industries, occupations, and professions; the installation and maintenance of the telegraph, telephone, electricity network, and railway routes; the construction or improvement of harbors and highways; the added number of educational institutions and a larger governmental apparatus—each of these factors, whatever might have been their mutual influence, represented the creation, at various levels, of work opportunities that previously had either not existed or only done so in a rudimentary form.

Thus the important changes in the economic structure in this period resulted in the increased complexity of the social stratification: the middle section of the social ladder became, we can assume, quantitatively broader, the number of rungs on it increased; in the higher and lower parts of the ladder new rungs appeared. So, through the creation of the modern, capitalist agricultural industry emerged a salaried proletariat that, although rural in origin and culture, had practically no knowledge of land tenancy and was incorporated completely into the growing money economy. In addition, there were the cane workers who with the slow season returned to their *conucos* in other regions of the country, thus creating the phenomenon of seasonal migration.

The growing demand for agricultural workers was filled in part by the Dominicans themselves, some dispossessed from their small plots as the sugar plantations in the South expanded and obliged to work for a salary, and others coming from other parts of the country, attracted by the prospect of a relatively high salary in the period of the sugar harvest. As for the rest, those who augmented the numbers of laborers were immigrants from other regions of the Caribbean, especially from the small British islands: the *cocolos*. At the other extreme of the socioeconomic scale emerged for the same reasons a group (composed partly of Dominicans, partly of immigrants) of owners of large agricultural enterprises; merchants and financiers of the new products; importers of materials used in infrastructure projects; and founders of small or medium-sized factories for beer, soft drinks, ice, soap, and so forth. This group turned out to be much more numerous than the comparable group that had existed previously—and that, like the tobacco merchants and rum makers, had lived principally in the Cibao—and was able to move the country's nucleus to the South, especially to the capital.

Regarding the intermediate section of the social scale, one must remember the *colonos* and the technical personnel of the *centrales*, the new technical occupations like telegraphers and electricians, the new groups of novice businessmen in the cities and the countryside, the increase in teaching personnel, and the growth of the tertiary sector of the economy in general. A city like Santiago had its first silversmith in 1878, its first tobacco shop in 1880, two years later its first billiard parlors and café-restaurants, its first tinsmith in 1886, the first lumber business in 1897, and in the following year cement was imported for the first time—all economic innovations that expanded the list of occupations.[15]

We already saw earlier how the numerous immigrant groups contributed to filling the gaps created in the economic structure. The urban descendants of the U.S. Methodists were employed in education, and later in the navy while others were artisans, with their daughters and sisters not infrequently nurses. The Sephardic Jews were largely in urban commerce, also contributing to intellectual life and more and more involved in holding public offices. The Canary Islanders, more recent immigrants, were in part *colonos* or autonomous farmers, in part in the cities as artisans and small merchants. Those from the Iberian peninsula were also active as urban merchants, but soon experienced strong competition from the Arabs. The Cubans are remembered principally for their role as pioneers in the sugar industry, but also for supplying many artisans. The Puerto Ricans made a similar contribution, but are associated especially with the education work of Hostos and Baldorioty de Castro and the diplomatic efforts of Betances. The Haitians, along with the immigrants from British islands, were workers on the large plantations and *conuqueros* in the western parts of the country. Curaçaoans above all were small merchants and artisans in the capital and contributed, like the Italians, to the organization of the navy. Finally, a small number of European technicians and doctors came to the country in the eighties for the construction of the railroad and remained. It is a known fact that the great majority of these immigrants were men, a factor that contributed to their mixing in a social and cultural sense with the Dominican population. Of the groups mentioned here, it was only the Arabs who, at least in the first generation— that is, until the beginning of the twentieth century—practiced endogamy.

However, it would be mistaken to assume that the immigrants occupied all the new positions in the expanding economy or that the economic betterment of the Dominicans could only be brought about by marrying an immigrant! Not only could many favored by the regime take advantage of the growing number of remunerative positions through the type of politico-social mobility noted earlier, but in addition many Dominicans found a more desirable social and economic position through their own initiative in this period of expansion. Among the first large producers of sugar, coffee, and cacao, there certainly were Dominicans. The greater demand for doctors, lawyers, and teaching personnel prompted by the rapid demographic growth and the increasing prosperity of some groups was met in greatest part by Dominicans. We already saw that the system of official and private assistance gave many the opportunity to ascend the social ladder in a short time.

The curious book of the "*memorioso*" Francisco Veloz, in which he meticulously brings together details about the inhabitants of the capital city *barrio* La Misericordia between the years 1894 and 1916 gives even more examples of such social ascents, also putting in relief the importance that the lower middle class of the urban population attributed to education and to the professions. The case of the shoemaker Pichardo, whom he mentions, and who became the solicitor general of the republic, is exceptional in itself and also illustrates the fact that in the period that we are examining the potential for mobility of both a politico-social and a structural nature made significant ascents possible. The fact that of Veloz's teachers in his *barrio*'s "primary school for males" three later became doctors, one a lawyer, one a notary public, and one a surveyor is a further illustration.

The institution of "*lector*" (or reader) in the tobacco shops offers a picturesque instance of stimulating love for education; it is described in detail with respect to Cuba by Fernando Ortiz, but was not missing from Santo Domingo either. Together the cigar makers paid this *lector*, who entertained them by reading to them during their monotonous work and moderating the discussions that the reading often occasioned. Veloz mentions one *lector* who was also a teacher and notes that "some" of the cigar makers from the tobacco shop he described later became school teachers.[16] In this context one should mention again the night schools, some of which were financed by Masonry, and the classes organized by the artisans' guilds. However, the demand for well-trained artisans was not adequately met by the Dominicans themselves. Bonó attributes this to the Spanish colonial past and to slavery, which made it so that manual work enjoyed little prestige: "a poor employee, a middle-level shopkeeper, or a produce speculator" would not want to put his son into a trade, and the earlier initiatives on the part of the government to teach soldiers a trade in the arsenals had foundered. Thus, Dominican mahogany was for a long time worked abroad—St. Thomas, Curaçao—for want of native cabinetmakers.[17] Accordingly it must have been foreigners (Cubans, Spaniards, Curaçaoans) who would have made up the majority of fine artisans in our period.

The phenomenon of social mobility noted up to now did not appear equally throughout the country. The most obvious changes took place, on one hand, in the new sugar area, where a new type of "capitalist" agrarian society emerged and, on the other hand, in the largest cities, where the growing number of well-to-do people and the economic sectors that provided services especially for that group were located.

One must remember that the expansion of education benefitted principally the cities in that period. In large parts of the country only slight changes occurred—weak vibrations derived from the dramatic economic events in the new economic centers. In the Cibao the growing importance of raising cacao and coffee brought about a population increase. A *común* like San Francisco de Macorís, which only had eight thousand people in 1849, had thirty thousand in 1881. Among them were many migrants from the western part of the country who had fled from the Haitian invasions that occurred between 1844 and 1856. There were also farmers from the rural areas of Santiago and Moca who had abandoned their fields after the Restoration and "the social revolution that implied the destruction of so much wealth and hierarchies in that city [Santiago] and its *común*," fleeing the "endemic anarchy" roiling up in these rural areas. The consequence of this migration was that the livestock raising that occupied so much land in the vicinity of San Francisco would disappear. Some of the traditional livestock breeders imitated the recent arrivals and devoted themselves to raising the new products; others sold their lands and departed for the interior, which was less densely populated, to continue their pastoral activities there. Thus, the *hatos* traditionally devoted to livestock in both the Cibao and the South were turned over to agriculture and converted into *estancias* (or farms), and new ranches were started in the mountains and mountainous country, that is, in the regions until then less populated. The developing agriculture drove away livestock raising, with its extensive use of land, to economically and geographically marginal regions, and the boundary between the two activities began a prolonged movement of expansion. In the Cibao, too, the emergence of modern agriculture prompted the departure of small farmers who sold their lands for prices that seemed high, or who sometimes were brutally dispossessed of their lands. They went to join the seasonal rural proletariat that "goes nomadically from mines to plantations; from plantations to railroads; from hogs to cutting logwood; that has forgotten its *bohío*, its farm, its *conucos*."[18]

One part of that group would have left for the cities, where they established their own *barrios*, built in the primitive rural tradition. At the end of the century the capital, viewed from the sea, seemed like a cluster of huts: "nothing is visible except the heap of ramshackle *bohíos* that occupies the entire southern side of the city"; they hid the colonial monuments and the center of the city from view.[19] But desires for greater material comfort awoke not only in the city: "Earlier . . . the slave or the overseer on the ranches needed only two pigsties: one for shutting in the hogs, the other for a dwelling; a plot of two to four *tareas* for bananas and the other daily supplies for *sancocho*, two changes of coarse clothing, a machete, and a knife with its sharpening steel, and tobacco to chew or smoke. . . . Today [1881] it is not like that, civilization has continued filtering in to them little by little with the immediate contact of the farmers who have emigrated to those places, with the journeys . . . that the wars obliged them to make into the cities and agricultural regions, and with the continuous, direct communication in which these very wars have kept him with cultured men."[20] Thus, finally even the *monteros*, personification of the soldier-like, coarse "cowboy" from the old livestock-raising *hatos*, "half-naked, machete in hand," who had formed the nucleus of the traditional guerrilla forces (like the *mambís* rebels of 1863) began to know and to feel the attraction of the greater comfort that others possessed.[21] But this did not mean either then or now that the growing aspirations would be fulfilled or that they would lead in some other way to social results. In fact, in large areas of the country the old social and economic structure with the corresponding social stratification predominated, while in others began the sometimes laborious accommodation of new social categories on the scale of social values, which consequently started to change.

Any attempt to describe the social structure that immediately preceded the agrarian and economic changes of the eighties cannot, because of lack of data, be anything but an outline. It seems certain that each region—Línea Noroeste,* the South, the Cibao, and so forth—had its own pattern of stratification and that it was difficult to conceive of a social hierarchy of a national sort, apart from the formal political one. One could mention, depending upon the economic and geographic characteristics of each region, in an ascending line, the poorest, the ones who lacked lands, who were ready "to work for food" or "to live as a dependent," willing to work a year for some product of value like a revolver;[22] then the peons and *monteros* from the *hatos*; the ranchers and the *conuqueros*; the overseers from the larger enterprises; and finally the owners of these enterprises, the *hateros*, who often lived in the nearby towns and invested their money in houses.

In the Cibao the tobacco growers whose enterprises were of intermediate size formed a rural middle class that practically did not exist in other parts of the country. In the villages themselves were the unspecialized workers, the male servants, the laundresses and ironers, as well as cooks and seamstresses; then a category of small artisans and grocers, some of whom tried to increase their incomes by acting as musicians; employees in the somewhat larger stores, employees of the government and in the small offices of lawyers and notaries, teaching personnel, and finally the more important merchants and the professionals; these last two groups also tended to own

---

*For interesting data about the different "cultural" phases in the Línea Noroeste and their influences on the landscape, see Gustavo A. Antonini, "Processes and Patterns of Landscape Change in the Línea Noroeste, Dominican Republic," mimeographed, 1968.

land. Money was scarce, social contact outside one's own village or region was infrequent, family life tended economically to autarchy and socially to the intimacy of its own *barrio* and of its own extended group of relatives. Social relations with subordinates had a very paternalistic character. The meager possibilities for obtaining social prestige by means of the emphatic consumption of commercial goods may have contributed to making those social dividing lines between social groups that were not of an economic nature more rigid.

Here we mention, for example, the time that a family had resided in a region or a village, the extent to which this factor identified it with the region where it lived, and thus the *"abolengo"* (or lineage) that this family had and that was recognized by regional, sometimes even national, collective memory—a recognition that, because of its scarcity, was of the greatest social importance, given that the turbulent history of the republic had made many of the "old" families disappear. "In the Dominican Republic," wrote Luperón, "there are numerous families who have earned well the indispensable privilege of always being noteworthy, through a continuity of interesting services that elevate them and single them out as meriting general consideration, each time that public need appeals to their principal figures." He mentions in this context the Moya family of La Vega, "one of the oldest and most memorable of the Province of La Vega Real. Its origins are lost with the primitive founders of La Vega."[23]

It is appropriate to wonder whether in the seventies of the nineteenth century there were more than a very few of these "noteworthy families" that would have been able to prove their descent from families of the colonial period. It seems more probable to assume that those among the relatively wealthy who in the subsequent period of jumbled immigrations could point out family ties with the country that dated back to the First Republic, already had a good chance of being envied and praised for their lineage, even more so if they found among their relations any who would have participated in the struggle against Haiti or against Spain. Once the prestige of the family name was established upon this basis, economic fortune could make it more impressive, but—at least for a few generations—economic reverses could not tarnish it. Outside the largest towns, some regional surnames also attained considerable prestige in this way, which assured those who bore them "certain considerations in any sector of the national territory." Examples are Bencosme from Moca, Goico from El Seibo, Monrrobel from Luperón, Minyetty and Custorios from Ocoa, Cid from El Copey, and Camilo from Salcedo.[24]

It seems, nevertheless, mistaken to attribute to this type of social collectivity in the period that we are treating the character of a social caste with all the social impenetrability and exclusivity this term implies. Rather, it is surprising in the last decades of the century to find an opposite tendency: the great porosity of the old nuclei of "respectable" families with respect to the recent immigrants, especially those from Europe and the surrounding Spanish-speaking region, who had very few difficulties in being able to marry members of those families. The poorest branches of these families perhaps came to the conclusion that the changing economic structure was going to give increasing importance to possession of money and that the prestige of merely a name was going to diminish more and more. The members of the "old" families that owned lands saw, as the value of these increased, that the economic factor supported their social position, quickly converting them into desirable matrimonial candidates for the well-to-do merchant-immigrants and their children. Undoubtedly, the desire on the part of the old families "to improve the stock" through ties with foreigners, preferably Europeans, played a role. Thus, marriage settlements based on mutual benefit occurred, with local prestige on one side, new fortune and European physical features on the other. From these only the Arabs and Chinese among the recent arrivals found themselves excluded for the moment.

The upper social stratum that began to take shape from this union of old *Dones* and new *Señores* was distinguished in two ways from the earlier elites. In the first place the improved methods in the national system of communication—roads, telephone, telegraph, and so forth—meant that the barriers between the various regional stratifications were slowly eroded so that for the first time since independence, a *national* bourgeoisie could *begin* to develop. In the second place, this group's numerical growth was such that it was placed in the position of being able to act more than before as an active instrument of social pressure and control. Numerical growth also resulted in a larger supply of "leading intellectuals"—previously closely linked with the few "old" families—this group becoming large enough to occupy the highest administrative levels of the government bureaucracy and to attempt at the same time to monopolize it. Thus we see operating at the end of the century a process that can be labelled the consolidation of the national bourgeoisie.

It is no coincidence that the most exclusive social clubs in the capital and in Santiago were established precisely during these years. This was, rather, the *final result* of that process, which led in the last decade of the nineteenth century and the first decade of the twentieth to an isolation of a "caste" nature of those who were considered, many of them since only recently, "*de primera*" (of the highest category). In a political sense this meant that the new bourgeoisie developed during Heureaux's dictatorship, and in part thanks to it, felt the need to assert its influence on the exercise of power, a factor that led—at least indirectly—to the regime's fall. Since that time it has proven much more improbable, even today, that a person of the social background of a Heureaux or a Guillermo might obtain the presidency.

In a social sense, the increasing national influence and exclusivity of the upper group naturally meant a clearer awareness of their own social position in those who, located directly below the first on the social ladder, could not ascend to the uppermost rung or did so, if by chance, with great difficulty:

those *"de segunda"* (second-class), a "middle group" that, as we saw before, must have grown considerably in that period. Nevertheless, this middle class was, in terms of its own composition, quite heterogeneous; it comprised artisans and small merchants and storekeepers, teachers, and even those lawyers whose reduced economic success or whose excessively dark features made their social ascent difficult, as well as those members of the groups of white immigrants whose economic luck had not been adequate to make them acceptable to the highest groups. When their number was sufficiently large, they continued, like the *isleños* in the capital, to live in their own *barrios*. Even the middle group's heterogeneous character hindered the existence of a lifestyle, an economic ethic, or a social solidarity that would include all.

Regarding social solidarity, it is necessary to note that *opportunities* for greater ascent were also so varied for the diverse groups of this conglomerate that the awareness of a common social destiny could not develop; moreover, the patron-client system implied that one would attempt to improve his chances by means of individual ties with one or more protectors rather than by the social action of the fellow members of his class. Even in 1953 Mejía-Ricart indicated that the members of this sector "seek their own means, which isolates them from those who are their fellows and are at the same stage of transition or aspiration, insofar as they try to raise themselves from the social plane on which they live . . . retaining profound gratitude and good friendship for one from a higher class who treats [them] on a basis of equality."[25]

Although *socially effective* resentment did not exist—or scarcely did—in that sector in the period we are considering, this did not mean that comments, often humorous ones, were not made about the changes that were occurring. Many anecdotes about President Heureaux have been preserved—ones in which he treats the *"honorables"* or "everyone said to be great in this country" with skepticism, putting them in their just place. In his appointments he was guided by considerations that were in themselves neutral with respect to the "lineage" of the candidates and that, before all, were supposed to guarantee loyalty to his person. In this sector of his activities he could, therefore, rely on the gratitude of many people from the middle and lower strata, as can be seen in an 1891 editorial from *El Eco del Pueblo* that commented on those appointments: "[Earlier] an individual was sought for his *categoría* [or status] (certainly rancid in those times), because he belonged to such and such a circle, because he was Don So-and-so or Don Such-and-such, toying in that way with public matters as if . . . dealing with slaves. Today, fortunately, things have changed, the slave has turned into a Señor."[26] It is in this period that the term *"tutumpote,"* which refers to the powerful rich[27] and has been popularized in our time by Juan Bosch, appears frequently. Similarly, the term *culebrón* (social climber): the person giving a party protected himself against these last, requiring a list of the guests beforehand.[28]

Thus we see that at the end of the century, when the consequences of the dramatic changes in the economic and demographic realm began to crystallize socially, the lines of demarcation between the social categories became more profound. The bourgeoisie began to shut itself off with respect to the upper level of the middle class; in the lower strata a similar process took place, the word *Señá* or *Señó* remaining reserved for "those persons from among the people who were distinguished by their respectability," raising them from what was called "*el montón anónimo*" (the anonymous crowd).[29] The expansion of the cities had also underscored geographically the line of demarcation between the groups, as new *barrios* for the rich were built and the "*rancherías*" of the rural immigrants added. It is not surprising that the social exclusivism of the upper class would prompt similar tendencies in the lower class: "The people of color also had their social centers and in their rules, the limitations stand out. One of these societies that attained prestige was . . . 'La Perla Negra' in 19 de Marzo Street" in the capital.[30] It is worthwhile pointing out that this sort of phenomenon was also limited principally to the largest cities. In a little village like Azua, where the changes had not caused so much commotion, the social boundaries continued to be those from before, and those who wanted to improve their economic luck had to resort to migration to other regions of the country. There were few jobs available in the village itself for the younger generations, even those from the "upper class"; "thus, these young people marry, in order to be able to live, for they know that the woman's family maintains both; . . . here, anyone who is not a merchant does not have enough even for cigarettes, because there are neither jobs nor businesses that employ them."[31]

In the preceding pages we have given special attention to the growth, in absolute terms, of the upper and middle classes of the society because the direct social consequences of this growth seem to be the most apparent. Nevertheless, one should not lose sight of the fact that the *relative* numerical growth of these sectors must have been much smaller than that of the lowest economic strata. The tripling of the population in the last quarter of the century has to be explained not so much by its own natural growth, but, above all, by immigration of (plantation) workers, especially from the surrounding Caribbean area. For each Arab merchant, European technician, or Cuban sugar entrepreneur must have entered tens of laborers, who mixed over the course of several decades with their Dominican fellow workers.

The diversity of origin of the lowest social class, as well as its roles in the so very diverse economic subsystems contributed to counteracting, at least in the eighties and nineties, the development of any effective class consciousness at the national level. A portion of them participated in the patron-client structure or through the possession of small plots of land was set apart from the rural proletariat on the plantations who lacked land. But it goes without question that the numbers of the poorest grew disproportionately in this period in comparison with the middle and higher sectors; that the distance between the wealthiest and the poorest became considerably greater; and that the rural regions remained far behind the two largest cities with respect to the expansion of education and other channels of mobility. Only the army and the police retained their attractiveness as institutions for betterment of position of the young *campesino*. The new bourgeoisie gave little prestige to the military forces, even at the highest ranks. To the extent that a process of bureaucratization of the apparatus of sanction was developing, partly in a later period, better education was being required of the officer corps—an advantageous thing for those who came from the village middle class; however, in more recent periods, internal training cancelled out this advantage, at least in part. At any rate, the immense majority of the *campesinos* continued to be employed, naturally, in agriculture; the access of many of them to the growing cash economy not only gave the itinerant Arabs new business, but also created more devotees of gambling and liquor, prompting worried commentaries on rural vices.

But it was naturally in the largest cities where the greatest distancing between rich and poor could be observed. In Santo Domingo the number of beggars, particularly children, increased in the nineties. The *Listín* organized a campaign to solve this problem and to prevent children from selling lottery tickets.[32] Charitable institutions were organized: Francisco Billini founded his Charity Home and his Orphans' Asylum; there was also a "Societé de Bienfaisance." Prostitution in the capital took on such proportions that officials resorted to compulsory registration.[33] Many of these prostitutes came from the neighboring islands, by whose names *barrios* in which they lived were called: "gay women, young, white, cultured, and pretty, who came from Puerto Rico and Cuba. Some of these girls had received careful education, spoke more than one language, could make agreeable conversation, and played the piano marvelously," writes the astonished Gómez Alfau,[34] but among them were some who in a drunken state threw themselves into the sea, thus provoking press commentaries about this sort of suicide attempt.[35]

Indeed, the news in the press of the nineties reveals that the frequency of suicides increased in a disquieting fashion on other social levels as well. Thus, in 1890 *El Porvenir* of Puerto Plata dedicated an editorial to this phenomenon, attributing it to moral perversion, bad examples, increased vice, poor domestic upbringing, and scorn for religion. And three years later *La Prensa* of Santiago asserted that suicide could be, it was sure, a heroic deed in some cases, "but the majority of instances are caused by an excess of alienation." In the last half-year of the century three suicides in the capital attracted the attention of the "upper circles": one for unknown reasons, one for alcoholism, another for honor.[36] In fact, suicide attempts were not infrequently the result of disappointments in love, like the one in March 1893 in which a Señorita Ramírez, twenty years old, "daughter of a reputable Spanish artisan and a poor, humble, though honorable woman," killed herself with a revolver. Other female suicides were carried out with this firearm, but there were also attempts to set oneself on fire. Men always used firearms; only one Tomás Domínguez from Mao, who failed on attempting suicide with a revolver and out of jealousy, took a Collins knife and cut off his own head.[37] The youth Joaquín Joubert (a) Blanco in Samaná acted more cautiously: "After arranging his affairs, dressing himself in black, giving food to an unfortunate, twenty-five centavos to an old beggar, studying his music lesson, practicing a funeral march, taking off his shoes, and locking himself in his room, he took his own life, firing a shot from a revolver."[38]

If the deduction that the press attention indicates a growing number of suicides is correct, the simpliest explanation would be to relate this phenomenon to the rapid social and economic changes and the arrival of new inhabitants. Many must have suffered a break with a past that was familiar to them and with a traditional social environment, and they must have interpreted this experience psychologically in terms of a greater solitude and uncertainty, an anomie for which the surest solution seemed to be provided by a shot from a revolver.* Indeed, although official publications and invitations still indicated social categories in a traditional way, being addressed to the "señoritas" and the "respectable matrons," to "la Juventud" (or young people), to the "People" and the "Associations,"[39] the conflict between the image of culturally determined stratification as static and the dynamism of the recent changes—no matter the form in which it was expressed or felt—had to produce psychological consequences. And for the moment these changes could only corroborate Bonó's careful analysis: "Dominican society does not have the cohesion indispensable for any human grouping that wants to be definitively independent, absolute owner of its destiny. Particularism, individualism, forms the basis of our national character."[40] It is not difficult to understand that in the period we are treating this individualism could easily become psychological isolation, when geographic and/or social mobility weakened the ties with the family environment more than the society and, consequently, the individual considered normal.

RACE RELATIONS AND THE ATTITUDE TOWARD HAITI

On 22 May 1893 María Nansi of Puerto Plata celebrated her 100th birthday. As a girl nine years old she had been abducted by a slave trader in Africa and brought to Santo Domingo.[41] At the end of the eighteenth century slaves were still imported with regularity, and there was a "commissioner of the Negro trade"; the last shipments probably took place in the period of "la España boba." On the day following his entry into Santo Domingo on 28 January 1801, Toussaint L'Ouverture had proclaimed the abolition of slavery—only to introduce later a system of compulsory labor. During the Fer-

---

*It is obvious from the facts presented, and from the publicity they received, that there is no basis for attributing the increase in suicides in the nineties to political factors.

rand regime slavery, as well as the slave trade, was reestablished, with Haitian prisoners (of war) defined as slaves and designated in part for export. In the first year of the Boyer government slavery was abolished for the second time, by then for good.

Slavery as a juridico-economic system depended, as far as the character of the dealings between master and slave are concerned, to a great extent on the relations of production. On the large plantations producing for a world market, the treatment of slaves was by and large more severely regimented and cruel than in the pastoral livestock enterprises. Moreover, the lot of the field slaves was generally sadder than that of slave artisans, while the household slaves received the best treatment. Closely related to these facts is the element of numerical relations: a terrifying mass of slaves and a small group of masters often prompted a terrorist regimen on the part of the latter. In the Dominican colonial period there are indications that in the first years of the economic flourishing of the plantations and mines the treatment of slaves was cruel. The first rebellion by blacks occurred as early as 1522, but as the colony went on in the following centuries to become more and more a livestock territory, relations with slaves became more benign and paternalistic—excepting perhaps the sugar-producing slaves like those west of the capital (Los Ingenios), where over the course of time several revolts occurred, the last at the end of the eighteenth century.

For the slaves it was not difficult to run away, since the country was underpopulated and nature untamed, and as in Surinam and Jamaica, the runaway slaves managed to form semi-autonomous communities like Maniel de Ocoa, "where four villages were leading a free life . . . , exceeding a thousand persons overall"; that community was wiped out in 1655. The independence of a group of rebel runaways in the sierras of Baoruco was recognized in the eighteenth century by the French authorities as well as the Spanish. Even in our day a stubborn tradition affirms that this area is populated by monstrous beings called *"bienbienes."* Moreover, the colonial authorities themselves sometimes formed black communities, like the one that in the seventeenth century was called San Lorenzo de los Negros Minas (Los Minas), on the left bank of the Ozama River north of the capital and the place where slaves who fled from the French sector were settled. Haiti's more severe regime of slavery prompted, especially in the eighteenth century, attempts at flight to the Spanish part of the island, where if only because of the scarcity of men, the authorities were not much disposed to extradite the fugitives, notwithstanding the fact that official agreements required it. These accords also stipulated that the person extradited could not be punished with a death sentence.[42]

In 1794 out of a total population of 103,000, the number of slaves was estimated at 30,000 and that of freedmen at 38,000. Slaves or former slaves were often put in charge of *hatos*; they, like the rest of the personnel on the *hatos*, went around openly armed with knives and machetes. In 1784 a law prohibiting slaves from buying their freedom "without the consent of their masters" was proposed, from which it can be deduced that this phenomenon occurred. In that period, each year there were ninety-three holidays on which the slaves did not have to work. In a "draft for a [Black] Code" that same year, it is proposed that schools not be open to blacks and first-generation mulattoes, something that apparently took place before. It was commented that "the white population does not have useful employment because the mechanical trades and retail business are in the hands of free blacks and dark-coloreds." It was further suggested that "The free blacks and the slaves called *vividores* [or spongers] who go about the countryside and rob the haciendas ought to be grouped together in settlements, to be reconcentrated in Los Minas, in particular the blacks of Montegrande, who are employed in the retailing of provisions that go on to the capital." Also mentioned: "Those who raise cotton for over twenty years, or their descendants, may be ranked as *whites*." Many slaves were used as *jornaleros* (or day laborers) in the cigar (*túbano*) factories or in other nonagricultural work "in which jobs whites or persons of intermediate color ought to be employed."

The image that these data evoke is of a very benign form of slavery, which even the protests at the end of the eighteenth century cited above would be unable to change, and also a position for freedmen quite tolerable for the era, since they—as long as they were among the lightest mulattoes—had already begun to penetrate into the priesthood and the teaching profession in the colonial period, a factor that provoked the corresponding protests on the part of the metropolitan authorities. Moreover, even in the seventeenth century a militia of blacks and mulattoes existed. The close personal contact between the master and his relatively reduced number of slaves, the work of the church, and the role of cultural transmitter that the intermediate racially mixed group played are three factors that contributed to the high degree of assimilation of Spanish colonial culture. Yet, if only because of the arrival of new slaves until the beginning of the nineteenth century, obviously African cultural traits remained in force until our time. In 1784 there was a proposal to prohibit "the ceremonies that the blacks hold in the houses when some relative dies . . . , then they pray and sing in their languages in praise of the deceased, all mixed with proper rites; they hold dances that they call '*ban-cos*.'" As late as 1844 Santana wrote about "the Africans" in his army, referring to the soldiers from Monte Grande, many of them in fact natives of the Congo.[43]

The religious *cofradías* (or associations) were at least from the sixteenth century on a vehicle for cultural and religious assimilation of the black population. At the beginning, they were organized according to African tribe or region of origin: the Cofradía de San Cosme y San Damián consisted of Arara blacks, that of Santa María Magdalena of Zape blacks, that of Nuestra Señora de La Candelaria of Biafra and Mandinga blacks. But time slowly erased the tribal differences and replaced them with solidarity among the members of the *cofradías*. In 1613 some distinguished whites also belonged to the *cofradía* of Nuestra Señora de La Candelaria. Until the nineteenth century there existed in the capital the *cofradía* of San Juan Bautista, whose rules had been approved by Pope Paul III in 1602:

> The *cofradía* is one for *criollo* dark-colored people; its seat is the Cathedral Church and the entry fee is four *reales* and two *reales* for mulattoes. The officers are two majordomos, two lesser deputies, and a treasurer, a free man. The day of San Juan is their feast day; on its eves are said masses that they apply to the living and dead *cofrades* [or members of the brotherhood] . . . ; the church is "hung" and "adorned with branches" that day at the same time as festival lights . . . are set up. On Corpus Day the procession of San Juan Bautista takes place. Celebration of masses on All Saints' Day. Asking for offerings, two months before San Juan Bautista's day; works of compassion for sick *cofrades*. . . . The *cofrades*' mothers can become members of the *cofradía*, "although whoever they may be, there must be no scorning of them. . . ."

In case of death the *cofradía* provided half the cost of the burial.[44]

On San Juan's day in addition to religious services there were dances and the running of bulls. Even after the *cofradía* had disappeared, in the second half of the nineteenth century, on that day "groups of Negroes in procession, accompanying the march with songs and to the rhythm of drums" came into the capital from the outskirts to attend church. The fiesta of San Juan was naturally celebrated by the whole Christian population, but it is curious to note that the more European groups celebrated it as a "festival of fire," jumping over or riding through fire, while the lower social strata celebrated it as a "festival of water," as it still is in Baní, where people bathe in the river and submerge the saint's image; later they dance the *"saradunga"*—a name also used to allude to the fiesta itself.[45]

The twenty-two year Haitian domination as well as the sizeable later immigration of workers from Haiti and other areas of the Caribbean must have contributed to keeping alive popular customs originating in Africa. Certain elements from the Haitian cult of *vodun*—belief in *"luas"* like Baron Samedi, Metre Sili (Maitresse Erzulie, identified with Santa Rosa de Lima in Santo Domingo), Balagrí, Balenóo, and so forth—penetrated the country and remained in it, the efforts of some governments to exterminate these beliefs notwithstanding. The Dominican word *papabocó*, which acquired the meaning of influential person or apparition, is derived from the Haitian term that refers to the priest-wizard.[46] But the burials of children (*baquiní*) and the vigils for dead or dying adults are much more universal in their characteristics and cannot be attributed exclusively to Haitian or African influence.*

---

*The complicated routes through which some cultural forms were transmitted becomes evident in the example of the *carabiné*, a dance apparently introduced into the country by Canarian immigrants but learned during the 1805 siege of the capital by the Haitian troops, who executed the dance with carbines on their shoulders—hence the name. Even the command words of the dance leader continued thereafter to be given in Haitian French.

The Haitian influence penetrated speech as well. In the *Listín* of 1 August 1899 Francisco Orteo wrote an article on the many French words that had been introduced into Spanish, especially in the coastal regions of the South (sugar!) and in Samaná, where even today a patois is spoken, resulting from the strong French influence in the seventeenth and eighteenth centuries. He gave examples: *sefolé* (soufflé), *briché* (soldier's saber), *gató* (*gateau*), *roti, canotié* (sailor), *ragú* (ragout), *peti-puá, ratape* (soldier's tricorn), *fricassé, rob de cham* (*robe de chambre*), *collier, bullón* (fish soup), *madama, marshé* (market).

Although undoubtedly more cultural elements of Haitian-African influence did and do exist than many Hispanophile authors want to admit, on the other hand, the fact that in a country with such a numerous black population the folklore in its strictest sense should be predominantly Spanish is noteworthy. On collecting some 400 popular songs, games, anecdotes, verses, riddles, sayings, and stories, Edna Garrido de Boggs found only a few Africanisms in the vocabulary and only three songs that deal with the black man; the Haitian border region was the exception to this apparent continuity of the Spanish tradition. Andrade arrives at similar conclusions.[47] Although the proximity of Haiti and the penetration of its inhabitants in war and in peace was on one hand a permanent source of cultural influence, on the other the fear of the neighboring country and the feeling of being threatened by a culture and a nation considered inferior were apparently strong psychological restraints on any tendency to unlimited assimilation.

There are few Dominicans who, as we have seen, would not have considered the period of the Haitian domination as a black page in the history of a people that would have liked to be white. But it is also possible to ask oneself whether this cultivation of a collective traumatic experience has not at the same time served as an escape valve to ease the republic's internal racial situation. Thus after 1822-44 the negroid features of members of "respectable" families could be explained as results of the Haitian conquerors' barbarous cruelties. Simultaneously—as Hostos already observed—the Haitian domination had a cohesive effect on the relations among the various Dominican racial groups. The blackest groups were Dominicans too; in the struggle against Haiti, the cultural identity was more important than the racial one, although—as the saying expresses it, "He who is dark had better speak clearly"—it was always more necessary for the Dominican black to demonstrate his cultural identity than for the other social groups.

The attitude toward Haiti and political relations with that country continued to be marked during the entire nineteenth century by fear of numerical might, mixed with a certain scorn for Haiti's supposed cultural inferiority—that is, an ambiguity of feelings that would have been better hidden, at least on the political level. As Heureaux—himself insulted by his enemies as *"mañé"* (perjorative for Haitian) because of his partly Haitian descent—observed: "When one is dealing with a neighboring nation with which one was at war for a long time, fighting it for autonomy, the inhabitants of which doubt our affection, with a neighbor that aspires to possession of what belongs to us by right; that believes that the rancors that our ancestors could have transmitted to us on account of the deeds done by theirs are still alive in Dominican hearts; that rarely sees in our press, not even in official publications, a simple sign of cordiality, and that for all that and much more has reasons for living in distrust, with such a nation diplomatic relations become by nature delicate in the extreme."[48]

A border conflict of long duration strongly influenced relations between the two countries, as did the Haitian preoccupation over foreign influences in its neighbor country. These fears reached their climax when in 1893 the San Domingo Improvement Co. took charge of the claims of den Tex Bondt, and rumors that U.S. bases were going to be established in Samaná circulated.[49] Often the Haitian government loaned money—as we saw in an earlier chapter—for the Dominican election campaigns; it was also common for the government of one of the two countries to plot with revolutionaries from the neighbor country. Heureaux, for his part, visited Haiti incognito "to act as godfather for some children" in that country, where he had many relatives.[50]

The same ambiguity toward Haiti that the country demonstrated in the political realm was found at an intellectual level in a writer like Bonó. He saw the "colored race" as the bearer of Haitian civilization, but feared the numerical predominance of the blacks who from time to time managed to seize power in order to carry out an "ultrablack policy" as an "exclusivist race," something that he felt inevitably had to lead to violent aggression. But once he also wrote that Boyer's mistake had been in wanting to annex Santo Domingo to Haiti instead of basing "the union of the two peoples on a more . . . advantageous base, for example, confederation. If it had been thus, we would be more tranquil, happier, more civilized. The diverse elements of the two peoples . . . would have come together to maintain the balance of the black and white races. At present it is not possible to dream of an impossible, impractical thing, and it is necessary for each person on our side to look for new solutions for resolving our domestic problems, which for the moment seem insoluble to me."[51]

Since long before, the immense majority of Dominicans were no longer either whites nor blacks, but in biological terms, mulattoes, mixed forms of both races. 'The "*mulatización*" that Pedro Andrés Pérez describes, not without disdain, in his book *La comunidad mulata*[52] had proceeded, in fact, from quite early on. Around 1845 the French consul in Haiti, Raybaud, described the social and racial situation in Santo Domingo at the end of the eighteenth century in the following terms, attempting to explain the differences from revolutionary Haiti:

> The double layer of free blood that the conquering race and the last nucleus of the indigenous race were mixing with African blood was so

little distinguished after the second generation—the bronzed complexion of the Spaniard, the copper complexion of the Indian, and the bistre complexion of the mulatto tended to be confused to such an extent under the influence of a common hygiene and climate—that interested observers, if there had been any, would have often found themselves with a problem in discovering in the faces the secret of a genealogy lost in the savannahs and forests. This labor of fusion, which was retarded by neither European immigration, from a moral point of view, nor African immigration, from a physiological point of view, was summed up at the time of the revolution in the following figures: 25,000 whites of pure Spanish stock; 15,000 Africans, who, by being scattered, were not victims of any insurrectionist propaganda and who, moreover, felt too proud of the social superiority that daily contact with their masters imparted them over the slaves in the French section to consent to imitate the latter, whom they haughtily called "*los negros*"; finally, 73,000 mestizos who said they were white and who, as they gave no cause for injurious objections regarding themselves, had ended up being considered just that. The separatist element of the French colony [the mulattoes] had thus become the conservative element of the Spanish colony. The vanity that had dug an abyss of hatred between the three classes there had operated for their cohesion here.[53]

In the proposal for a Code of 1784 it was stipulated that "the mulattoes or *pardos* constitute the people of the Spanish island; the intermediate classes are the balance between the blacks and whites and never mix at all with the blacks, whom they hate."[54]

The lines of demarcation between white and mulatto and between mulatto and black were not, nor are they, rigidly drawn; rather, it is a matter of an extensive, fluid series of shades and racial characteristics that make any strict social division between the three principal categories impossible in practice. The social definition of "white"—what I have called in another context the normative somatic image[55]—was and is sufficiently broad to include light mulattoes as well and to make them acceptable as marriage partners. In this sense, D'Alaux's observation that the mulattoes are considered white is a description of the situation, exaggerated to be sure, that basically reflects the sociological essence—that is, the absence of a rigid barrier between the two groups. And the native blacks, thus differentiating them from those coming from the surrounding Caribbean region, he readily described as less pure racially and, consequently, more attractive aesthetically, because, in a few words, they are en route to "*mulatización*." They are more heavily concentrated in the country's southern and eastern regions and in the western border area, owing, respectively, to the sugar plantation economy and the proximity of Haiti (rather than in the Cibao).

From the foregoing material, one should not draw the conclusion that the racial factor had no social importance in the nineteenth century. Although race relations were more benign and paternalistic than in the majority of other Caribbean societies (and certainly more so than in the non-Iberian areas) being white continued to be the social and aesthetic ideal, defined as such by society. Social prejudice against the black was and is, rather, phrased in terms of aesthetic aversion.

Although in the Spanish colonial period, bureaucratic and political power was in the hands of a white elite, the vicissitudes of the first half of the nineteenth century and the emigration of many white families had changed this situation. The War of Restoration against Spain resulted in a new social cataclysm, given that the whites who remained in the country or who had returned to it were compromised as collaborators with Spain, while at the same time the war and its consequences brought numerous colored and black men to positions of great power, although frequently of short duration. The growing social and political influence of men of color in this period, added to their awareness of numerical superiority, made them proclaim more bluntly than before that their group was the "real" people. Luperón even pointed to an supposedly scientific link between men of color and the Indians: the mulattoes, "through the law of climates, [tend] to return to the primitive race of the island."[56] Luperón's candidacy for the presidency in 1887 was welcomed by Bonó in the following terms:

> It is good that the government . . . begin to think seriously about the destinies that Providence is setting aside for the blacks and mulattoes in America. From this point on these destinies are manifest, given the current numbers of this race; and I believe the island of Santo Domingo is called upon to be the nucleus, the model of its exaltation, and its embodiment in this hemisphere. And who better than you will be able to begin to place the first stones, to establish the bases of this grandeur? Who better than you can know just how necessary the white race is for attaining it, but at the same time know the superiority of combinations of this so superior race; and who better than you will be able to fuse, amalgamate, and shape a homogeneous whole out of the wisdom and the ignorance of both families so that, model of tolerance and of contention, we might place ourselves in an enviable position in the Universe?[57]

This argument in favor of the cooperation and amalgamation of the races under the direction of men of color and whites (the superiority of the latter was admitted beforehand) continued to be a favorite topic of the intellectual circles to which Bonó belonged. In the face of Haitian "black exclusivism" he liked to point to his own country, which encouraged "the spread of all the races on its soil" and which, thus, was supposed to be the nucleus of a "powerful" Antillian "confederation," for which Hostos and Betances also fought.[58]

But in their subsequent philippics against Heureaux—who for that time proved too black to be considered mulatto—several of these liberal thinkers did not abstain from using a good number of racist insults. Eugenio Deschamps called him a monkey; Betances observed that this "unworthy farceur" "hates foreigners because they are whites, and blacks because he is one." Juan María Jiménez spoke of his "anthropoid face," and even Hostos spoke in veiled terms of "that blackener of Quisqueyanismo."[59] In 1886 Heureaux wrote to Luperón (who still supported him at the time) that the partisans of Casimiro de Moya "resort even to ridiculous lies, to abominable infamies. They put signs on my house 'Down with the negro!', shout out 'Down with *el mañé.*' "[60]

In the many anecdotes about Heureaux that form part of the Dominican political folklore even today, this racial factor forms an important element. Heureaux's ambiguous position once he had risen to power is confirmed in these anecdotes. At times he seems to be conforming to the existing prejudices—didn't they used to say that he sometimes slept in open air at night to make himself white?—at times he takes revenge upon "respectable" vilifiers.

In foreign policy, particularly in the numerous plans to make the country a protectorate of a foreign power or to annex it, the future of the colored part of the population was always a topic of discussion, with the apparent aim of influencing the political opinion of the larger public. When rumors went around in the nineties that Heureaux had secret contacts with the United States in order to rent Samaná Bay, Luperón tried to mobilize public opinion by declaring that "[the plan of the United States] is to take possession of the whole island . . . in order to bring to it the four million emancipated Africans they have. The Yankees [would exterminate our] race because it is not theirs. It is that North American people, enemy of the Indian race, of the yellow race, of the mestizo race, of the African race, and above all, of the Latin race, to whom the traitor General Heureaux is attempting to sell and surrender the Dominican Republic."[61] In another context Luperón accused Heureaux of being too passive with regard to the infiltration of Haitians into Dominican territory, an accusation that was probably not free from racial emphasis, although Luperón admitted that President Cabral, who was not black, had also demonstrated laxity in another period.

Sumner Welles refers to advertisements Heureaux published in the U.S. press to encourage immigration of "persons of the colored race" into Santo Domingo, thus following the footsteps of Boyer's policy that had brought the Methodists to Samaná. The response to one of these advertisements sent by a man from Texas to the American consul is pathetic: this gentleman sold portraits of Toussaint L'Ouverture in San Marcos, Texas, and wondered whether there would be a good market in Santo Domingo for this article. In his postscript he said: "The bill for a 'Separate Coach' Law* has been

---

*Segregation of public transportation.

approved, and I am anxious to leave Texas"[62]. But Heureaux's publicity campaign does not seem to have had much success.

The considerable number of white immigrants who entered the country beginning in the seventies strengthened the economic and political power of whites compared with that of men of color, in such a way that Hostos could assert around 1890 that "The white portion . . . in the current population of the Dominican Republic is struggling to recover its old privileges and primacies."[63] In those years, the external manifestations of racial prejudice (often called "*preocupación*" and the topic of an article in *El Eco del Pueblo* in 1891) increased. The Cubans in particular had the reputation of being anti-black, as illustrated in the famous anecdote in which Heureaux asks a Cuban how many courses are needed in Cuba for a high school diploma. When he finds out the number, Heureaux asks: "And don't you believe that for me they would require two more subjects at the least?"[64] Also explicit is the *décima* by the popular singer Alix, which dates from 1883:

> Todo aquel que es blanco fino
> Jamás se fija en blancura
> Y el que no es de sangre pura
> Por ser blanco pierde el tino
> Si hay baile en algún CASINO
> Alguno siempre se queja,
> Pues a la blanca siempre aconseja
> Que no baile con el negrillo.
> Teniendo, aunque es amarillo,
> "El negro tras la oreja."
> *
> El que se crea preocupado
> que se largue allá a La Habana
> Que en tierra dominicana
> No le da buen resultado
> Y el bizcochuelo lustrado
> Aunque sea con miel de abeja,
> No dé motivo de queja
> Que todo esto es tontería,
> Pues está a la moda hoy día
> "El negro tras la oreja". *[65]

In the final decades of the century, as social stratification was crystallizing, especially with regard to the recently formed bourgeoisie, the opportunities

---

*Everyone who is pure white/Never pays attention to whiteness/And he who is not of pure blood/In his eagerness to be white takes leave of his senses/If there is a dance in some CASINO,/Someone always complains,/Because the white woman is always advised/Not to dance with the young black/For even if he is yellow, he has /"Black behind his ears."/Anyone who grows up prejudiced/Let him go to Havana/Because on Dominican soil/It isn't going to turn out well for him/And the little cake/Even if it's coated with honey/Gives no grounds for complaint/Because all that is ridiculous/For these days it's fashionable:/"Black behind the ears."

for *maximum* social ascent for obviously black persons must have been diminished. The racial factor became, as in earlier periods of political stability, an important determinant of social status, although undoubtedly the fact that the president was black could be considered a mitigating circumstance. But in the future it would prove less easy for a president as black as Heureaux to ascend to power.

Even today the army has continued to be one of the principal channels of mobility, but the change in the military apparatus from a "marketplace" structure to an "organizational" one brought about by Heureaux probably involved a greater emphasis on the racial factor in selection. The incipient bureaucratization of the military apparatus required a cadre of better-educated officers, so that a relatively larger number of colored men than of blacks was able to ascend to higher positions. Moreover, once organized, the military sector will tend to utilize the same criteria for social promotion that the society as a whole uses. On the other hand, a military career was not going to enjoy for very long the social prestige that the traditional bourgeois professions had, so that the number of whites in the military apparatus continued to be relatively low. When José Martí inspected one of Heureaux's battalions in 1895, he observed that among the officers there were mestizos and blacks, among the soldiers only blacks.[66]

Moreover, it is probable that the numerical growth of the recently formed national bourgeoisie and its growing consciousness of its social position would increase the social importance of the racial factor, if only because the mechanisms of social control could then be manipulated more effectively.

Lastly, the growth of the cities must have prompted more pronounced segregation, particularly between blacks and other groups, in the eighties and nineties through the construction of the new suburbs, which were more homogeneous in an economic, and thus racial, sense than the old urban central districts. But there were always exceptions: a black family was living in San Carlos, the *barrio* of Canary Islanders, at the end of the century: "they called them the dark-complexioned Islanders, because they were honorable, hardworking, and decent."[67]

We already saw that in the nineties the exclusive clubs of the upper social class found their reflections in colored people's clubs like La Perla Negra. In popular speech, too, the color black found its defenders, by way of counterbalance and consolation:

> Si el color negro te causa espanto
> No le muestra tu nobleza
> de negro viten la iglesia
> ei Jueves y ei Vieines Santo
> de negro ponen ei manto
> ei aquei sagrado atai*

*If the color black frightens you/You aren't showing good character/In black they deck the church/On Holy Thursday and Good Friday/Black the cloth they put/On that sacred Altar.

So they sang in the Cibao.[68]

It seems justifiable to conclude that the changes described earlier in the social and economic structure in the last quarter of the nineteenth century created a situation in which the racial factor acquired more importance in social life than it had had in the first three decades after 1844 (excepting the Spanish Annexation):

> Si ves a la mesa un blanco
> y a un negro en su compañía,
> o el blanco le debe al negro,
> o es del negro la comida.*

As the national bourgeoisie was gaining awareness of its importance and was behaving in a more exclusive manner, Mejía-Ricart's (contemporary) observation acquired more validity than it had had all along: "The Dominicans have an ethnic complex. . . . As racial purity does not abound, but a mix between hues: white, almost white, mulatto, and black, it means that differences regarding complexion, hair texture, and more or less clear origins are constantly being noted. Such importance given to this element of the personality consequently produces an aspiration in those who do not have white coloring to acquire it, in those who almost possess it to improve it; and in those who form the small groups of white ancestral stock, that of conserving that gift,"[69] a phenomenon characteristic of any multiracial society where one racial group is dominant and its physical features are considered desirable. But the extent to which this leads to an "ethnic complex" depends on the exclusivity that the dominant group appropriates for itself. And although in the Dominican Republic this exclusivity was, we repeat, *grosso modo* of a different, more benign quality than that of the non-Iberian societies of the Caribbean, its relative rigidification at the end of the century is, nonetheless, a noteworthy fact.

One retains the impression (without making an in-depth study) that several of the historians that the new bourgeoisie produced in our century have shown greater racial prejudice than their nineteenth-century colleagues. Still, the latter were not free of it either: in the last century, too, the benefit of European immigration "in order to improve the race" was freely praised. If this impression is correct, it would be a logical and psychological result of the position of security in which the bourgeoisie found themselves, particularly in the first decades of the twentieth century. It was only in the 1960s that a new generation of historians arose to submit learned judgments to new analysis and perhaps to discover a certain intellectual kinship with some nineteenth-century predecessors who had, after all, suffered some healthy doubts and anxieties.

---

*If you see at table a white/And a black man in his company,/Either the white man is in debt to the black/Or the black is paying for the meal.

CHAPTER NINE

Family and Daily Life

The period of pregnancy was surrounded with superstitious taboos, and it was not uncommon for the woman to spend it withdrawn in her house. In the countryside an illegitimate child was sometimes called "*hijo del mundo*" (or child of the world) and the legitimate child "*hijo de bendición*" (or blessed child). The newborn's umbilical cord was carefully saved and given to him at seven years of age by his mother "to rip up and to acquire in that way the secret virtue that 'would open all roads' to him." The first nine days after the birth the mother—in all social classes—shut herself away hermetically, avoiding contacts with the outside world, and with the night air; she even stopped up her ears with cotton. Before the birth the godparents for the baptism had already been chosen "among the most beloved, suitable, well-to-do persons of the village, since they rarely chose poor people so that such an obligation would not fall upon individuals who "*no tienen en que caeise mueito*" (did not have a cent to their names). After the baptismal ceremony the child was presented by the godparents to the parents, who had remained at home, with the words: "*Comadre*, here you have your child, you gave him to me a Moor, I turn him over to you a Christian. What I entrust to you is teaching him the catechism." Then the rural godfather gave his godchild a heifer or a sow. "From then on the *compadres* will take off their hats in greeting, they will never quarrel, and the godchild will later have to kneel before those who made him a Christian, and will say 'Sión, padrino' or 'Sión, madrina' . . . ," and likewise will ask for a blessing from any respected adult as well.[1] In the city too the ties of co-parenthood were strong: "The godparents were the godchild's second parents and had duties and rights regarding them, being able to correct and punish them. In case of the father's death the godparents took care of the bodily and spiritual health of the godchild." Sometimes it even came to adopting the child. No conflict was supposed to stain the relation between godchild and godparents:

> Si tienes algún tormento
> tu no te apures por nada.
> Entre madrina y ahijada
> no puede haber sentimiento.*[2]

*If you have some problem/Don't worry at all./Between godmother and goddaughter/ There cannot be any resentment.

The special tie that joined the godfather and the mother carried with it a risk of erotic interest, but "between a *compadre* and a *comadre* no carnal feeling was possible, and in case, both being free, some interest arose, amorous relations were not established as long as the Church had not issued . . . the necessary dispensations."[3] Men of influence and prestige like Heureaux had hundreds of godchildren and were united by ties of co-parenthood with families of all the social levels. But one must conclude, and Jiménez does, that in the countryside and in some villages the duties of the baptismal godparent during the godchild's whole life were greater than in the city.

We saw earlier that more or less half of the births were illegitimate. This must be attributed in greatest part to the low number of marriages among the poor groups of the population, but on the other hand, it was also due to the extremely widespread institution of concubinage, a situation in which the man—from the higher groups as well as from the lower ones—lived before his marriage and after it, not to mention less enduring extramarital relationships. In 1891 in San Pedro de Macorís, a sailor-carpenter died, leaving forty-two children from two marriages "and a few missteps," as the newspaper said.[4] Luperón had two legitimate children and six illegitimate ones; the number of Heureaux's illegitimate children would not be any lower. A simple Curaçao immigrant in Neyba had a legitimate wife with seven children as well as two concubines with whom he had three children.[5]

Infant mortality was high, and the death of a small child, *un angelito*, was not supposed to cause great sorrow. The child's corpse was dressed like an angel "with its wings in a flying position." In the cities an orchestra that accompanied with "happy pieces, *danzas*, and waltzes" was hired for such children's funerals.[6] In the rural areas the *angelito*'s wake was a pleasant fiesta, and "the neighborhood gathered night after night at the so-called wake, in which one danced, sang, gambled, and consumed a great deal of rum. For these events the unfortunate child was prepared in the most criminal, crude fashion so that it would last through the nine days of the fiesta without beginning to decay. This preparation after the fashion of embalming was performed by persons already skilled in the method by dint of ground salt and lime juice. Some went as far as opening the belly and filling it with rags soaked in these substances, and cases were even seen in which the practical preparers of these sacrileges had introduced a stick with a sharpened point through the rectum, leading it through the belly and the neck to the head in order to place the little corpse, upright like a doll, on an altar full of flowers and candles. . . . In the workers' quarters of La Angelina hacienda . . . they gave the mother, ignorant or perverted, the following command: '*Señá* Juana, your *comadre* Munda says for you to loan her the little corpse for tonight.'"[7] At the beginning of September 1896 a bacchanal of this sort was held in Puerto Plata, and as the fiesta was forbidden by law, "especially on weekdays," the mayor went there accompanied by two soldiers. He was shot by the revelers.[8]

How did the children who survived the dangerous first years of life grow up in their rural or urban environment? Before learning the alphabet they already knew how to make the sign of the cross under the severe vigilance of the adults, but they sought, like all young people, routes of escape from a discipline they considered excessive. In the city they organized stone-throwing fights between *barrios*: Migueletes against Barbareños, Reginistas against Carmelitas and Misericordes.[9] Sometimes they caused disturbances in church, shouting and interrupting with whistling during the Mass in Regina Angelorum.[10] The seclusion of Holy Week, which was very difficult for children to endure, demanded some compensation on the following Sunday, when the boys of Santiago headed in groups to the market in order to steal fruit there under the shouts of "Alleluia" in a more of less accepted ritual.[11] Amusements for girls were limited to the house, and many of their games must naturally have consisted of children's imitation of adult life. Such games became news only exceptionally, as when some rich Sephardic girls organized a luxurious baptism for their female cat, which received the names Dominicana Aurora and then was married to another cat in a splendid ceremony.[12] Rich youths sometimes rode Arab horses, imported from Puerto Rico, on their Sunday rides—"well-dressed in white drill, heads covered with a fine Panama hats, shining patent leather boots, feet in the burnished copper stirrups, revolvers at their belts, whips in hands."

The strict social control made free contact between young people of both sexes impossible, and for the highest urban groups there seem to have been only two places where young people could meet: the church, where lovesick glances were exchanged and little notes furtively delivered, and the newspaper, where young people sent one another verses, riddles (*charadas*), and flirtatious compliments. Thus, in March 1899 B. saw arriving on the boat from Curaçao the "ideal of my hopes . . . who has black eyes that are so beautiful and seductive, but which according to the current fashion she veils with glasses, which although transparent, do not have the diaphanousness of her shining glance."[13] Often the enamored young man could not at first do anything more than stand waiting anxiously at the corner near his adored's house: *hacer esquina* (doing the corner). The romantic love letter was a carefully wrought work of art, and as late as the year of his death Heureaux was showing himself a master in this art when he wrote to the young Olga Clan in Jacmel, Haiti: "As long as a man has not passed too far beyond the meridian of life he cannot see as daughters the beautiful and charming young ladies whom he has the fortune to know. A more demanding and passionate god than the one who presides over paternal loves, a god who neither sees nor thinks, it is he who ignites his torch in the flame of the looks that cross one another's paths between a gentleman and a young woman, if she is beautiful like the dawn of spring days."[14]

As soon as a young man was frequently visiting a home where there were daughters of marriageable age, public opinion became an important factor, as J. E. Julia recognized in a letter to his beloved's brother: "In view of the numerous and varied comments that the public is making about my frequent visits to your home and heeding the just reproach that you recently gave me, I beg that you deign to permit me to continue visiting your estimable family not only as its friend but also as a suitor of your sister Virginia, whom I love in all sincerity and good faith. I assure you beforehand that up until today only the bonds of true friendship have united me to her."[15]

Once the betrothal was accepted by the members of the two families and the falling in love made public, the young man visited his fiancée's home every night, "forming what they called the altar, that is, the lovers' being seated in the drawing room, settled in the comfortable rockers."[16] Going out together was not permitted for the engaged couple: a chaperone always had to accompany them. In the city as well as in the countryside the bride-to-be withdrew into her house from the moment the priest announced the date of the wedding until the ninth day after it. Naturally in the country the ritual of the betrothal was less subject than that of the urban bourgeoisie to the impact of writing, although the formalities in the behavior of the future spouses were not any the less for that. Ramón Emilio Jiménez has described rural love affairs in a most sympathetic and touching way, from the first gallant phrase, "I would give my saddle horse to be able to see you every day," by way of the serenade:

> Ere chiquita y bonita
> ere como yo te quiero,
> que parece campanita
> de la mano de un platero,*

Jiménez then follows these courtships up to the construction of the *bohío* and its furnishing with "rustic chairs," a mahogany bed, a dining table, "and a big earthen water jar atop a trunk with three inverted branch-stumps, over which many calabash vessels and coconut shells are visible," and the planting of the *conuco*. The baptismal godparents were in time advised of the wedding date, new godparents for the wedding were sought, and the young man had already asked his father beforehand for permission to "tie on the revolver" and to buy a horse and a saddle because:

> Ei que quiera sei un hombre
> necesita poseei
> buen caballo, su revoive,
> una silla y su mujei.†[17]

---

*You are little and pretty/You are the way I want you,/Who seem like a little bell/ From the hand of a silversmith.

†Anyone who wants to be a man/Needs to possess/A good horse, his revolver,/A saddle and his woman.

An entire year could easily elapse between the moment of the start of amorous relations and that of the wedding, even among the *campesinos*.

The route to the altar was not always travelled so happily. Opposition
from the parents, especially the girl's father, led, even among the uppermost
urban groups, to abduction. On 18 September 1896 the *Listín* reported:
"Last night at eight-thirty a young woman, a minor, who belongs to one of
the leading families of the capital, was taken from her home by a young man
with whom she was carrying on a courtship. The police knew to stop the
lovers en route to Santiago." Abduction knew its subtle nuances: "When
certain considerations intervened or the lover felt true love and respect for
the girl, the abduction took place with the lover accompanied by one of his
intimate friends of recognized social solvency, and the young woman was
placed for safekeeping in the home of a woman friend of recognized seriousness, while the procedures for the wedding, which the bride's family did not
attend, were carried out."[18] Article 355 of the penal code did not consider
abduction a crime if it was followed by marriage; whoever "would seize from
the paternal home a young woman less than sixteen years old with a promise
of matrimony and does not celebrate the latter in the term of one month
after being required to by her parents will incur a punishment of from one to
two years in prison."[19] Sometimes the abduction seemed to be punished in a
supernatural way: "On 24 January the youth Isidro López, a native of and
resident of the Cachón section (near Barahona) . . . took a girl from her
paternal home, and the following day the above-mentioned López went to
the village called Caballero to see some oxen that he had there, and it is said
that these oxen spoke to him from the mountain, calling him by his name.
The shock that it caused him was so great . . . that he headed back to his
house and when he arrived there he passed out, and when he returned to
consciousness he told what happened, but remained so gravely affected
that he died the following day."[20]

But neither judge nor ox could halt the seduction of young women, much
less when the country's powerful men were the ones who were setting the
example. When Heureaux had evidently seduced a friend's daughter, another
man had immediately had "the daring to make use of my name as a pretext
for seducing his beloved," the very same girl. Heureaux, in denying the
accusation, could not refrain from pointing out that the other suitor did not
"have the caliber to be my rival nor my protegé on that path . . . I repeat my
advice to you and to Hormesinda," he wrote to the father, "you should leave
that Señor Caballero in peace and to her that she endure the consequences of
her girlhood and resign herself to living under the paternal roof, abandoning
any pretense of reparation, etc., on the part of the author of her disgrace. . . ."[21]
Resignation: the word that was the watchword of woman as a sexual partner,
even if she were unwilling. Nonetheless, some fathers succeeded in obtaining
some indemnification, as Juan Antonio Alix lamented in an explicitly titled
décima: "To a very rich man from whom they took two hundred odd pesos

because his son dishonored a girl, with him alleging that he found her dishonored already." It begins this way:

Al que le sienten dinero
Le arman tamaño proceso
Y le muerden por un cuero
Dos cientos y tantos pesos.*[22]

Once he had become a husband and father, the man watched over his wife and his daughters jealously. If on some occasion he surprised his wife in the crime of adultery, the killing of the lover was carried out without delay and was socially accepted as revenge, although quite often the woman was pardoned. In Guayabín José Martí knew a general who, when he had to flee from his village, left his wife under the care of a *compadre*: "the woman gave herself to the *compadre*, he returned, found out, and with one carbine shot at the door of his own house, he shut the eyes of his unfaithful friend, 'and to you, goodbye! I'm not killing you because you are a woman.'"[23] Even the rumor of the wife's adultery had to lead to some public action, as is seen in the following letter to a newspaper, the aim of which was to satisfy public opinion and to save the honor of both spouses.

> Señora: A vile slander that a vile servant raised against you, the furies of unjustified jealousy have allowed me to be driven by anger, and without realizing my actions, I have offended you and have even raised my hand to you. . . . My duty as a gentleman and an honorable man is to confess my error. Today I am convinced that you are as pure as you always have been . . . some forgiveness in the persons of honor who know me . . . and my unfortunate character that does not know how to master itself and that in questions of honor can even impel me toward crime. In spite of my unjust conduct, believe, Señora, that I have always loved you. Your husband, José Ma. Rodríguez. I authorize you to make whatever use of this letter best suits you.[24]

The man and his sons, on the other hand, were free in their sexual explorations before marriage and outside it, as long as the social priorities of the legitimate wife were not attacked excessively. There were even families in which the illegimate child of the husband or a son was accepted in order to raise it along with the legitimate children. Heureaux had various lovers to whom he tended to write in the tone of a worried husband: "In no way do I want you to continue devoting yourself to those rice and corn crops that require you to take a lot of sun and to get very tired. I believe that around the middle of the month next January I will be able to come to spend a few days with you. At that time I myself will bring you your Christmas present.[25] He gave his illegitimate sons a good education, and several of them later bore his surname with pride. Not all good illegitimate children were so

---

*Against one whom they sense has money/They start up a great big lawsuit/And they put the bite on him through a prostitute/For two hundred some odd pesos.

fortunate, and the pride or jealousy of the legal wife could be merciless: "María E. Franco de Burgos . . . is kind enough to make clear to a group of sons without surnames that, since they were born out of concubinage, in the future they ought to sign the name of their mother, Señora Julia Saldaña, and not make further use of the surname Burgos, which solely and legitimately belongs to those from the marriage. If this is not sufficient we will find ourselves obliged to have them make use of their surname through the Law."[26]

There were undoubtedly young women from among the common people and the lower middle class to whom the "answer of a young woman to a married man" that appeared in one of Alix's *décimas* could be applied:

> Si de mi está enamorado
> Váyase desengañando
> No quiero a hombre casado
> Porque nada voy buscando*[27]

But there were also many who were "looking for" the possibility of association with a man from the higher social classes, the prestige that this gave them in their own environment, and the economic improvement that could accompany concubinage. A. Plaza wrote the following poem about them in the *Listín* on 14 February 1896:

> Enseñanza superior
>
> Muchachas sin camisas ni tomines
> Concepciones de honrada figonera
> Que no saben mover una tijera
> Ni remendar siquiera calcetines.
>
> Tus armadas de lazos y botines
> Pretenden sacudir su pobre esfera
> Aprendiendo posturas de bolera
> Y a cantar una ópera y maitines.
>
> Luego que esas chiquillas relamidas
> Se convierten en hembras pretenciosas
> Prima-donas con puff marisabidas
>
> Y nieguen a sus madres haraposas
> Para los ricos sobrarán queridas
> Para los pobres faltarán esposas.†

---

*If you are in love with me/You'd better not fool yourself,/I don't want a married man/Because I'm not looking for anything.

†"Higher Education": Girls without chemises or a penny,/The very images of the honorable food-vendor,/Who don't know how to use scissors/Or how to mend even socks./Your armadas of laces and boots/Strive to shake off your sphere of poverty/Learning the postures of a bolero dancer/And to sing an opera and matins./As soon as those slicked up little girls/Become pretentious females/Primadonnas with puff, blue-stockings/And deny their raggedy mothers,/For the rich there will be mistresses to spare,/For the poor there will be a shortage of wives.

In addition to these concubinages, which were often permanent, there were also more casual relations with prostitutes, who sometimes succeeded in making a man abandon his family, a topic that Alix also commented upon in a tone of regret in one of his *décimas.* [28]

It is not surprising that such a great stress on machismo and potency would lead to advertisements for a (U.S.) product addressed to "weak men" that began this way: "It seems that the Creator has ordained that, after the blood, the vital seminal fluid is the most precious substance in man's body." [29]

Nor is it surprising that the woman of the highest social groups, whose freedoms were so restricted while she was supposed to tolerate her husband's liberties, would adopt an attitude that would denote her patiently born sufferings, behavior that the repercussions of the Romantic era also encouraged: "Sadness was a mark of distinction in a lady, and the favorite conversations of the feminine sex were those in which sad episodes that stunned the happiness of homes came to light." [30] Indeed, a woman of forty was old, a situation that the powder made of *cascarilla*, finely ground eggshells, could not remedy.

Just as youth had its routes of escape from parental discipline, the woman had them from matrimonial discipline: "Carnival is the period of relaxing for women, since it is the only time that, under disguise, they are permitted jumps, leaps, racing around and shouting in a happy uproar, dispensing with the routine, customary seclusion of the entire year." [31] But even in 1893 there were some enterprising women who had sought consolation and recreation in ocean swimming spots in Güibia, although complaining about the presence of curious fishermen. [32] Men also swam, naked, on the coast at the capital. One quite well-used bay had two little islands nearby to which the best athletes used to swim; these islets bore the meaningful names "Curaçao" and "St. Thomas." In 1893 the ladies could enjoy Emile Zola's novel *Le Débacle*, which appeared serialized in the newspaper, perhaps identifying themselves with the heroine, and maintaining the "modest silence" that "does honor to womankind," the slogan from Sophocles that Father Billini's magazine liked to print. [33]

Distance—that key concept in this sort of society—was emphasized in the paternalist family in a formal way: "on awaking, on arriving from school, from the street, at the ringing of the Angelus, and before going to bed, the child was required to kiss the hands of his parents. The hand-kissing was performed in deed or by word, and when, through distraction, the child did not comply with this precept, he was punished." With regard to his male children—even if they were married—the father retained his authority in the home. He gave permission for the first shave; they could not smoke or drink in the house without his prior authorization. But it is significant that the worst punishment for a small boy was to dress him like a woman. And daughters who for their part were sometimes condemned to a cloistered life, without ever receiving permission to go to some dance or other gathering,

gave their fathers nicknames like Herod, Caiphas, and Nero, and they cultivated "dissembling and hypocrisy" as indispensable characteristics.[34] This
discipline, which can hardly be distinguished from male jealousy, makes the
custom of abduction more explicable.

Respect for adult authority was not limited to any social group. We
already saw how formalistic norms of conduct characterized the relations
between father and child and between the latter and his godfather in the
rural areas. And in the less well-off families in the city, too, paternal authority was indisputable. It was only after the ritual of the first long trousers
that the son—at fifteen or sixteen years of age—was given the right of going
to bed after nine at night and of standing in the doorway to watch the
dances. Parental authority was easily delegated: "the parents gave all the
rights, from reprimands to the greatest punishments to the teachers where
one went to learn any trade."[35] Widows or women whose husbands were
absent for a long period sent their sons to be punished by the "whipper of
naughty boys," which no neighborhood was without.[36]

Although, as we have seen, the women seemed to have a masochistic
delight in exposing their sufferings in their conversations and although their
sexual freedom and freedom of movement were in fact minimal in comparison with those of their husbands, one should not therefore draw the conclusion that their influence, even power, within their homes was similarly
reduced. The husband's numerous absences made the woman, especially the
older one, a central, not infrequently dominant, even matriarchal figure, who
watched over the interests of her children and to whom it was often due that
the family's possessions were not lost through the husband's gambling and
drinking debts. In periods of revolution it was she who went to ask the
general or the president for clemency in order to save husband or son from
prison or imminent execution. In a time of economic adversity she could
provide additional necessary income by preparing meals, or sweets, or sewing,
and sending her products to her clients by a maid. And one must recall that in
the last decade of the century the first female teachers were graduated, as
we saw earlier, and that the cultural life was influenced to a great extent by
a woman poet.

Just as the social—even political—influence of the urban "matrons" was
considerable, in the rural areas as well one could sometimes find women with
regional reputations, like Ceferina Chaves, who kept up an intense political
correspondence with Heureaux and of whose image in the Línea Noroeste
José Martí has left us a description:

> Everyone in the region talks about Ceferina Chaves: hers is the most
> pleasant home, with a wide compound and garden and big house at the
> rear, where on fine chairs she receives travelers . . . and gives them
> sweet wine to drink, served by her daughter: she buys at a good price
> what the region offers and she sells at a profit, and has her sons in fine
> schools, so that later they come to live as she does, in the healthiness of

the countryside, in the house that dominates, with its luxuries and hospitality, the pallid region; Ceferina's fame and power extend throughout the entire vicinity. We stop at a fence, and she comes from a distance from her *conuco*, passing among her men who are cutting tobacco for her. She leans on the fence . . . and speaks easily and as if the open countryside were a salon and she the natural owner of it. The husband appears infrequently or goes about his own tasks: Ceferina, who rides with gloves and riding habit when she goes to town, is the one who, out of her own ownership, and by strength of will, has set the idle land to growing . . . she will marry her daughter to a lawyer [Eugenio Deschamps]; but she will not give up productive work nor pride in it. *El sillón, junto al pilón.* [The easy chair, along with the watering-trough.] In the salon porcelain, and to the *conuco* in the mornings. "To the poor man, something must be left, and the divvying up of my lands, let the poor take it for themselves." Her conversation, with a natural authority, flows and sparkles. . . . The mother [Ceferina] is saying: "It is necessary to see whether we are sowing good men."

Even earlier Martí had admiringly seen Nené, the "doting mother of the people of Pena, the mother in twenty or more rearings," who had worked all day in the *conuco*, "swinging the machete."[37]

But the most characteristic relation between man and woman—of all the social classes—was painted for Martí by "general" Corona of Monte Cristi: "Thirteen children I have, but not by the same woman: because that's the way I am, when I look at my assignment, and I see that I am going to have to be in a place more than a month or two, right away I look out for my greatest possible comfort." Then at the farewell: "She sees that she has no choice, and I leave her with her little house and with some money: because for nothing in this world will I let my legitimate wife go wanting." To her he always returns; she took care of the hacienda during his exile, she paid his debts, helped him in all his efforts, and "She has my very own dignity, and if I have to give myself over to the bad life to get along with work, I know that my children remain behind very well taken care of and that that woman would not object if I behave like a man."[38]

Family feeling was strongly developed, and particularly those who found themselves in an inferior economic position found social satisfaction in proudly mentioning in their conversation their real or imagine relation with persons of higher status. In his chapter *"El inquiridor de linajes,"* Jiménez even speaks of a "mania about kinship." Given the noteworthy political and social mobility in certain periods, a person in humble economic circumstances could easily be able to say: "That happened when my uncle was a deputy" or "when my grandfather was minister." Or he was able to point proudly to some relative who had been "the girlfriend" of some distinguished person. If kinship with persons of importance could not be mentioned, ties that denoted a relationship of familiarity could also be brought to light: The old servant could say, "That one I saw born and I raised him," or "I was his maid when he was baptized," or some could say, "When your father was persecuted as a politican, mine served him as guarantor."[39] In this way, by means of the extended system of kinship or *compadrazgo*, or by means of vaguer, sometimes imagined relations, an individual could identify himself with the fortune and interests of more distinguished persons and share in their social prestige, even if it were on a minimal level. This phenomenon also worked against the creation of strong class resentments.

The term "family" was and is readily used to emphasize the solidarity that should exist between members of groups that are not based on kinship: "the Dominican family," "the university family," and so forth. Moreover, the intensity of an intimate friendship is expressed in terms of kinship: "Friend So-and-so and I are like brothers." The use of these familial terms gives the term "brother," current in ecclesiastical and Masonic circles, an affective connotation that it lacks in societies where family structure is less developed. Furthermore, the number of "friends" that individuals tend to attribute to themselves leads to an inflation of the affective ties with those whom they denote. "It is curious to observe on the subject of friendship how it has its variants and limits, for example, there are those for cafés, parks, outings, churches, and theatres; in emergency situations, like cyclones, storms, earthquakes, and in everything for purposes of taking care of one's 'hide', we are equal; but when it is a matter of visiting social centers, here the wagon stops. Since the fellow from the wealthy class has the right to be anywhere, he is able to indulge in the pleasure of having friends or friendships of all kinds, and if they are bohemians, better yet."[40]

Indeed, direct social contact on an (almost) equal footing, within socially delimited activities and areas—like the cockpit, the *tertulia*, the café, the *barrio* festival—among persons of different social status was much more common and intensive than in societies with a greater degree of urbanization, where the criteria of social prestige are based more on economic well-being than on descent from people all well-known. The social prestige of a man with a good name did not suffer if he was seen in the company of a social inferior, treating him as a "friend" under certain circumstances. The old city, with its almost total absence of economically segregated *barrios* gave a "democratic" character to social life—outside the recently created exclusive social clubs. Thus, the "dignity" of everyone was guaranteed, within, I repeat, the boundaries of certain activities, notwithstanding one's humble situation (which, moreover, was assumed to be subject to rapid improvement through political or some other sort of good luck). "Don't ask too much from your friend or your horse," it was said.

Intimate social contact with social inferiors was encouraged even more in the domestic sphere by the institution of the *"criado,"* according to which the son or daughter of some poor relative or *compadre*, or even of some person with whom patron-client ties were maintained, was taken into the house from the time he or she was very small. The position of these children within the family could vary from that of an exploited, free servant or maid to that of an adopted child and in the majority of cases must have oscillated between the two extremes—the *padres de crianza* (parents for rearing) receiving service, companionship, and affection, the *"criado"* getting nourishment and often receiving as well instruction and training in forms of conduct and behavior that he would have lacked in his paternal home. But the relationship was not always satisfactory, and at times a *padre de crianza* had to publicize the flight of a *"criado"*: "Federico Camacho, 12 years old, swarthy coloring, has run away from the home of Señor Cecilio Martínez."[41]

And finally the family regularly received visits or letters from persons belonging to the circle of its clients—a considerable group for the most well-to-do—who requested all kinds of favors from them: "Señor, by virtue of the good friendship that I profess for you, I go so far as to trouble you for your attention, begging you that you do me the favor, if it would be possible for you, of lending me three pesos that I need to begin to operate my shoestore; for I have been in this capital for a few days and I have not been able to get started in my work for lack of resources. However, as you and your family must need slippers, I can reciprocate the $3—in work as you appraise it. Moreover, you should know that if you might need me as a musician for some function in the church, you can send for me as you please. Without more ado, I am your most humble and obedient servant, Rafael Cáceres." And: "the twenty-seventh of this month I am going to San Cristóbal to spend a month, which the doctor orders for me so that I can take the waters, and my position is bad for that journey . . . as it is the blood that I have disordered. . . ."[42] But one always had to distinguish the "recognized" clients clearly from the "spongers" and "grubs," parasitic individuals who sought the attention of influential persons, trying to live off their money or their favors.

It would be totally incorrect to conclude that daily social life was idyllic by putting emphasis on its "democratic" aspects. There were also considerable distrust and venom, exploited by the neighborhood newspapers that the citizens read in great detail. Veloz even ends up speaking of "minimal sociability": in a capital city *barrio* like La Misericordia "one lived amidst distrusts and rancors, occasioned by the egoisms produced principally by the '*correos*,' who in such isolated circumstances took on authority and sometimes said what was the truth and what a lie. (The *correos* were people who gossiped. There were families obliged to pay off similar services, which were sometimes the provokers of unforgiveable sorrows.)"[43] The "gossip" of "evil tongues" could bring about catastrophes in the small villages with their families jealous of their pride and dignity, and they could lead to prolonged quarrels in the heart of the family or between one family and another. In fact, one retains the impression that the much exaggerated "harmony" (with which name or a similar one many associations adorned themselves), whether within the environment of the family, the *barrio*, or the political apparatus, had more the function of repressing the potential of omnipresent tensions than of reflecting a real, "natural" harmony of a pastoral sort.

But life also had its happy compensations. One could go pigeon hunting, play dominoes or chess, visit the ladies, or go to the billiard hall. Or they played card games: ombre, poker, baccarat, seven-up, or *nalilla*, as did the upper social groups, the games usually for money, but not—as among some urban middle groups—as a profession.[44] A number of foreign lotteries and a domestic one partly satiated the eagerness for gambling and were surrounded by many superstitions: with a new moon, low numbers won, and vice-versa. Bets were made at the cockpits, which during the nineties increased in number and in size of the public that they drew from all the social classes.[45] Many presidents and "aristocractic" ministers like, for example, Jiménez senior and Manuel María Gautier were known for their passion for cockfighting. Sometimes the cockpits were the setting for serious fights, as in 1899 when there were two dead and nine wounded in San Francisco de Macorís.[46]

Calmer men (and women) could frequent the "*veladas lírico-literarias*" (or lyrico-literary soirées) that were organized often, or they could read the summary of foreign politics ("Cosmorámico") that the *Listín* published from April 1893 on, or, instead, the weekly literary page that the newspaper began to publish in 1896. Also in 1893 the first 3,200 gallons of beer from the capital city plant had finished brewing, and the first cigarettes had just appeared. But cigarette smoking was only done at home, because a person who arrived at the Club Juventud with cigarette in hand had been turned away from the ballroom without hesitation.[47] (The cigar, naturally, was native, and in the lower classes women, even young girls, also smoked it.) The circuses and zarzuelas—as we already saw in another context—began to visit the country, although sometimes one had to wait four months for the advertised Compañía de Zarzuelas to arrive from Cuba. But the pleasure of seeing a work like "*El reloj de Lucerna*" ("The Clock of Lucerne") would have compensated for the long wait.[48] The actual public clocks prompted an ambiguous reaction: the people were proud of having them (Alix praised Heureaux in a *décima* for giving a clock to Santiago in 1885),[49] but the rhythm of the society made knowing the exact hour superfluous. In the capital, the cathedral's public clock was sometimes forty-five minutes fast.[50] The *campesinos* deduced the time by measuring their shadows or by the opening of certain flowers.

And lastly there were music and dancing as universal diversions. In the sixties and seventies the harp had been the favorite instrument in some wealthy homes; later pianos from France and Germany arrived. The elegant dances were waltzes, schottisches, mazurkas, polkas, lancers, and quadrilles, but *la danza* (a slow dance, and the tune for it) alone commonly filled three quarters of the program. In 1899 Heureaux sent the *danza* "Germania" and the waltz "Maine" to a nephew in Port-au-Prince who had requested them for himself. Only the "lower classes" danced, along with the *yuca, sarambo, guarapo, zapateo*, and *fandango*, the *merengue* in their "*bachatas*" or *barrio* festivals. At the beginning they were played only by a *cuatro* (four-stringed guitar), a violin, a bombardon, a regular guitar, and the native percussion instruments such as maracas, *palitos*, güira, and so forth. In the nineties the accordion became the principal melodic instrument in the local bands, with the saxophone added in the second quarter of the twentieth century. By that time the *merengue* had become socially acceptable: it was danced for the first time in La Vega in 1922 in the Casino Central; in Puerto Plata it had been danced a little before then in the Club de Comercio.[51] Along with the obvious subjects like love and the landscape, politics were often commented on in the lyrics of the *merengues*. The dances generally lasted from 10 p.m. until 2 or 3 in the morning. If some fight had a fatal outcome, the corpse was taken out and the party went on, "to the extreme [that there are] women whom the rapid, voluptuous strutting of the dance scarcely permits drying the tears that are drawn from them thus, dancing and all, by the death of the friend whom they just carried out of there, perhaps their partner moments before."[52] "*Armar la fiesta*" (or starting a row at the fiesta) was a very common phenomenon because even when it was the government that was organizing the dances in the provincial governor's hall, the newspaper felt obliged to remark that "The order that has reigned in the festival, . . . speaks very highly in favor of the culture and advancement of our country."[53]

But just as the man of the cities had his refined diversions, the *campesino* had his: one must recall the *mediatuna*, the contest among *décima* singers of regional fame who tried to outdo one another in singing and in the improvisation of verses, all in the midst of a critical audience that determined the winner.[54] The work of the teams, or *convites*, who helped some neighbor in the *común* prepare his land for planting, was eased by work songs, which also existed for other kinds of labor. Even oaths, which the *campesino* viewed with great respect, were sometimes translated into poetic form, like this one from a woman in love:

> Poi ese sol que está alumbrando
> por ese dió que me está viendo
> que como tú me siga amando
> te seguiré siempre queriendo.*[55]

Considerable time and pleasure were dedicated to the preparation of food, particularly on festive occasions in the rural areas. The urban kitchen was well equipped: "kettles, clay pots, stoves, kitchen grates, glazed earthen tubs in different sizes, a great round slab of lignum vitae for chopping and pounding meat, the little copper kettle, tin-plated on the inside, cylindrical in the upper

---

*By that sun that is giving light, / By that God who is looking at me, / As long as you keep loving me / I will always keep on loving you.

part and spherical in the lower or base, with its *molinillo* for beating choco-
late, the spatulas of white wood. . . . In a corner, the large, pot-bellied earthen
jar for water, and the mortar for the heavy pestle for milling rice, grinding
coffee, etc." (There was also always a bunch of coco-palm switches at hand
for killing mosquitoes.)[56]

In the country the daily diet was frugal. In the morning one had coffee,
ginger, or brews of orange leaves or of guanabanas, sweetened with sugar,
syrup, or honey. One worked in the field until three or four in the afternoon,
and afterwards the hot meal was prepared: parboiled vegetables and, once a
week, meat.[57] In the home of General Gómez, José Martí ate white rice and
chicken with yeren, a tuber about the size of a hen's egg, as well as sweet
potato and auyama, a type of pumpkin.[58] In the city the breakfast of the
most well-to-do was more extensive: *arepas* (or corn griddle-cakes), tripe,
bread, cheese, corn fritters, and so forth, "at a cost of pennies"; after the
siesta there was a *merienda* (or snack) with crackers, cheese, tea, coffee.[59]
The state banquets given by Heureaux on the occasion of visits of foreigners
(and I mention them to point out the other extreme of the culinary tradition)
were quite refined, sometimes with twelve courses ("Poisson sauce tartare,
filets maitre d'hotel, asperges a l'huile . . .") and seven wines (Haut Sauterne,
Th. Roederer frappé, champagne . . .),[60] but even in the outskirts of the
capital there were "many people from the countryside who, in the rainy
months, which are the ones of idleness, have to feed themselves with a wild
species of yuca called *guáyiga* in order not to die of starvation (. . . such is
the lack of steady work, such the indolence, such the lack of incentives)."[61]

The bourgeoisie allowed itself to be caught up in these years—as we
already saw—by the European mania for hygiene. The newspaper gave advice
on the way to control the purity of milk, in some schools hygiene was taught
as a subject, and in 1892 the capital's city government asked the Congress to
"forbid once and for all" burials in the churches. This custom, notwithstanding the amount of 300 pesos with which it had been taxed since 1883,
seemed impossible to wipe out, owing to the prestige that it carried with it.
But "the unhealthy emanations that the lack of ventilation . . . makes so
dangerous because of the crowd of people that come together under their
arches" finally made the drastic intervention of the authorities indispensable.[62]

Among the village and rural lower classes the interest in hygiene was minimal. The *campesinos* bathed rarely and sometimes made good use of the
natural consequences of the absence of hygiene: "The organic secretions
produce stenches of an unendurable intensity, particularly under the armpits, where body odor grows and achieves its essence. When the body odor
is strong, a species of fine powder, like a tiny fungus, grows in the soft hair
of the armpits, adhering tightly to the hair. The stench that body odor gives
off is an insupportable, nauseating, loathsome, and contagious thing. Wasps
and bees are subdued with that odor; thus, before handing these insects one

who has the arsenal of such an asphyxiating pestilence under his arm rubs the palm of his hand there vigorously in order to saturate it with the powder's stench." Body odor was also used to make a dog become accustomed to his new master; a piece of bread rubbed under the armpit made the animal forget the odor of his former owner.[63]

But with or without new concepts of hygiene, contagious diseases continued to claim a high number of victims. Here is a selection of press items from one year: February 1893, Guayabín: "The disease known by the name of whooping-cough is wreaking havoc in the children of that whole District"; March 1893: "In Mao, whooping-cough is spreading among the children and causing many deaths"; July 1893: "between El Seybo and Higuey there is a young woman who suffers from leprosy stretched out in the road, begging for alms"; September 1893: various cases of typhus in the capital, with tetanus and smallpox also occurring regularly. In 1881/82 there had been a true smallpox epidemic in Puerto Plata, Santiago, and the capital; there was not enough vaccine, and the people used carbolic acid and camphor. Heureaux warned his minister Marchena, whose wife suffered the dreaded disease, not to the make the case too public: "It is appropriate to create the least possible alarm regarding smallpox, for, as you will understand, the impression that it causes abroad is always unfavorable."[64] Also common was tuberculosis: in an advertisement a woman thanked Dr. Francisco Carvajal for what she considered the curing of her son: she had already lost five children because of the "*tisis.*"[65]

Meriño enumerated the most common diseases thus: "Endemic diseases: intermittent fevers, pulmonary consumption, digestive tract disorders, tetanus. In the July-October heat: typhoid fevers, although those whom these normally attack are Europeans who are incautious about the climate."[66]

Not only in the case of smallpox, but also in other epidemics the people believed in the protection of camphor (as did the doctors), carrying it in a little sack they hung around the neck. Many illnesses that today are rarely fatal at that time inevitably led to death—like appendicitis, which was sometimes called "*cólico miserere.*" It was quite common to hear it said that "So-and-so died of an ache."[67]

On New Year's Day 1893 Dr. Henríquez y Carvajal performed the first ovariotomy in the country; the patient died. A not very lofty medical dispute between this doctor and his colleague Xigues that was carried on publicly in the newspaper developed in that year. In fact, the growing number of doctors competing in all the largest cities for the favors of the most well-to-do created a strong internal competition, and perhaps for that reason many doctors were at the same time agents for imported medicines like the Scott Emulsion, which Henríquez y Carvajal constantly advertised in the newspaper, or "specific salves for wounds and tumors" that another doctor advertised.[68] The numerous wounds from shootings and stabbings resulting from the political and other types of quarrels gave some wealthy women an opportunity to devote themselves to a philanthropic activity: the preparation of bandages from strips of white material. In the rural areas bullet wounds were covered with handfuls of dirt, and just as in the cities, urine was used for massages and sometimes for injection as a medicine; the urine had to be from a small child or from a pregnant women or an old person, or, instead, from a person who had a certain trade: shoemaker, smith.[69]

Here we are entering into the wide realm of popular medicine; the boundaries between this and "official" medicine were in reality vague, as were the categories of the practitioners of both types of medicine. In turn, the boundaries between medicine and magic were also vague, for it is obvious that the many diseases that threatened the people, as well as dangers of other types—political, amorous—readily put them in contact with those who promised to help them by supernatural means. Seen regularly in the newspaper were items like the one about "the Witch Damiana" who lived in Mao and who asked twenty-five centavos for her consultations, or about the imprisonment of a Haitian like San Cristóbal's Pedro David, known as a "*bocó*," practitioner of *vodun* ("*jodú*") religion, and accused of infanticide.[70]

If the illness was very grave, in the cities traffic was halted on the street where the patient lived and ropes were placed at each corner. The family and friends (and the inevitable "night birds") spent the *velorio*, the vigil while awaiting the death, drinking coffee, eating cheese, and smoking cigars. After the death the women were supposed to weep, screaming at times hysterically, something that occasionally brought on "attacks" ("A man's strength is needed here"); reviving the fainted woman was attempted with salts or the smell of burnt chicken feathers. Sometimes a bleeding, performed by the doctor, was necessary. If the weeping had been insufficient one heard it said scornfully, "Here there was nothing but misty eyes." As there was no ice (before the establishment of the first ice plant, this product was only occasionally brought aboard schooners by speculators), the body was conserved by placing lemon or orange juice poultices in the belly.

The period of mourning by widows, mothers, fathers, and children varied from five to ten years and by brothers, sisters, aunts and uncles, from two to three. During mourning the women did not use earrings or covered the earrings with black cloth (so that the holes in their ears would not close up).[71] The bourgeoisie attended the burial dressed in black formal wear, a custom that the *Listín* protested in 1893 because of the high prices of this clothing and because it was difficult to get. The newspaper wondered whether one could go to a burial in ordinary clothing, as in Caracas.[72] The poor were transported in the casket itself: "There was a rustic, anti-hygienic coffin, outfitted with a litter, painted black, that the people gave the name of "*El Negrito*" and those disowned by fortune, who, in the most absolute poverty, died in the hospitals or in some wretched *barrio* were carried to the tomb in it."[73]

In the rural areas Jiménez distinguished three classes of public in the *velorios*: "those who honestly share the sorrow of the mourners," the "*velor-iómanos* [or the wake-lovers] who go to eat and tell stories," and "opportunistic lovers." The female relatives of the deceased withdrew into some room during the *velorio*, as well as during the *"vela"* (or vigil) nine days after the death. During these nine days the neighbors took care of the work and came in the early evening and during the night in groups to keep the relatives company. On the day of the burial, as in the city, extravagant weeping by the women was considered a social obligation, to "demonstrate feeling." If someone had buried his money or valuables—a widespread custom because of the absence of banks and because of the frequent revolutions—and if this person died, the popular belief was that his soul could not enter heaven until someone found his treasure. The one who found it ordered a Mass said for the deceased; thus, the one gained paradise, the other a fortune. In addition to the *"velas"* nine days after the death and on the first day of the death (*velas de muertos*), there were also "vigils of offerings" or "of song" for "attaining a vehemently requested grace from Heaven." In the home an altar was improvised with a white tablecloth over a table, on top a crucifix flanked by two large candles. For a few hours there was praying, then began the story telling and prophecies and singing, and in some regions of the country, dancing, at times until dawn.[74]

Thus, the life force sprang up, death notwithstanding, love blossomed in the midst of mourners, dancing commanded respect after devotion, and the Dominican archetype of the fortune hunter found a moral justification for appropriating another's goods.

This chapter does not claim to give an extensive description of the extremely rich popular culture from the quite varied urban and village traditions at the end of the nineteenth century. For that one must read the books cited here. The "daily life" could only be outlined here in bold strokes, illustrated here and there with examples that I hope were interesting and with some peculiarities that may perhaps be little known.

Contrary to what I have done in the earlier chapters, here I have not spoken of "changes." Perhaps the available material is insufficient to make us conclude that there were important changes in family and daily life in the second half of the nineteenth century. It may also be—and this seems more probable to me—that the changes that may be somewhat noteworthy could only be found by analyzing a longer period. The greater and more intensive foreign influences that the country has had in the twentieth century—one must think of the period of U.S. intervention (1916-24) but also of the impact of radio and television, of the airplane and of films—and, in internal terms, the steadily improving communication between the cities and rural areas that has reduced the distance between them and has brought many *campesinos* to the city: all these influences have undoubtedly had consequences. The authoritarian character of the father figure has changed; abductions are no longer normal; the strong tie between co-parents in the countryside has been weakened and the godchild is no longer required to kneel, to mention only a few examples here. Summarizing, and using Mannheim's terms, it could perhaps be said that Dominican culture has lost something of it characteristic emphasis upon social distance, that it has become less "aristocratic" (observing that in this terminology the *campesinos*, too, were "aristocratic" within their culture).

But certainly it seems justifiable to point out that the area these changes encompass should not be overestimated. For the generation that has lived and has suffered this process of transformation, the changes seem like cataclysms, while one who observes from some distance does not see drastic changes in the landscape, and the analyst notes that the composition of the land has also remained almost the same. The changes—economic, agrarian, demographic, politico-ideological—have in fact been notable in the last 100 years. But have there been intrinsic changes in essential attitudes within the family; the attitude between protector and client, between political friend or enemy; the attitudes toward poetry and the natural sciences, toward the priest and the woman, toward mother and daughter? If it were so, one would have to suppose that the way the individual perceives his environment and which thus determines the "basic personality type" or—an even riskier term—the "character of a people" would have a rate of change parallel to that of the changes (determined principally by external causes) in the economic, technological, and demographic structure. When reading a description of economic life that dates from eighty years ago the contemporary reader will feel himself instantly transported into the past, but this sensation will be considerably less when he reads that:

> The Dominican is hospitable, honest, and affable . . . , being active and hardworking when it pleases him to be. He ardently loves music and fiestas . . . ; as noble as brave; as sly as suspicious, as sprightly as astute; as daring as benevolent. Fearless and terrible in battle, he is humanitarian and compassionate in victory. . . . He proves hardy in working, but without the spirit of order or of thrift. . . . He loves poetry . . . , it impels him to love the beautiful. . . . The Dominicans are deeply religious, without ever losing sight of God, who, in their judgment, helps them in their miseries and joys. Unfortunately, the Dominicans are generally passionate to an excess, always struggling between the extremes of volubility and of the ambitions. . . ."[75]

A description like the foregoing one of the Dominican in his psychological relation to the social environment that dates from seventy-five years ago can prompt arguments today—as at any other time—but it cannot be discarded as antiquated or because it can be said *a priori* that it is inapplicable to the present. It should not be concluded from the aforesaid that the social sciences' crucial question regarding the primacy of culture (or superstructure) as opposed to structure thus stands answered for me. But the compiled material certainly indicates that this question has no easy answers. Each social institution has its own culture and structure, and the impact that a certain institution has on the rest of social reality depends on many factors. We could compare social institutions with trees whose roots reach different depths and whose foliage covers areas of different sizes. There seem to be some—like the patron-client institution (complemented by the Catholic church's system of patron saints), like the institution of the extended family and that of co-parenthood, and the institution that can be summed up in the terms personalism and *caudillismo*—that have influenced the society for such a long time and so profoundly that the recent social innovations have been molded or transformed according to the example of these old, tested forms and attitudes.

If only the material collected in this book would inspire a discussion of this and other similar hypotheses based on empirical reality!

PREFACE

1. E. De Vries and J. Medina Echevarría, eds., *Social Aspects of Economic Development in Latin America* (Paris: UNESCO, 1963), vol. 1, p. 395.

CHAPTER 1

1. With this step a measure taken by the Haitian government was confirmed. However, after 1844 the Church was allowed to acquire new properties.

2. Alcibíades Albuquerque, *Títulos de los terrenos comuneros de la República Dominicana* (Ciudad Trujillo: Impresora Dominicana, 1961), pp. 14-15.

3. However, lumber was also cut into pieces that were transported by mules.

4. Albuquerque, *Títulos*, p. 17.

5. Antonio del Monte y Tejada, *Historia de Santo Domingo*, 4 vols. (Santo Domingo: Imprenta de García Hermanos, 1890), vol. 3, p. 19. See Albuquerque, *Títulos*, p. 19. See also on *terrenos comuneros*: J. R. Abad, *La República Dominicana: Reseña general geográfico-estadística* (Santo Domingo: n.p., 1888); M. R. Ruiz Tejada, *Estudio sobre la propiedad inmobiliaria en la República Dominicana* (Ciudad Trujillo: n.p., 1952).

6. Albuquerque, *Títulos*, p. 28.

7. Ibid., p. 29.

8. Samuel Hazard, *Santo Domingo, Past and Present, with a Glance at Hayti* (London: Sampson Low, Marston, Low & Searle, 1873), p. 483. See also Academia Dominicana de la Historia, vol. 9, *Informe de la Comisión de Investigación de los E.U.A. en Santo Domingo en 1871,* preface and notes of Emilo Rodríguez Demorizi (Ciudad Trujillo: Editora Montalvo, 1960), p. 583. This is a translation of the *Report of the Commission of Inquiry to Santo Domingo etc.* (Washington, D.C.: U.S. Government Printing Office, 1871) and will hereafter be referred to as *Informe*.

9. Hazard, *Santo Domingo*, p. 484.

10. *Informe*, p. 548.

11. Ibid., p. 230.

12. Ibid., p. 258.

13. Ibid., p. 347.

14. Ibid., p. 559.

15. Hazard, *Santo Domingo*, p. 320.

16. *Informe*, pp. 469, 486.

17. Ibid., pp. 585-86.

18. Luis Emilio Gómez Alfau, *Ayer, o el Santo Domingo de hace 50 años* (Ciudad Trujillo: Pol Hermanos, Editores, 1944), p. 83.

19. *Informe*, p. 256.

20. Ibid., p. 197.

21. Arturo Bueno, *Santiago, quien te vió y quien te ve* (Santiago de los Caballeros: Impresora Comercial, 1961), p. 135.

22. *Informe*, pp. 75, 362.

23. "This old black, with his wife and two adult sons lived in a field of more than 200 acres (near the capital); the only building of any importance on this land was one of these typical simple houses of palm with two rooms. He raised some cattle and grew some cane, coffee, and a little produce, without much energy and without any system in his labor. On asking him why, with so much land and so many apparently appropriate means, he did not have a real house and a garden and improve his farm, he told us the same story, heard so many times, of revolutions and attacks, and forced recruitments" (Hazard, *Santo Domingo*, pp. 282-83).

24. Fernando Arturo de Meriño, *Elementos de geografía física, política e histórica de la República Dominicana, precedidos de las nociones generales de geografía*, 3d ed. rev. (Santo Domingo: Imprenta de García Hermanos, 1898), p. 104.

25. A *tarea* is approximately 629 square meters. All these data from the Ministry of Public Works, *Estadística agrícola e industrial: Cuadro de las haciendas de azúcar establecidas en la República desde el año 1875 hasta abril del 1882, Actas del Congreso Nacional*, no. 205, 1882, Archivo General de la Nación. (Hereafter referred to as AGN.)

26. Read was a native of Boston and came to the country in 1846. See *Informe*, p. 483.

27. *Listín Diario*, 22 June 1893. (Hereafter referred to as *Listín*.)

28. *Listín*, 27 April 1893.

29. *Listín*, 9 March 1896.

30. *Libreta de las resoluciones de Hacienda dictadas por el Poder Ejecutivo*, no. 81, 25 June 1887, AGN. (Also called *Libreta de Hacienda y Comercio*.)

31. *Listín*, 1 December 1893.

32. *Actas del Congreso Nacional*, 30 July 1897, AGN.

33. Heureaux to Delgado, 23 February 1888, Copiador de cartas del Presidente Heureaux, AGN. (Hereafter referred to as Cartas Heureaux.)

34. *La República Dominicana en la Exposición Internacional de Bruselas: Memoria descriptiva y catálogo de la sección dominicana, publicada por la Junta Central Organizadora del Concurso de la Exposición de Bruselas* (Santo Domingo: Imprenta Cuna de América, 1897). (Hereafter referred to as *Exposición*.)

35. *Listín*, 1 December 1893.

36. *Listín*, 1 December 1893.

37. *Listín*, 15 June 1893.

38. *Exposición*, p. 176.

39. *Actas del Congreso Nacional*, Sección de Fomento, 1885, AGN.

40. *Exposición*, pp. 184 ff.

41. Gregorio Luperón, *Notas autobiográficas y apuntes históricos*, 2d ed. in 3 vols. (Santiago: Editorial El Diario, 1939), vol. 3, p. 44. Second edition ordered by the Dominican government on the centennial of Luperón's birth (1839-1939). Vol. 1 of the original edition was published in 1895, vols. 2 and 3 in 1896 in Ponce, Puerto Rico. (Hereafter referred to as Luperón.)

42. Heureaux to J. M. Glas, 29 July 1882, Cartas Heureaux.

43. He came to the country in 1888 as director of the Caja de Recaudación.

44. Under the Luperón provisional government "agricultural commissions . . . composed of Dominicans, Cubans, and Puerto Ricans, making use of Moca in particular" had been established "in the provinces and principal centers" (Luperón, vol. 3, p. 44).

45. *Actas del Congreso Nacional*, Comisión de Fomento, 1888/89. Correspondence with Farensbach, 23 February 1889 and 27 May 1889, AGN.

46. *Listín*, 21 October 1893. Between 1879 and 1882 a total of ten cacao planta-tions, comprising 265,000 plants, had been founded, especially in the Samaná District, but also around Santo Domingo and San Pedro de Macorís (Ministry of Public Works, *Estadística agrícola e industrial*, AGN).

47. *Listín*, 6 November 1893.

48. *Listín*, open letter, 15 November 1893.

49. *Actas del Congreso Nacional*, 13 March 1888, AGN.

50. *Actas del Congreso Nacional*, Sección de Fomento, 20 February 1885, AGN.

51. Luperón, vol. 3, p. 121.

52. *Listín*, 21 May 1896.

53. Albuquerque, *Títulos*, p. 32.

54. Ibid., p. 36.

55. Ibid., pp. 39 ff.

56. Ibid., p. 131.

57. *Listín*, 8 June 1899.

58. *Listín*, 27 April 1893.

59. Luperón, vol. 3, p. 149. In this same letter Bonó refuses to run as a candidate for the subsequent presidential elections.

60. This and the following citations are from Eugenio María de Hostos, "Falsa Alarma. Crisis Agrícola," *El Eco de la Opinión* (Santo Domingo), November 1884, in Emilio Rodríguez Demorizi, ed., *Hostos en Santo Domingo*, 2 vols. (Ciudad Trujillo: Imprenta J. R. vda. García Sucs., 1939), vol. 1, pp. 159-76.

61. Memoria del Gobernador Civil y Militar de la Provincia de Santo Domingo al Ministro de lo Interior y Policía, no. 115, 8 February 1898, AGN.

62. On the other hand, the governor appears satisfied with the effects of the Central Dominican Railroad between Santiago and Puerto Plata, which had been inaugurated on 16 August 1897: that "gigantic and daring project of General Heureaux" that increases interest in agriculture. The tobacco harvest is larger than that of the previous year, and coffee was also exported in larger quantities, "if one realizes that perhaps a decade ago none was exported at all." The selection technology also advanced: "separating machines are already being introduced." Also, "lumber of value" could not be easily transported to the coast (Memoria del Gobernador Civil y Militar de la Provincia de Santiago al Ministro de lo Interior y Policía, January 1898, AGN).

63. Memoria del Gobernador Civil y Militar de Samaná al Ministro de lo Interior y Policía, 7 January 1898, AGN.

64. Ramón Marrero Aristy, *Over* (Santo Domingo: Librería Dominicana, 1963).

65. *Listín*, 25 September 1893.

66. *Actas del Congreso Nacional*, no. 42, 22 May 1897, AGN.

67. *Actas del Congreso Nacional*, 19 May 1897, AGN.

68. Gómez Alfau, *Ayer*, pp. 42, 44.

69. *Actas del Congreso Nacional*, no. 24, 1896, AGN.

CHAPTER 2

1. M.L.E. Moreau de Saint-Mery, *Descriptions de la partie espagnole de l'isle de Saint-Domingue* (Philadelphia, n.p., 1799).

2. *La República Dominicana en la Exposición Internacional de Bruselas: Memoria descriptiva y catálogo de la sección dominicana, publicada por la Junta Central Organi-zadora del Concurso de la Exposición de Bruselas* (Santo Domingo: Imprenta Cuna de América, 1897), p. 98. (Hereafter referred to as *Exposición*.)

3. Academia Dominicana de la Historia, vol. 9, *Informe de la Comisión de Investi-gación de los E.U.A. en Santo Domingo en 1871*, preface and notes of Emilio Rodríguez

Demorizi (Ciudad Trujillo. Editora Montalvo, 1960). This is a translation of the *Report of the Commission of Inquiry to Santo Domingo etc.* (Washington, D.C.: U.S. Government Printing Office, 1871) and will hereafter be referred to as *Informe*.

4. J. R. Abad, *La República Dominicana: Reseña general geográfico-estadística* (Santo Domingo: n.p., 1888).

5. *Exposición*, p. 98.

6. Fernando Arturo de Meriño, *Elementos de geografía física, política e histórica de la República Dominicana, precedidos de las nociones generales de geografía*, 3d ed. rev. (Santo Domingo. Imprenta de García Hermanos, 1898). The population count of 585,000 that resulted from the 1908 census lends credibility to the figures from the nineties. See also Manuel A. Amiama, "La población de Santo Domingo," *Clío*, no. 155 (1959).

7. In 1893 a Methodist congregation still existed in the capital. That year a collection for the purchase of a site was taken up under the direction of the pastor, Gooding. On the occasion of this action references were made to the 1824 immigrants; among the surnames of organizers of this collection are some (Phipp, Hamilton) that are also found in Samaná (*Listín Diario*, 28 November 1893. Hereafter *Listín*).

8. Heureaux went to the "English" school of a Mr. Thauller in Puerto Plata. As Rufino Martínez observes, "English teachers . . . were the only ones Puerto Plata had in the First Republic. Those teachers, formal and stern, like good Saxons, . . . developed in the child a lofty concept of duty, which was of no little value in an environment where the disorderly life accepted the need to trample and spoil everything in order to triumph." See Rufino Martínez, *Hombres dominicanos: Deschamps, Heureaux, Luperón* (Ciudad Trujillo: Imprenta Montalvo, 1936) vol. 1, p. 76.

9. For more detailed data on the colonization of Samaná, see H. Hoetink, "Americans in Samaná," *Caribbean Studies*, vol. 2, no. 1 (April 1962), pp. 3-22, and the literature mentioned there.

10. *Informe*, pp. 521 ff.

11. "Historia de la medicina en Santo Domingo," study by university students under Dr. H. Pieter, ms. no. 496, Archivo General de la Nación (hereafter AGN).

12. Until 1915 the Jewish cemetery of Santo Domingo was dependent on the British crown; the English subject and vice-consul Abraham León had made this arrangement. His younger brother, Benjamín León, was in charge of the cemetery until that year; he was one of the few who was then practicing the Jewish religion. In 1915 the cemetery was given to the ayuntamiento of Santo Domingo, by agreement with the British consul. The greater part of this data comes from Enrique Ucko, *La fusión de los sefardíes con los dominicanos* (Ciudad Trujillo: Impr. La Opinión, 1944). I possess only a typewritten copy of this article.

13. Ucko, *La fusión*. The original is found in the AGN.

14. *Informe*, p. 92.

15. For more details see César A. Herrera, *De Hartmont a Trujillo* (Ciudad Trujillo: Impresora Dominicana, 1953), pp. 13-57. After a certain period Marchena fell into disgrace and was executed by order of President Heureaux.

16. For other key positions held by the Jewish group, see Ucko, *La fusión*, p. 25.

17. See H. Hoetink, *Het Patroon van de oude Curaçaose Samenleving*, 2d ed. (Aruba/Tiel: De Wit, 1966), pp. 42-43.

18. We shall treat the importance of Masonry more extensively later on. Here we shall mention only that a descendant of the Sephardim did a study of it: Haim H. López-Penha, *La masonería en Santo Domingo*, vol. 1 (Ciudad Trujillo: Edit. Stella, 1956).

19. Francisco Henríquez y Carvajal came to be president; another grandson of Sephardim, Monsignor Armando Lamarche y Marchena, was ecclesiastical governor.

20. See also Ucko, *La fusión*, p. 26.

21. Meriño, *Elementos*, pp. 110-11.

22. M. A. González Rodríguez, "Apuntes y recuerdos de San Carlos," *Clío*, no. 106 (January-March 1956), pp. 93-95.

23. Not only *isleños* lived in San Carlos; for example, the famous Puerto Rican immigrant Hostos lived there for a while.

24. Samuel Hazard, *Santo Domingo, Past and Present, with a Glance at Hayti* (London: Sampson Low, Marston, Low & Searle, (1873), p. 204.

25. Emilio Rodríguez Demorizi, ed., *Baní y la novela de Billini* (Santo Domingo: Editora del Caribe, 1964), pp. 5, 6.

26. *Actas del Congreso Nacional*, Sección de Fomento, 20 February 1885, AGN.

27. Eugenio María de Hostos, "Centro de inmigración y colonias agrícolas," in Rodríguez Demorizi, ed., *Hostos en Santo Domingo*, 2 vols. (Ciudad Trujillo: Imprenta J. R. vda. García Sucs., 1939), vol. 1, pp. 177 ff.

28. Gregorio Luperón, *Notas autobiográficas y apuntes históricos*, 2d ed. in 3 vols. (Santiago: Editorial El Diario, 1939), vol. 2, p. 178. (Hereafter referred to as Luperón.)

29. Luperón, vol. 2, p. 286.

30. *Informe*, p. 286.

31. Luperón, vol. 1, p. 358.

32. Emilio Rodríguez Demorizi, ed., *Hostos en Santo Domingo*, vol. 1, p. 9; elsewhere Hostos affirms that the Cuban immigration into Puerto Plata represented an increase in capital "two million pesos strong" (Ibid., vol. 1, p. 89).

33. Ibid., vol. 2, p. xi.

34. Ibid., vol. 1, p. 310.

35. These and the following items are from ibid., vol. 2, pp. xi-xix. For the international policy ideals of Hostos, Betances, and Luperón, see Thomas Mathews, "The Project for a Confederation of the Greater Antilles," *Caribbean Historical Review*, vols. 3-4 (December 1954), pp. 70-107.

36. Luperón, vol. 2, p. 294.

37. Rodríguez Demorizi, ed., *Hostos en Santo Domingo*, vol. 1, p. 267.

38. Emilio Rodríguez Demorizi, ed., *Papeles de Pedro F. Bonó* (Santo Domingo: Editora del Caribe, 1964), pp. 215 ff. Hereafter referred to as Bonó.

39. Ibid., p. 253.

40. Ibid., p. 256. For Puerto Rican participation in sugar and coffee plantations, see the preceding chapter.

41. Also among the immigrants from the sister islands who arrived in the country later were some who worked for the independence of Cuba and Puerto Rico. On 23 June 1880 *El Porvenir* published a letter mentioning their "banditry" and counselling the government to close the ports to any Cuban or Puerto Rican "who is not widely known." In his journal *El Mensajero* Federico Henríquez y Carvajal opposed this idea violently. See Federico Henríquez y Carvajal, *El Mensajero*, 1886-89, 2 vols. (Havana: Instituto de Historia, 1964), vol. 2, p. 144. (Hereafter referred to as *Mensajero*.)

42. *Listín*, 1 April 1896.

43. Rodríguez Demorizi, ed., *Hostos en Santo Domingo*, vol. 2, p. 273.

44. *Informe*, p. 286.

45. Bonó, p. 280.

46. Francisco X. Billini, ed., *La Crónica—Religión, Ciencias, Artes y Literatura* (Santo Domingo: 1884-86). Hereafter referred to as *La Crónica*.

47. This term is still in vogue and is also applied to the descendants of the Samaná colonists. Furthermore, by 1871 "a large number of blacks from the British islands Nassau, St. Thomas, Jamaica, etc., the majority of them speaking English well," was found in Puerto Plata (Hazard, *Santo Domingo*, p. 181).

48. *Listín*, 2 January 1899.

49. Luis Emilio Gómez Alfau, *Ayer, o el Santo Domingo de hace 50 años* (Ciudad Trujillo: Pol Hermanos, Editores, 1944), p. 124.

50. "Historia de la medicina." Perhaps it might be good to observe here that bearing a typically Sephardic surname does not always mean that the person in question came to the Dominican Republic as a Jewish immigrant. In Curaçao these surnames are also found among the rest of the population, generally as a consequence of the recognition of illegitimate children.

51. Rufino Martínez, *Del Puerto Plata de ayer* (Santo Domingo: Editora del Caribe, 1963), p. 40.

52. Heureaux to Lorenzo Sánchez, 18 January 1899, Copiador de cartas del Presidente Heureaux (hereafter Cartas Heureaux, AGN).

53. *Listín*, 25 November 1896.

54. *Listín*, 14 July 1899.

55. See Arturo Bueno, *Santiago, quien te vió y quien te ve* (Santiago de los Caballeros: Impresora Comercial, 1961), pp. 160ff., for the data mentioned here.

56. Rodríguez Demorizi, ed., *Hostos en Santo Domingo*, vol. 2, p. 5.

57. Bueno, *Santiago*, pp. 139, 140. However, in 1899 mention is still (or again) made of an "Italian colony" in Santiago (*Listín*, 2 March 1899).

58. Ibid., pp. 189, 190.

59. In 1899 a "German colony" in San Pedro de Macorís is mentioned (*Listín*, 21 July 1899).

60. *El Eco del Pueblo* (Santiago: 1888-92), 11 August 1888.

61. *La Paz*, 8 September 1875.

62. Luperón, vol. 3, p. 56.

63. Heureaux to Hostos, 21 June 1882, Cartas Heureaux, AGN.

64. *El Eco del Pueblo*, 20 February 1892.

65. Heureaux to Luperón, 28 June 1882, Cartas Heureaux, AGN.

66. Heureaux to Luis R. Marión, 28 June 1882, Cartas Heureaux, AGN. (A "stamp law" was rejected by the National Convention during the Luperón government [Luperón, vol. 3, p. 57].)

67. Heureaux to S. S. Marsán, June 1882, Cartas Heureaux, AGN.

68. Heureaux to Luperón, 5 August 1882, Cartas Heureaux, AGN.

69. Heureaux to Leoncio Julia, 24 October 1888, Cartas Heureaux, AGN.

70. Heureaux to H. Gamby, November 1888, Cartas Heureaux, AGN.

71. Heureaux to Abraham C. León, 12 January 1899, Cartas Heureaux, AGN.

72. Rodríguez Demorizi, ed., *Hostos en Santo Domingo*, vol. 1, p. 95.

73. Ibid., vol. 1, p. 91.

74. Cited in ibid., vol. 1, p. 96.

75. Bonó, p. 279. In this article published in *El Eco del Pueblo*, Bonó points out that "in Colombia, with its adjacent Panama canal" foreign workers were certainly welcome.

76. Rodríguez Demorizi, ed., *Hostos en Santo Domingo*, vol. 1, p. 267.

77. See Mark Wischnitzer, "The Historical Background of the Immigration of Jewish Refugees in Santo Domingo," ms., n.d. Copy in author's possession.

78. Rodríguez Demorizi, ed., *Hostos en Santo Domingo*, vol. 1, p. 269.

79. Bueno, *Santiago*, appendix.

80. Personal communication.

81. The numerous Haitian cultural influences cannot be attributed (exclusively) to immigration; I hope to deal with this topic in another context.

82. Abad, *La República Dominicana*.

83. Enrique Deschamps, *La República Dominicana: directorio y guía general*, 2 vols. (Santiago: n.p., [1906?]), vol. 1.

84. *Listín*, 19 January 1899.

85. Deschamps, *La República Dominicana*, vol. 2, pp. 269ff.

86. *Informe*, p. 229.

87. Ibid., p. 223. In La Vega Real, however, no disproportion was noted in that year (p. 198).

88. Abad, *La República Dominicana*.

89. *Listín*, 16 February 1899.

90. *Informe*, p. 285.

91. Ibid., p. 235.

92. Deschamps, *La República Dominicana*, vol. 1.

93. All the data mentioned here and the calculations are based on Meriño, *Elementos*. We have retained the 1898 division into provinces and districts.

94. Hazard, *Santo Domingo*, pp. 324-25. In 1871 Puerto Plata had only two or three thousand inhabitants (Ibid., p. 180).

95. *El Eco del Pueblo*, 24 July 1889.

96. Ibid., 17 September 1890.

97. *Listín*, 16 February 1899.

98. Deschamps *La República Dominicana*, vol. 2, p. 269.

99. *Informe*, p. 74.

100. Hazard, *Santo Domingo*, pp. 212ff.

101. *Listín*, 16 February 1893. Based on *Censo de población y otros datos estadísticos de la Ciudad de Santo Domingo, por el Ayuntamiento de Santo Domingo*. Original unavailable.

102. Meriño, *Elementos*, p. 109.

103. Deschamps, *La República Dominicana*, vol. 2, p. 115.

104. Gómez Alfau, *Ayer*, pp. 116, 55.

105. See also the preceding article in this series, pp. 19-20.

106. Hazard, *Santo Domingo*, pp. 306ff.

107. *Informe*, p. 282.

108. *Listín*, 8 June 1899. The census dates from 1898.

109. Rodríguez Demorizi, ed., *Hostos en Santo Domingo*, vol. 1, p. 291.

110. Ibid., vol. 1, pp. 300ff.

CHAPTER 3

1. Emilio Rodríguez Demorizi, ed., *Papeles de Pedro F. Bonó* (Santo Domingo: Editora del Caribe, 1964), p. 206. Hereafter referred to as Bonó.

2. Gregorio Luperón, *Notas autobiográficas y apuntes históricos*, 2d ed. in 3 vols. (Santiago: Editorial El Diario, 1939), vol. 3, p. 114. (Hereafter referred to as Luperón.) See also Heureaux to Lithgow, 14 September 1887, Copiador de cartas del Presidente Heureaux (hereafter Cartas Heureaux), Archivo General de la Nación (hereafter AGN).

3. Emilio Rodríguez Demorizi, ed., *Hostos en Santo Domingo*, 2 vols. (Ciudad Trujillo: Imprenta J. R. vda. García Sucs., 1939), vol. 1, pp. 113-14. See also Bonó, pp. 270ff.

4. *Informe anual del Gobernador Civil i Militar de la Provincia de Espaillat, Actas del Congreso Nacional*, no. 5, 5 February 1887, AGN.

5. Luis Emilio Gómez Alfau, *Ayer, o el Santo Domingo de hace 50 años* (Ciudad Trujillo: Pol Hermanos, Editores, 1944), p. 91.

6. Luperón, vol 3, p. 287.

7. See Emilio Rodríguez Demorizi, ed., *Enciclopedia dominicana del caballo* Ciudad Trujillo: n.p., 1955). It was the requisitioning of horses during the numerous internal disturbances that greatly reduced the interest in breeding quality horses that had existed at first.

8. Samuel Hazard, *Santo Domingo, Past and Present, with a Glance at Hayti* (London: Sampson Low, Marston, Low & Searle, 1873), p. 383.

9. The first grand piano, also German, had been imported to Santiago around 1876 by Juan Antonio de Lora by way of Samaná Bay and La Vega, "drawn by oxen." See Arturo Bueno, *Santiago, quien te vió y quien te ve* (Santiago de los Caballeros: Impresora Comercial, 1961).

10. Gómez Alfau, *Ayer*, pp. 8, 7.

11. *El Eco del Pueblo*, (Santiago: 1888-92), 17 September 1890.

12. Gómez Alfau, *Ayer*, pp. 116ff.

13. Heureaux to district prefect of Guayabín, 9 October 1893, Cartas Heureaux, AGN.

14. Heureaux to Tiresias Simón Sam, 30 April 1888, Cartas Heureaux, AGN.

15. Heureaux to Auguste, 20 January 1899, Cartas Heureaux, AGN.

16. *Informe anual del Gobernador Civil i Militar de la Provincia de Azua*, 20 January 1896, AGN.

17. Rodríguez Demorizi, ed., *Hostos en Santo Domingo*, vol. 1, pp. 117-28.

18. Luperón, vol. 3, pp. 70.

19. Ibid., vol. 3, p. 96.

20. Heureaux to Teófilo Cordero y Bidó, minister of public works, 15 December 1898, Cartas Heureaux, AGN.

21. Bonó, pp. 215-16.

22. The private railways of the new sugar industries were already treated in the first chapter.

23. Bonó, p. 210.

24. Ibid., p. 385.

25. Rodríguez Demorizi, ed., *Hostos en Santo Domingo*, vol. 1, pp. 228ff.

26. *Actas del Congreso Nacional*, Sección de Fomento, 20 February 1885, AGN.

27. Rodríguez Demorizi, ed., *Hostos en Santo Domingo*, vol. 1, pp. 235ff.

28. *Listín Diario*, 11 March 1896 (hereafter *Listín*).

29. Memoria del Gobernador de Santiago, January 1898, AGN.

30. *Informe*, p. 100 .

31. Bueno, *Santiago*.

32. *Actas del Congreso Nacional*, Sección de Fomento, 1885.

33. Copiador de Oficios, Ministerio de Correos y Telégrafos, 1893 and following years, AGN. (Hereafter referred to as Correos.)

34. Memoria del Gobernador de Samaná, 7 January 1898, AGN.

35. Correos, 12 May 1893, AGN.

36. *Listín*, 23 February 1893, 29 April 1893.

37. It must have been the same man who was president from 1940-42 during the Trujillo regime. Trujillo also worked as a telegrapher (1907-10).

38. Correos, 1889, AGN.

39. Later governments also made use of an adapted edition of the *Código*: data taken from *Código telegráfico: uso oficial y privado del Gobierno* (n.p.: Imprenta de El Liberal, 1900).

40. Francisco X. Billini, ed., *La Crónica—Religión, Ciencias, Artes y Literatura* (Santo Domingo: 1884-86), 12 January 1886. Hereafter *La Crónica*.

41. Emilio Rodríguez Demorizi, ed., *San Cristóbal de antaño* (Ciudad Trujillo: Editora Montalvo, 1946), p. 147.

42. Fernando Arturo de Meriño, *Elementos de geografía física, política e histórica de la República Dominicana, precedidos de las nociones generales de geografía*, 3d ed. rev. (Santo Domingo. Imprenta de García Hermanos, 1898), p. 183.

43. Bueno, *Santiago*.

44. *Listín*, 6 January 1893.

45. Correos, 1893, AGN.

46. Memoria del Gobernador Civil i Militar del Distrito Marítimo de Montecristi, *Actas del Congreso Nacional*, 19 January 1898, no. 5, AGN.

47. Rodríguez Demorizi, ed., *Hostos en Santo Domingo*, vol. 2, p. 48.

48. Heureaux to I. Mendel 15 January 1898, Cartas Heureaux, AGN. In a letter of 29 December 1898 to Alejandro Woss y Gil, consul and chargé d'affaires in New York, he speaks, nevertheless, of "the third payment that is to be met" (AGN). Even years after his death there were difficulties regarding this matter.

49. Rodríguez Demorizi, ed., *San Cristóbal*, p. 148.

50. *Actas del Congreso Nacional*, Sección de Fomento, 1885, AGN.

51. *Listín*, 6 April 1893.

52. *Actas del Congreso Nacional*, Sección de Fomento, 1885, AGN.

53. See the preceding chapter.

54. Arturo Bueno, *Santiago*.

55. *La República Dominicana en la Exposición Internacional de Bruselas: Memoria descriptiva y catálogo de la sección dominicana, publicada por la Junta Central Organizadora del Concurso de la Exposición de Bruselas* (Santo Domingo: Imprenta Cuna de América 1897), p. 175. (Hereafter referred to as *Exposición*.)

56. *Listín*, 11 March 1896, 6 November 1896.

57. *Listín*, 9 June 1893.

58. *Libro de Secretaría de Hacienda y Comercio*, no. 110, 1 September 1896, AGN.

59. Ibid., 9 April 1896, AGN.

60. Heureaux to Marchena, 2 February 1882, Cartas Heureaux, AGN.

61. Heureaux to Wanamaker, 22 October 1887, Cartas Heureaux, AGN.

62. *Listín*, 2 January 1899.

63. Luperón, vol. 3, p. 38.

64. Ibid., vol. 3, p. 79.

65. "Baron de Almeida . . . came to acquire such authority that many times he scolded the government for making decisions relative to diplomatic appointments in Europe without having consulted him." See César A. Herrera, *De Hartmont a Trujillo* (Ciudad Trujillo: Impresora Dominicana, 1953), p. 47; see also Herrera, *Cuadros históricos dominicanos* (Ciudad Trujillo: n.p., 1949).

66. Heureaux to editor of *Le Nouveau Monde*, 13 December 1892, Cartas Heureaux, AGN. In 1893 100 francs were sent to the editor of this periodical "for efforts for the Dominican government" (*Libreta de las resoluciones de Hacienda dictadas por el Poder Ejecutivo*, no. 101, 14 December 1893, AGN).

67. Rodríguez Demorizi, ed., *Hostos en Santo Domingo*, vol. 1, p. 250.

68. *Informe*, p. 100.

69. This firm was active with its ship in combating Luperón's revolution against Báez on board the *Telégrafo* in 1869. The same firm offered free passage to each U.S. agent who would encourage the annexation of the republic to the United States (Sumner B. Welles, *La viña de Naboth*, trans. M. A. Moore, 2 vols. (Santiago: Editorial El Diario, 1939), vol. 1, pp. 345, 352).

70. Gómez Alfau, *Ayer*, p. 91.

71. *Exposición*, p. 91.

72. See Gómez Alfau, *Ayer*, p. 141.

73. *Listín*, 10 May 1893.

CHAPTER 4

1. Fernando Ortiz, *Contrapunteo cubano del tabaco y el azúcar* (Havana: Jésus Montero, 1940).

2. Emilio Rodríguez Demorizi, ed., *Papeles de Pedro F. Bonó* (Santo Domingo: Editora del Caribe, 1964), p. 363 (hereafter Bonó).

3. Ibid., pp. 197ff. See also the first chapter.

4. Bonó, p. 363.

5. Ibid., pp. 280ff.

6. Ibid., p. 380.

7. Academia Dominicana de la Historia, vol. 9, *Informe de la Comisión de Investigación de los E.U.A. en Santo Domingo en 1871*, preface and notes of Emilio Rodríguez Demorizi (Ciudad Trujillo: Editora Montalvo, 1960), p. 283. This is a translation of the *Report of the Commission of Inquiry to Santo Domingo etc.* (Washington, D.C.: U.S. Government Printing Office, 1871) and will hereafter be referred to as *Informe*.

8. Gregorio Luperón, *Notas autobiográficas y apuntes históricos*, 2d ed. in 3 vols. (Santiago: Editorial El Diario, 1939), vol. 3, pp. 34, 84-85. (Hereafter referred to as Luperón.)

9. Ibid., vol. 3, pp. 86.

10. *Libreta de las resoluciones de Hacienda dictadas por el Poder Ejecutivo*, no. 81, 3 June 1887, Archivo General de la Nación (hereafter AGN). (Also called *Libreta de Hacienda y Comercio*.)

11. Ibid., 22 June 1887, AGN.

12. Luperón, vol. 3, pp. 122ff.

13. Heureaux to Luperón, 5 May 1882, Copiador de cartas del Presidente Heureaux (hereafter Cartas Heureaux), AGN.

14. Heureaux to Luperón, 14 September 1887, Cartas Heureaux, AGN.

15. Federico Henríquez y Carvajal, *El Mensajero*, 1886-89, 2 vols. (Havana: Instituto de Historia, 1964), vol. 2, pp. 100ff. (hereafter *Mensajero*).

16. Ibid., p. 53.

17. Ibid., pp. 156ff., 177ff.

18. Luperón, vol. 3, pp. 289ff.

19. Heureaux to Boscowitz, 15 July 1882, Cartas Heureaux, AGN. Heureaux to Gen. Segundo Imbert, 23 July 1887, Cartas Heureaux, AGN.

20. Heureaux to Batlle, 26 October 1887, Cartas Heureaux, AGN.

21. *Libreta Secretaría de Hacienda y Comercio*, no. 110, 19 February 1896, AGN.

22. Ibid., 5 March 1895, AGN.

23. Heureaux wrote to Cosme Batlle and Co. about a loan from this company on 10 March 1888: "I offer you my thanks, reserving the right to complain about how high the sort of premium you will charge me is . . . and I harbor the hope that in another negotiation you will be a little more liberal with your most affectionate friend" (Cartas Heureaux, AGN).

24. Heureaux to Batlle and Co., 26 October 1887, Cartas Heureaux, AGN.

25. Heureaux to Batlle and Co., 30 June 1888, Cartas Heureaux, AGN.

26. Heureaux to Batlle and Co., 16 February 1888, Cartas Heureaux, AGN.

27. *Libreta de las resoluciones de Hacienda*, no. 101, 26 December 1891, AGN.

28. Heureaux to M. A. Pichardo, 25 July 1887, Cartas Heureaux, AGN.

29. Heureaux to Customs Inspector, Sánchez, 10 January 1899, Cartas Heureaux, AGN.

30. Heureaux to Wanamaker and Brown, 2 August 1881, Cartas Heureaux, AGN.

31. Heureaux to H. Billini, 12 July 1882, Cartas Heureaux, AGN. See also first chapter.

32. Heureaux to J. B. Vicini, 28 January 1893, Cartas Heureaux, AGN.

33. *Libreta de las resoluciones de Hacienda*, no. 101, 8 June 1893, AGN.

34. *Libreta Secretaría de Hacienda y Comercio*, no. 110, February 1897, AGN.

35. *Resumen general del activo y pasivo de la sucesión Heureaux, hecho por el notario Miguel Joaquín Alfau a requerimiento de la Comisión Judicial designada para*

la formación del inventario (Santo Domingo: Imprenta de García Hermanos, 1900). (Hereafter referred to as *Sucesión Heureaux*.)

36. Heureaux to A. Brea, 11 January 1899, Cartas Heureaux, AGN.

37. Minister of Treasury and Commerce to president of the Congress, 29 April 1892, *Actas del Congreso Nacional*, AGN.

38. *Libreta Secretaría de Hacienda y Comercio*, no. 110, 1 July 1896, AGN.

39. Heureaux to I. Mendel, 15 December 1898, Cartas Heureaux, AGN.

40. Heureaux to de Lemos, 30 December 1898, Cartas Heureaux, AGN.

41. Heureaux to Customs Administrator, Sánchez, 12 January 1899, Cartas Heureaux, AGN.

42. *Sucesión Heureaux*.

43. *Actas del Congreso Nacional*, Sección de Fomento, 10 February 1885, AGN.

44. Ibid., 9 May 1898, AGN.

45. *Listín Diario*, 17 April 1899 (hereafter *Listín)*.

46. *Listín*, 17 January 1899.

47. *Sucesión Heureaux*.

48. Dubocq to Canon Carlos Nouel, n.d., *Epistolario de Carlos Nouel*, vol. 1, p. D 58, AGN. (Hereafter referred to as *Epistolario Nouel*.)

49. *Listín*, 20 November 1893.

50. *Listín*, 6 October 1896.

51. *Listín*, 19 January 1899.

52. Rufino Martínez, *Hombres dominicanos: Deschamps, Heureaux, Luperón*, (Ciudad Trujillo: Imprenta Montalvo, 1936), vol. 1, p. 135.

53. Heureaux to Bernardini and Marietti, 18 January 1899, Cartas Heureaux, AGN.

54. *Listín*, 31 August 1899.

55. *Actas del Congreso Nacional*, 17 March 1889, AGN.

56. Arturo Bueno, *Santiago, quien te vió y quien te ve* (Santiago de los Caballeros: Impresora Comercial, 1961).

57. Cited in M. A. González Rodríguez, "Apuntes y recuerdos de San Carlos," *Clío*, no. 106 (January-March, 1956).

58. *Listín*, 10 July 1893, 4 April 1899.

59. Antonio Masturzi to Canon Nouel, 29 August 1887 and 6 April 1888, *Epistolario Nouel*, vol. 2, pp. M 16, 17, AGN.

60. R. Emilio Jiménez, *Al amor del bohío*, 2 vols. (Santo Domingo: Editora Montalvo, 1927), vol. 1, pp. 201, 235. In a *décima* supposedly written in Italian that the popular singer Juan Antonio Alix dedicated to the Italian colony of Santiago in 1891 he says: Como tuti santiagueri/A di colone apreciata/Pur le vende dimaciata/A lo gente sin dinero. See Juan Antonio Alix, *Décimas*, ed. Joaquín Balaguer, 2 vols. (Ciudad Trujillo: Librería Dominicana, 1961), vol. 1, p. 59.

61. *Listín*, 11 February 1893, 25 May 1893.

62. Heureaux to Pereyra, 24 May 1882, Cartas Heureaux, AGN.

63. Heureaux to Wanamaker, 26 February 1887, Cartas Heureaux, AGN.

64. Heureaux to War Minister Pichardo, 13 September 1887, Cartas Heureaux, AGN.

65. Heureaux to Batlle, 23 July 1887, Cartas Heureaux, AGN.

66. *Sucesión Heureaux*.

67. Heureaux to Meriño, 15 February 1882, Cartas Heureaux, AGN.

68. *Sucesión Heureaux*, pp. 397 ff; *Listín*, 15 May 1899, 29 March 1899, 4 April 1899, 5 April 1899.

69. Heureaux to Daniel Ortiz, 14 March 1893, Cartas Heureaux, AGN.

70. *Listín*, 11 June 1896.

71. José Ramón López, "Moralidad social," in *Cuentos de la política criolla*, ed. Emilio Rodríguez Demorizi (Santo Domingo: Librería Dominicana, 1963), p. 78.

72. Heureaux to Luperón, 14 September 1887, Cartas Heureaux, AGN.

73. Heureaux to Imbert, 13 September 1887, Cartas Heureaux, AGN.

74. Minister of Treasury and Commerce to president of the Congress, *Actas del Congreso Nacional*, 7 May 1888, AGN.

75. *Libreta de las resoluciones de Hacienda*, no. 101, 27 September 1893, AGN.

76. J. R. Abad, *La República Dominicana: Reseña general geográfico-estadística* (Santo Domingo: n.p., 1888), cited in *Mensajero*, p. 269.

77. *Libreta Secretaría de Hacienda y Comercio*, no. 110, 12 November 1896, AGN.

78. *La República Dominicana en la Exposición Internacional de Bruselas: Memoria descriptiva y catálogo de la sección dominicana, publicada por la Junta Central Organizadora del Concurso de la Exposición de Bruselas* (Santo Domingo: Imprenta Cuna de América, 1897), p. 179. (Hereafter referred to as *Exposición*.)

79. Cited in *Mensajero*, pp. 272-73.

80. *Mensajero*, pp. 42 ff.

81. Heureaux to J. M. Glas, 6 October 1887, Cartas Heureaux, AGN.

82. Heureaux to Dr. Ramón E. Betances, 24 October 1887, Cartas Heureaux, AGN.

83. *Mensajero*, p. 273.

84. *El Eco del Pueblo*, 24 November 1888.

85. Luperón, vol. 3, p. 323.

86. *Libreta de las resoluciones de Hacienda*, no. 101, 4 July 1893, AGN.

87. In 1897 the popular singer Juan Antonio Alix wrote a *décima* called "Manifestación de la moneda mejicana," which began this way: "Señores, ya voy de ruta,/Para otra tierra lejana./Queda hoy con la batuta,/La plata dominicana" (Alix, p. 122). ["Folks, now I'm on the way/To another distant land./Dominican money/Remains the boss today."]

88. *Listín*, 17 October 1896, 24 August 1899.

89. Heureaux to Cordero y Bidó, 19 January 1899, Copiador de cartas del Presidente Heureaux con Gobernadores y Jefes militares, AGN.

90. Ramón Marrero Aristy even speaks of a strike by merchants who did not want to accept the *"papeletas de Lilís"* from the 1897 emission and of numerous small merchants who for the same reason would have been killed on Heureaux's orders. See Ramón Marrero Aristy, *La República Dominicana*, 2 vols. (Ciudad Trujillo: Editora del Caribe, 1958), vol. 2, p. 263.

91. *Listín*, 1 March 1899.

92. César A. Herrera, *De Hartmont a Trujillo* (Ciudad Trujillo: Impresora Dominicana, 1953), p. 89.

93. *Listín*, 15 April 1899, 22 March 1899, 21 July 1899, 26 July 1899, 28 July 1899.

94. *Listín*, 1 August 1899, 3 August 1899.

95. Marrero Aristy, *La República Dominicana*, p. 269. See also Banco Central de la República Dominicana, *Legislación monetaria y bancaria de la República Dominicana* (Ciudad Trujillo: n.p., 1955), pp. 5-51.

96. Marrero Aristy, *La República Dominicana*, p. 229.

97. Heureaux to Marchena, 31 July 1889, Copiador de cartas del Presidente Heureaux con Gobernadores y Jefes militares, AGN. Heureaux to Marchena, 28 July 1889, Cartas Heureaux, AGN.

98. Marrero Aristy, *La República Dominicana*, pp. 229 ff.

99. According to Luperón, however, Heureaux was not only aware of the transfer, but had prompted it in order thus to facilitate the leasing of Samaná Bay. Wanamaker, then postmaster general of the U.S. and an old friend of Heureaux, would have been involved in this (Luperón, vol. 3, p. 295). See also Marrero Aristy, *La República Dominicana*, p. 232.

100. *Libreta de las resoluciones de Hacienda*, no. 101, AGN.

101. Heureaux to Garrido, Pérez, Bidó, and Galván, 12 January 1893 and 24 January 1893, Cartas Heureaux, AGN.

102. Den Tex Bondt entered the services of the Improvement Co. A search in Dutch archives did not produce new documents. His descendants residing in the United States possess only an "Obsequio a la señora C. J. den Tex Bondt" from April 1898 with the signatures of, among others, Heureaux, the José A. Puente family, Francisco Gregorio Billini, and Statkowski (N. J. den Tex to the author).

103. Heureaux to Marchena, 8 July 1889, Cartas Heureaux, AGN.

104. See Marrero Aristy, *La República Dominicana*, p. 236.

105. Heureaux to I. Mendel, 13 December 1893, Cartas Heureaux, AGN.

106. Luperón, vol. 3, p. 146.

107. *Libreta de Hacienda y Comercio*, no. 81, 18 April 1887, AGN.

108. His sister was living in Santo Domingo.

109. Heureaux to I. Mendel, 14 January 1899, Cartas Heureaux, AGN.

110. Heureaux to Cordero y Bidó, 17 January 1899, Cartas Heureaux, AGN.

111. *Sucesión Heureaux*.

112. Herrera, *De Hartmont*, pp. 124ff. See also Antonio de la Rosa, *Las finanzas de Santo Domingo y el control americano* (1915; reprint ed., Santo Domingo: Editora Nacional, 1969).

113. *Listín*, 5 January 1899.

114. Heureaux to I. Mendel, 11 February 1893, Cartas Heureaux, AGN.

115. *Listín*, 30 September 1899, 11 November 1899.

CHAPTER 5

1. Emilio Rodríguez Demorizi, ed., *Guerra dominico-haitiana: Documentos para su estudio*, 2 vols. (Ciudad Trujillo: Impresora Dominicana, 1957), vol. 2, pp. 134, 144.

2. Ibid.

3. Ibid., pp. 168ff.

4. Ibid., p. 200.

5. Ibid., p. 134.

6. Academia Dominicana de la Historia, vol. 9, *Informe de la Comisión de Investigación de los E.U.A. en Santo Domingo en 1871*, preface and notes of Emilio Rodríguez Demorizi (Ciudad Trujillo: Editora Montalvo, 1960), p. 339. This is a translation of the *Report of the Commission of Inquiry to Santo Domingo etc.* (Washington, D.C.: U.S. Government Printing Office, 1871) and will hereafter to referred to as *Informe*.

7. Gregorio Luperón, *Notas autobiográficas y apuntes históricos*, 2d ed. in 3 vols. (Santiago: Editorial El Diario, 1939), vol. 1, pp. 120, 133. (Hereafter referred to as Luperón.)

8. *Informe*, p. 340.

9. Ibid., p. 340.

10. Luperón, vol. 2, p. 292.

11. *Informe*, p. 340.

12. Ibid., p. 340.

13. Ibid., pp. 63-64.

14. Luperón, vol. 1, p. 374.

15. Ibid., vol. 3, p. 35.

16. Emilio Rodríguez Demorizi, ed., *San Cristóbal de antaño* (Ciudad Trujillo: Editora Montalvo, 1946), p. 102.

17. Luperón, vol. 3, p. 324.

18. Heureaux to Gen. Andrés P. Péres, 6 June 1882, Copiador de cartas del Presidente Heureaux (hereafter Cartas Heureaux), Archivo General de la Nación (hereafter AGN).

19. Heureaux to Gen. A. Matos, 24 December 1892, Cartas Heureaux, AGN; *Libreta de las Resoluciones de Hacienda dictadas por el Poder Ejecutivo*, 16 March 1887, 26 March 1887, 13 February 1896, AGN. (Also called *Libreta de Hacienda y Comercio*); Heureaux letters, 6 February 1893, 8 March 1893, 16 December 1898, 30 December 1898, 31 December 1898, 10 January 1899, Cartas Heureaux, AGN.

20. Heureaux letters, 31 October 1887, 11 February 1893, Cartas Heureaux, AGN.

21. José Martí, *Apuntes de un viaje* (Havana: Secretaría de Educación, División de Cultura, 1938), pp. 60 ff.

22. Vigil Díaz, *Lilís y Alejandrito* (Ciudad Trujillo: Editora Montalvo, 1956), p. 47.

23. R. Emilio Jiménez, *Al amor del bohío*, 2 vols. (Santo Domingo: Editora Montalvo, 1927), vol. 1, pp. 247 ff.

24. Victor M. de Castro, *Cosas de Lilís* (Santo Domingo: Imprenta Cuna de América, 1919); *Informe*, pp. 252 ff.; Jiménez, *Al amor*, vol. 1, pp. 195 ff.; Emilio Rodríguez Demorizi, ed., *Hostos en Santo Domingo*, 2 vols. (Ciudad Trujillo: Imprenta J. R. vda. García Sucs., 1939), vol. 1, pp. 285 ff.

25. Jiménez, *Al amor*, vol. 1, pp. 197 ff., 251.

26. Luperón, vol. 3, p. 34.

27. Ibid., vol. 3, p. 404.

28. Luis Emilio Gómez Alfau, *Ayer, o el Santo Domingo de hace 50 años* (Ciudad Trujillo: Pol Hermanos, Editores, 1944), pp. 120 ff.

29. Rodríguez Demorizi, ed., *Hostos en Santo Domingo*, vol. 1, p. 285; Samuel Hazard, *Santo Domingo, Past and President, with a Glance at Hayti* (London: Sampson Low, Marston, Low & Searle, 1873), p. 367.

30. Luperón, vol. 1; vol. 3, p. 236.

31. Ibid., vol. 3, p. 225; vol. 1, p. 127.

32. Ibid., vol. 1, pp. 345, 221.

33. Martí, *Apuntes de un viaje*, p. 45; Jiménez, *Al amor*, vol. 1, p. 248.

34. Jiménez, *Al amor*, vol. 1, p. 248.

35. Heureaux to F. Lithgow, 22 March 1882, Cartas Heureaux, AGN.

36. *Libreta de Hacienda y Comercio*, no. 81, 12 March 1887, AGN.

37. Heureaux to treasury administrator of Monte Cristi, 24 April 1889, Cartas Heureaux, AGN.

38. Heureaux to Imbert, 18 May 1888, Cartas Heureaux, AGN.

39. *Actas del Congreso Nacional*, 27 June 1889, AGN.

40. Heureaux to A. Bertrand & Fils, 18 January 1893, Cartas Heureaux, AGN. Heureaux letters, 17 December 1898, 10 January 1899, 27 January 1899, Cartas Heureaux, AGN.

41. *Libreta Secretaría de Hacienda y Comercio*, no. 93, 30 June 1895, AGN. In 1899 there was a weekly called *El Pacificador* for the army (*Listín Diario*, 17 April 1899; hereafter *Listín*).

42. Martí, *Apuntes de un viaje*, p. 40.

43. Arturo Bueno, *Santiago, quien te vió y quien te ve* (Santiago de los Caballeros: Impresora Comercial, 1961), pp. 384 ff.

44. *Libreta Secretaría de Hacienda y Comercio*, no. 110, 29 May 1896, AGN.

45. *La República Dominicana en la Exposición Internacional de Bruselas: Memoria descriptiva y catálogo de la sección dominicana, publicada por la Junta Central Organizadora del Concurso de la Exposición de Bruselas* (Santo Domingo: Imprenta Cuna de América, 1897), p. 138.

46. Rufino Martínez, *Hombres dominicanos: Deschamps, Heureaux, Luperón*, (Ciudad Trujillo: Imprenta Montalvo, 1936), vol. 1, p. 125.

47. Rodríguez Demorizi, ed., *Guerra dominico-haitiana*, vol. 2, p. 200.

48. Emilio Rodríguez Demorizi, ed., *La Marina de Guerra dominicana: 1844-1861*, 3 vols. (Ciudad Trujillo: Editora Montalvo, 1958), vol. 3, pp. 177 ff.

49. *Informe*, p. 340.

50. Luperón, vol. 2, p. 292.

51. Rodríguez Demorizi, ed., *La Marina de Guerra*, vol. 3, p. 262. The notable Curaçaoan influence on the Dominican navy continued to be felt until within the current century; a Curaçaoan named De Windt was until recently one of the principal naval officers.

52. *Listín*, 13 March 1893.

53. *El Eco del Pueblo*, 12 January 1889; Rodríguez Demorizi, ed., *La Marina de Guerra*, vol. 3, pp. 273 ff.

54. This commander was Gen. M. A. Anderson, governor of Samaná and a member of the group of U.S. Methodist immigrants (Heureaux to Anderson, 13 March 1893, Cartas Heureaux, AGN).

55. See Ramón Marrero Aristy, *La República Dominicana*, 2 vols. (Ciudad Trujillo: Editora del Caribe, 1958), vol. 2, pp. 268, 330.

56. *Código telegráfico: uso oficial y privado del Gobierno* (n.p.: Imprenta de El Liberal, 1900).

57. Heureaux to Lithgow, 25 March 1882; Heureaux to Moca officials, 14 April 1882; Heureaux to general, 23 June 1882; Heureaux to Gen. Pedro A. Lluberes, minister of the interior and police, 8 May 1893, Cartas Heureaux, AGN.

58. Martínez, *Hombres dominicanos*, p. 125.

59. Sumner A. Welles, *La viña de Naboth*, trans. M. A. Moore, 2 vols. (Santiago: Editorial El Diario, 1939), vol. 1, p. 488.

60. Informe Gobernador Civil i Militar al Ministro del Interior y Policía, *Actas del Congreso Nacional*, 8 February 1898, AGN.

61. Luperón, vol. 3, p. 39.

62. *Informe*, p. 57.

63. See E. C. Joubert, *Cosas que fueron* (Ciudad Trujillo: Imprenta J. R. vda. García Sucs., 1936), pp. 73 ff.

64. Heureaux to Luperón, 5 April 1888, Cartas Heureaux, AGN.

65. Heureaux to Juan Tomás Mejía, 12 October 1887 and 24 October 1887; Heureaux to Glas, 31 October 1887, Cartas Heureaux, AGN.

66. Luperón, vol. 3, p. 303.

67. Heureaux letters, 20 May 1882, April 1888, 29 December 1892, 7 February 1893, 20 January 1899, 11 January 1899, 23 January 1899, Cartas Heureaux, AGN.

68. Welles, *La viña*, vol. 2, p. 13.

69. *El Eco del Pueblo*, 24 July 1889.

70. *Listín*, 1 November 1893, 16 February 1899.

71. Enrique Deschamps, *La República Dominicana: directorio y guía general*, 2 vols. (Santiago: n.p., [1906?]), vol. 1, p. 197.

72. Informe Gobernador Civil i Militar de la Provincia de Santiago, *Actas del Congreso Nacional*, January 1898, AGN.

73. Jiménez, *Al amor*, vol. 1, p. 68.

74. Rodríguez Demorizi, ed., *Hostos en Santo Domingo*, vol. 1, pp. 287 ff.

75. Mensaje del Gobernador de la Provincia de La Vega a los Ciudadanos diputados, *Actas del Congreso Nacional*, no. 99, 1890, AGN.

76. *El Eco del Pueblo*, 26 May 1888.

CHAPTER 6

1. Emilio Rodríguez Demorizi, ed., *Hostos en Santo Domingo*, 2 vols. (Ciudad Trujillo: Imprenta J. R. vda. García Sucs., 1939), vol. 2, pp. 57 ff.

2. Emilio Rodríguez Demorizi, ed., *Papeles de Pedro F. Bonó* (Santo Domingo: Editora del Caribe, 1964), p. 228 (hereafter Bonó).

3. Gregorio Luperón, *Notas autobiográficas y apuntes históricos,* 2d ed. in 3 vols. (Santiago: Editorial El Diario, 1939), vol. 2, pp. 280ff., 328, 275. (Hereafter referred to as Luperón.)

4. Ibid., vol. 3, p. 330.

5. Eugenio Deschamps in *La República* (Santiago), 21 February 1885.

6. Luperón, vol. 1, p. 348. [Italics mine, H.H.]

7. Ibid., vol. 1, p. 341.

8. Sumner Welles, *La viña de Naboth,* trans. M. A. Moore, 2 vols. (Santiago: Editorial El Diario, 1939), p. 331.

9. Academia Dominicana de la Historia, vol. 9, *Informe de la Comisión de Investigación de los E.U.A. en Santo Domingo en 1871,* preface and notes of Emilio Rodríguez Demorizi (Ciudad Trujillo: Editora Montalvo, 1960), p. 542. This is a translation of the *Report of the Commission of Inquiry to Santo Domingo etc.* (Washington, D.C.: U.S. Government Printing Office, 1871) and will hereafter be referred to as *Informe.*

10. Bonó, p. 461.

11. Ibid., pp. 472ff.

12. Welles, *La viña,* pp. 430ff.

13. Luperón, vol. 3, pp. 182ff. In April 1884 there were rumors that Meriño was supporting Billini in exchange for the archbishopric (*La República,* 30 April 1844).

14. Welles, *La viña,* p. 421.

15. Luperón, vol. 3, p. 421.

16. Ibid., vol. 3, p. 225.

17. Bonó, pp. 517ff.

18. Luperón, vol. 2, p. 405.

19. Ibid., vol. 3, p. 176.

20. *La República,* 17 January 1885.

21. Bonó, p. 275.

22. R. Emilio Jiménez, *Al amor del bohío,* 2 vols. (Santo Domingo: Editora Montalvo, 1927), vol. 1, p. 249.

23. Bonó, p. 289.

24. Ibid., p. 492.

25. See Emilio Rodríguez Demorizi, *El Cancionero de Lilís: Poesía, dictadura y libertad* (Santo Domingo: Editora del Caribe, 1962) and Juan Antonio Alix, *Décimas,* ed. Joaquín Balaguer, 2 vols. (Ciudad Trujillo: Libería Dominicana, 1961).

26. Jiménez, *Al amor,* vol. 1, p. 68.

27. Bonó, p. 235.

28. For this last point, see *Informe* and Bonó, pp. 283ff.

29. Welles, *La viña,* p. 367.

30. Luperón, vol. 2, pp. 107, 189.

31. R. Damirón, *Cronicones de antaño* (Ciudad Trujillo: Imprenta Dominicana, 1949), pp. 127ff.

32. Heureaux to Salomón, 5 April 1882, Copiador de cartas del Presidente Heureaux (hereafter Cartas Heureaux), Archivo General de la Nación (hereafter AGN).

33. Heureaux to Luperón, 5 May 1882, Cartas Heureaux, AGN.

34. See Miguel Angel Monclús, *El caudillismo en la República Dominicana,* 3d ed. (Santo Domingo: Editora del Caribe, 1962), pp. 144ff.

35. Ulises Heureaux, Jr., "Rafael Leonidas Trujillo Molina," in *Cromos* (Santo Domingo: n.p., 1933), pp. 2, 4, 5. The author mentioned one difference between the two *caudillos:* Trujillo was a better administrator (p. 14). However, Trujillo does not seem to have appreciated the comparison.

36. Luperón, vol. 1, p. 101.

37. Ibid., vol. 1, p. 89.

38. Ibid., vol. 1, pp. 103, 53.

39. Ibid., vol. 1, pp. 88, 242.
40. Ibid., vol. 1, p. 88; vol. 2, p. 355.
41. Ibid., vol. 1, p. 117.
42. Ibid., vol. 2, p. 18.
43. Heureaux to Glas, 30 September 1887, Cartas Heureaux, AGN.
44. Heureaux to Luperón, 3 March 1882, Cartas Heureaux, AGN.
45. Luperón, vol. 1, p. 118.
46. Heureaux to Juan F. Mejía, 8 May 1888, Heureaux to Ceferina C. de Chaves, 16 February 1887, Cartas Heureaux, AGN.
47. Among others: *El Eco del Pueblo*, April 1889. Heureaux to Luperón, 5 April 1888; Heureaux to Pedro Pepín, 6 February 1893, Cartas Heureaux, AGN.
48. Heureaux to Glas, 14 February 1887, Cartas Heureaux, AGN.
49. Luperón, vol. 2, p. 238.
50. Heureaux to Glas, 9 December 1892, Cartas Heureaux, AGN.
51. Rufino Martínez, *Hombres dominicanos: Deschamps, Heureaux, Luperón* (Ciudad Trujillo: Imprenta Montalvo, 1936), vol. 1, p. 154.
52. Heureaux to Juan A. de Lora, 4 May 1888, Cartas Heureaux, AGN.
53. For example, in Copiador de Oficios, Ministerio de Correos y Telégrafos, 1897/98, AGN.
54. Luperón, vol. 1, p. 56.
55. Heureaux to Gertrudis Calderín, 1893, reproduced in *Clío*, January/February, 1940.
56. Martínez, *Hombres dominicanos*, p. 192.
57. *Listín Diario*, 6 January 1893 (hereafter *Listín*).
58. Ibid., 4 January 1896.
59. Ibid., 12 January 1893.
60. Ibid., 11 January 1896, 20 May 1899.
61. Ibid., 5 October 1896.
62. *La República*, 21 June 1884.
63. *Epistolario de Carlos Nouel*, vol. 2, p. N28, AGN.
64. Luperón, vol. 2, p. 22.
65. *Listín*, 1 September 1899, 3 August 1899.
66. Presbyter Eliseo E. Echevarría in *Listín*, 15 September 1899.
67. *Listín*, 13 September 1899.
68. Heureaux to Isaías Franco, 24 March 1882, Cartas Heureaux, AGN.
69. Heureaux to Franco, 10 April 1882, Cartas Heureaux, AGN.
70. Heureaux to Luperón, 28 June 1882, Cartas Heureaux, AGN.
71. Heureaux to Imbert, 13 March 1888, Cartas Heureaux, AGN.
72. Heureaux to Manuel J. Jiménez, 22 June 1888, Cartas Heureaux, AGN.
73. Heureaux to U. Bidó, 22 February 1887; Heureaux letters, 29 May 1882, 25 March 1882, 30 December 1898, Cartas Heureaux, AGN. *El Eco del Pueblo*, 20 March 1888.
74. Heureaux letters, 20 June 1882, 2 August 1882, 8 August 1882, Cartas Heureaux, AGN.
75. Heureaux letters, 8 August 1882, 30 April 1888, 3 August 1882, Cartas Heureaux, AGN.
76. Heureaux to Francisco A. Rodríguez, 4 January 1889; Heureaux to Pedro Pepín, 6 February 1893, Cartas Heureaux, AGN.
77. Luperón, vol. 3, pp. 66ff.
78. Heureaux letters, 24 October 1887, 28 December 1892, Cartas Heureaux, AGN.
79. Heureaux letters, 4 May 1888, 18 April 1888, Cartas Heureaux, AGN.
80. Heureaux to Washington Lithgow, 7 June 1882; Heureaux to Federico Lithgow, 21 June 1882; Heureaux letter, 23 April 1888, Cartas Heureaux, AGN.

81. Heureaux to Telésforo Objío, 4 June 1887, Cartas Heureaux, AGN.
82. *Epistolario Nouel*, vol. 2, p. N19, 7 December 1892; vol. 2, p N24, 8 March 1893, AGN.
83. *Listín*, 16 May 1893.
84. Message to President Ulises Heureaux, *Actas del Congreso Nacional*, 22 April 1889, AGN.
85. *Actas del Congreso Nacional*, no. 168, 1892. As far as the capital was concerned, these complaints were rejected by J. B. Vicini, president of the ayuntamiento. The selling of votes also took place (see *La República*, 2 June 1883).
86. Rodríguez Demorizi, ed., *Hostos en Santo Domingo*, vol. 1, p. 276 (1892).
87. *Actas del Congreso Nacional*, no. 115, 8 February 1898.
88. *La República Dominicana en la Exposición Internacional de Bruselas: Memoria descriptiva y catálogo de la sección dominicana, publicada por la Junta Central Organizadora del Concurso de la Exposición de Bruselas* (Santo Domingo: Imprenta Cuna de América, 1897), p. 147.
89. Heureaux to Manuel J. Jiménez, 22 June 1888; Heureaux to Imbert, 9 May 1888, Cartas Heureaux, AGN.
90. Heureaux to R. D'assas Heureaux, 26 January 1893, Cartas Heureaux, AGN.
91. *Actas del Congreso Nacional*, 24 December 1898, AGN. Heureaux to Washington Lithgow, Heureaux to Jacobo de Lara, Heureaux to commander at arms, Puerto Plata, 29 December 1898, Cartas Heureaux, AGN.
92. Heureaux to J. I. Marsán, 18 January 1899, Cartas Heureaux, AGN.
93. Heureaux to Gen. Juan de Lora, 20 June 1888, Cartas Heureaux, AGN.
94. *Listín*, 31 July 1899, 7 August 1899.
95. *Resumen general del activo y pasivo de la sucesión Heureaux, hecho por el notario Miguel Joaquín Alfau a requerimiento de la Comisión Judicial designada para la formación del inventario* (Santo Domingo: Imprenta de García Hermanos, 1900).
96. Damirón, *Cronicones de antaño*, p. 46.
97. Jiménez, *Hombres dominicanos*, vol. 1, p. 164.
98. José M. Nouel to Carlos Nouel, 24 October 1893, *Epistolario Nouel*, vol. 2, p. N28, AGN.

CHAPTER 7

1. Academia Dominicana de la Historia, vol. 9, *Informe de la Comisión de Investigación de los E.U.A. en Santo Domingo en 1871*, preface and notes of Emilio Rodríguez Demorizi (Ciudad Trujillo: Editora Montalvo, 1960), pp. 347 ff. This is a translation of the *Report of the Commission of Inquiry to Santo Domingo etc.* (Washington, D.C.: U.S. Government Printing Office, 1871) and will hereafter be referred to as *Informe*.
2. Emilio Rodríguez Demorizi, ed., *Papeles de Pedro F. Bonó* (Santo Domingo: Editora del Caribe, 1964), pp. 145 ff. (hereafter Bonó).
3. Ibid., pp. 153, 151.
4. *Informe*, p. 225; Emilio Rodríguez Demorizi, ed., *San Cristóbal de antaño* (Ciudad Trujillo: Editora Montalvo, 1946); Emilio Rodríguez Demorizi, ed., *Hostos en Santo Domingo*, 2 vols. (Ciudad Truillo: Imprenta J. R. vda. García Sucs., 1939), vol. 1, p. 78.
5. *Informe*, p. 130; Rodríguez Demorizi, ed., *Hostos en Santo Domingo*, vol. 1, p. 78.
6. *Informe*, p. 236; Rodríguez Demorizi, ed., *Hostos en Santo Domingo*, vol. 1, p. 78.

7. *La República Dominicana en la Exposición Internacional de Bruselas: Memoria descriptiva y catálogo de la sección dominicana, publicada por la Junta Central Organizadora del Concurso de la Exposición de Bruselas* (Santo Domingo: Imprenta Cuna de América, 1897), p. 154.

8. Fernando Arturo de Meriño, *Elementos de geografía física, política e histórica de la República Dominicana, precedidos de las nociones generales de geografía*, 3d ed. rev. (Santo Domingo: Imprenta de García Hermanos, 1898), p. 103.

9. Based on population figures (see chapter 2) and on the data mentioned above, assuming a number of thirty pupils per school.

10. Bonó, p. 147; *Informe*, p. 358; *Informe del Gobernador Civil y Militar de la Provincia de Santiago al Ministro de lo Interior y Policía, Actas del Congreso Nacional*, no. 5, January 1898, Archivo General de Nación (hereafter AGN). *Listín Diario*, 16 February 1899 (hereafter *Listín*).

11. Bonó, p. 147; *Informe*, p. 348; *Listín*, 16 February 1893: *Informe del Gobernador de la Provincia de Santo Domingo al Ministro de los Interior y Policía, Actas del Congreso Nacional*, no. 115, 8 February 1898, AGN.

12. Luis Emilio Gómez Alfau, *Ayer, o el Santo Domingo de hace 50 años* (Ciudad Trujillo: Pol Hermanos, Editores, 1944), pp. 15 ff.

13. *Listín*, 13 January 1899.

14. *Actas del Congreso Nacional*, nos. 12 and 23, 24 April 1895, AGN.

15. *Listín*, 8 June 1899.

16. Bonó, pp. 291 ff.

17. Francisco X. Billini, ed., *La Crónica–Religión, Ciencias, Artes y Literatura* (Santo Domingo: 1884-86), 28 October 1885, 27 November 1884, June 1884 (hereafter *La Crónica*).

18. Fernando Arturo de Meriño, *Obras* (Ciudad Trujillo: Editora La Nación, 1960), pp. 127, 134.

19. *Actas del Congreso Nacional*, 24 April 1895, AGN.

20. Meriño, *Obras*, pp. 294 ff.

21. Vigil Díaz, *Lilís y Alejandrito* (Ciudad Trujillo: Editora Montalvo, 1956), p. 53.

22. *Listín*, 19 May 1893.

23. Rodríguez Demorizi, ed., *Hostos en Santo Domingo*, vol. 2, pp. lxvii, lxviii ff.; vol. 1, p. xxxi.

24. Heureaux to Baron de Almeida, 20 July 1887, Copiador de cartas del Presidente Heureaux (hereafter Cartas Heureaux), AGN.

25. Heureaux to F. Hohlt, 14 December 1898, 14 January 1899, Cartas Heureaux, AGN.

26. Emilio Rodríguez Demorizi, ed., *Salomé Ureña y el Instituto de Señoritas* (Ciudad Trujillo: Impresora Dominicana, 1960), pp. 133 ff.

27. Data from "Historia de la medicina en Santo Domingo," study by university students under Dr. H. Pieter, ms. no. 496, AGN.

28. See, for example, Heureaux to A. Soto, 20 December 1892, Cartas Heureaux, AGN, on the medical activities of Linares.

29. E. C. Joubert, *Cosas que fueron* (Ciudad Trujillo: Imprenta J. R. vda. García Sucs., 1936), pp. 79-80.

30. Heureaux to Glas, 21 March 1888, Cartas Heureaux, AGN; *El Eco del Pueblo*, 24 August 1888.

31. *Libreta de las resoluciones de Hacienda dictadas por el Poder Ejecutivo*, 16 March 1887, AGN, illuminating expenses of Prof. J. J. Cortés. (Also called *Libreta de Hacienda y Comercio*.)

32. Gregorio Luperón, *Notas autobiográficas y apuntes históricos*, 2d ed. in 3 vols. (Santiago: Editorial El Diario, 1939), vol. 3, p. 37. (Hereafter referred to as *Luperón*.)

33. *Listín*, 13 May 1896.

34. Bonó, appendix. But L. García Lluberes in his *Crítica histórica* (Santo Domingo: Editora Montalvo, 1964), criticizing a pamphlet by Manuel A. Amiama, "El periodismo en la República Dominicana," mentioned for the nineties alone forty newspapers in the capital, a dozen in Santiago, four in La Vega, six in Moca, and seven in San Pedro de Macorís that Amiama does not mention in his pamphlet!

35. *Listín*, 16 February 1893.

36. Emilio Rodríguez Demorizi, ed., *San Cristóbal de antaño* (Ciudad Trujillo: Editora Montalvo, 1946), p. 21.

37. Rodríguez Demorizi, ed., *Hostos en Santo Domingo*, vol. 1, pp. 277 ff.

38. Díaz, *Lilís*, p. 53.

39. These and the following data from Haim H. López-Penha, *La masonería en Santo Domingo*, vol. 1 (Ciudad Trujillo: Edit. Stella, 1956).

40. Rodríguez Demorizi, ed., *Hostos en Santo Domingo*, vol. 1, p. 276.

41. López-Penha, *La masonería*, pp. 77-78.

42. *Libreta de Hacienda y Comercio*, 21 June 1887, AGN.

43. López-Penha, *La masonería*, p. 108.

44. Eugenio María de Hostos, *Moral social* (Santo Domingo: Imprenta de García Hermanos, 1888), p. 153.

45. Ibid., p. 148.

46. Luperón, vol. 1, pp. 82 ff.

47. López-Penha, *La masonería*, pp. 171 ff.

48. Heureaux to Meriño, 18 February 1887, Cartas Heureaux, AGN.

49. Heureaux to Meriño, 24 October 1887, Cartas Heureaux, AGN.

50. Heureaux to Manuel María Castillo, 9 May 1889, Cartas Heureaux, AGN.

51. Meriño, *Obras*, p. 21.

52. Heureaux to Luperón, 5 April 1888, Copiador de cartas del Presidente Heureaux con Gobernadores y Jefes militares, AGN.

53. Meriño, *Obras*, pp. 295-96.

54. Ibid., p. 311.

55. Juan Antonio Alix, *Décimas*, ed. Joaquín Balaguer, 2 vols. (Ciudad Trujillo: Librería Dominicana, 1961), vol. 1, p. 142.

56. *Epistolario de Carlos Nouel*, vol. 2, p. Q6, AGN.

57. Letter of Fr. Otero Nolasco, 1887, *Epistolario Nouel*, vol. 1, p. N4, AGN.

58. Letter of Fr. Nolasco, 25 May 1886, *Epistolario Nouel*, vol. 2, p. Z4, AGN.

59. Heureaux to Moreno del Christo, 29 July 1882, Cartas Heureaux, AGN.

60. Fr. Quezada to Canon Nouel, *Epistolario Nouel*, vol. 2, pp. Q2, 20, AGN.

61. García Lluberes, *Crítica histórica*, p. 177.

62. *Listín*, 30 April 1896.

63. *Epistolario Nouel*, vol. 1, p. I4, AGN.

64. Fr. Eliseo Echevarría to Canon Nouel, 3 May 1893, *Epistolario Nouel*, vol. 1, p. E6, AGN.

65. See *Listín*, 3 April 1899, regarding the Moca hermitage with an image of San Isidro.

66. One hundred-twenty children from the Colegio San Luis Gonzaga also participated, by requirement (*La Crónica*, July 1884).

67. Quotations and data on the various festivals are from Gómez Alfau, *Ayer*, pp. 94 ff., 137.

68. Bonó, p. 161.

69. *Listín*, 22 March 1899. I do not know whether the law was passed.

70. *Listín*, 11 June 1893, 28 November 1893.

71. See H. Hoetink, "Americans in Samaná," *Caribbean Studies*, vol. 2, no. 1 (April 1962).

72. See Emilio Rodríguez Demorizi's preface to Pedro F. Bonó, *El Montero* (Santo Domingo: Julio D. Postigo, 1968).

73. Joaquín Balaguer, *Historia de la literatura dominicana*, 2d ed. (Ciudad Trujillo: Librería Dominicana, 1958). For the following data also see Max Henríquez Ureña, *Panorama histórico de la literatura dominicana*, 2 vols. (Santo Domingo: Librería Dominicana, 1965).

74. Emilio Rodríguez Demorizi, ed., *Poesía popular dominicana* (Ciudad Trujillo: Edit. La Nación, 1938), vol. 1.

75. Henríquez Ureña, *Panorama histórico*, vol. 1, p. 182.

76. Rodríguez Demorizi, ed., *Poesía popular*, p. 259.

77. *Listín*, 2 August 1893.

78. *Listín*, 9 March 1896.

79. *Informe*, p. 563.

80. Bonó, p. 606.

81. Díaz, *Lilís*, p. 86.

82. *Listín*, 10 February 1896.

83. Bonó, pp. 287, 291-93.

84. Luperón, vol. 3, pp. 258 ff.

85. Ibid., vol. 3, pp. 54, 240-42, 327 ff.

86. Ibid., vol. 3, pp. 269-70.

87. Heureaux to Jacobo Pereyra, 16 February 1882, Cartas Heureaux, AGN.

88. Heureaux to Rodolfo O. Limardo, 10 February 1882, Cartas Heureaux, AGN.

89. Heureaux to Luperón, 5 May 1882, Cartas Heureaux, AGN.

CHAPTER 8

1. Karl Mannheim, *Ensayos de sociología de la cultura*, trans. by Manuel Suárez (Madrid: Aguilar, 1957).

2. R. Emilio Jiménez, *Al amor del bohío*, 2 vols. (Santo Domingo: Editora Montalvo, 1927), vol. 2, pp. 107 ff.

3. J. M. Briceño Guerrero, *América Latina en el mundo* (Caracas: Editorial Arte, 1966), p. 179.

4. Emilio Rodríguez Demorizi, ed., *Papeles de Pedro F. Bonó* (Santo Domingo: Editora del Caribe, 1964), p. 391 (hereafter Bonó).

5. Gregorio Luperón, *Notas autobiográficas y apuntes históricos*, 2d ed. in 3 vols. (Santiago: Editorial El Diario, 1939), vol. 2, pp. 258 ff. (Hereafter referred to as Luperón.)

6. Sumner B. Welles, *La viña de Naboth*, trans. M. A. Moore, 2 vols. (Santiago: Editorial El Diario, 1939), vol. 1, p. 58.

7. Luperón, vol. 1, pp. 37 ff.

8. Emilio Rodríguez Demorizi, ed., *Hostos en Santo Domingo*, 2 vols. (Ciudad Trujillo: Imprenta J. R. vda. García Sucs., 1939), vol. 1, pp. 265-66.

9. Juan Bosch, *Trujillo: causas de una tiranía sin ejemplo* (Caracas: Librería "Las Novedades," 1959), p. 75. See also Franklin J. Franco, *Los negros, los mulatos, y la nación dominicana* (Santo Domingo: Editora Nacional, 1969), pp. 101 ff.

10. Bosch, *Trujillo*, p. 76.

11. Rodríguez Demorizi, ed., *Hostos en Santo Domingo*, vol. 1, p. 266.

12. Bonó, p. 391.

13. Luperón, vol. 1, p. 88.

14. Rodríguez Demorizi, ed., *Hostos en Santo Domingo*, vol. 1, p. 275.

15. Arturo Bueno, *Santiago, quien te vió y quien te ve* (Santiago de los Caballeros: Impresora Comercial, 1961).

16. Francisco Veloz Maggiolo, *La Misericordia y sus contornos* (Santo Domingo: Edit. Arte y Cine, 1967), pp. 180, 33, 152. For a general history of the streets and *barrios*, see Luis E. Alemán, *Santo Domingo, Ciudad Trujillo* (Santiago: Impr. Moreno, 1966).

17. Bonó, pp. 283 ff. In 1893 a scissors sharpener was advertising his services: he would remain in the capital only a short time (*Listín Diario*, 17 August 1893; hereafter *Listín*).

18. Bonó, pp. 263, 342, 223.

19. Rodríguez Demorizi, ed., *Hostos en Santo Domingo*, vol. 1, p. 297.

20. Bonó, p. 221.

21. See Rodríguez Demorizi's preface to Pedro F. Bonó, *El Montero*, (Santo Domingo: Julio D. Postigo, 1968), for a description of the nineteenth-century *montero*.

22. Rodríguez Demorizi in Bonó, *El Montero*, p. 31.

23. Luperón, vol. 1, p. 165.

24. Marco Antonio Mejía-Ricart, *Las clases sociales en Santo Domingo* (Ciudad Trujillo: Librería Dominicana, 1953), p. 37.

25. Ibid., pp. 45, 47.

26. *El Eco del Pueblo*, 15 March 1891.

27. R. Damirón, *Cronicones de antaño* (Ciudad Trujillo: Imprenta Dominicana, 1949), p. 103.

28. Luis Emilio Gómez Alfau, *Ayer, o el Santo Domingo de hace 50 años* (Ciudad Trujillo: Pol Hermanos, Editores, 1944), p. 123.

29. Ibid., p. 124.

30. Ibid., p. 124.

31. Fr. Pedro Suazo to Nouel, 7 April 1893, *Epistolario de Carlos Nouel*, (Archivo General de la Nación (hereafter AGN).

32. *Listín*, 19 January 1899.

33. *Listín*, 29 April 1893.

34. Gómez Alfau, *Ayer*, p. 86.

35. *Listín*, 18 September 1893. Generally the women were rescued in time.

36. *Listín*, December 1893.

37. *Listín*, 16 May 1893.

38. *Listín*, 5 April 1893.

39. *El Eco del Pueblo*, 24 July 1889.

40. Bonó, p. 393.

41. *Listín*, 22 May 1893.

42. For this and the following data see Carlos Larrazabal Blanco, *Los negros y la esclavitud en Santo Domingo* (Santo Domingo: Julio D. Postigo, 1967). See also Franco, *Los negros*.

43. Emilio Rodríguez Demorizi, ed., *Guerra dominico-haitiana: Documentos para su estudio*, 2 vols. (Ciudad Trujillo: Impresora Dominicana, 1957), p. 125.

44. Larrazabal, *Los negros y la esclavitud*, pp. 137, 195.

45. Ibid., p. 195. See also Julio Alberto Hernández, *Música tradicional dominicana* (Santo Domingo: Julio D. Postigo, 1969), pp. 19 ff.

46. Larrazabal, *Los negros y la esclavitud*, p. 190.

47. Edna Garrido de Boggs, *Folklore infantil de Santo Domingo* (Madrid: Ediciones Cultura Hispánica, 1955), pp. 24, 25. M. J. Andrade, *Folklore de la República Dominicana* (Ciudad Trujillo: n.p., 1948), p. 44. Also Emilio Rodríguez Demorizi, ed., *Refranero dominicano* (Rome: Stab. Tipográfico G. Menaglia, 1950), introduction.

48. Heureaux to J. M. Glas, 30 September 1887, Copiador de cartas del Presidente Heureaux (hereafter Cartas Heureaux), AGN.

49. See Heureaux to B. G. Gost Konst, 13 March 1893, Cartas Heureaux, AGN.

50. Heureaux to Hortencia García, 29 December 1898, Cartas Heureaux, AGN.

51. Bonó, pp. 344, 610.

52. Pedro Andrés Pérez Cabral, *La comunidad mulata* (Caracas: Gráfica Americana, 1967).

53. Gustave d'Alaux [pseud.], *L'Empereur Soulouque et son empire*, trans. and ed. Emilio Rodríguez Demorizi, in *Documentos para la historia de la República Dominicana* (Ciudad Trujillo: Impr. Dominicana, 1959), vol. 3, pp. 359-60.

54. Larrazabal, *Los negros y la esclavitud*, p. 122.

55. H. Hoetink, *The Two Variants in Caribbean Race Relations* (London: Oxford University Press, 1967).

56. Luperón, vol. 1, p. 27.

57. Ibid., vol. 3, p. 250.

58. Bonó, p. 392.

59. Luperón, vol. 3, pp. 370, 385; Rodríguez Demorizi, ed., *Hostos en Santo Domingo*, vol. 2, p. 203.

60. Luperón, vol. 3, p. 202.

61. Ibid., vol. 3, pp. 328, 329.

62. Welles, *La viña*, vol. 1, p. 444.

63. Rodríguez Demorizi, ed., *Hostos en Santo Domingo*, p. 185.

64. Rufino Martínez, *Hombres dominicanos: Deschamps, Heureaux, Luperón*, vol. 1 (Ciudad Trujillo: Imprenta Montalvo, 1936), vol. 1, p. 185.

65. Juan Antonio Alix, *Décimas*, ed. Joaquín Balaguer, 2 vols. (Ciudad Trujillo: Librería Dominicana, 1961), vol. 1, pp. 28 ff.

66. José Martí, *Apuntes de un viaje* (Havana: Secretaría de Educación, División de Cultura, 1938), p. 40. Needless to say, after Heureaux's death the "market" character of the military apparatus as well as that of the political apparatus predominated again for a considerable period.

67. M. A. González Rodríguez, "Apuntes y recuerdos de San Carlos," *Clío*, no. 106.

68. R. Emilio Jiménez, *Al amor del bohío* 2 vols. (Santo Domingo: Editora Montalvo, 1927), vol. 1, p. 95.

69. Mejía-Ricart, *Las clases sociales*, pp. 27, 28.

CHAPTER 9

1. R. Emilio Jiménez, *Al amor del bohío*, 2 vols. (Santo Domingo: Editora Montalvo, 1927), vol. 1, pp. 20, 12 ff.

2. Juan Antonio Alix, *Décimas inéditas* (Santo Domingo: Impr. Moreno, 1966), p. 164.

3. Luis Emilio Gómez Alfau, *Ayer, o el Santo Domingo de hace 50 años* (Ciudad Trujillo: Pol Hermanos, Editores, 1944), p. 133.

4. *Listín Diario*, 28 June 1893 (hereafter *Listín*).

5. *Listín*, 10 July 1899.

6. Gómez Alfau, *Ayer*, p. 114.

7. Ibid., pp. 61 ff.

8. *Listín*, 5 September 1896.

9. Gómez Alfau, *Ayer*, p. 50.

10. *Listín*, 7 January 1893.

11. Jiménez, *Al amor*, vol. 1, p. 297.

12. *Listín*, 13 July 1893.

13. *Listín*, 29 March 1899.

14. Heureaux to Olga Clan, 23 January 1899, Copiador de cartas del Presidente Heureaux (hereafter Cartas Heureaux), Archivo General de la Nación (hereafter AGN).

15. Letter from J. E. Julia, 1 October 1893, *Epistolario de Carlos Nouel*, vol. 1, p. J11, AGN.

16. Gómez Alfau, *Ayer*, p. 29.
17. Jiménez, *Al amor*, vol. 1, pp. 5 ff.
18. Gómez Alfau, *Ayer*, p. 28.
19. *Actas del Congreso Nacional*, Jurisprudence, 23 January 1885, AGN.
20. *Listín*, 4 February 1893.
21. Letter from Heureaux, 22 February 1887, Cartas Heureaux, AGN.
22. Alix, *Décimas inéditas*, p. 34.
23. José Martí, *Apuntes de un viaje* (Havana: Secretaría de Educación, División de Cultura, 1938), p. 31.
24. *Listín*, 4 April 1893.
25. Heureaux to Juana Ogander, 30 December 1898, Cartas Heureaux, AGN.
26. *Listín*, 6 February 1896.
27. Alix, *Décimas inéditas*, p. 47.
28. Ibid., p. 127.
29. *Listín*, January 1899.
30. Gómez Alfau, *Ayer*, p. 41.
31. *Listín*, 17 February 1896.
32. *Listín*, 13 January 1893.
33. Francisco X. Billini, ed., *La Crónica—Religión, Ciencias, Artes y Literatura* (Santo Domingo: 1884-86).
34. Gómez Alfau, *Ayer*, pp. 46 ff.
35. Francisco Veloz Maggiolo, *La Misericordia y sus contornos* (Santo Domingo: Edit. Arte y Cine, 1967), p. 241.
36. Jiménez, *Al amor*, vol. 2, p. 65.
37. Martí, *Apuntes de un viaje*, p. 50.
38. Ibid., pp. 60 ff.
39. Jiménez, *Al amor*, vol. 1, pp. 286 ff.
40. Arturo Bueno, *Santiago, quien te vió y quien te ve* (Santiago de los Caballeros: Impresora Comercial, 1961), pp. 446 ff.
41. *Listín*, 9 March 1896.
42. *Epistolario Nouel*, 12 May 1887, 12 July 1887, vol. 1, p. A14, AGN.
43. Veloz Maggiolo, *La Misericordia*, p. 71.
44. Enrique Deschamps, *La República Dominicana: directorio y guía general*, 2 vols. (Santiago: [1906?]), vol. 1, pp. 283 ff.
45. *Listín*, 5 April 1899.
46. *Listín*, 2 March 1899.
47. *Listín*, 23 March 1893, January 1896.
48. *Listín*, 26 January 1893.
49. Alix, *Décimas inéditas*, p. 157.
50. *Listín*, 2 January 1899.
51. Julio Alberto Hernández, *Música tradicional dominicana* (Santo Domingo: Julio D. Postigo, 1969), pp. 53 ff.
52. Deschamps, *La República Dominicana*, vol. 1, pp. 278 ff.
53. *Listín*, 17 August 1893.
54. Jiménez, *Al amor*, vol. 1, pp. 92 ff.
55. Ibid., p. 64.
56. Gómez Alfau, *Ayer*, pp. 33 ff.
57. Ibid., p. 66.
58. Martí, *Apuntes de un viaje*, p. 34.
59. Gómez Alfau, *Ayer*, pp. 70 ff.
60. *Listín*, 27 March 1893.
61. Emilio Rodríguez Demorizi, ed., *Hostos en Santo Domingo*, 2 vols. (Ciudad Trujillo: Imprenta J. R. vda. García Sucs., 1939), vol. 1, p. 286.

62. *Actas del Congreso Nacional*, 12 May 1892, AGN.
63. Gómez Alfau, *Ayer*, pp. 64 ff.
64. Heureaux to Marchena, 14 March 1882, Cartas Heureaux, AGN.
65. *Listín*, 3 January 1893.
66. Fernando Arturo de Meriño, *Elementos de geografía física, política e histórica de la República Dominicana, precedidos de las nociones generales de geografía*, 3d ed. rev. (Santo Domingo: Imprenta de García Hermanos, 1898), pp. 86, 87.
67. Gómez Alfau, *Ayer*, pp. 53 ff.
68. *Listín*, 2 January 1893, 3 January 1893, July 1896.
69. Gómez Alfau, *Ayer*, pp. 61 ff.
70. *Listín*, 10 May 1893, 24 April 1893.
71. Gómez Alfau, *Ayer*, pp. 110 ff.
72. *Listín*, 20 May 1893.
73. Gómez Alfau, *Ayer*, p. 115.
74. Jiménez, *Al amor*, vol. 1, pp. 23 ff., 158 ff.
75. Luperón, vol. 1, p. 117.

ARCHIVES

Archivo General de la Nación

Congreso Nacional. 1882: article 205; 1885: 6, 18; 1886: 78; 1887: 5, 8, 101, 182; 1888: 7, 11, 43, 80; 1889: 34, 49, 93, 196; 1890: 56, 99; 1892: 9, 12, 18, 66, 68; 1893: 13, 61; 1894: 48; 1895: 22, 23, 24; 1896: 1, 24, 29; 1897: 7, 20, 39, 42, 44, 45, 64; 1898: 1, 2, 3, 5, 26, 29; 1899: 22.
Copiador de cartas del Presidente Heureaux. 1882; 1887/88; 1888/89; 1892/93; 1898/99.
Copiador de cartas del Presidente Heureaux con Gobernadores y Jefes militares. 1888/89.
Copiador de Oficios, Ministerio de Correos y Telégrafos. 1893-99.
Epistolario de Carlos Nouel.
Libreta de las resoluciones de Hacienda dictadas por el Poder Ejecutivo (or *Libreta de Hacienda y Comercio*). No. 81, 1887; No. 101, 1891/92, 1893.
Libreta Secretaría de Hacienda y Comercio. No. 93, 1894/95.
Libreta Secretaría de Hacienda y Comercio, No. 110, 1895, 1896, 1897.

Archives of Lic. Emilio Rodríguez Demorizi

Historic documents, the Carlos Nouel collection.

NEWSPAPERS AND MAGAZINES

La Crónica: Religión, Ciencias, Artes y Literature. Edited by F. X. Billini. Santo Domingo: 1884-86.
El Eco del Pueblo. Edited by J. J. Hungría. Santiago: 1888-92.
Listín Diario. Edited by A. J. Pellerano. Santo Domingo: 1893-99.
El Porvenir. Puerto Plata: 1890.
La República. Edited by E. Deschamps. Santiago: 1883-85.

BOOKS AND ARTICLES

Abad, J. R. *La República Dominicana: Reseña general geográfico-estadística.* Santo Domingo: n.p., 1888.

Academia Dominicana de la Historia. *Informe de la Comisión de Investigación de los E.U.A. en Santo Domingo en 1871*. Preface and notes by Emilio Rodríguez Demorizi. Ciudad Trujillo: Editora Montalvo, 1960. Translation of the *Report of the Commission of Inquiry to Santo Domingo, etc.* Washington, D.C.: U.S. Government Printing Office, 1871.

D'Alaux, Gustave [pseud.]. *L'Empereur Soulouque et son empire*. Translated and edited by Emilio Rodríguez Demorizi. In *Documentos para la historia de la República Dominicana*. Vol. 3. Ciudad Trujillo: Impresora Dominicana, 1959.

Albuquerque, Alcibíades. *Títulos de los terrenos comuneros de la República Dominicana*. Ciudad Trujillo: Impresora Dominicana, 1961.

Alemán, Luis E. *Santo Domingo, Ciudad Trujillo*. Santiago: Impr. Moreno, 1966.

Alix, Juan Antonio. *Décimas*. Edited by Joaquín Balaguer. 2 vols. Ciudad Trujillo: Librería Dominicana, 1961.

——————. *Décimas inéditas*. Santo Domingo: Impr. Moreno, 1966.

Amiama, Manuel A. "La población de Santo Domingo." *Clío*, no. 115 (1959).

Andrade, M. J. *Folklore de la República Dominicana*. Ciudad Trujillo: n.p., 1948.

Antonini, Gustavo Arthur. "Processes and Patterns of Landscape Change in the Línea Noroeste, Dominican Republic." Mimeographed. 1968.

Balaguer, Joaquín. *Historia de la literatura dominicana*. 2d ed. Ciudad Trujillo: Librería Dominicana, 1958.

Banco Central de la República Dominicana. *Legislación monetaria y bancaria de la República Dominicana*. Ciudad Trujillo: n.p., 1955.

Bonó, Pedro F. *El Montero*. Preface by Emilio Rodríguez Demorizi. Santo Domingo: Julio D. Postigo, 1968.

Bosch, Juan. *Trujillo: causas de una tiranía sin ejemplo*. Caracas: Librería "Las Novedades," 1959.

Briceño Guerrero, J. M. *América Latina en el mundo*. Caracas: Editorial Arte, 1966.

Bueno, Arturo. *Santiago, quien te vió y quien te ve*. Santiago de los Caballeros: Impresora Comercial, 1961.

Cabral, Manuel del. *Compadre Mon*. 4th ed. Buenos Aires: Losada, 1957.

Castro, Victor M. de. *Cosas de Lilís*. Santo Domingo: Imprenta Cuna de América, 1919.

Código telegráfico, uso oficial y privado del Gobierno. n.p.: Imprenta de El Liberal, 1900.

Crasweller, R. D. *Trujillo: The Life and Times of a Caribbean Dictator*. New York: Macmillan, 1966.

Damirón, R. *Cronicones de antaño*. Ciudad Trujillo: Imprenta Dominicana, 1949.

Deschamps, Enrique. *La República Dominicana, directorio y guía general*. 2 vols. Santiago: n.p., [1906?].

De Vries, E., and Medina Echevarría, J., eds. *Social Aspects of Economic Development in Latin America*. Paris: UNESCO, 1963.

Díaz, Vigil. *Lilís y Alejandrito*. Ciudad Trujillo: Editora Montalvo, 1956.

Franco, Franklin J. *Los negros, los mulatos, y la nación dominicana.* Santo Domingo: Editora Nacional, 1969.

García Lluberes, L. *Crítica histórica.* Santo Domingo: Editora Montalvo, 1964.

Garrido de Boggs, Edna. *Folklore infantil de Santo Domingo.* Madrid: Ediciones Cultura Hispánica, 1955.

Gómez Alfau, Luis Emilio. *Ayer, o el Santo Domingo de hace 50 años.* Ciudad Trujillo: Pol Hermanos, Editores, 1944.

González Rodríguez, M. A. "Apuntes y recuerdos de San Carlos," *Clío,* no. 106 (January-March 1956).

Hazard, Samuel. *Santo Domingo, Past and Present, with a Glance at Hayti.* London: Sampson Low, Marston, Low & Searle, 1873.

Henríquez Ureña, Max. *Panorama histórico de la literatura dominicana.* 2 vols. Santo Domingo: Librería Dominicana, 1965.

Henríquez y Carvajal, Federico. *El Mensajero.* 1886-1889. 2 vols. Havana: Instituto de Historia, 1964.

Hernández, Julio Alberto. *Música tradicional dominicana.* Santo Domingo: Julio D. Postigo, 1969.

Herrera, César A. *Cuadros históricos dominicanos.* Ciudad Trujillo: n.p., 1949.

————. *De Hartmont a Trujillo.* Ciudad Trujillo: Impresora Dominicana, 1953.

Heureaux, Ulises, Jr. "Rafael Leonidas Trujillo Molina," in *Cromos.* Santo Domingo: n.p., 1933.

"Historia de la medicina en Santo Domingo." A study by university students under Dr. H. Pieter. Manuscript no. 496. Archivo General de la Nación.

Hoetink, H. "Americans in Samaná," *Caribbean Studies.* Vol. 2, no. 1 (April 1962).

———— *Het patroon van de oude Curaçaose Samenleving.* 2d ed. Aruba/Tiel: De Wit, 1966.

———— *The Two Variants in Caribbean Race Relations.* London: Oxford University Press, 1967. (New York, 1971).

Hostos, Eugenio María de. *Moral social.* Santo Domingo: Imprenta de García Hermanos, 1888.

————. *Tratado de sociología.* Buenos Aires: Losada, 1941.

La influencia de Hostos en la cultura dominicana: respuestas a la encuesta de El Caribe. Ciudad Trujillo: Editora del Caribe, 1956.

Jiménez, R. Emilio. *Al amor del bohío.* 2 vols. Santo Domingo: Editora Montalvo, 1927.

Joubert, E. C., *Cosas que fueron.* Ciudad Trujillo: Impr. J. R. vda García Sucs., 1936.

Larrazabal Blanco, Carlos. *Los negros y la esclavitud en Santo Domingo.* Santo Domingo: Julio D. Postigo, 1967.

López-Penha, Haim H. *La masonería en Santo Domingo.* Vol. 1. Ciudad Trujillo: Edit. Stella, 1956.

Luperón, Gregorio. *Notas autobiográficas y apuntes históricos.* 2d ed. 3 vols. Santiago: Editorial El Diario, 1939.

Mannheim, Karl. *Ensayos de sociología de la cultura*. Translated by Manuel Suárez. Madrid: Aguilar, 1957.

Marrero Aristy, Ramón. *Over*. Santo Domingo: Librería Dominicana, 1963.

_____. *La República Dominicana*. 2 vols. Ciudad Trujillo: Editora del Caribe, 1958.

Martí, José. *Apuntes de un viaje*. Havana: Secretaría de Educación, División de Cultura, 1938.

Martínez, Rufino. *Hombres dominicanos: Deschamps, Heureaux, Luperón*. Vol. 1. Ciudad Trujillo: Imprenta Montalvo, 1936.

_____. *Del Puerto Plata de ayer*. Santo Domingo: Editora del Caribe, 1963.

Mathews, Thomas. "The Project for a Confederation of the Greater Antilles," *Caribbean Historical Review*. Vols. 3-4 (December 1954).

Mejía-Ricart, Marco Antonio. *Las clases sociales en Santo Domingo*. Ciudad Trujillo: Librería Dominicana, 1953.

Meriño, Fernando Arturo de. *Elementos de geografía física, política e história de la República Dominicana, precedidos de las nociones generales de geografía*. 3d ed. rev. Santo Domingo: Imprenta de García Hermanos, 1898.

_____. *Obras*. Ciudad Trujillo: Edit. La Nación, 1960.

Monclús, Miguel Angel. *El caudillismo en la República Dominicana*. 3d ed. Santo Domingo: Editora del Caribe, 1962.

Monte y Tejada, Antonio del. *Historia de Santo Domingo*. 4 vols. Santo Domingo: Imprenta de García Hermanos, 1890.

Moreau de Saint-Mery, M.L.E. *Descriptions de la partie espagnole de l'isle de Saint-Domingue*. Philadelphia: n.p., 1799.

Nouel, Canon Carlos. *Historia eclesiástica de la Arquidiócesis de Santo Domingo, Primada de América*. Santo Domingo: Tip. El Progreso, Emilio Espinal, 1915.

Ortiz, Fernando. *Contrapunteo cubano del tabaco y el azúcar*. Havana: Jesús Montero, 1940.

Penson, César Nicolás. *Reseña histórico-crítica de la poesía en Santo Domingo*. Santo Domingo: n.p., 1892.

Pérez Cabral, Pedro Andrés. *La comunidad mulata*. Caracas: Gráfica Americana, 1967.

La República Dominicana en la Exposición Internacional de Bruselas: Memoria descriptiva y catálogo de la sección dominicana, publicada por la Junta Central Organizadora del Concurso de la Exposición de Bruselas. Santo Domingo: Imprenta Cuna de América, 1897.

Resumen general del activo y pasivo de la sucesión Heureaux, hecho por el notario Miguel Joaquín Alfau a requerimiento de la Comisión Judicial designada para la formación del inventario. Santo Domingo: Imprenta de García Hermanos, 1900.

Rodríguez Demorizi, Emilio. *El Cancionero de Lilís: Poesía, dictadura y libertad*. Santo Domingo: Editora del Caribe, 1962.

Rodríguez Demorizi, Emilio, ed. *Baní y la novela de Billini*. Santo Domingo: Editora del Caribe, 1964.

_____.*Cuentos de política criolla.* Santo Domingo: Librería Dominicana, 1963.

_____. *Enciclopedia dominicana del caballo.* Ciudad Trujillo: n.p., 1955.

_____. *Guerra dominico-haitiana: Documentos para su estudio.* 2 vols. Ciudad Trujillo: Impresora Dominicana, 1957.

_____. *Hostos en Santo Domingo.* 2 vols. Ciudad Trujillo: Impr. J. R. vda. García Sucs., 1939.

_____. *La Marina de Guerra dominicana: 1844-1861.* 3 vols. Ciudad Trujillo: Editora Montalvo, 1958.

_____. *Papeles de Pedro F. Bonó.* Santo Domingo: Editora del Caribe, 1964.

_____. *Poesía popular dominicana.* Ciudad Trujillo: Edit. La Nación, 1938.

_____. *Refranero dominicano.* Rome: Stab. Tipográfico G. Menaglia, 1950.

_____. *Salomé Ureña y el Instituto de Señoritas.* Ciudad Trujillo: Impresora Dominicana, 1960.

_____. *San Cristóbal de antaño.* Ciudad Trujillo: Editora Montalvo, 1946.

Rosa, Antonio de la. *Las finanzas de Santo Domingo y el control americano.* Santo Domingo: Editora Nacional, 1969.

Ruiz Tejada, M. R. *Estudio sobre la propiedad inmobiliaria en la República Dominicana.* Ciudad Trujillo: n.p., 1952.

Troncoso Sánchez, Pedro. *Ramon Cáceres.* Santo Domingo: Edit. Stella, 1964.

Ucko, Enrique, *La fusión de los sefardíes con los dominicanos.* Ciudad Trujillo: Impr. La Opinión, 1944.

Veloz Maggiolo, Francisco. *La Misericordia y sus contornos.* Santo Domingo: Edit. Arte y Cine, 1967.

Welles, Sumner B. *La viña de Naboth.* Translated by M. A. Moore. Santiago: Editorial El Diario, 1939.

Wischnitzer, Mark. "The Historical Background of the Immigration of Jewish Refugees in Santo Domingo." Manuscript, n.d.